Bridging Tourism Theory and Practice
Volume 2

Tourism in the Muslim World

Series Editors:
Jafar Jafari
Department of Hospitality and Tourism, University of Wisconsin-Stout, Menomonie WI 54751, USA. Tel: (715) 232 2339; Fax: (715) 232-3200; Email: <jafari@uwstout.edu> Universidade do Algarve, Portugal

Liping A. Cai
Purdue Tourism and Hospitality Research Center, Purdue University, West Lafayette, Indiana 47907, USA. Tel (765) 494 8384; Fax (765) 496 1168; Email: <liping@purdue.edu>

Associate Editor (this volume):
Eric Laws
James Cook University, Australia

Recognizing the increasing gap between what is researched in academic community and what is practiced in industry, this series aims to bring together academic and industry leaders in their respective fields to discuss, exchange, and debate issues critical to the advancement of tourism. The book series intends to not only create a platform for the academics and practitioners to share theories and practices with each other, but more importantly serve as a collaborative venue for meaningful synthesis.

Each volume will feature a distinct theme by focusing on a current or upcoming niche or "hot" topic. It shows how theories and practices inform each other; how both have evolved, advanced, and been applied; and how industry best practices have benefited from, and contributed to, theoretical developments. Volume editors have both strong academic credentials and significant consulting or other industry engagement experiences. Chapter contributors will be identified through professional conferences and trade conventions. In general, the book series seeks a synergy of how concepts can inform actions, and vice versa. The book series will inspire a new generation of researchers who can translate academic discoveries to deliverable results valuable to practitioners.

Forthcoming volumes in this book series

Tourism and the Implications of Climate Change
Christian Schott, ed.

Tourism as an Instrument of Development: A Case Study
Eduardo Fayos-Solà, ed.

Bridging Tourism Theory and Practice
Volume 2

Tourism in the Muslim World

NOEL SCOTT
University of Queensland, Australia

JAFAR JAFARI
University of Wisconsin-Stout, USA, Universidade do Algarve, Portugal

United Kingdom • North America • Japan
India • Malaysia • China

Emerald Group Publishing Limited
Howard House, Wagon Lane, Bingley BD16 1WA, UK

First edition 2010

British Library Cataloguing in Publication Data
A catalogue record for this book is available from the British Library

ISBN: 978-1-84950-920-6
ISSN: 2042-1443 (Series)

Emerald Group Publishing
Limited, Howard House,
Environmental Management
System has been certified by
ISOQAR to ISO 14001:2004
standards

Awarded in recognition of
Emerald's production
department's adherence to
quality systems and processes
when preparing scholarly
journals for print

INVESTOR IN PEOPLE

Contents

Acknowledgments

This book has a long and complicated history. In early 1990s, the second editor of this volume, along with Salah Wahab (Egypt), Turgut Var (USA, Turkey), and Kadir Din (Malaysia) tried to organize a conference on Islam and tourism—not as a religious treatment of the subject, but as a dialogue between Islam and tourism. The proposal was discussed with representatives from a few Muslim countries, but a host could not be found. In late 1990s, another attempt was made to have this conference hosted, but its faith remained the same. In addition to the conference, the idea was to publish a book based on its proceedings. While the conference never took off, the present volume is not so different from what the conference would have produced.

For the first editor, the idea for this book began during a visit to Prince Sultan College, Abha, Kingdom of Saudi Arabia, in 2004, to attend a symposium held under the auspices of HRH Prince Faisal Bin Abdul Aziz in the presence of Prince Sultan Bin Salman Bin Abdul Aziz. This event examined both the importance of education for the developing tourism industry in the country, and the need for increased links between tourism scholars interested in this topic around the world. Serendipitously, both of the editors of this book were speakers at the Abha Symposium.

From this beginning, the idea for an edited book was shared with our colleagues Ali Al-Shabi and Yasin Al-Jefri of Prince Sultan College, and with their encouragement, the ideas for this project began. Its proposal was shaped by conversations with numerous people, in particular the comments and suggestions of Eric Laws. The editors issued a call for papers in 2008, and this resulted in over 50 expressions of interest, and eventually the chapters of the book came together. Here gratitude is expressed to the reviewers who gave their time so generously to read and report on the manuscripts under review. Their many comments and suggestions have been invaluable, and their names are listed below.

Avcikurt, Cevdet: Balikesir University, Turkey
Ahmad, Rozila: Universiti Utara Malaysia, Malaysia

Aktas, Ahmet: Akdeniz Üniversitesi, Turkey
Albawardi, Saif: The University of Queensland, Australia
Alvarez, Maria: Bogaziçi University, Turkey
Ashton, Ann: Southland Institute of Technology, New Zealand
Baggio, Rodolfo: Boccioni University, Italy
Bianchi, Raoul: University of East London, United Kingdom
Boksberger, Philipp: University of Applied Sciences, Switzerland
Bristol-Rhys, Jane: Zayed University, United Arab Emirates
Carson, Dean: Charles Darwin University, Australia
Comparinon, Kom: DPU International College, Thailand
Demir, Cengiz: EGE University, Turkey
Din, Kadir: Universiti Utara Malaysia, Malaysia
Dabphet, Siriphen: The University of Queensland, Australia
Digance, Justine: Tourism, Leisure, Hotel and Sport Management, Griffith
University, Australia
Elsaban, Sharif: University of Bahrain, Bahrain
Fowler, Elizabeth: The University of Queensland, Australia
Gao, Jun: Shanghai Normal University, China
Hazbun, Waleed: Johns Hopkins University, United States of America
Kang, Eun Jun: The University of Queensland, Australia
Kantarci, Kemal: Akdeniz University, Turkey
Laws, Eric: James Cook University, Australia
Marzano, Giuseppe: Universidad San Francisco de Quito, Ecuador
Monshi, Emad: The University of Queensland, Australia
Mounir, Ayman: Helwan University, Egypt
Robinson, Richard: The University of Queensland, Australia
Sharif, Masih: formerly with the UNWTO Regional Representations for
Asia and the Pacific, Spain
Sheridan, Lorraine: University of Leicester, United Kingdom
Shihab, Aminath: The University of Queensland, Australia
Tanrisevdi, Abdullah: Adnan Menderes University, Turkey
Wickens, Eugenia: Buckinghamshire New University, United Kingdom
Yaghmour, Samer: King Abdul Aziz University, Kingdom of Saudi Arabia
Yutyunyong, Tranakjit: The University of Queensland, Australia
Zamani-Farahani, Hamira: Astiaj Tourism Consultancy and Research
Centre, Iran
Xu, Hongang: Sun Yat Sen University, People's Republic of China

Several years after this project was conceived, it is rewarding to see the
idea come to fruition in a collection of chapters from authors around the

world. Efforts and contributions of the authors are sincerely appreciated and valued. A project such as this book takes a significant amount of time, often on weekends and at night, and inevitably erodes the time available to be spent with family members. Such is true for editors as well; their families' patience, support, and understanding made all the difference. Thanks are also extended to the editors' universities and to Sue Melloy for her administrative and editorial work. The valuable advice and support of Professor Eric Laws is also acknowledged.

Preface

Tourism in the Muslim World presents the first collection of scholarly writings concerning tourism in the Muslim world. Its chapters provide a synthesis of thought on this important issue for tourism and indeed for our times, offering a point of focus for tourism students, researchers, managers, and developers in Muslim countries and beyond, eager to increase their share in this 1.6-billion-strong tourism market.

The 21 chapters of this book have been contributed by scholars from 16 countries: Australia, Brunei, China, Croatia, Egypt, France, Germany, Iran, Japan, Malaysia, Saudi Arabia, Singapore, Turkey, the United Arab Emirates, the United Kingdom, and the United States of America. Each chapter sets out a distinct view of tourism in the Muslim world, indicating a vibrant and developing field of study.

Tourism is a powerful tool in poverty alleviation, economic growth, and mutual understanding, but requires responsible and considered development—one that respects the cultural heritage and the environment, while benefiting local communities and promoting tolerance. Understanding the development of tourism in Muslim countries, the experiences of Muslim travelers, and the role of tourism in fostering mutual understanding is therefore of vital importance for scholars and policymakers.

Tourism development requires a trained workforce, which is able to address complex practical and policy problems in a dynamic environment, and hence the need for graduate programs and postgraduate study relevant to the Muslim world. *Hajj* and *Umrah*, for example, entail the management of large numbers of travelers and have important implications when dealing with pandemics. The chapters of this book provide a useful basis for tourism students for advancing academic thought and will surely become required reading for future tourism stakeholders. At the same time, the growth of tourist numbers from the Muslim world implies that Islamic values must be considered in all destinations. As such, the insight of *Tourism in the Muslim*

World into the particularities of Muslim travelers presents a welcome contribution to tourism scholarship.

Yet this book goes beyond the purely academic, serving also as a practical tool for policymakers and tourism stakeholders. The Middle East, North Africa, and much of Central, Southern, and Southeast Asia have seen increasing and rapid tourism development over the past years. It is vital that tourism stakeholders have a comprehensive knowledge regarding the attitudes of residents when developing tourism and hosting tourists in these predominantly Muslim countries.

The UNWTO Global Code of Ethics for Tourism states that "an attitude of tolerance and respect for the diversity of religious, philosophical and moral beliefs, are the foundation and the consequence of responsible tourism." This important study of the interaction between tourism and the Muslim world represents a determined step toward greater understanding between the host and the tourist.

Taleb Rifai
Secretary-General
United Nations World Tourism Organization, Madrid, Spain

Chapter 1

INTRODUCTION
Islam and Tourism

Noel Scott
The University of Queensland, Australia
Jafar Jafari
University of Wisconsin-Stout, USA
University of Algarve, Portugal

This introductory chapter discusses the significance of tourism in the Muslim world and provides some basic information that will help non-Muslim readers to understand the later chapters. This is followed by an introduction to the four parts of the book: Part I examines the characteristics of Islamic religious practices; Part II discusses tourism development in various Muslim countries; Part III examines the experiences of Muslim travelers; and Part IV discusses the issues related to tourism promotion in Muslim countries.

Following the groundbreaking book *Tourism and Religion* by Boris Vukonić (1996), a few recent volumes have explored the intersection of tourism and religion, including *Religious Tourism and Pilgrimage Festivals Management* (Raj and Morpeth 2007) and *Tourism, Religion and Spiritual Journeys* (Timothy and Olsen 2006). This book also shares the idea that the study of the intersection of tourism and religion, spirituality, and pilgrimage can illuminate many topics of interest to the social sciences, as well as important from a policy and industry viewpoint. These topics include heritage and identity; community development; regional, national, and global economic and political systems; spiritual experiences and their effects; and the development, promotion, and marketing of tourism destinations. They allow the conceptual and theoretical foundations of tourism to be better understood.

This book, therefore, puts tourism in the foreground and looks at how Islam is affecting the direction of tourism development and various choices

Tourism in the Muslim World
Bridging Tourism Theory and Practice, Volume 2, 1–13
Copyright © 2010 by Emerald Group Publishing Limited
All rights of reproduction in any form reserved
ISSN: 2042-1443/doi:10.1108/S2042-1443(2010)0000002004

that both individuals and governments are making about the types of travel they prefer. Topics such as religion (Alipour and Heydari 2005; Bandyopadhyay, Morais and Chick 2008; Din 1989; Francis, Williams, Annis and Robbins 2008; Poria, Butler and Airey 2003; Raj and Morpeth 2007; Rinschede 1992; Shani, Rivera and Severt 2007; Timothy and Olsen 2006; Turner 1973; Woodward 2004) and pilgrimage (Ahmed 1992; Belhassen, Caton and Stewart 2008; Bhardwaj 1998; Collins-Kreiner 2010; Collins-Kreiner and Gatrell 2006; Delaney 1990; Digance 2003; Doron 2005; Fleischer 2000; Haq and Jackson 2009; McDonnell 1990; Metcalf 1990; Pinto 2007; Raj and Morpeth 2007; Rinschede 1992; Tapper 1990; Turner 1973) have been important themes of the tourism literature and, indeed, may have been historically the impetus and origin for what is now called tourism. So why then should one concentrate on Islam?

In order to address this question, this chapter first provides some background information on the political, cultural, and social significance of tourism for Muslims. It is written for a global audience and thus initially discusses some aspects of Islam that Muslims (Islam refers to the religion and Muslims are its adherents) are well familiar with but might not be clearly understood by non-Muslims of the world. It is likely that non-Muslim readers are aware of the *Hajj* as a pilgrimage undertaken to Makkah in the Kingdom of Saudi Arabia, but many may be unfamiliar with the history of Islam, and the population size and geographical extent of the Muslims today.

It is important to recognize the central importance of Islam and the role of *Shari'a* (law) in the daily lives of its 1.6 billion adherents worldwide. In Islam, there is no separation of religious and secular laws; instead, the *Qur'an* identifies objects or actions that are permissible to use or engage in. As such, undertaking tourism is not merely a personal decision but must be permissible by law, which emphasizes the personal and social significance of tourism for Muslims. In order to clarify the position of tourism, Chapter 2 discusses whether it is "legal" for Muslims to undertake tourism—a question that may seem strange for non-Muslim readers. Chapter 3 provides a call for religious tolerance in dealing with other faiths. Given this discussion of the centrality of religion in the life of Muslims, this chapter provides brief details of the history of Islam.

ISLAM AND ITS SPREAD

Islam began in western Arabia with the preaching of Prophet Muhammad (ca. 570–632 CE) and has since spread through expansion, economic trade, missionaries, and migration. CE is an abbreviation of Common Era and is the system used in this book. In this system for recording dates, 2009 CE represents 1430 after Hegira (abbreviated as AH). During his life, Mohammad was able to unite virtually the whole of the Arabian Peninsula under Islam. After his death, Islam expanded north into Syria (636 CE), east into Persia and beyond (636 CE), and west into Egypt (640 CE), and then into Spain (711 CE). Dissention about the procedure for choice of the Muslim leader (caliph) led to the proclamation of a rival caliph in Damascus in 661 and the establishment of the Shia faith (Donner 2004). Islam arrived in the area known today as Pakistan in 711 when the Umayyad dynasty sent a Muslim Arab army that conquered the northwestern part of Indus Valley from Kashmir to the Arabian Sea (Esposito and Donner 1999). Today, the majority of Muslims worldwide are Sunni but Shia Muslims constitute the majority of the population in Iran as well as are significant minorities in Pakistan, India, Iraq, and Afghanistan.

Although such expansion was important to the spread of Islam, trade was also an important factor especially in India, Malaysia, Indonesia, and China. Numerous Muslim merchants, usually of Arab or Persian origin, established trading colonies particularly along the west coast of India. These outposts were important catalysts for the conversion to Islam of many people in India (Donner 2004). Arab merchants established a colony in eastern Sumatra in the 7th century (Gardet 2005). The trading port of Malacca—which controlled the crucial shipping lane through the narrow strait separating Malaya and Sumatra—had a Muslim ruler by the early 15th century. In both cases, the wealth and commercially based assertiveness of these trading cities resulted in the spread of Islam to neighboring areas (Donner 2004). The historical development of Islam in China is discussed further in Chapter 8 and that in Turkministan in Chapter 9.

The Five Pillars

The Islamic faith is articulated in the *Qur'an*, a book that for Muslims contains the written words of God. God's word was revealed to many, including Adam, Moses, and Jesus who are also revered by people of the other faiths. The basic spiritual duties of all Muslims consist of five pillars of faith:

1. Declaring one's complete faith that Allah is the only Supreme Being and Muhammad is the messenger of Allah;
2. Performing five prayers a day;

3. Donating 2.5% of annual income through *Zakat*, a charity tax to help the needy;
4. Fasting (which includes no eating, drinking, or intimacy) during the daytime in Ramadan; and
5. Making a pilgrimage to Makkah (Muhammad's birthplace) at least once, if one has the financial capability and is physically able.

As noted above, Muslims do not distinguish between the religious and the secular but consider Islam to be a complete way of life (Hussain 1999). This way of life is derived from the teachings of the *Qur'an* and from the *Sunnah* (the recorded sayings and behavior of Prophet Muhammad). Islam is based on concepts of human well-being and a good life that stress brotherhood and socioeconomic justice. This requires a balanced satisfaction of both the material and spiritual needs of all humans (Rice and Al-Mossawi 2002). In the Islamic world, adherents must follow many rules in order to gain access to divine reality and religion is an integral part of daily life. Islamic teachings forbid the consumption of alcohol and pork, and prohibit gambling. Alcoholic beverages, like any intoxicant or narcotic, are believed to be harmful to the health. They take away an individual's productivity and cause much harm to society (Yu 1999). The issue of permissible food is taken up again in Chapter 4.

The Hajj

Apart from the number of adherents and their geographic spread, another important reason to study Islam and tourism is that the *Hajj* is one of the largest religious pilgrimage today. Religious tourism is one of the oldest types and "probably as old as religion" itself (Rinschede 1992:53). Pilgrimage was a fundamental component of life for ancient Assyrians and Babylonians (Rinschede 1992). Tourism and Islam "naturally" fit together as Islam also expects pilgrimage by its adherents to Makkah.

The central Muslim pilgrimage or *Hajj* is a journey obligatory on every Muslim, man or woman, who has reached the age of puberty and is of sound mind, and must be performed at least once in his or her life provided that they have the means to do so. In addition to the obligatory *Hajj*, there is a lesser pilgrimage to Makkah, *Umrah*, and Muslims may take other religiously motivated trips known as *ziarat* (Bhardwaj 1998). The *Qur'an* often refers to travel, and Muslims are encouraged to travel for cultural encounters, to gain knowledge to associate with other Muslims, to spread

God's word, and to enjoy and appreciate God's creations (Timothy and Iverson 2006).

In 2008, around 2.5 million adherents made the *Hajj* pilgrimage, with around 1.7 million of these from outside the Kingdom of Saudi Arabia (Kingdom of Saudi Arabia Central Department of Statistics and Information 2009; Kingdom of Saudi Arabia Ministry of Hajj 2009). This annual event of great importance influences the lives of Muslims from around the world. A massive logistical undertaking, it is organized by the Saudi Ministry of Hajj. Today most foreign pilgrims arrive by air. In addition, each year millions choose to undertake *Umrah*, which may be performed multiple times and all year round. Beyond this pilgrimage, Muslims globally are also influenced by their religion in their day-to-day activities, while traveling, as well as in the choice of a destination for discretionary travel. Two chapters of this book discuss aspects of the *Hajj* pilgrimage (Chapters 14 and 20). Visits to local or regional shrines (Bhardwaj 1998) and travel in search of knowledge (*Rihia*) provide further examples of religiously inspired tourism (Din 1989).

However, beyond all the economic, political, and cultural significance of Muslim tourism, such travel and the *Hajj*, in particular, create an intense personal experience (Digance 2006) and shared understanding of the core of Islam (Metcalf 1990). This view is supported in Chapter 14, which examines the experiences of Muslim women during the *Hajj*.

Islam has adherents in many countries, cultures, and ethnic groups. Thus, it is important to distinguish between issues of culture or ethnicity and religion. In particular, some may think that Islam is a faith of the Arabic peoples. It is true that it originated in the Middle East and specifically in the western coast of the Arabian Peninsula; however, today, the country with the largest Muslim population is Indonesia. The religion includes Sunnis, Shi'as, and other groups that vary in their sizes and beliefs, as is commonly found in other religions. Shi'as are concentrated geographically in Iran and Iraq, while the peoples of Indonesia and Malaysia, for example, are predominately Sunni.

A recent study has estimated that there are 1.57 billion Muslims in the world today, representing 23% of an estimated 2009 world population of 6.8 billion (Pew Research Centre 2009). The study found that more than 60% of Muslims live in Asia and about 20% in the Middle East and North Africa. More than 300 million, or one-fifth of the world's Muslim people, live in countries where Islam is not the majority religion and these minority groups are often quite large. India, for example, has the third-largest number of Muslim citizens worldwide (Table 1) (Pew Research Centre 2009).

According the Pew Research Centre (2009), of the 10 countries with the largest Muslim populations, 5 are in Asia: Indonesia (203 million), Pakistan

Table 1. Muslim Populations of the World[a]

Countries	Estimated 2009 Muslim Population	Percentage of Muslims in the Total Population	Percentage of World Muslim Population
Asia-Pacific	972,537,000	24.10	61.9
Afghanistan	28,072,000	99.7	1.8
Azerbaijan	8,765,000	99.2	0.6
Bangladesh	145,312,000	89.6	9.3
Burma (Myanmar)	1,889,000	3.8	0.1
China	21,667,000	1.6	1.4
India	160,945,000	13.4	10.3
Indonesia	202,867,000	88.2	12.9
Iran	73,777,000	99.4	4.7
Kazakhstan	8,822,000	56.4	0.6
Kyrgyzstan	4,734,000	86.3	0.3
Malaysia	16,581,000	60.4	1.1
Nepal	1,231,000	4.2	0.1
Pakistan	174,082,000	96.3	11.1
Philippines	4,654,000	5.1	0.3
Sri Lanka	1,711,000	8.5	0.1
Tajikistan	5,848,000	84.1	0.4
Thailand	3,930,000	5.8	0.3
Turkey	73,619,000	~98	4.7
Turkmenistan	4,757,000	93.1	0.3
Uzbekistan	26,469,000	96.3	1.7
Middle East–North Africa	315,322,000	91.20	20.1
Algeria	34,199,000	98	2.2
Egypt	78,513,000	94.6	5
Iraq	30,428,000	~99	~2
Israel	1,194,000	16.7	0.1
Jordan	6,202,000	98.2	0.4
Kuwait	2,824,000	~95	<1
Lebanon	2,504,000	59.3	0.2
Libya	6,203,000	96.6	0.4
Morocco	31,993,000	~99	~2
Oman	2,494,000	87.7	0.2
Palestinian territories	4,173,000	~98	<1
Qatar	1,092,000	77.5	0.1
Saudi Arabia	24,949,000	~97	~2
Sudan	30,121,000	71.3	1.9
Syria	20,196,000	92.2	1.3
Tunisia	10,216,000	99.5	0.7

Table 1. (*Continued*)

Countries	Estimated 2009 Muslim Population	Percentage of Muslims in the Total Population	Percentage of World Muslim Population
United Arab Emirates	3,504,000	76.2	0.2
Yemen	23,363,000	99.1	1.5
Sub-Saharan Africa	240,632,000	30.10	15.3
Benin	2,182,000	24.4	0.1
Burkina Faso	9,292,000	59	0.6
Cameroon	3,498,000	17.9	0.2
Chad	6,257,000	55.8	0.4
Eritrea	1,854,000	36.5	0.1
Ethiopia	28,063,000	33.9	1.8
Gambia	1,625,000	~95	<1
Ghana	3,787,000	15.9	0.2
Guinea	8,502,000	84.4	0.5
Ivory Coast	7,745,000	36.7	0.5
Kenya	2,793,000	7	0.2
Malawi	1,955,000	12.8	0.1
Mali	12,040,000	92.5	0.8
Mauritania	3,261,000	99.1	0.2
Mozambique	5,224,000	22.8	0.3
Niger	15,075,000	98.6	1
Nigeria	78,056,000	50.4	5
Senegal	12,028,000	96	0.8
Sierra Leone	4,059,000	71.3	0.3
Somalia	8,995,000	98.5	0.6
Tanzania	13,218,000	30.2	0.8
Uganda	3,958,000	12.1	0.3
Europe	38,112,000	5.20	2.40
Albania	2,522,000	79.9	0.2
Bosnia-Herzegovina	1,522,000	~40	<1
France	3,554,000	~6	<1
Germany	4,026,000	~5	<1
Kosovo	1,999,000	89.6	0.1
Russia	16,482,000	11.7	1
United Kingdom	1,647,000	2.7	0.1
Americas	4,596,000	0.50	0.30
United States	2,454,000	0.8	0.2
World	1,571,198,000	22.90	100.00

Source: Pew Research Center (2009)
[a]Countries with over 1,000,000 Muslims.

(174 million), India (161 million), Bangladesh (145 million), and Iran (74 million). Of the remaining five, three are in North Africa (Egypt, Algeria, and Morocco), one in Europe (Turkey), and one in Sub-Saharan Africa (Nigeria). Those living in the Asia-Pacific region constitute over 50% of all Muslims worldwide. About half of the Muslim population within Asia lives in South Asia and the remainder are somewhat equally divided between this region (26%) and Central-Western Asia (24%)—see Figure 1. Very few (<1%), however, live in the Pacific region (Pew Research Centre 2009).

About 13% of all Muslims in the world live in Indonesia, while Pakistan, India, and Bangladesh together are home to nearly a third (31%). Indonesia also accounts for about 80% of Muslims living in Southeast Asia. Other Asian countries with more than 20 million Muslims include Afghanistan (28 million) and China (22 million).

Tourism Development in Muslim Countries

The Muslim market, both for religious and personal reasons, is of great significance. The number of Muslim travelers is expected to increase in future as the global population increases, along with prosperity in Muslim countries. Further, as Al-Hamarneh and Steiner (2004) note, "The importance of intra-Muslim traffic has led to a focus in some countries on Islamic tourism." This concept discussed in Chapter 12 is due to a confluence of factors, including the discomfort some Muslims feel in resorts and places where the behavior of other guests is inconsistent with Islam principles; a reaction to difficulties of traveling to some countries after September 11, 2001; Muslim countries recognizing an opportunity for tourism development consistent with Islamic principles; and the growing populations and economies of countries with large Muslim populations.

Developing tourism in Islamic countries may create tensions between economic and social development. In many nations, where Islam is the foundation of society and order of law, countries are increasingly considering tourism as a source of development and hence these Islamic principles are influencing tourism policy, development objectives, and the management and operation of the industry. A number of studies have examined the dynamics of tourism in countries where Islam is the majority religion (Alavi and Yasin 2000; Burns and Cooper 1997; Din 1982, 1989; Henderson 2003; Sharpley 2008). A number of chapters of this book discuss aspects of tourism development in various countries, including Brunei, Indonesia, Malaysia, and Singapore (Chapter 6), the Kingdom of Saudi Arabia (Chapters 7 and 16),

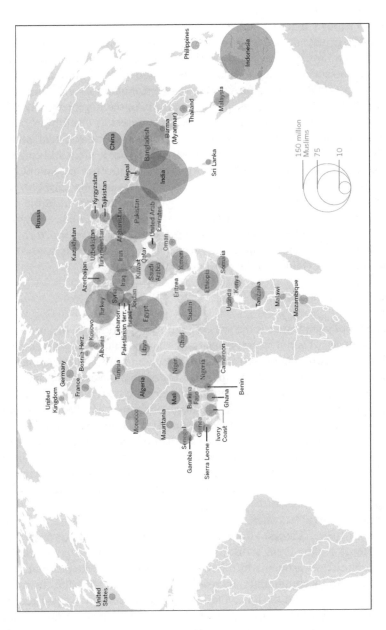

Figure 1. Muslim Populations of the World
Source: Pew Research Center (2009)

China (Chapter 8), Turkmenistan (Chapter 9), Jordon (Chapter 10), Iran (Chapters 11 and 13), and Maldives (Chapter 5).

Din (1989) argues that, due to religious beliefs, tourism is discouraged in some Muslim countries because of its impact on the local community. This raises issues of social sustainability also discussed in the context of other religious visitations. Joseph and Kavoosi (2001), for example, examined the impact of Western tourism on the host community in the pilgrimage town of Pushkar, India. Here, tourism is perceived as a threat to "tradition" and religion even while a large segment of the population is dependent on its economic benefits. In the Islamic context, Muslim social leaders and citizens are concerned that tourism will lead to drug and alcohol consumption, spread unacceptable behavior and immodest dress, open displays of affection between males and females, and lead to sexual prostitution and gambling that are forbidden by Islamic law (Henderson 2003). A better outcome would be that tourism in Islamic countries develops through consultation and planning where the local social and religious context is taken into account (Shunnaq, Schwab and Reid 2008).

Outbound Travel by Muslims

Another area of significance is the growing outbound travel by Muslims from Islamic countries. Today, improvements in the economies of "developing countries" are creating increased self-confidence and pushing to prominence values and cultures different from a previously dominant Western perspective associated with liberalism, consumption, and arguably excess. These values have been to some extent reflected in the image of tourism as a hedonistic and excessive activity (Mazrui 1997). A discussion of the Islamic religion and its relation to tourism emphasizes reflection on the popular "Western" image of tourism and its values and the discourse that surrounds it, such as that Islam is incompatible with the decadent Western practices of commercial tourism. This view of tourism emphasizes holidays as a context for escape from social bounds.

Muslims are avid travelers and today tourism for pleasure is more acceptable in their societies. However, their behavior in terms of food and travel patterns makes them a distinct group (Timothy and Iverson 2006). This may require adjustments in the tourism offering of some destinations. Additionally, to accommodate increasing numbers of Muslim tourists, especially from the Middle East, Destination Management Organizations are advised to add Muslim information to their websites such as prayer times and locations where mosques and *halal* food can be found. Further, tourism operators are encouraged to educate their staff on cross-cultural communication to allow them to treat Muslim tourists with respect (Timothy and Iverson 2006). As Muslims observe a dress code and avoid free mixing, hotels depending on this market may offer separate swimming pool and recreational facilities (Hashim, Murphy and Hashim 2007).

Islamic Travel

As briefly noted earlier, there is a growing trend among Muslims toward travel to other Islamic countries for their holidays. This growth of the Muslim market helps to encourage the development of other Islamic countries through the expenditure provided by Muslim tourists traveling and holidaying in such destinations, and is also likely to create less social impacts because the customs and social mores of such tourists are similar. Thus growth in "Islamic tourism" has been noted by some authors (Al-Hamarneh and Steiner 2004; Zamani-Farahani and Henderson 2010). One reason for this trend is that for Muslims, "the spiritual goal is to reinforce one's submission to the ways of God, the social goal which follows is to encourage and strengthen the bond of *sillaturrahim* (Muslim fraternity) among the *Ummah* (Muslim community)" (Din 1989:552).

This trend is not simply based on religious pilgrimage (though this may be an element) but also to give more local and regional social context to cultures of travel. As Al-Hamarneh and Steiner note, "Part of the vision includes reorienting tourist destinations towards less consumption and 'Western culture loaded' sites and towards more Islamic historical religious and cultural sites…. A special place in this concept is held by the new 'touristic' interpretations of pilgrimage and efforts to merge religious and leisure tourism in joint programs" (Al-Hamarneh and Steiner 2004:183).

Another impetus to travel between Islamic countries is due to the consequences of the September 11 incident in 2001 (Steiner 2007). Terrorism and political instability, according to Al-Hamarneh and Steiner (2004), added to the fear, particularly by Western tourists, of visiting Muslim countries (Chapter 12). At the same time, tight security and travel regulations (see Chapter 15) increased the number of Muslim tourists holidaying in Muslim countries such as Malaysia. Responding to these effects, Malaysia promotes its tourism as "Muslim-friendly" (Timothy and Iverson 2006).

The four countries that dominate inbound Islamic tourism globally (Morocco, Egypt, Turkey, and Malaysia) received 17.5 million tourists in 2004. There is a call to open and promote Muslim countries' tourism attractions, as reflected, for example, by the November 2005 inaugural Tourism Fair of Islamic Countries in Istanbul (Hashim, Murphy and Muhammad 2003). Serious discussions about boosting Islamic tourism in Malaysia began in the middle of 2008, during the inaugural Global Islamic Tourism Conference and Exhibition held in Kuala Lumpur. An Islamic Civilization Theme Park in Kuala Terengganu attracted 1.9 million tourists in 18 months from February 2008 when it opened (Taman Tamadun Islam 2009). Singapore holds the Hari Raya Festival annually, a month-long cultural event celebrating the country's rich Muslim roots. In 2007, the largest destination for Saudi travelers in the region was Malaysia (78,298), followed by Indonesia (39,238).

Issues in Tourism Marketing

Apart from the important issue of tourism development, Muslim countries will often develop promotional material for their country and this raises issues of what images to use to attract tourists from overseas. A number of prior studies have examined the destination images used in Muslim countries (Burns and Cooper 1997; Cohen-Hattab and Katz 2001; Din 1982; Hashim et al 2007; Schneider and Sönmez 1999), finding that they focus on four categories: arts and architectures, festivals, conduct, and dress code. The area of destination promotion also then highlights the potential conflict between using (for example) women in bikinis in destination images as possibly attractive to people from Western cultures versus images of a more traditional nature. However, for Muslims, "even when the religious-political motivation is absent, religious attributes in the guise of architectural forms, history, festivals and rituals and lifestyles have always featured prominently in promotional literature" (Din 1989:543). Thus, "unlike mass tourism which for Muslims is 'characterized by hedonism, permissiveness, lavishness'" (Sonmez 2001:127) religion plays a role in tourism decisions regardless of whether the motivation to travel is religious or not. This issue is discussed in Chapters 17, 18, 19, and 20 from a tourist perspective and in Chapter 5 from an employee viewpoint.

Finally, the editors would like to note that this is an academic treatment of tourism in the Muslim world. For this reason, the abbreviation PBUH used in conjunction with the name of Prophet Muhammad is not included, although no disrespect is intended from this omission. Further, the opinions of the authors are their own and they do not represent the views of the volume and series editors.

CONCLUSION

The size and growth in the populations of Muslim countries and their increasing economic wealth indicates that there is likely to be growth in both the *Hajj* and *Umrah* in Saudi Arabia. This suggests a need to increase the capacity of infrastructure to cater to increased numbers of pilgrims, a situation known to the Kingdom and reflected in its tourism master plan.

It is also likely that shrine tourism in Asia will grow in popularity among both Muslims and non-Muslims. The local or regional nature of the visits to shrines offers opportunities for many destinations in the study area to develop new products and services, such as events that complement the religious observances. However, such development must be sensitive to both the wishes of the local people and to the needs of Muslim travelers.

To accommodate increasing numbers of Muslim tourists, especially from the Middle East, Destination Management Organizations, particularly in Western countries, may wish to add Muslim-relevant information to their websites (Timothy and Iverson 2006). These organizations need to understand and respect Muslim attitudes when choosing visual images and text for the purpose of promotion.

Tourism operators may also educate their staff on cross-cultural communication to allow them to accommodate Muslim tourists appropriately (Timothy and Iverson 2006). Hotels that cater to the Islamic market are now found in a number of countries. It is also recommended that tourism authorities become more aware of the variation in attitudes and behaviors among Muslims from different countries.

Clearly, the growth of Muslim tourism is a topic of global religious and socioeconomic significance, and one about which there is a lack of detailed information and research. This calls for further investigation of Islamic tourism, fostered in academic circles and put into practice in the field of operation.

Acknowledgments

This work draws on a chapter entitled "Islam and Tourism: Asia and the Pacific in Focus" that was prepared for a book edited by the United Nations World Tourism Organization (Scott and Jafari 2010).

PART I

ISLAM AND TRAVEL & TOURISM

Chapter 2

TOURISM AND ISLAMIC LAW

Hassan Saad Sanad
Ayman Mounier Kassem
Minya University, Egypt
Noel Scott
The University of Queensland, Australia

Abridgement: There has been much controversy, if not dispute, especially among non-Muslims over the attitude of Islam to tourism. One may claim that this debate is mainly due to non-Muslims' misunderstanding of the true nature of the religion and its *Shari'a* or Islamic law. This chapter attempts to show in some detail tourism from the perspective of the Islamic creed and to demonstrate that the religion does encourage tourism and regards it as legal. To do this the chapter reviews a number of sources including the holy *Qur'an*. **Keywords:** *Shari'a* law; Islamic law

INTRODUCTION

Political and religious systems are two forces that institutionalize the way of life of people. The prevailing systems of thought influence many social and individual behaviors and this is commonly discussed in the tourism research literature in relation to the behavior of travelers and tourism business operators and their staff. What is not often discussed, however, is the effect of these belief systems on the appropriate methods and objects suitable for scholarly debate.

Scholars in Western society may take for granted the separation of religious beliefs and legal and political systems, but this duality is not universal. Indeed, the degree of interrelationship among religion, politics, and

Tourism in the Muslim World
Bridging Tourism Theory and Practice, Volume 2, 17–30
Copyright © 2010 by Emerald Group Publishing Limited
All rights of reproduction in any form reserved
ISSN: 2042-1443/doi:10.1108/S2042-1443(2010)0000002005

the law varies greatly from a country like China, where religion and political law are completely separate, to the Islamic Republic of Iran, where church and state are based on Islamic law (Hudman and Jackson 2002).

One basic difference between Western law and *Shari'a* or Islamic law is that the former is essentially secular while the latter is essentially religious. The laws of the United States and the countries of Europe are based on a system of codes as enacted by legislature and interpreted and applied through courts. It is a human and secular law that can be changed by the same authority that enacted it. Islamic law is essentially different as it is fundamentally divine law and as such is basically immutable (Anderson 1959).

To a Muslim there is an ethical quality in every human action, characterized by *qubh* (literally, ugliness, unsuitability) on the one hand or *husn* (literally, beauty, suitability) on the other. This ethical quality is not such as can be perceived by human reason; instead, it is dependent on divine revelation. Thus, all human actions are subsumed under five categories; as commanded, recommended, left legally indifferent, reprehended, or else prohibited. It is only the middle category (things that are legally indifferent) for which there is any scope for human legislation. However, because Islamic law deals with the whole of human conduct, it therefore covers matters that Western people would not consider law at all. Islamic law determines what foods and drinks are legal or permitted (*halal*) and may be consumed by Muslims, the way to dress, what entertainments may be seen, and how to behave. Islamic law prohibits gambling, the giving or taking of interest in financial transactions, and certain types of personal relationships. The extent to which these laws are enforced varies from country to country.

Islamic law withholds legislative power from the ruler, the government, or the state; it only allows these bodies to make administrative regulations within the limits that it itself assigns and on the subjects that it itself refers—regulations that by definition must never come into conflict with its own enactments. Some Islamic rulers in the past have given little heed to this restriction, but they have always been careful to pay lip service to it (Schacht 1959).

These matters are important for a number of reasons. First, Muslims constitute around 25% of the population of the world and Indonesia, the largest Muslim country, has a population that exceeds 200 million, and 88% of these are Muslims. Further, Muslim countries are developing economically, with Saudi Arabia, the United Arab Emirates, Iraq, and Iran controlling a substantial percentage of the world's oil supplies.

Countries as diverse as Malaysia, Egypt, and the Maldives are also embracing tourism as a developing segment of their economy and must reconcile its benefits with the social impacts on the local population. Tourism may, therefore, be a source of political tension. Since the 1970s the Muslim world has experienced an Islamic revival that has slowed and even reversed the rush toward uncritical Westernization. For a number of complex reasons many Muslim countries have embarked upon a program of part or complete "Islamization" of their societies, economies, and legal systems. Examples include the revolution in Iran in 1979 when the country was declared an Islamic State. In Pakistan, Malaysia, Indonesia, and even secular Turkey, Islamist parties are gaining popular support. Therefore, it is important to understand the culture and way of life of these countries, which are at least partly determined by Islamic religious laws that are taken very seriously by governments and local populations (Hussain 1999).

This chapter examines the source and nature of Islamic law and discusses an important question for tourists and the tourism industry in interacting with it. This question is whether it is "legal" for Muslims to undertake tourism. Such a question may be seen as unnecessary for many scholars embedded in a Western ethos and, indeed, may be seen as an assault on freedom of choice and personal liberty. Further, it may not be seen as a question suitable for academic discussion, as it resides in the domain of ethics and the law not that of tourism research.

However, it is argued here that the question is important for consideration by tourism scholars for a number of reasons. First, it is important as it confronts a central issue for a globalizing world where acceptance of Western philosophy cannot be taken for granted; that is, how do tourism scholars deal with a context where Western values are in the minority? Second, by making problematic the structures and influences that determine tourism flows, it may provide insight on their likely future developments.

SHARI'A LAW

The first source of Islamic law is the holy *Qur'an*. The second is the *Sunnah* or customs of Prophet Mohammed. The third is the consensus of jurists (or the Muslim Community). The fourth is that which follows from the above and together these four sources form *Shari'a* or the holy Islamic law, which occupies an essential part of the lives of Muslims and therefore its features are agents in determining social order and community life. This theology and law go hand in hand in Muslim countries. There is a common view that *Shari'a* is fixed. But in fact this holy law has coexisted and interacted with statute law issued by rulers, as well as customary conduct (Hashim et al 2007; Schacht 1959; Zubaida 2003).

The Muslim nation agrees unanimously that *Shari'a* is a mercy and is intended for the interests of people in both life and the hereafter. It is neither harsh nor strangling. This is apparent in God's ensuing words: "We have sent you [i.e., Prophet Mohammed] down as a mercy for people" (*The Chapter of Prophets*, 107). In his exegesis, Al-Qurtubi, a famous Muslim scholar, is quoted as saying: "The wise are unanimous that the religious laws of the prophets are verily for the good and interests of creatures in both life and the hereafter." Likewise, according to Imam Al-Shatibi, another Muslim scholar, "The Lawmaker [i.e., God] has based the [Islamic] law on the goods [of creatures]" (Al-Shatibi 1960:134). Similarly, Ibn Al-Qaiem (1940a) stresses: "*Shari'a* is mainly based on the interests of bondsmen in both life and the hereafter. It is all justice, mercy and good incarnate. Henceforth, everything that goes beyond justice, mercy, good and wisdom has nothing to do with *Shari'a*" (*I'alam Al-Moaqaien*, literally declaration of jurisprudents).

The reason and wisdom of these religious commands are very significant. Thus, a subject entitled "*maqasid Al-Shari'a*" (literally, the intentions of *Shari'a*) is now taught at universities concerned with Islamic studies. In brief, there is no restraint imposed on reason. Likewise, every (religious) command has its significance, which is mainly dedicated for the good of people. Islamic *Shari'a* abounds in many examples demonstrating that it aims at the good of people. To help people work harder, Islam urges Muslims to roam about the land and move from one place to another for pleasure (i.e., tourism). Moreover, it permits Muslims to break their fasting or to bring together or shorten their prayers in case of travel, even when on pleasure trips.

Islamic Law and Tourism

Tourism is an activity guaranteed by both Islam and international law, although some Muslims may look at international law with suspicion or consider it as not a lawful or useful activity. Tourism development and its overall benefits are a source of both envy and suspicion in many Islamic countries. The reasons for this uncertainty are based on arguments both about its moral and legal status, as well as its economic and environmental impact. Tourism has been viewed by some Muslims as a means of leisure and entertainment that does not have any real or lasting value. This view is held despite the benefits of tourism to the national economy as well as the propagation of cultural values and opportunity to build good relationships between people and nations of different cultures (Sanad 2008).

Tourism is also considered by others to be harmful to the environment because it requires extra construction of buildings and other activities that will produce pollution. Some Islamic scholars fear tourism because they think that it would lead inevitably to an exchange or mixing of various cultural traditions, values, beliefs, and attitudes. Hence, they oppose such things for fear of diluting Islamic values and culture. Development of tourism is also opposed on the basis that the income from it will not be retained but transferred to Western companies in the United States and Europe, since they are usually responsible for building hotels and operating airlines for tourists. Further, others consider that the General Agreement on Tariff and Trade (GATT), the General Agreement of Trade in Services (GATS), the Trade-Related Aspects of Intellectual Property Rights (TRIPS), and electronic trade laws are set up to favor Western countries (Badawi 2006:5).

On the other hand, scholars from countries such as Egypt have emphasized the overall benefits of tourism, especially due to its contribution to the national economy and the development of infrastructure (Badawi 2006:6). However, they warn against the overdependency on tourism as a primary activity and source of income and advocate a balanced approach to economic development, involving trade and development of manufacturing industry as well as tourism. They fear that overdependence is dangerous because it opens the country to the possibility of foreign action, leading to a major economic crisis or indeed economic ruin. A second criticism, which forms the focus of this chapter, concerns the lawfulness of tourism and whether there is or is not a basic human right to practice it similar to the right to life, the right of dignity, integrity, the right of freedom, and the right of human expression.

Islamic View of Tourism

A point to stress right here is that Islam entitles the right of moving from one place to another (i.e., tourism). Nevertheless, it puts boundaries, rules, and regulations for this right. A reading of the holy *Qur'an* reveals that Islam encourages tourism. The very word is literally mentioned in the holy *Qur'an*. *Siyaha* (literally, tourism) in Arabic is derived from the word *yasih*, which literally means "to travel, journey, rove and roam about" (Cowan 1976:446). This word is mentioned in the holy *Qur'an* in *Surat Al-Tawba* (literally, the Chapter of Repentance) in which Allah says in the second *ayah*, *fasiyhou fi al-ard* (travel freely in the land) (*Surat Al-Tawba*, 2).

Although Islam entitles the right to journey from one place to another, tourism has to be of some purpose. It is not encouraged to escape from one's duties or to get away from one's day-to-day responsibilities. To put it another way, Islam does not encourage tourism to isolate oneself from the rest of the community. Although isolation or hermitage is allowed in some religions, it is prohibited in Islam. This is well illustrated in *Surat Al-Hadeed* (literally, The Chapter of Iron), which stresses:

> Then We caused Our messengers to follow in their footsteps; and We caused Jesus, son of Mary, to follow, and gave him the Gospel, and placed compassion and mercy in the hearts of those who followed him. But monasticism they invented. We ordained it not for them. Only seeking Allah's pleasure, and they observed it not with right observance (*Surat Al-Hadeed*, 27).

This isolation is also prohibited by the traditions of Prophet Mohammed. Saad ibn Abi-Wakkaas, another companion, reports that when the Prophet was told that Uthman ibn Mazoon, his other companion, left his work, family, everything and left enjoyable things, the Prophet sent for Othman and reprimanded him:

> I am against isolation—that is my *Sunnah*. In my *Sunnah*, I must pray, sleep, fast, eat, marry women and fulfill my responsibility. Anyone not doing these is outside my *Sunnah*. Oh Othman! Your family has a right and you must give them their rights; your body has a right and you must give it its rights (Al-Bukhari, The Chapter of Sunnah of Marriage, 1402).

As mentioned earlier, Islam encourages tourism for beneficial purposes including *Hajj* and *Umrah* (literally, the Higher and Lesser Pilgrimages, respectively), remedy, education, business, trade, entertainment, fun, and interest. However, words like "fun" and "entertainment" are not to be misunderstood here. Muslims are ordered to seek fun and entertainment. But this is to be done according to regulations. In other words, Muslims are to seek fun and entertainment in a way that does not go beyond the rules and obligations of Islamic *Shari'a*. For example, a Muslim cannot go somewhere and have sex or drink alcohol and claim that this was fun or entertainment, simply because such matters are banned in Islam. But they can go somewhere for refreshment, which can be through swimming, riding horses, practicing sports, etc. Rather, doing such matters is much encouraged in Islam. It was reported that Umar Ibn al-Khattab, one of the Prophet's famous and close companions, and the second caliph in Islam, said, "Teach your children swimming, shooting and horse riding." Doubtless, all such matters are sorts of fun and entertainment. Thus, fun is legitimate, but regulated and organized in Islam.

Surat Al-Ankabout (literally, The Spider) informs of another purpose of tourism: consideration and contemplation. The ensuing *ayah* asks people to journey here and there in the world to contemplate the creation of God. To quote it:

> Say: "*Travel* through the earth and see how Allah did originate creation; so will Allah produce a later creation: for Allah has power over all things" (*Surat Al-Ankabout*, 20; italics added).

Likewise, *Surat Al-An'am* (literally, The Cattle) urges people to roam about the earth to consider the destiny of those who preceded them, especially those who cast aspersions on God's Word:

> Say: "*Travel* through the earth and see what was the end of those who rejected Truth" (*Surat Al-An'am*, 11; italics added).

The same thing is stressed in *Surat Mohammed*:

> Do they not travel through the earth, and see what was the end of those before them? (*Surat Mohammed*, 10).

In his interpretation of this *ayah*, Sheikh Muhammad Rasheed Redda, a Muslim scholar, writes:

> Allah ordered us to work and made tourism as a must. Tourism is not just classable but obligatory in Islam, as the Zmakhshary said.

Tourism According to Islamic Shari'a

Regardless of whether tourism is encouraged, desirable, or obligatory, a Muslim must follow the rules and regulations given by the *Shari'a* (Mehmet 1991). Islam is a universal religion. Thus, one of the main purposes of tourism in Islam is to introduce the religion of Islam and the Word of God to all people. This is an order from Allah to Prophet Mohammed in the holy *Qur'an*. In *Surat Sabaa* (literally, Sheba), Allah says:

> We have not sent thee but as a universal (Messenger) to men, giving them glad tidings, and warning them (against sin), but most men understand not (*Surat Sabaa*, 28).

Also, in *Surat Al-Aaraf* (literally, The Heights), Allah stresses:

> Say: "O men! I am sent unto you all, as the Apostle of Allah, to Whom belongeth the dominion of the heavens and the earth: there is no god but He: it is He That giveth both life and death. So believe in Allah and His Apostle, the Unlettered Prophet, who believeth in Allah and His words: follow him that (so) ye may be guided.

These *ayahs* highlight the universality of Islam and that Islam has a universal message for the whole of mankind regardless of their race, color, creed, social status, and location. Hence, this message is to be transferred to all people peacefully without threat, obligation, or force. Then this is a type of tourism with a specific mission, religious in this case.

Of the other *ayahs* that stress this fact are *Surat Al-Baqara* (literally, The Cow):

> Let there be no compulsion in religion: Truth stands out clear from Error: whoever rejects evil and believes in Allah hath grasped the most trustworthy handhold, that never breaks. And Allah heareth and knoweth all things (*Surat Al-Baqara*, 256).

Surat Al-Imran (literally, The Family of Imran):

> Let there arise out of you a band of people inviting to all that is good, enjoining what is right, and forbidding what is wrong: They are the ones to attain felicity (*Surat Al-Imran*, 88).

Surat Al-Baqara:

> Thus, have We made of you an *Ummat* justly balanced, that ye
> might be witnesses over the nations, and the Apostle a witness
> over yourselves; and We appointed the *Qibla* to which thou
> wast used, only to test those who followed the Apostle from
> those who would turn on their heels (From the Faith). Indeed
> it was (A change) momentous, except to those guided by
> Allah. And never would Allah make your faith of no effect.
> For Allah is to all people most surely full of kindness, Most
> Merciful (*Surat Al-Baqa*, 100).

Tourism and Promotion of Science

The first *ayah* of the holy *Qur'an* encourages Muslims to seek all forms of
beneficial knowledge and strive toward that purpose even if one has to travel
to China; in those times China was far away and very difficult to get to.
However, with the advent of technology and air travel, no land is now difficult
to reach. Likewise, travel to space is encouraged in Islam to seek knowledge.
The first *ayahs* of the holy *Qur'an* urge Muslims to read and learn:

> *Read* in the name of thy Lord who createth. He createth man
> from a clot. Read: And thy Lord is the Most Bounteous, Who
> teacheth by the pen, [He] teacheth man that which he knew
> not (*Surat Al-Alaque*, 1–5; italics added).

This is one of the purposes of tourism—seeking knowledge. Thus,
learning and seeking knowledge is one type of tourism in Islam. It is
unreasonable, therefore, to consider Islam as being against tourism. As
mentioned above, all Islamic principles urge people to travel and see the
other nations. How can one know and experience the *ayahs* of the holy
Qur'an without traveling to various places? For example, in the holy *Qur'an*
Allah tells His Prophet to go to the sea and experience things he did not
know. Consider, for example, the ensuing *ayahs* from *Surat Fousselat*
(literally, They are Explained in Detail):

> Soon will We show them our Signs in the (furthest) regions
> (of the earth), and in their own souls, until it becomes manifest
> to them that this is the Truth. Is it not enough that thy Lord
> doth witness all things? (*Surat Fousselat*, 53).

As mentioned here, Muslims can travel anywhere in the world, stipulated that they do not go beyond the rules and obligations of Islamic *Shari'a*. The early Muslims were very advanced in many different fields such as geography, medicine, chemistry, and so forth. They traveled here and there in the world whether for the sake of knowledge, development, or trade. This, then, is the benefit of traveling—tourism. To give examples:

- Sulayman Al Bahar traveled by ship between China and India to study life and the aquatic world.
- Abu Zayd Al-Sarafy gathered a lot of knowledge about India and other countries surrounding it.
- Similarly, Ali ibn Hasan Al-Masudi traveled to many world countries to learn as much as he could about science. His book, *Moroog Al-Zahab*, is considered one of the well-known books in this field.
- Ibn Joubair and Ibn Battoota wrote a popular book on the morals of traveling, something that is considered a travel guidebook.
- Al-Hassan ibn Wazaanand Al-Jabarty and Ahmed ibn Majed developed maps that helped the first explorers to discover India and the other civilizations.
- In the field of medicine, physics, and chemistry, there are famous scientists of the sort of Al-Hassan ibn Al-Haytham, Abu Bakr, Al-Razy, and Ibn Al-Nafees who are well known in Europe and many other parts in the world.

Main Purposes of Tourism in Islam

Islam allows tourism for the purpose of amusement and entertainment. From time immemorial, people have moved from place to place. Even before the advent of Islam, the Arabs visited the holy city of Makkah in Saudi Arabia to perform *Hajj* (i.e., pilgrimage), trade, and entertainment.

The Arabs visited Makkah for the so-called "two journeys of winter and summer." This continued before as well as after Islam. In *Surat Al-Hajj* (literally, The Higher Pilgrimage), Allah says:

> And proclaim unto mankind the Pilgrimage. They will come unto thee on foot and on every lean camel; they will come from every deep ravine. That they may witness things that are of benefit to them, and mention the name of Allah on appointed days over the beast of cattle that He hath bestowed upon them.

Then eat thereof and feed therewith the poor unfortunate (*Surat Al-Hajj*, 27–28).

Also, in *Surat Al-Mulk* (literally, Dominion), Allah stresses:

It is He Who hath made the earth subservient unto you, so walk in the paths thereof and eat of His providence. And unto Him will be the resurrection (of the dead) (*Al-Mulk*, 15).

Likewise, in *Surat Al-Nessaa* (literally, Women), Allah pronounces:

Whoso migrateth for the cause of Allah will find much refuge and abundance in the earth, and whoso forsaketh his home, a fugitive unto Allah and His messenger, and death overtaketh him, his reward is then incumbent on Allah. Allah is ever Forgiving, Merciful. And when ye go forth in the land, it is no sin for you to curtail (your) worship if ye fear that those who disbelieve may attack you. In truth the disbelievers are an open enemy to you (*Surat Al-Nessaa*, 100–101).

Islam orders people to have fun, to find amusement meaning, and to travel from place to place so as to see and enjoy what Allah has created for man. This is mentioned in many verses. To give just one example, *Surat Al-Naml* (literally, The Ants) stresses:

Is not He (best) who created the heavens and the earth, and sendeth down for you water from the sky wherewith We cause to spring forth joyous orchards, whose trees it never hath been yours to cause to grow. Is there any God beside Allah? Nay, but they are folk who ascribe equals (unto Him)! 61. Is not He (best) Who made the earth a fixed abode, and placed rivers in the folds thereof, and placed firm hills therein, and hath set a barrier between the two seas? Is there any God beside Allah? Nay, but most of them know not! (*Surat Al-Naml*, 60–61).

All human beings in Islam throughout the world are brothers and sisters. They are equals exactly as the teeth of the comb regardless of their color, gender, creed, etc. Therefore, nothing should separate them. People in Islam, thus, are to move from one place to another to communicate with one another. This fact is stressed by the ensuing verses in *Surat Al-Hojrat* (literally, The Dwellings):

> O mankind! Lo! We have created you male and female, and have made you nations and tribes that ye may know one another. Lo! the noblest of you, in the sight of Allah, is the best in conduct. Lo! Allah is Knower, Aware (*Surat Al-Hojrat*, 13).

So, Islamic law or *Shari'a* allows Muslims to travel. But if they must travel during the holy month of *Ramadan*, they can break their fasting. Also, there are other facilities during travel in Islam because travel is, indeed, difficult.

Prophet Muhammad orders Muslims to have entertainment. He is quoted as saying:

> Have fun, have a good time and enjoy yourselves because if the heart is bored or fatigued, it could not be good (Hadith ibn Majah).

As mentioned before, this is a carte blanch for Muslims to amuse themselves and have fun as long as they get away from all that which may anger Allah and goes beyond His orders and rules.

Also, the Prophet is reported as saying:

> Your body has a right on you; your soul has a right on you; your wife has a right on you. So, you must give every of these their rights (Al-Bukhari).

Man's right to move from one place to another and the right of amusement is a legal right because a tourist is the most important one to spread peace and friendship among nations. This is an order from Allah. This is mentioned in *Surat Al-Hojrat*, which informs people:

> O mankind! We created you from a single (pair) of a male and a female, and made you into nations and tribes, that ye may know each other (not that ye may despise (each other)). Verily the most honored of you in the sight of Allah is (he who is) the most righteous of you. And Allah has full knowledge and is well acquainted with all things (*Surat Al-Hojrat*, 13).

Rights of Non-Muslim Tourists in Islam

In Islam all humans are brothers and sisters. The differences among different cultures, languages, and traditions must be, then, an invitation for cooperation. So, the message of Islam is not restricted to the Arab nations or Muslims. Rather, it addresses all beings in the universe. Islam considers that Christianity and Judaism as correct religions. Accordingly, Muslims can take some principles from both of these religions (Al-Gendy 2005). Islam orders Muslims to respect these religions. This respect is an important aspect of Islam (Shehata 2005). There are many verses in the holy *Qur'an* that speak of Jesus the Christ, his mother Lady Mary the Virgin, and Moses. Islam appreciates these three and all the other holy people. For example, Allah says in *Surat Al-Imran* (literally, The Family of Imran):

> Allah preferred Adam and Noah and the Family of Abraham and the Family of Imran above (all His) creatures. They were descendants one of another. Allah is Hearer, Knower. (Remember) when the wife of Imran said: My Lord I have vowed unto Thee that which is in my belly as a consecrated (offering). Accept it from me. Lo! Thou, only Thou, art the Hearer, the Knower! And when she was delivered she said: My Lord! Lo! I am delivered of a female. Allah knew best of what she was delivered. The male is not as the female; and Lo! I have named her Mary, and Lo! I crave Thy protection for her and for her offspring from Satan the outcast (*Surat Al-Imran*, 33–36).

Freedom of Religion in Islam

Every person has the freedom of religion. So all tourists from all sources (religion or otherwise) are respectable in Islam. Moreover, Islam forbids Muslims to fight against non-Muslims except for self-defense (Uriely, Israeli and Reichel 2003). The holy *Qur'an* abounds in many *ayahs* that urge Muslims to such principles. Of such *ayahs* are *Surat Al-Hajj* (literally, The Pilgrimage):

> Sanction is given unto those who fight because they have been wronged; and Allah is indeed Able to give them victory. Those who have been driven from their homes unjustly only because they said: Our Lord is Allah. For had it not been for Allah's repelling some men by means of others, cloisters and churches and oratories and mosques, wherein the name of Allah is oft

mentioned, would assuredly have been pulled down. Verily Allah helpeth one who helpeth Him. Lo! Allah is Strong, Almighty (*Surat Al-Hajj*, 39–40).

Also *Surat Al-Baqara* stresses:

> Fight in the way of Allah against those who fight against you, but begin not hostilities. Lo! Allah loveth not, aggressors (*Surat Al-Baqara*, 190).

Islam allows Muslims to have good relations with non-Muslims, whether they are people of the "book" or not. Also, it urges them to be indulgent in dealings with them including trade, travel, and daily experiences, such as eating. It orders Muslims to respect the traditions and dogma of other religions. Muslims are ordered to be polite, decent, wise, and peaceful while discussing religion with non-Muslims (Mawlawy 1987). Thus, Muslim tourists are ordered to show respect to the customs and traditions of the countries they visit irrespective of the religion adopted in this country.

This is mentioned in many *ayahs*. To give just an example, Allah says in *Surat Al-Mumtahana* (literally, The Woman to be Examined):

> Allah forbiddeth you not those who warred not against you on account of religion and drove you not out from your homes, that ye should show them kindness and deal justly with them. Lo! Allah loveth the just dealers. Allah forbiddeth you only those who warred against you on account of religion and have driven you out from your homes and helped to drive you out, that ye make friends of them. Whosoever maketh friends of them (All) such are wrong-doers (*Surat Al-Mumtahana*, 8–9).

CONCLUSION

This chapter examined the interaction of *Shari'a* (Islamic law) and tourism as a lawful activity. Based on its discussion, one can conclude that tourism is a human right under Islamic law and that those Muslims who prohibit tourism are ignorant of the true nature of *Shari'a*. Islam regards the differences in culture, language, race, and status between human beings as an invitation for cooperation not a reason for fighting.

Chapter 3

DO WE ALWAYS UNDERSTAND EACH OTHER?

Boris Vukonić
Business School for Tourism and Hotel Management, Croatia

Abridgement: This chapter discusses the importance and the strength of the interaction between tourism and the Muslim world, as well as the importance of tourism to overcome misunderstanding between the peoples in Islamic and non-Islamic countries. The objectives of this chapter are to look at the connections between tourism and Islam and to try to determine how these connections may develop. Tourism has brought many changes in Islamic countries. Traditionally conservative religions are particularly sensitive to such changes. This includes the Muslim world, deeply rooted in certain countries and parts of the world. As a precondition for future tourism developments, the tolerance among peoples and religions is of great importance. Better understanding will bring benefit to all. **Keywords:** tolerance; religion; conservatism

> Nobody has an exclusive right in the field of religion, but everyone can contribute to searching for this truth (Jakov Jukić 1977).

INTRODUCTION

Religion has always been a constituent part of the social system of the world. Hence there is the view that religion will be alive for as long as the smallest

Tourism in the Muslim World
Bridging Tourism Theory and Practice, Volume 2, 31–45
Copyright © 2010 by Emerald Group Publishing Limited
All rights of reproduction in any form reserved
ISSN: 2042-1443/doi:10.1108/S2042-1443(2010)0000002006

vestige of this traditional system exists. Starting from the same sociological standpoint, it seems that every important movement has long had religious attributes, or has sprung up within a religious framework, or has at least looked for a foundation or justification in religion. This link between the social system, on one hand, and religion and the church, on the other, has been sustained, renewed, and reborn many times.

Throughout history, all forms of rule have attempted to legitimize themselves through religion. For its part, religion has made efforts to be an intermediary between cult and the community, and has directed its endeavors to creating cultures (art, philosophy, music, poetry), and toward different forms of social life. Through its association with culture and by intermingling with social systems, religion has often acquired a privileged place and has become an irreplaceable spiritual force. In this way, religion has created conditions for the future movements of people, and not only for adherents. To explain many phenomena, man has invariably first turned to religion, and after that to philosophy, art, law, politics, and science. Attempting to master reality, he has continually constructed his own awareness of that reality. It was precisely basic needs, the need to survive and maintain life, that created and reshaped his belief. So, the first links between religion and tourism were probably rooted in this context.

The breadth of religious teachings and the science of tourism clearly show that a vast framework exists for discussion. The objective of this chapter is not to provide definitive and comprehensive conclusions, but to emphasize the importance and strength of the interrelations between tourism and one religion, in particular, that of the Muslim world, viewed from the present positions of their roles and global significance, and to point to the possible future development of these interrelations.

Tourism and the Muslim World

Religion and tourism are two pronounced aspects of contemporary civilization, although they have entirely different goals and different contents. Both phenomena are an essential part of modern mankind, interlocked in the very logic of life, with sometimes positive and sometimes negative consequences for one or both of them. Although only a few would probably admit it, a keen observer has nevertheless to conclude that certain similarities exist between religion and tourism: their extent, the large number of participants, and their significance in human life.

In the contemporary world, religions not only survive, but also are gaining in strength and influence, though not all religions equally.

Differences exist in certain communities and countries. Some religions, like Islam, and the Muslim world itself, are more keenly present. Some of them are even more assertive today in man's life than they were at the beginning of the previous century. The strength of a certain religion is often measured by a national leader's or a famous politician's affiliation to it. Obviously, this does not have to, and indeed does not, reflect the power of the religion to which such an individual belongs, but mirrors his political status and, with it, his influence. The latter statement is true for Islam. In the Western world, we witness that political events in a Muslim country are *a priori* linked to the religion there. The best known examples of such opinions are the terrorist attacks undertaken by individuals or groups: because the protagonists belong to a religion (Islam, in this case), their deeds are considered to be inherent to the religion itself and to stem from it, and not from the political or other beliefs and goals of the individual or group. Many people tend to endorse such a general picture of religion and will not analyze the real and deeper reasons and motives for the behavior of such individuals and groups.

Tourism in the world today follows a trend similar to the trend of religion: it is continuously gaining in importance and in its number of participants. It is interesting to note that philosophers and other experts did not expect religions to expand to such a degree, particularly not in the environments where religion has been strictly separated from the state. It was believed that interest in religious beliefs would diminish for many reasons. However, some of these reasons, all of them beyond the direct influence of religion—for example, events related to the collapse of communism in Eastern Europe, political crises that have frequently escalated into wars between nations—have strengthened the importance of certain religions. The relations between tourism and religion have followed a similar pattern: this interrelation has strengthened or loosened depending on the environment and circumstances. It seems that this link has been more the result of circumstances than of tourism or religion in itself. The first task of this chapter is to investigate the links between just one religion, Islam, and tourism, without bringing any long-term and final conclusions. Another task is to try to establish how the links between tourism and the Muslim world will develop in the future.

According to the United Nations World Tourism Organization, 300–330 million pilgrims visit the world's key religious sites every year. In 2005, according to the same source, tourist arrivals in the Middle East have increased at a much faster rate over the past five decades than in the rest of the world. The average annual increase in the Middle East, the heart of the Muslim world, was 10%.

In the long history of mankind, religion has shaped almost all forms of man's life, has set criteria of behavior both for individuals and for entire nations, and has created value systems. Depending on the development of a certain community or nation, religious canons have changed with time, sometimes together with religious views, but sometimes against them. In the 20th century, religion's dominant role in the developed world weakened, although in some less-developed regions this influence actually grew. The impact of religion on tourism should be viewed in this context, and has carried more weight than tourism's impact on religion. In radical communities, the influence of religious views and their use in everyday life can be strong in the extreme and can turn into intolerance. As tourism has expanded and penetrated almost every corner of the globe, it is clear that where it has met orthodox beliefs, in sharp contrast to the tourist way of life, tourism and tourists have had more communication difficulties with the local population. Islam, with its religious views spreading in different areas, has not responded to tourists in only one way. The reason lies in the circumstances prevailing in these areas, not necessarily arising from religious beliefs. It is interesting that in Muslim countries where tourism started early, as in Egypt or Morocco, tourism has been more easily accepted than in countries where tourism arrived relatively late.

It is no easy task to write about Islam and tourism. The reason is very simple: there are no official views. Incidental remarks by authors on tourism exist, and admittedly these are no mere subjective opinions but scientifically argued positions. However, the largest part of the work on Islam and tourism involves lamentations on the problems encountered by Muslim tourists. But of all religions, Christians, and in particular the Catholic Church, have the most extensive body of work on tourism.

DO WE ALWAYS UNDERSTAND EACH OTHER?

In order to carry out this task, the official Catholic views will be compared with Islamic practice, coupled with the authors' personal experience gained through traveling to Muslim countries. There are great differences actually in practicing one's religion. In countries with more orthodox religious beliefs, which means stronger, and mostly intolerant (not to mention exclusive) positions, the relation toward tourism is not clearly defined, but local attitudes toward tourists of other faiths is much more disapproving than in countries where religious beliefs are less strict. In the latter countries, opinions on the relations to other faiths are much more realistic, and definitely more tolerant. In the Muslim countries where tourism is more developed (such as Indonesia and Malaysia), the relation of the Muslim religious community toward all forms of tourism, and toward those from other faiths, is very liberal, particularly if compared to orthodox religious views. Egypt, where tourism has been developing for more than 150 years, also shows great tolerance. The views raised here concern primarily the behavior of Islamic hosts toward all forms of tourism and tourists who visit an Islamic tourism destination.

Before the end of the 20th century, there was little research or writing on the relation between tourism and religion. At the end of the century, a small number of theoreticians emerged, later growing to a larger number, who deemed it necessary to call attention to, and then to research, the relation between tourism and religion as two important phenomena of contemporary life. Depending on their answers, these theoreticians can be grouped into three general groups: those who believe that religion somehow supports tourism; those who consider that tourism somehow influences religion; and those who maintain that religion and tourism oppose each other. The views on the relation between tourism and religion are expounded by different authors regardless of their religious affiliation.

Religion Somehow Supports Tourism. This view starts from the actual practice of religion and from participating in religious customs. Inspired by such motives, an adherent submits himself or herself to the whole range of norms, from moral to practical and technological ones. Most of the so-called big or revealed religions in their basic teaching directly require their followers to visit "holy places." The spatial dispersion of sacred buildings and holy places has been the main reason for movement to have been built into every religious teaching and has sometimes even caused entire migrations. Moving has thus become inherent to each of the major religions.

Migrations can be considered a tool by which a follower can adhere to his or her religious norms. If we add here the fear that they feel and the threat of punishment if norms are not observed, it can reasonably assume that for these reasons religions encourage movement, which, in one of its forms, has the attribute of tourism. Although the fear of nonobservance of certain religious norms has weakened over time, nevertheless the consequences are still felt on migrations and individual religious teachings.

Tourism Somehow Influences Religion. The advocates of this thesis—tourism has an impact on religion—start from the viewpoint that participants in tourism movements are adherents, members of different religions, as well as atheists, and that their common characteristic is the wish to "broaden their horizon" through such travels and to learn about different attitudes to life and religion. This new knowledge will make them more tolerant of others, and will make other religious beliefs more comprehensible and acceptable to them, without in any way making them abandon their own faith.

In a way, tourism has a stronger impact on religion in destinations where, apart from religious reasons, other preconditions exist for its various forms. Tourism has a particularly strong impact on religion if we compare the views of the theory of tourism and religions concerning the need for peace and understanding among people and the possible impact of religion in achieving such understanding. Widely accepted theses on the need for understanding among the peoples of the world, regardless of their national, cultural, political, or religious belonging, could help the tourist masses to learn and understand different religious beliefs and teachings.

Religion and Tourism Stand in Opposition. This view surfaces every time tourists are harmed in religious conflicts or in political conflicts incited by religious belief. Although the number of adherents who participate in tourism flows is indeed large, the unfortunate incidents prompt views that tourism and religion are in opposition. In some religions, particularly in Christianity, frequent negative tones toward tourism arise from ecclesiastic circles. Objections are made that tourists behave aggressively in destinations and in places of pilgrimage, and do not observe religious dogma when touring its facilities. On the other hand, tourists are also reprimanded for not performing all their religious duties during tourist visits and stays.

But, another question could be posed: does not religion often fuel conflicts among people and adherents? We can follow with another one: does not it fit with tourism and tourist "ideology"? Both answers lead to one simple possible conclusion: tourism could bring people together and enhance understanding of each other. Tourist experts often say that travel is a way for clearing misconceptions, but do not say exactly what we are supposed to do in practice to make these words truthful. Each of these views can easily be applied to Islam and in its relation to tourism, and vice versa.

In the world where tourism has been growing in importance, with a still growing number of tourists, it is logical to expect that this trend of opposition will also occur in the Muslim world that encompasses millions of people. Most Muslims live in less-developed countries where their limited material situation determines their interest in tourism. This is the main reason for the relatively few Muslim tourists seen in foreign destinations. Nevertheless, there are exceptions, and many do travel abroad, particularly in the case of the oil-rich Arab countries that have achieved an enviable level of economic development and a high standard of living enjoyed by the majority of their population. For such countries, touristic journeys are a part of everyday life, just as they are in other countries of the developed world.

Due to the material situation in which most of the Muslim population has been living, they first took part in international tourism as hosts. Another reason why they have primarily been destinations is that their countries abound in rich natural, cultural, and historical resources. To begin with, the fact that the religion of the host country was different from that of the guests did not have a great impact on tourists from Western countries. The first questions and misunderstandings arose with the first terrorist attacks, when, in the perception of the Western world, Islam began to be identified with the concept of terrorism. Particularly negative effects were produced by attacks in some Muslim tourism destinations where it was mainly the tourists of other religions that were targeted. Through such attacks, destinations in Muslim countries were directly associated with the idea of terrorism.

The logic of tourism and of tourist behavior demands a peaceful environment where tourists feel satisfied, but, above all, safe. Any alarming situation in the closer or wider surroundings, of a political nature (or any other nature), automatically excludes a peaceful environment, for a shorter or longer period, from the circle of interest of potential tourists, depending on how grave the disturbing event is. Islamic countries, in such a context, find themselves in a special and a very serious situation, with regards to the development of world tourism.

In the second half of the 20th century, and particularly at its end, many Muslim countries reached significant levels of economic development that secured a higher standard for at least a part of their citizens, which has enabled them to embark on tourism journeys. Generally, since Muslims first choose a destination in neighboring Muslim countries, there is no reason for problems based on religion. If problems arise, they spring from situations where a host country's population and foreign tourists belong to different religions. Problems may also occur during political tension between countries, in particular, between a Muslim and a non-Muslim country. In such situations, a religion is identified with a political system and the perception of one is transferred to the other.

The largest countries with a majority Muslim population, which are at the same time highly popular destinations, are Malaysia, Indonesia, Turkey, and the United Arab Emirates. It is interesting that Turkey is the only Muslim country among the first 10 in the world's most visited countries, and it is worth noting that it experienced its true tourism boom only toward the end of the 20th century. Among the most visited attractions in the world, only Giza in Cairo is in the Muslim world, with about 3 million tourists each year.

Even without a detailed analysis of the main directions of global tourism development, it can easily be seen that tourism has established ways of growing in all parts of the world, regardless of the local situation and local religious beliefs. This is the starting point for all other conclusions. Even where huge local differences exist, tourism has not been thrown off course but has been able to fulfill one of its basic tasks: to establish better understanding among peoples and countries of the world. This task has been mentioned by almost all theoreticians of tourism, regardless of their nationality or religion, who research tourism as a relatively new social and economic phenomenon of the contemporary world.

Why is it then important to insist on differences and on a possible lack of understanding, or even misunderstanding, as in this chapter? The reason is precisely the surprising, continuous, and massive development of tourism, and its geographic expansion, which is greater and more rapid than that of any other industry. This development has literally embraced the peoples of the world, their way of life, their cultures, and religious beliefs. These developments have, among other effects, left room for wrong interpretations of the strength of the tourism impact on contemporary society. The misinterpretations have partially occurred due to man's imperfection, but also because of the rapid development of human civilization. What formerly needed centuries to evolve is today compressed into decades or even years. Traditionally conservative religions, deeply rooted in certain countries or parts of the world, are particularly sensitive to such changes. When they come into contact with the impulsive development of tourism, they have difficulty in accommodating the changes brought by it.

At the beginning of the 20th century, the traditional countries of Islam attracted tourists far more than they included their own local populations in tourism flows. This can be explained in part by religion. Another part of the explanation lies in the many historical, cultural, and natural attractions these countries offer, as was mentioned above. Today, modern tourists, including those from the Muslim world, are no longer limited by their faith. Previously, the arrival of international tourists could have caused certain conflicts and *faux pas* in terms of standard customs and etiquette, specifically those introduced by religion, which have in the past proved difficult for the other side to accept. The more conservative a community, the more it considered that tourism was bringing unacceptable and insulting novelties. The deeply rooted religious consciousness of the local population has often considered itself to be the ideal guardian of its own views and behavior.

However, these are the general characteristics of "the relation between tourist visitors and the local population in tourist receptive areas" (Vukonić 1996:36). This issue is primarily of a sociological nature. In the destination itself, numerous contacts are made that engage tourists in social relationships, although these are not the regular contacts such as those that people establish in their permanent place of residence (at work, with friends, neighbors, etc.) and that occur continuously (Scheuch 1976:305). These differences are clearly visible when tourists bring certain negative habits and behavior to a destination (gambling, prostitution, illegal trade, etc.) to which religion is particularly sensitive (Vukonić 1996:62).

On the other hand, the expansion of Islam for most of the 20th century attempted for its own sake to neutralize such orthodox religious beliefs that could hamper or slow the desired intensity and directions of this expansion. Today, Islam is perceived differently in the world. Saudi Arabia, Egypt, the United Arab Emirates, Indonesia, and Malaysia have remained devout Muslim countries, but their views on tourism have changed and have acquired new and different qualities. However, the intensified flows of Western tourists to traditional Muslim countries have brought about similar changes, predominantly influenced by the positive economic impact that tourism has created. This pragmatic reason (creating better conditions for survival) has become even stronger than religious or political beliefs. The tolerance threshold on both sides has improved, although we cannot always say that this holds true for some religious beliefs and for mutual religious understanding. Recent evidence has shown that there are those in the world, including Muslims, who maintain that one of the most important roles of tourism, and of religion, is to build bridges, understanding, and cooperation among peoples. Examples of increased awareness abound, and one of the most recent occurred in a speech by the Vice President of the Iran Tour Operators Congress. Speaking at its First Annual gathering in Tehran, in December 2008, it is reported that he "offered insight on Iran's desire to use its growing tourism industry as a bridge to create dialogue and understanding among nations and peoples." He pointed out that through cultural, historical, and religious understanding, countries could bridge gaps and create "peace and understanding" (Chevalier 2008).

If we omit for a moment the tacit centuries-old antagonism between Islam and Christianity, we can easily see the differences that can lead to such conflict. However, their number is not nearly as great as it might at first appear. For convenience sake, this chapter shall discuss just some which can have a direct impact on relations between the non-Muslim and Muslim world when their members participate in international tourism.

The method of practicing the faith in Islam is relatively simple in its approach because it does not always unconditionally require physical presence in "God's temple," since, according to Islam's teaching, "encounter" with Allah can occur in any space, on any occasion. This aspect of religion is much more difficult for a non-Muslim tourist in Islamic destinations, and this difficulty can pose a serious problem for the orthodox. On the other hand, ignorance of how Islam is practiced can hurt the Muslim population and many times it reinforces the attitude that foreign tourists intentionally disrespect Islam. Taken to the extreme, this misunderstanding can cause conflict.

The field of morality is one of the vast and important areas of learning and interest for all religions. In its relation to tourism, morality is discussed within the specific circumstances of tourism, seen through the behavior of tourists-adherents. The hedonist call to man, felt during his leisure time and in his travels and stays, leads tourists to temptations that are great and that often contradict the morality taught by religion. Such deviations from religious teachings are easier when people are far from their place of residence, without religious "controls" and in more permissive settings.

In this context, tourism can be a threat for every religion. The Catholic Church, for example, has designated *pastorization* as a way to come closer to adherents when they are on their travels, thus bridging the spatial gap that occurs when tourists leave their domiciles. "Like a bird that strays from its nests, is a man who strays from his home" (Proverbs, 27, 8). Muslims should keep "more firmly" to their religious requirements (food, drink) during their time spent as tourists. This can directly lessen tourist consumption in the Western destinations, notwithstanding that this consumption is one of the prime motives of a destination in developing tourism. On the other hand, the nonacceptance of tourists' religious principles (those of Muslims, for example) and their dietary needs decreases the interest of such tourists in certain destinations, but it also weakens the interest of these destinations in attracting tourists of different faiths.

The idea of hospitality is another basic concept in the relationship between tourism and religion. The attitude of Islam toward hospitality arises from the *Hajj*, which is one of the basic obligations for an Islamic follower. One of the ways for a Muslim to reach *Jannah* (paradise) is "by showing hospitality (to a traveler or a guest)" (Selection of the Prophet's *Hadith, hadith* 146). Hadith 146 explicitly states: "There is no wellbeing in a family which does not welcome and treat guests well." It is understandable that special care should be provided to people on the

Hajj, but Islam is categorical here: "Hospitality extends for three days. What is beyond that is charity" (Selection of the Prophet's Hadith, hadith 1000). In this context, the positions of almost all religions on hospitality are the same, yet in non-Islamic countries favoring *Hajj* pilgrims is not expected.

Christianity holds very similar positions on hospitality and requires Christians to be hospitable. The Bible talks about hospitality as an act of charity and as Testimony of Faith. The basis of these teachings can be condensed in a message that a guest should be welcomed and treated with love (Deuteronomy, 10, 18). Through a guest and in a guest, a Christian accepts or denies Christ (Matthew, 25, 35–42). That is why hospitality is embedded in the deepest religious conceptions and considerations, and denying hospitality means denying the foundation of religious life. The Epistle to the Hebrews contains the following: "Remember to welcome strangers in your homes. There were some who did that and welcomed angels without knowing" (13, 2). From this viewpoint, we can find no good reasons for any lack of understanding between the followers of either Islam or Christianity.

Based on these brief explanations, one may suggest that the differences between the important canons in both Islam and the Christian faith, at least those differences that can be related to tourism, are not of such a character to cause intolerance or conflicts between the tourists and hosts of these two faiths. Since practice shows that misunderstandings exist, it would be difficult not to conclude that the reasons lie beyond the religions themselves, or that misunderstandings and lack of understanding arise from equating religion with political views on both sides. Rigid or orthodox religious viewpoints can indeed reinforce such behavior among adherents, but the frequent repetition of certain political views, supported by religious terms, create an illusion of truth in what they advocate or preach. An additional problem is that a superficial observer in both cases accuses either religion or tourism, and not the real causes that lead to misunderstanding and lack of understanding. To put out "the fire of conflict" we need to go back to the roots, to Abraham, to the three monotheistic religions, to the novelty, to the morals of old stories, to the New Testament, to the *Qur'an*, to ancient history to understand each other. "Hence, peace through tourism has been so effective lately," explained Akel el Baltaji, Tourism Committee chairman, Upper House of Parliament for the Hasemite Kingdom of Jordan, "because with faith in our part of the world, people are driven by strong values—not that they go endangering themselves." He added, "When they try looking for answers, they find out the differences are small. And this whole business of conflict should not have been there in the first place.... Once you politicize faith, it gets messy."

When we call for faith tourism, which now forms the basis of many people's lives (as people are now going back to faith while they are disturbed and distressed), nations support the idea. Traveling to a religious destination is very comforting to tourists. Christians go to sites related to Moses and Jesus; Muslims go to Makkah for pilgrimage. For most peoples of the world today faith is very important to their lives; we can just convert it then to tourism and eventually peace in the region.

The answer to the development of tourism in the Muslim world lies in the latter statement, in not seeing the real causes of misunderstanding. The conclusion is that the future of tourism is necessarily linked to the development of the general political situation and to the international position of a particular community with a majority Muslim population. The first part of the solution is to change the entrenched attitudes held by a large part of the non-Muslim world that Islam is a faith that supports or even preaches negative political views, thereby undermining peace in the world. Without this change, it is not possible to see any serious and economically viable development of tourism destinations in the Muslim world. The second part of the conclusion is derived from the first. It requires that primarily politics and politicians invest efforts in changing such attitudes, since tourism is rather inefficient in carrying out this big task. Tourism requires stable political and economic conditions, and its development ensues from such positive favorable conditions. Both Muslim and Christian religious institutions can contribute to creating a favorable climate by publicly proclaiming their positive views and by materializing them in their daily activities.

Finally, to try to answer the question posed in the title of this chapter, do we understand each other?, we must say, not yet. After September 11 we understand each other even less than before this date. But the truth is that the people who have carried out the bombings are not moderate Muslims or Muslim followers. Islam does not allow this, no matter if they call it *Jihad*. Simply, it was not a holy war! Their misinterpretation is what made them terrorists. For an understanding, first we must know much more about each other, about our histories, about our cultures, our religions, our lifestyle, and our civilizations. Tourism is or could be a good tool for obtaining this knowledge. Without such knowledge we would never be able to answer differently by saying: yes we understand each other, if not completely but to the point of necessary tolerance.

CONCLUSION

The potential scope of discussion on religion and tourism is obviously vast. However, this chapter has no presumptions to provide all-encompassing and final arguments on the topic. In the modern world, religions have not only survived but are gaining in strength and influence. This general statement does not imply that all religions have evolved equally. Some, like Islam and the Muslim world itself, are very much more present in the life of mankind today than any time in the past.

The starting point of this analysis was the present situation and the events that marked the relation between global tourism and the Muslim world at the end of the 20th century and the beginning of the third millennium. The chapter has analyzed tourism development and its relations with the Western world, the lifestyle in the West and its spiritual pursuits on the one hand, and those in the Muslim world on the other. Even without a detailed analysis of the main directions of global tourism development, it is reasonable to conclude that tourism has found a way to grow in all parts of the world, regardless of local material wealth or religious beliefs. This is the key starting point for all other conclusions, since it shows that even when differences were huge, tourism was not halted by them, but was able to perform one of its basic tasks: to establish better understanding between the peoples and countries of the world. This task has been mentioned by almost all theoreticians, regardless of their nationality or religion, who have analyzed tourism as a new social and economic phenomenon of the contemporary world.

Why, then, would anyone insist on the differences and potential lack of understanding, or even misunderstandings, as in this chapter? Undoubtedly this is because this surprisingly huge tourism development and its geographic expansion have, more than the developments in any other branch of the economy, literally entwined the peoples of the world, their ways of life, their cultures and religious features. This interlocking has, among other consequences, provided grounds for misinterpretations and failure to grasp other cultures, due to man's imperfection and the rapid development of human civilization. What formerly needed centuries to evolve is today compressed in decades or even years. Traditionally conservative religions, deeply rooted in certain countries or parts of the world, are particularly sensitive to such changes. When in contact with the impulsive development of tourism, they have difficulty in accommodating the changes brought by tourism.

However, perceptions of tourism do not remain the same. Saudi Arabia, Egypt, the United Arab Emirates, Indonesia, and Malaysia remain dedicated Muslim countries but with their views of tourism have developed new aspects. The increased numbers of Western tourists to Muslim countries have also brought about changes, due mostly to tourism's positive economic impact. The tolerance threshold on both sides has increased, although we cannot always say that this holds true for some religious beliefs and for mutual religious understanding.

In this context, it seems realistic that receptive tourism in Muslim countries will grow faster than the flow of tourists from those countries to destinations in non-Muslim countries. Establishing such a flow from Muslim countries will signify real tourism development in the Muslim world. The same pattern was seen for more than a century in the development of European tourism, in all European countries where tourism is now developed, regardless of dominant or less-dominant religious beliefs. Perhaps in the light of current events and the present global political situation, tolerance among peoples and religions as a precondition for the future development of tourism in the Muslim world may seem far-fetched. However, it should not be forgotten that a similar belief was widespread in Europe in the middle of the 20th century, which today seems entirely unreal.

How the future relationship between tourism and the Muslim world will develop, how tourism is going to fit it with the Muslim world, and whether the level of understanding among tourists of various nations and religions will increase depend on three key factors: the will to change; the benefit, or lack of benefit, that certain changes have, or whether developing better understanding is more or less beneficial than keeping the *status quo*; and the time needed for both sides to accept change and for these changes to be integrated into everyday life.

When looking at the situation in the world today, it is difficult to objectively believe that this will significantly change in the next few decades. Many orthodox views certainly do not speak in favor of greater understanding in the future. It seems there is a lack of true will to change relationships and to develop better understanding to enable people to become more tolerant of others. If signs of goodwill do sporadically appear, these are usually "one-way streets." This is especially true of all those countries—including Islamic ones—where the political establishment uses religion as a means of political struggle. If we add to this the threat of terrorism, which, in the perception of many countries, right or wrong, is related to religious beliefs, it is evident that currently in most Islamic countries there are still too many obstacles preventing international tourism from being activated as an instrument of better understanding among peoples. To insist on the exclusivity of one's views, which is the basic behavioral characteristic of the political and religious leaderships of these countries, is certainly the wrong approach to resolve the issue of lack of understanding, from whatever side it comes. It is wrong for many reasons, one of them being that it will provoke a counter reaction from the other side that will, as is usual in such situations, entrench itself in its own different position, thus leading to a standstill in the process of mutual understanding.

To begin any rapprochement and to ensure better understanding on both sides, it is crucial to identify the benefits of any future relationships compared with those of maintaining the present state of affairs. Naturally, better understanding between Islamic and non-Islamic countries would bring about a greater and safer tourism flow, and consequently produce new and larger masses of potential tourists. This would surely result in increased tourist consumption, which would provide economic benefit from tourism in host countries. Such conditions correspond to the general desire of mankind to enjoy free and totally safe movement in the world, and opens up new values for tourists: the values of another religion, which create new strands of interest and meet the wishes of potential tourists.

The time needed to establish better understanding is a very important factor that must be taken into account. A relatively long adjustment is to be expected, and history teaches us that religions have a hard time adjusting to other teachings and beliefs. This means that a relatively long period will be needed for new understandings to reach a realistic and high tolerance threshold of the beliefs of the other side. It is presently difficult to see whether the 21st century will provide sufficient room at least to loosen up these very rigid beliefs.

Chapter 4

HALAL FOOD AND TOURISM
Prospects and Challenges

Maedeh Bon
University of Tehran, Iran
Mazhar Hussain
SESRIC, Turkey

Abridgement: *Halal* food despite its undeniable importance for Muslims is largely absent in the tourism development and planning literature. Given the fact that today Muslims represent more than 20% of world population and the number of Muslim tourists has grown significantly over recent years, there is a dire need to investigate the *halal* food's potential for both the tourism industry and world trade. Furthermore, it is important to investigate at both Muslim and non-Muslim tourism sites how availability of *halal* food has influenced the selection of a particular destination for vacation by Muslims. **Keywords:** food tourism; Muslims; *halal*; religion

INTRODUCTION

In today's modern world, tourists are more knowledgeable about travel and may consider many factors before selecting a place to spend their leisure time and discretionary income. Food is one important factor that influences the choice to visit a particular place and affects tourist's attitudes, decisions, and behavior (Henderson 2009; Hjalanger and Corigliano 2000). Food and wine have historically tended to be in the background of the tourist

Tourism in the Muslim World
Bridging Tourism Theory and Practice, Volume 2, 47–59
Copyright © 2010 by Emerald Group Publishing Limited
All rights of reproduction in any form reserved
ISSN: 2042-1443/doi:10.1108/S2042-1443(2010)0000002007

experience as a part of the overall hospitality service provided to tourists (Hall and Mitchell 2005). More recently, some authors have indicated that food has potential to enhance the sustainability of tourism destinations (Du Rand, Heath and Alberts 2003) and indeed may represent a competitive advantage. As a basic necessity of life, tourist food demand is inelastic in price (Au and Law 2002), and spending on dining out during a holiday constitutes approximately one-third of all tourist expenditure in a destination (Quan and Wang 2004). Increasingly, researchers are examining the relations between food and tourism (Matson and Vermignon 2006) although most of the studies in this field have been limited to food safety; hygiene issues; analyses of food and wine festival attendance; examination of supply-side issues such as business networks, food production, and its role in tourism (Mitchell and Hall 2003); cross-promotion between food and tourism; and the impact of the world's cuisines on tourism. Clearly, much light is being thrown on explaining the importance of various socioeconomic factors in shaping food consumption behavior and choices and its impacts on tourism industry. However, the role of religious beliefs on tourist food consumption behavior and its impacts on the tourism industry has gained less attention.

Carmouche and Kelly (1995) suggested a list of factors that shape the food consumption behavior: social class, gender, age, culture, race, and religion (also considered a cultural factor). Ample evidence has been found that religion can influence consumer attitude and behavior in general and food purchasing decisions and eating habits in particular (Bonne and Verbeke 2008b).

In many societies, religion plays one of the most influential roles in shaping food choices and consumption behavior: the types of food that can be consumed, who should prepare and cook the food at what times, and how and when to eat it. However, different religions have different rules and teachings about food consumption behavior. Followers of religions also differ in observance of these rules: some follow the rules strictly, while others behave with more flexibility, and few may not care at all. Hence, in order to investigate the relationship between food consumption behavior and religion, it is important to give ample consideration to this religious diversity both within and among the followers of each religion.

This relationship also implies that significance of food in destination development is of paramount importance, due not only to its direct relationship with the biological need of tourists but also to tourists' religious beliefs. Hence, in order to maximize the potential of the relationship between food and tourism, it is necessary to recognize the religious aspect of food demand. In this regard, measures should be taken to educate the travel agents and guides about food eating preferences based on religious beliefs of tourists, and destinations should also recognize the commercial opportunities available when they offer food choices compliant with tourists' beliefs.

Islam is a complete code of life and it provides guidance that should be followed by Muslims in all spheres of life. Islamic teachings about eating behavior have classified the food broadly into two categories: *halal* (permissible) and *haram* (prohibited). The former is a crucial aspect of Islamic life and it is obligatory for all Muslims to eat only *halal* food. Hence, determining if a food product is *halal* or *haram* is of paramount importance.

Islam is the fastest growing religion in the world, and a large percentage of Muslims (estimated 70% worldwide) largely obey the dietary rules of Islam (Minkus McKenna 2007). Whether in the majority or minority in their societies, they obey Islamic dietary rules and eat only *halal* food. Today, around 23% of world total population is Muslim, and the numbers traveling for leisure, both domestic and outbound, are also increasing. However, food can be an important concern when traveling abroad (Henderson 2009). In non-Muslim countries, these tourists may face hardships in finding food that is *halal* according to their religion.

A review of the literature of the role of *halal* food in tourism found there was just one previous study on this subject: the book *Food Tourism Around the World: Development, Management, and Markets* (Wan Hassan and Hall 2003). Chapter four of this book entitled "The Demand for *Halal* Food among Muslim Travelers in New Zealand" surveyed its availability. The results of the survey showed that in spite of this country's significant market share in providing *halal* meat around the world, the majority of Muslim tourists did not have easy access to it and Muslim consumers in New Zealand are today in urgent need of statutory or legislative regulations and stronger guidelines pertaining to the issue of *halal* food.

Hence, it is reasonable to suggest that despite the fact that the concept/ practice of *halal* is of paramount importance for Muslims, its relationship with hospitality and tourism industry has been largely ignored. However, due to increasing number of Muslim tourists and migrant workers, the demand for *halal* food is growing, even in non-Muslim countries. This lucrative market provides a very high potential for businesses, especially in the tourism industry, to ensure the availability of *halal* food at destinations.

DEVELOPMENT OF *HALAL* FOOD AND TOURISM

In Islam, Muslims must follow a set of *halal* dietary laws intended to advance their well being (Bonne and Verbeke 2008a). These laws are almost 1,400 years old and are found in the *Qur'an* and in the *Sunnah*, the practice of holy Prophet Muhammad (PBUH) as recorded in the books of *Hadith* according to Islamic rulings (Bonne, Vermeir, Bergeaud-Blackler and Verbeke 2007a). In the English language, *halal* most frequently refers to food that is permissible according to Islamic law. In the Arabic language, it refers to anything that is permissible under Islam (Lewis 2007:19). These dietary laws determine which food is *halal* and which is *haram*. However, instead of giving a list of what is *halal*, the *Qur'an* and *Sunnah* described what *haram* is, because only a few are *haram* and rest are *halal*. Hence, the basic ruling is "All is *halal* except as prohibited by the *Qur'an* or *Sunnah*." By following this rule, Islamic jurists have worked out a list of *halal* and *haram* food in the Islamic *fiqh* (Jurisprudence) literature and despite minor differences among different schools of thoughts, this classification is being largely accepted and practiced across the Islamic world.

Halal animals include:

- Domesticated animals such as cows, buffalos, sheep, goats, camels, chicken, geese, ducks, and turkeys.
- Nonpredatory wild animals such as deer, antelope, chamois, wild cows, and zebras.
- Nonpredatory birds such as pigeons, sparrows, quails, starlings, and ostriches.
- Grasshoppers.
- All fish with scales (including their eggs), as well as shrimps.

Haram and non-*halal* animals include:

- Pigs, dogs, and their descendants.
- Animals not slaughtered in the name of Allah.
- Animals not slaughtered according to Islamic rules.
- Dead animals.
- Animals with long pointed teeth or tusks that are used to kill prey or defend themselves, such as tigers, bears, elephants, cats, monkeys, wolves, lions, tigers, panthers, jackals, bears, foxes, squirrels, martens, weasels, and moles.
- Predatory birds with sharp claws, such as hawks, falcons, eagles, vultures, ravens, crows, kites, and owls.
- Lizards, snails, insects, mouse, crocodiles, and alligators.

- Pests and venomous animals such as rats, centipedes, scorpions, snake, wasps, and similar animals.
- Animals that are considered repulsive, such as flies, maggots, ticks, spiders, and the like.
- Animals that are forbidden to be killed in Islam, such as honeybees and hoopoe (*Upupa epops*).
- Donkeys and mules.
- Any ingredient derived from non-*halal* animals is not *permissible*.
- Poisonous aquatic animals harmful to human health (unless the harmful or poisonous material is removed).
- All amphibious animals.

Haram and non-*halal* substances, apart from animals, include:

- All types of products made from blood.
- Any liquid and objects discharged from the orifices of human beings or animals such as urine, placenta, excrement, vomit, pus, sperm, and ova.
- Poisonous and harmful plants, unless the poisonous and harmful materials are removed. [According to Organization of the Islamic Conference (OIC) Standards—General Guidelines on *Halal* Food (2009)].
- Alcohol. Whether in food or beverages, alcohol is clearly forbidden in the *Qur'an*. Islam takes an uncompromising stand in the prohibition of intoxicants and stipulates that whatever intoxicates people in large amounts is *haram* and forbidden in any amount, even in minute quantities (Wan Hassan and Hall 2003).

In addition, it is also mandatory that *halal* products are "processed, produced, manufactured and/or stored by using utensils, equipments, and/or machineries that have been cleansed according to Islamic law" (Wan Hassan and Hall 2003). The main idea behind this is that manufactured products should be free of contamination and must not come into contact with *haram* substances during its preparation, production, and/or storage. In addition, *halal* ingredients should also not be mixed with objectionable or *haram* ingredients like enzymes and emulsifiers of porcine origin or other non-*halal* animals (Wan Hassan and Hall 2003).

Development of the Halal Food Market

Halal food is clearly not a recent concept, and a market for it exists wherever there are Muslim consumers with tastes and preferences that are governed by *halal* rules on food and beverages (Wan Hassan and Hall 2003). As eating *halal* food is compulsory for Muslims, in the past they simply avoided foods that did not meet their dietary standards (Bonne et al 2007b), or used to eat only vegetarian meals, especially while traveling in non-Muslim countries. However, with the passage of time the number of Muslim tourists and migrant workers has increased in non-Muslim countries, and awareness of their food preferences has also spread. Because of this *halal* food production has gained popularity in both Muslim and non-Muslim countries.

According to recent estimates (Sungkar 2009), the *halal* food industry has shown promising growth and has increased from US$587.2 billion in 2004 to $634.5 billion in 2009 (Table 1). At the same time, the world food market has increased from $3,842.6 billion in 2004 to $3,992.2 billion in 2009. In 2010, the size of the global *halal* food market is projected to continue increasing to reach $641.5 billion, while world food market is projected to reach $4,021.3 in the same year.

Despite showing an increasing trend, the *halal* food market is still relatively small and accounts for 16% of the world food market. This can be attributed mainly to the lower purchasing power of majority of Muslims living mostly in low-income developing countries in Asian and African

Table 1. Global *Halal* Food Markets (US$ Billions)

Region/Year	2004	2005	2009	2010 (Projected)
Africa	136.9	139.5	150.3	153.4
Asian countries	369.6	375.8	400.1	406.1
GCC countries	38.4	39.5	43.8	44.7
Indonesia	72.9	73.9	77.6	78.5
China	18.5	18.9	20.8	21.2
India	21.8	22.1	23.6	24.0
Malaysia	6.6	6.9	8.2	8.4
European countries	64.3	64.4	66.6	67.0
France	16.4	16.5	17.4	17.6
Russian Federation	20.7	20.8	21.7	21.9
United Kingdom	3.4	3.5	4.1	4.2
Australia/Oceania	1.1	1.1	1.5	1.6
American countries	15.3	15.5	16.1	16.2
USA	12.3	12.5	12.9	31.1
Canada	1.4	1.5	1.8	1.9
Global halal food market	*587.2*	*596.1*	*634.5*	*641.5*
Global food market	3,842.6	3,872.8	3,992.2	4,021.3

region. However, it has growth potential due to the increasing Muslim populations and increasing awareness about *halal* food, among both Muslims and non-Muslims worldwide.

Key Markets

Demand for *halal* food products has shown tremendous growth in some countries, especially in those that are members of the Gulf Cooperation Council (GCC). Rising income levels due to strong economic growth in these markets have led to higher consumption rates and more opportunities for *halal* food producers. Currently, this food market is concentrated mainly in Asian and African region where the majority of Muslims live.

As shown in Table 1, of the total *halal* food market in 2009, Asian countries represent the largest share (63% or $400.1 billion), and of this Asian *halal* market, Indonesia alone accounts for 19%, followed by GCC countries (11%), India (6%), and China (5%). The GCC countries import more than 90% of their total food consumption and thus constitute an important market, while India and China, with Muslim population estimated at 161 million and 22 million respectively, are two important non-GCC member *halal* food markets in this region.

Africa is the second largest consumer of *halal* food and represents a 24% share, or $150.3 billion, of the total *halal* food market in 2009. The predominantly Muslim North African region represents the largest share of this market. The European region, with more than 38 million Muslims represented 10% or $66.6 billion of the total *halal* market in 2009. The higher purchasing power of European Muslims and the growing number of educated Muslims in the labor market have resulted in a market where the growth of *halal* food consumption is strong, while the trade potential is rapidly increasing. In this region, the Russian Federation, with around 16.5 million Muslims, represents 33% of the total market.

Despite accounting for more than 80% of global *halal* food demand, Islamic countries have very low share compared to their non-Islamic counterparts on the supply side of *halal* food chain. According to some estimates, nearly 85% of the total *halal* food is produced by the non-Muslim countries. For example, Australia and New Zealand are the leading suppliers of *halal* meat since 2003 (Halal Focus 2009). Australia is exporting *halal* meat worth of $570 million a year, while The Economist (2009) reported that Brazil alone accounts for 54% of the global market for *halal* meat.

However, due to lack of global *halal* brand and uniform standardization methodology, there is confusion about these food products among both consumers and producers. According to the World *Halal* Forum chairman, a lack of consensus on a global *halal* standard is one of the major hindrances in the development of this market despite growing demand (Wan Hassan 2007). *Halal* food certification was first launched in Singapore, a predominantly non-Muslim country, and today there is a wide variety of Islamic centers and organizations along with governmental bodies issuing different types of *halal* certificates in more than 60 countries across the globe (Today's Zaman 2009). According to The Economist (2009), there are more than 50 certification bodies in France that are in competition with each other to issue *halal* certificates. Similarly, the United Kingdom has 20 different such certification bodies in operation. On the other hand, in Malaysia, Thailand, Indonesia, Singapore, and the Philippines there are special government institutions for *halal* certification. This diversity leads to differences on issues like animal feed, slaughtering methods, packaging, and logistics.

Halal Food Policy in the Tourism Industry

Over the years, awareness about the Muslims' food consumption behavior and preferences has increased across the globe. Today, there are many companies and retailers even in the non-Muslim countries who have entered the lucrative business of *halal* food. Among these big companies and retailers, Nestlé has produced *halal* products since the 1980s, and 75 out of its 456 factories have *halal* certification. French supermarket chain Casino and British outfits Tesco and Sainsbury's have *halal* product lines. All restaurants of KFC, an American fast-food chain, in France are *halal* certified and KFC also serves such food in eight of its British restaurants on a trial basis (The Economist 2009). Similarly, The Currumbin Wildlife Sanctuary in Australia, Hilton Glasgow, and The Intercontinental Hotel in Prague have started to offer *halal* meals (Hashim et al 2003). Thailand and Philippines have also developed restaurants and hotels serving *halal* food. However, despite these developments, this is still an unknown concept for many destinations.

On the demand side, considering the high number of Muslim travelers from both Muslim and non-Muslim regions and their insistence on using only *halal* food products, its availability has become an important issue in relation to their travel choice. While on the supply side, there is a lot of untapped potential for *halal* products in the food service sector, which includes various subsectors such as travel food services that are mainly comprised of food-related services in hotels and motels, roadside service to automobile travelers, and all food service on airplanes, trains, and ships. Another major subsector of this sector is related to restaurants and includes fast-food units, coffee shops, specialty restaurants, family restaurants, cafeterias, and full-service restaurants (Goeldner and Ritchie 2006).

For these subsectors, it may be difficult to incorporate *halal* products in their food preparation systems due to strict regulations about ingredients, and the cooking and storage process for *halal* food. In fact, due to a lack of an integrated global supply chain and also a lack of global awareness of its importance for Muslims, the food services sector at large finds it difficult to comply with *halal* standards. There is no unique global trademark for *halal* food available and no common standard or a global institution to issue and regulate the certificates. In recent years, the OIC has undertaken many initiatives to address this problem by establishing a global *halal* brand based on unanimously agreed upon standards, along with a global body to issue *halal* certification for companies interested in this sector, but still there is very little on the ground in this regard. The challenge of a lack of interest and awareness may be solved by clarification of *halal* and its dimensions for all authorities and activities in this sector.

Basic knowledge and information about *halal* food and its importance for the Muslims is necessary for those working in tourism and hospitality businesses, as lack of knowledge about this expectation may lead to misunderstandings and conflict. According to Timothy and Iverson (2006), a young server in a Chinese-American restaurant was instructed to insure that there was no pork in the meal being ordered. When the meal arrived there were pieces of ham in the food, and the server's response was "yes, ham, but not pork." When informed that ham is pork, she innocently replied: "Oh, I didn't know that, actually I'm a vegetarian." On another occasion, a flight attendant seemed disinterested when asked by Iverson if the meat in a sandwich was pork. She replied simply that she did not know and did not bother to find out.

Therefore, the matter of *halal* is not limited just to food service sector. After establishing its needed structure and considering its aspects from the stage of preparing the ingredients to the stage of serving food at the table, a system of informing customers about its availability is also needed. Customers should be informed about places delivering *halal* foods and their accessibility. Possible measures to aid in this process are the publication of guidebooks, installation of foreign language signage, and multilingual menus with ingredients and prices clearly marked (Henderson 2009). By including the availability of *halal* foods in advertising when promoting a destination, stress before traveling in the matter of its availability will be reduced.

Fasting in Ramadan is another important dietary rule, which should be kept in consideration while planning for Muslim tourists or for a trip to any

Muslim country. Fasting from dawn to dusk during the holy month of Ramadan is the fourth pillar of Islam. This includes abstaining from worldly desires, as exemplified by adults avoiding food and drink between sunrise and sunset each day of the holy month. As the matter of fasting in Ramadan is directly related to food consumption, two main considerations need to be considered by tourism planners. First, although Muslims can delay their fasting till they return from their travel, most prefer not to arrange their trips during Ramadan and there is always a decrease in their numbers during this month. Second, as eating and drinking during Ramadan should not be done in public, most Islamic countries limit their food availability in restaurants and other food service centers during the daylight hours, which may cause some problems for non-Muslim tourists. Considering the effect of Ramadan on both Muslim and non-Muslim destinations is a necessity for all those interested in tourism.

Halal *Food at Muslim Destinations*

Hospitality is an important characteristic of good Muslims (Timothy and Iverson 2006) as their religion teaches them to be hospitable and treat people with respect. They are instructed by the *Qur'an* and Prophet Muhammad (PBUH) to be good to other fellow human beings and offer hospitality to travelers in the form of food, water, shelter, and by helping them carrying their luggage (Din 1989; Timothy and Iverson 2006). In addition, the Islamic world has also been the center of many ancient civilizations and has a very rich heritage to share. Due to its rich and diverse social, cultural, and historical heritage, the Islamic world has always remained a very attractive place for tourists. In December 2004, the World Tourism Organization nominated 10 Muslim countries, Algeria, Iran, Malaysia, Turkey, Oman, Syria, United Arab Emirates, Bahrain, Lebanon, and Egypt, among 38 countries as the world's top emerging destinations (Hashim et al 2005). Four countries, Morocco, Egypt, Turkey, and Malaysia dominate other Muslim countries, receiving 17.5 million guests in 2004, particularly Western tourists (Al-Hamarneh and Steiner 2004).

Among the Muslim countries there are different approaches to *halal* food. In fact, these different policies relate to their different perspective to tourism in particular and to Islamic law in general. For example, laws about *halal* and non-*halal* are more relaxed in countries such as Malaysia, United Arab Emirates, Oman, Indonesia, and Turkey (Hashim et al 2005). Alcohol and non-*halal* foods are widely available in these countries and openly served at most of their touristic sites. On the other hand, most Muslim countries have very strict laws about delivering non-*halal* products.

Keeping in view these two different approaches about delivery of *halal* and non-*halal* food in the Muslim countries, there is a need to educate the non-Muslim tourists about both types of destinations. For countries with relaxed rules about the delivery of non-*halal* food, system of supplying food and beverage may not vary much from non-Muslims countries, but for the second group of destinations, while some tourists would enjoy the experience of understanding and showing their appreciation of Islamic concepts (Hashim et al 2005), others may find it hard to abide these restrictions. Therefore, clarifying and informing the non-Muslim tourists about these issues would be very helpful to prevent misunderstandings.

Today, Islamic countries in the Middle East region have great potential for the development of tourism. Along with many social, cultural, and historical attractions, this region also has a very rich heritage of ancient cuisines from Mesopotamian, Persian, Egyptian, and Phoenician civilizations. Most of these cousins were developed by Arabs from the local food of the countries they conquered, which is why these cuisines represent the eating habits and products from ancient Greece, Rome, and many Asian and Mediterranean cultures. Hence, by keeping in mind the eating preferences of modern tourists, it may be possible that these cuisines are developed and promoted as ancient *halal* foods, and thus be a very effective source of attraction for non-Muslims and Muslims living in non-Muslim countries. In this way, Islamic countries can increase their share of the global tourism market along with promotion of *halal* food products around the world.

Halal *Catering Policies at Some Destinations*

Considering the demand for *halal* food, especially by the tourists from the Gulf with high level of income, some Muslim and non-Muslim destinations have started more active commitment to *halal* catering. Here are some examples:

- In order to attract more tourists from the Middle East, New Zealand, one of the major *halal* meat producer and exporter, has recently taken an interest in the supply of *halal* food for Muslim tourists in restaurants. Tourism New Zealand Chief Executive, George Hickton, believes that by ensuring the availability of *halal* food in restaurants, New Zealand can be promoted as an attractive destination for Muslim travelers (Wan Hassan and Hall 2003).

- In order to promote *halal*-based tourism, The Emirates Investment Group plans to build 150 Islamic hotels around the world by 2013. This project is planned to start in Egypt, the United Arab Emirates, and Malaysia, then moving on to Europe, the United States, and China (The Halal Journal 2009a). These hotels will be in total compliance with the Islamic laws and only *halal* food will be served.
- Keeping in view the potential of the inbound Muslim market, Tourism Authority of Thailand has urged restaurant owners to improve the quality of their food to meet Muslim standards. Currently, only 30 restaurants in five provinces meet the *Halal* Food Services Standard for Tourism developed by the Tourism Authority of Thailand and the *Halal* Standard Institute of Thailand. The authority is preparing to approach more restaurants, particularly on tourist routes, to encourage them to adopt *halal* standards.
- Malaysia's *halal* food, extensively promoted in the Middle East, is considered a draw for tourists from that region, especially those from the United Arab Emirates, Syria, and Saudi Arabia. There were 340,000 tourists from the Middle East in 2008, and the number is expected to increase in 2009 to 400,000 (The Halal Journal 2009b).

CONCLUSION

Food catering has always been important for tourism as it is directly related to tourists' satisfaction with their experience. However, food selection by tourists also has religious aspects that play a very crucial role in shaping a tourist's destination selection criteria. Hence, there is a need to give ample consideration to this dimension of the relationship between food and the tourism industry while designing policies to promote destinations. The religious aspect of food selection criteria is very visible for Muslim tourists. According to Islamic teachings, Muslims can only consume the variety of permitted foods called *halal*. However, In spite of the importance of *halal* food for Muslims, it has not yet become an important consideration in tourism planning in many countries and there is still a low degree of awareness about this concept for most non-Muslim destinations. However, there are initiatives being undertaken by some Muslim and non-Muslim destinations to improve *halal* delivery for Muslim tourists, but there remain a need for radical changes in tourism planning at the global level to attract Muslim tourists. On the other hand, Islamic countries as tourists destinations have applied different policies for this matter; some of them act more relaxed about Islamic laws and openly deliver non-*halal* foods to tourists, while others strictly ban it.

Halal food provides the tourism industry with both opportunities and challenges. For the Muslim countries, especially in the Middle East, *halal* food can be an attraction as they are located in the heart of ancient Mesopotamian, Persian, Egyptian, and Phoenician civilizations. These civilizations have left a valuable heritage in their cuisines, which can be developed and promoted as a *halal* attraction. Similarly, non-Muslim countries can also tap into increasing number of Muslim tourists by ensuring the availability of food and other hospitality services compliant with Islamic laws.

On the academic side, there is not a single study based on empirical evidence to investigate the exact nature and type of relationship between availability or unavailability of *halal* food and Muslim tourist's destination selection criteria. Therefore, there is a need to conduct surveys at both national and international level to gather firsthand information and explore the potential of *halal* food in development and promotion of tourism sector in both Muslim and non-Muslim countries. In addition, lack of common *halal* standards and a global *halal* body is another major topic that demands scholars' due attention to work out some general guidelines in the light of *Qur'an* and *Sunnah* for such global standards, which should be formulated by keeping in mind their application and compliance by the food industry. There is also need to establish academies and training institutes to educate the people working in tourism about the *halal* food and its importance for their Muslim customers. Similarly, there is very little progress to develop scientific laboratory-based tests and procedures to certify that *halal* standards are being upheld during the manufacturing process of a particular product. Therefore, it is reasonable to say that in coming days, progress on these issues will be crucial not only for the development of *halal* food, but also for the recognition of its true potential in the development of the tourism industry.

Note

The views expressed in this article are the author's own and not necessarily those of The Statistical, Economic and Social Research and Training Centre for Islamic Countries.

Chapter 5

WOMEN'S PARTICIPATION IN TOURISM
A Case from the Maldives

Aishath Shakeela
Lisa Ruhanen
Noreen Breakey
The University of Queensland, Australia

Abridgement: Women are key participants in the tourism labor market. Maldivian women are recognized as being among the most emancipated in South Asia and the Islamic world. There is no institutional discrimination along gender lines in access to education, health services, or for jobs in the public sector (The World Bank 2004). However, the proportion of women working in the Maldivian tourism industry is relatively low. This chapter explores one of the key outcomes of a broader study on the participation of locals in the Maldivian tourism industry. The role of government in balancing religion, politics, and economy is considered imperative in positively influencing local tourism labor market participation and employment for women. **Keywords:** women; tourism employment; Islam; Maldives

INTRODUCTION

Islam is one of the major religions in the world. For "outsiders," Islam is often associated with ultraconservatism, anti-Western sentiment, terrorism, and oppression of women (Armstrong 2002). Certainly these perceptions have influenced tourism demand and activity for Islamic countries, with some

Tourism in the Muslim World
Bridging Tourism Theory and Practice, Volume 2, 61–71
Copyright © 2010 by Emerald Group Publishing Limited
All rights of reproduction in any form reserved
ISSN: 2042-1443/doi:10.1108/S2042-1443(2010)0000002008

claims that Islamic societies are not major destinations (Burton 1995). Yet, there is a growing body of literature on tourism and Islam (Al-Hamarneh and Steiner 2004; Alavi and Yasin 2000; Cooper 2008; Wilson 2006; Yaapar 2005; Zamani-Farahani and Henderson 2010), focusing on issues as diverse as the impact on international tourism market in the Middle East countries following the September 11 terrorist attack in the United States, effect of religion on tourism development, and use of Islamic identity as a marketing tool. Despite authors such as Burton (1995) claiming that Islamic societies are not major destinations, research indicates otherwise. For example, Al-Hamarneh and Steiner (2004) found that the Middle East tourism industry did not suffer wide-ranging collapse as was envisaged following the terrorist attack in the United States in 2001. In 2002, international tourist arrivals to the Middle East increased by 17%, reaching almost 28 million, which can be considered an extraordinary performance under the difficult world tourism conditions, constrained by the economic slowdown and the geopolitical instability affecting this region (UNWTO 2003). Indeed, the region has remained a popular destination. While there is a small but growing body of literature on Islam and tourism more generally, little attention has yet been paid to religion and its impact on Islamic women's labor market participation and employment in the tourism industry.

Women are acknowledged as key participants in the tourism labor market (Ashley, Roe and Goodwin 2001; Jamieson 2003), yet the nature and extent of their involvement is often a point of contention. For instance, Sinclair (1997) found that women have been excluded from some occupations within the tourism industry due to traditional ideologies of gender and social sexuality. There also continues to be wide discrepancies in remuneration between the genders (Muñoz-Bullón 2009; Tugores 2008). Furthermore, research indicates that religion, culture, and society can influence women's employment (Constance 2005; Feldmann 2007; Foroutan 2008; Read and Oselin 2008; Read 2004).

Today there are inequalities within the world's labor force that result in disparities between countries and worker segments. For example, a large gender gap continues to remain in many labor markets, indicating limited opportunities for women (ILO 2007). In this context, religion also plays a crucial role in the extent to which women are employed. For example, Murphy (1995) researching religion and female labor force participation and unemployment in Northern Ireland found that Catholic females were significantly less likely to be employed than single Protestant females, and further being married also affected whether a woman was employed or not. In recent research, Feldmann (2007) found that female participation in employment was higher among Protestants in 19 industrial countries. Researching the effects of religion and family among Arab American women, Read (2004) found that religiosity exerted a negative influence on women's labor force participation if children were present at home. In the context of Malaysia, Amin and Alam (2008) also found that religion significantly influenced a woman's decision regarding employment.

In terms of Islam, gender differences associated with religion are apparent in Malaysia, and this has been found to make working in tourism unfavorable for women (Henderson 2003). Indeed, indigenous Malaysians do not perceive tourism activity as a positive way to create jobs as the activity conflicts with their religious beliefs. Similarly, there are virtually no indigenous women working in Iran's tourism industry (Zadeh 2001). However, "the culturally induced absence of working women in the services sectors of some countries is tempered by evidence of gradual change in, for example, Iran and Saudi Arabia" (Baum 2007:1395).

THE REPUBLIC OF MALDIVES

The archipelagic nation of the Republic of Maldives, an Islamic country located in the Indian Ocean, is officially recognized as "a unitary, sovereign, independent, democratic republic based on the principles of Islam" (Constitution of the Republic of Maldives 2008:1). However, before the people embraced Islam through a Moroccan traveler Abul Barkat Yoosuf Al Barbary in 1153 CE, they were of different religions, with the majority Buddhists (Heyerdahl 1986).

The Maldives relies on tourism as the mainstay of its economy. This important industry began in 1972 with the opening of two resorts, a total of 280 beds and 1,097 international arrivals (Ministry of Tourism 1998). By the end of 2008, the Maldives had a total bed capacity of 23,464 (Department of National Planning 2009a; Ministry of Tourism Arts and Culture 2009). In the same period, tourism contributed 27% to GDP and 29% to government revenue and generated some 70% of the country's foreign currency earnings (DNP 2009b; MTAC 2009). The significance of the tourism industry can be seen when compared to other major economic sectors such as fishing which contributed only 5% to the country's GDP during the same period.

An important feature of the Maldivian tourism industry is that the country is one of the few that practices "enclave tourism," under which islands developed for tourism are "off-limits to the local people" (UNWTO 1997:13), unless they are employed at the resort. Only 194 islands are inhabited by local people. Of the remaining 996 islands, 94 have been developed as individual, self-contained resorts under the country's "one island–one resort policy" (DNP 2009a; MTAC 2009). The Maldives is often cited as a model for island tourism development (UNWTO 2000). However, the Maldivian enclave tourism approach was due to the small size of individual islands that make up the country. Using the "smallness" of the islands, the Maldivian government developed the enclave island tourism strategy to ensure that the economic benefits of tourism were obtained without impacting the culture and environment of the country.

With a population of just over 310,000 people, nearly 40% are under the age of 18 in 2006; the country had an economically active population of just over 129,000 (DNP 2009a), with an unemployment rate of 14% (DNP 2009b). Yet, despite this high unemployment rate, by the end of 2008 the Maldives had an expatriate workforce of nearly 81,000 (DNP 2009b; MHRYS 2009), with the majority directly or indirectly employed in tourism. While exact figures for Maldivians employed in the industry are unavailable, considering the local/foreign employment structure in tourism, it was estimated that some 53% of this workforce was comprised of expatriate labor (CATC 2007).

Although women in the Maldives are recognized as being among the most emancipated in the Islamic world (Dayal and Didi 2001), and there is no institutional discrimination in access to education, health services, or for jobs in the public sector (The World Bank 2004), their proportion working in the industry is relatively low. Government statistics estimate that only 7% of resort employees are females and only 2% of these are local (MTCA 2007). "Apart from cultural factors, in general, the type of accommodation provided by tourist resorts is not suitable for female employees. That makes it difficult for most of the resorts to attract women" (MTCA 2007:53). Yet, no research has been previously undertaken to understand the reasons why women have such low participation rates in tourism.

The Maldivian Women's Labor Study

Given this context, this chapter explores the participation and employment of local women in the Maldivian tourism industry. Based on primary research undertaken as part of a broader study on the participation of local people in tourism, this chapter explores one of the key outcomes of the research related to religion and its impact on the participation and employment of women in this industry. These results are considered in the context of Islam and the entrenched societal beliefs surrounding women's participation in tourism employment in the Maldives. The role of government in balancing religion, politics, and economy are considered imperative in positively influencing local tourism labor market participation and employment for women.

Primary research utilizing a mixed methodology (28 in-depth face-to-face interviews with tourism educators; eight focus groups with local community group representatives; and 74 survey questionnaires with resort managers) was undertaken in 2007 to examine the attraction and retention of local people in tourism employment in the Maldives. The research elicited a range of findings regarding local labor market participation in tourism. While the scope of this chapter does not permit discussion of each of these aspects, a number of issues and challenges regarding the participation and employment of local Maldivians in this industry were highlighted. These included local employee's lack of vocational skills and commitment to industry jobs, unavailability of skilled local employees including inadequate professional experience and lack of academic qualifications, as well as the locals' negative images regarding employment in tourism. The qualitative components of the research elicited further themes including social, human resource, economic, institutional, and religious factors as impacting the participation of local people in tourism (Figure 1).

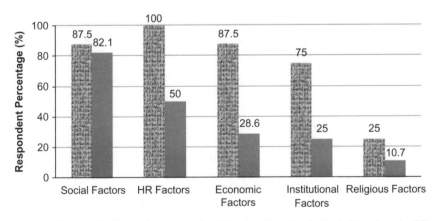

Figure 1. The Attraction and Retention Factors of Local Employees
Note: Multiple Responses Included

Religion as an Influencing Factor

In this study, religion did emerge as a key factor influencing the attraction and retention of Maldivians in the tourism industry. Importantly, most respondents who discussed the impact of religion did so in the context of women and the religious and societal boundaries associated with Islam "Individual women are reluctant in joining the tourism industry due to cultural/religious conflicts" (Interview Number 01 [INT01]). For instance, while Islam does not exert any significant influence on the operation of tourism-related activities (Din 1989), "non-Islamic behavior" such as gambling, prostitution, nudism, consumption of pork, and alcohol may clash with traditional values (Burns 2007). This was identified in Pulau Redang (Malaysia), Bali (Indonesia), as well as in Egypt (Aziz 1995; Fisher, Nawaz, Fauzi, Nawaz, Eran Sadek, Zulkiflee Abd and Blackett 2008; Hitchcock and Putra 2007) where cultural and religious frictions with tourism development have emerged. In the Maldives, the government walks a fine line in balancing the needs of the international tourists and that of the local inhabitants. The government prohibits prostitution, gambling, and nude bathing in public areas. On the other hand, pork and alcohol considered *haram* (forbidden) are available to tourists. As CATC aptly noted:

> tourist resort jobs were not popular with the public (especially parents) who held traditional Islamic values due to aspects of the industry being unIslamic; service of alcohol, sunbathers' attire and the holidaymakers way of life in general (2007:4).

Similar sentiments are evident in the following interview excerpt:

> The other is women ... because 50% of the working population [are] women and they don't work in the resorts, mainly because the public perception of the resort in the Maldives is something very different from what we know it is ... it is just a place you go and work and you stay, not mingling with the guests except at the time of service ... but the perception in the country is that, these are places where people are drinking and running around naked, illegal things going on, it's an immoral industry, this is not a proper place for people to work, especially young women to go and work. That attitude is something which is

ingrained in the national conscious and national attitude. That will take time to change (INT24).

Yet, religion is not the only factor at play in dissuading women from joining the tourism labor market. For instance, the enclave resort approach is another strong inhibitor, as employees working on resort islands can be estranged from their families and communities for extended periods of time. In addition to poor employee facilities and the absence of childcare facilities available in the country (Dayal and Didi 2001), the lack of an internal transport system linking employees to their home islands is an ongoing challenge in engaging and retaining Maldivians in the tourism labor market (Shakeela, Breakey and Ruhanen 2010; Shakeela and Cooper 2009).

Given the geographically disperse nature of the country's tourism businesses, coupled with religious influences, women are excluded or dissuaded from joining the industry. As they have to leave home for extended periods of time to stay on the resort island where they are employed, they are generally traveling unaccompanied. As one respondent noted:

> Parents from those kinds of families will not send their daughters to work because in their belief a woman cannot travel alone. And this will be a hindrance for a woman to work in any industry. I think that is already happening here (FG04).

Similarly:

> I don't foresee Maldives ever having 25% women participation in the tourism and hospitality industry or any actual direct employment in the resorts. That would be ideal if we could. As you know, our culture, our religion, our values, a lot of things hinder that (INT13).

In fact, so strong are these influences that a woman working in tourism is regarded with less dignity than one employed in a public sector position, and local women comprise 47% of the public service workforce as opposed to 2% of tourism employment (DNP 2009b; MTCA 2007). One reason that women are so strongly represented in the public service sector is that such positions generally do not require daily commuting to work from one island to another.

The notion that religion should affect women's participation in tourism employment in the Maldives is an interesting phenomenon, particularly given the history of Islam. A Muslim's life is guided by the *Qur'an*, the *Sunnah*, and the *Hadith*, containing the sayings and deeds of Prophet Muhammad, set down by his companions and family (IslamiCity 2010; University of Southern California 2010). Indeed, the first wife of Prophet Mohammed, Khadeeja, was a renowned businesswoman. Further, the *Qur'an* permits women to work away from their home, outlines women's right to financial security and inheritance, and also emphasizes their rights to their own earnings, property, and wealth (*Qur'an* 4:32). Therefore, it is argued that notions such as women traveling alone suggested by respondents as precluding her from working in the industry are not in fact based on the *Qur'an*, the *Sunnah*, or the *Hadith*, but are instead societal and cultural interpretations that have been retrospectively linked to religion. Indeed, interpretations of Islamic philosophy are not uniform, with variations within and among various countries and cultures (Hassan 2005; Mazari 1983). However, if a literal interpretation of the *Qur'an* and teachings of Prophet Mohammed are to be taken, then women leaving home to work in tourism should not be a religious issue.

The Role of Government

According to Jenkins and Henry (1982), the potential opportunities for local employment cannot be fully realized without active government intervention. Echoing these sentiments, Scheyvens and Momsen (2008) argued that governments need to establish an effective policy environment and play a stronger regulatory role if sustainable, equity-enhancing tourism is to emerge. In the case of the Maldives, the government plays the role of planner, promoter, regulator, controller, facilitator, and educator in tourism. Yet up until early 2007, student rules and regulations set by the Ministry of Education in the Maldives prohibited students from visiting resorts unless accompanied by a parent or a guardian. The government's intention was to avoid acculturation processes. However, such measures can deter potential employees from joining the industry.

It is widely accepted that some degree of government intervention, appropriate to the sociopolitical ideology as well as economic and developmental goals of the destination, is necessary for tourism to be developed on a sustainable platform (Buhalis 2000; Gee 1997; Gunn and Var 2002; Hall 2008; Jenkins 2008; Jenkins and Henry 1982). However, in the Maldives, during the initial stages of tourism development, the government did not have an active role, leaving industry development to the private entrepreneurs, both local and international.

An extreme case of tourism development that created negative sentiments among locals when it was just starting to be introduced is that of the Club Méditerranée (now known as Club Med). With the emergence of Maldives as a destination, Club Méditerranée, by an agreement with a French national and a local entrepreneur, started a resort operation in Malé atoll in 1973 called "Club Nature," which was known a nudist colony. Using the isolated geographic configuration of the resort island, a unique tourism product was created. In the Club, clients and key customer contact staff were required to stay without clothing, except at meal times. A relaxed, money-less, free lifestyle atmosphere was created to provide a contrast to the busy urban lifestyle of the Europeans (MOT 1996). While it might have been a desirable product for tourists who chose to stay in the resort, the approach conflicted with staff and the wider community's religious and cultural beliefs.

As negative impacts of tourism, such as aspects of acculturation, emerged in the early 1980s, the government intervened and enacted laws to prohibit tourists from staying in locally inhabited islands other than Malé. The government also restricted the safari *dhoni* boats, which provide accommodation, food and beverages, and normally are accompanied by a smaller vessel with diving facilities, to certain zones of the country for travel (MTCA 2008; Niyaz 2002). With this policy change, enclave tourism emerged, and the tourists were confined to resorts, hotels, guesthouses, and safari *dhonis*. This further entrenched the image of tourism as a "necessary evil" among the general population. While tourism created the much needed job opportunities and foreign currency, it was concomitantly seen as negatively impacting on local cultures and beliefs, which required it to be separated from the local community.

Both anecdotal and scholarly accounts indicate that in the past and present, religion is used as a political power tool. An example of this is the complex interplay between religion and politics in Turkey. On the one hand, policies put forward by political parties on the center right and the religious activities of various government institutions have tended to heighten religious consciousness, increase levels of its observance, and reinforce identity with it among the locals. On the other hand, some political parties call for compartmentalization of religion and the state (Ayata 1996). Indeed, religion adds another dimension to the multifaceted process of tourism development in Islamic countries. In this regard, Saeidi (2002) notes that in the case of Iran, tourism cannot be separated from the processes of political power struggles. In a similar manner, as evident in the Maldives, religion is often used for political gain (Henderson 2008c). Indeed, debates on the Parliament floor with regard to allowing the sale of alcohol in hotels and guesthouses on inhabited islands also took a political angle with all the parties using religion to gain political points (Hamdhoon 2010; Wajdhee 2010). As one interviewee highlighted:

> The government has not whole heartedly accepted the tourism industry, if not for that, today tourism should have been one of the subjects taught in the schools. The government has always used religion as a tool of governance in this country, and therefore tourism has been one of the victims of this ... tourism was regarded as a step-son of the economy, not a full child (INT28).

One of the major challenges facing tourism development in an Islamic country is how to create a more culturally friendly tourism work environment for the indigenous Muslim population. Often in Islamic countries, such as Malaysia, Indonesia, and the Maldives, the government tends to take the view that the economic significance of tourism is more important than cultural values. Such an approach does not facilitate increasing the participation of workers who are culturally sensitive to tourism activity (Liu and Wall 2006).

Yet, tourism has the potential to reduce ethnic differences and create equitable economic income. For this reason, in Malaysia the government has tried to promote tourism employment to its Malay population, despite the religious difficulties. Slowly changing societal views in Malaysia have allowed some Muslim Malays, particularly females, to enter into employment in tourism. Certainly the role of government in balancing religion, politics, and the economy, as well as responding to societal interpretations of Islam, are crucial as this undoubtedly influences local tourism labor market participation and employment, particularly for women. While political stability is crucial to the sustainable development of tourism in any destination (Hall 2008), a key role of the government is also to ensure that cultural and religious values do not erode with the inception of tourism.

CONCLUSION

Using qualitative data gathered in the Maldives, this chapter has explored the impact of religion on women's participation and employment in the Maldivian tourism labor market. Religion was found to be a significant factor influencing their employment in the industry, particularly in terms of a woman working at an enclave tourism operation. However, there are other crucial factors also affecting women's employment in the industry, namely the country's enclave resort policy and the government attempts to separate religion and tourism development. Not only does the one island–one resort policy dissuade or exclude women's participation in the industry, it also severely inhibits its sustainability with ongoing challenges in attracting and retaining the local workforce in the industry.

The findings suggest that a core issue is how the government balances religion and tourism development policy in the country. As women account for nearly 50% of the working population in the Maldives, the government needs to present tourism as a viable and sustainable source of employment, rather than use religion as a power tool for political gain.

PART II

MUSLIM COUNTRIES

Chapter 6

ISLAM AND TOURISM
Brunei, Indonesia,
Malaysia, and Singapore

Joan C. Henderson
Nanyang Technological University, Singapore

Abridgement: This chapter discusses aspects of the relationship between Islam and tourism in Brunei, Indonesia, Malaysia, and Singapore. Islam is shown to exercise considerable influence over social and political systems in the first three countries, in addition to affecting the tourism industry. It also gives rise to a series of particular demands from adherents, reflected in a movement termed Islamic tourism that encompasses product development and marketing efforts designed for and directed at Muslims. The activities of the four countries in the field are reviewed, revealing an appreciation of the volume and value of Muslim markets. However, there are challenges to overcome if the prospects for future growth are to be fully realized. **Keywords:** Brunei; Indonesia; Islamic tourism; Malaysia; Singapore

INTRODUCTION

Islam is one of the world's major religions and a powerful social and political force. Its influence extends to the domain of tourism where it can help to determine demand for travel among Muslims and the direction of their domestic and international tourist flows. The religion also affects formal tourism policymaking and industry operations in countries where

Tourism in the Muslim World
Bridging Tourism Theory and Practice, Volume 2, 75–89
Copyright © 2010 by Emerald Group Publishing Limited
All rights of reproduction in any form reserved
ISSN: 2042-1443/doi:10.1108/S2042-1443(2010)0000002009

state institutions and value systems are closely linked to Islam, or where there are significant numbers of Muslim citizens. This chapter examines such situations and interactions within the context of Southeast Asian destinations. It focuses on Brunei, Indonesia, and Malaysia, which have predominantly Muslim populations, and Singapore where Malay Muslims constitute a sizeable minority. Religion allied to race is a sensitive issue across much of the region and has political ramifications, introducing another dimension to discussions of the relationship between tourism and Islam and interpretations of Islamic tourism.

There are definitional ambiguities surrounding the concept of Islamic tourism, which is a relatively new phrase, generally describing tourism primarily undertaken by its followers within the Muslim world. The emphasis is on leisure and the status of business travel is uncertain, as is the contribution of non-Muslims visiting places with connections to Islam. Some supporters of this version of tourism envisage an industry funded and owned by Islamic financial institutions, operated in strict accordance with Muslim codes of conduct, and ultimately directed toward religious ends. However, individual Muslims may be prepared to overlook certain doctrinal matters while still regarding themselves as Islamic tourists. This chapter adopts a broad notion of Islamic tourism in which motivations are not always or entirely religious. Participants could be pursuing similar leisure experiences to non-Muslims, albeit within parameters set by Islam, and destinations are not necessarily locations where *Shari'a* or full Islamic law is enacted. Many providers, exemplified by the cases in the chapter, need to cater to Muslims of a spectrum of conservatism and may also have to satisfy non-Muslim customers, giving rise to management and marketing dilemmas.

ISLAM, SOCIETY, AND POLITICS IN SOUTHEAST ASIA

Islam initially spread from Arabia to other regions of the world, not least Southeast Asia. Historians suggest that it was brought there by Arab traders in the 8th century, although missionaries were also at work, and became more firmly established from 12th century onwards. The adoption of the faith three centuries later by the rulers of Malacca, powerful figures who controlled the key port on the Malay Peninsula, encouraged its dissemination and it became a unifying force in many of the territories which make up present day Malaysia and Indonesia (Lawrence 1999; Somers Heidhues 2001). There are now Muslim communities in the 10 countries of the Association of Southeast

Asian Nations (ASEAN), but these are very small in Cambodia, Laos, and Vietnam where the religion is closely associated with the Cham ethnic groups. An unspecified number of Muslims reside in Myanmar/Burma and about 5% of Philippine and 4% of Thai nationals are Muslims (Kramer and Allen 2009). In contrast, 67% of Brunei's 383,000 citizens are Malays and these are largely Muslim, but the category does encompass indigenous peoples who do not follow Islam (EIU 2008a). Malaysia and Indonesia have populations of 27.2 million and 235 million respectively; around 60% of the former are Muslims (EIU 2008b) and 87% of the latter (EIU 2008c), with the remainder mainly of Chinese or Indian origin. These statistics account for the inclusion of the three countries in the chapter alongside Singapore where almost 14% of the total population of just over 4 million are Malay Muslims (EIU 2008d).

Governments in Brunei and Malaysia hail Islam as the official religion and it is accepted as one of the principal faiths in Indonesia and Singapore. Applications of the religion and its effects on everyday life are not uniform, but the rigidity and ultraorthodoxy, which characterizes versions such as the strict Wahhabism of Saudi Arabia, are less evident in Southeast Asia. Indeed, there is a tradition of religious diversity and tolerance, and constitutions guarantee freedom of worship so that Christianity, Buddhism, and Hinduism are also openly practiced. However, Islam pervades societies and cultures in which there are assorted degrees of conformity to its regulations about dress, food, prayer, and conduct. Muslim residents tend to be conservative by Western standards, especially outside larger cities, and observers have commented on a religious resurgence and mounting orthodoxy whereby Islam has acquired greater prominence in public life. At the same time, modernization and the consumerism it engenders are occurring, which can produce sociocultural strains.

Islam impacts on politics and the Sultan of Brunei introduced an ideology termed Malay Muslim Monarchy in 1991, which is founded on "strong Malay cultural influences, stressing the importance of Islam in daily life and governance, and respect for the monarchy as represented by His Majesty" (Brunei Tourism 2008). The sultan's rule is autocratic, despite the reopening of Parliament in 2004 after 20 years of suspension, whereas governments in Malaysia and Indonesia have to contend with opposition parties, some of which champion more radical readings of the religion. Under the leadership of a Malay Muslim party, the long-standing coalition in the parliamentary democracy of Malaysia has traditionally been moderate. However, the Prime Minister's 2001 pronouncement that it was an Islamic state and subsequent similar avowals are perceived to be a bid to counter the popularity of Parti Islam SeMalaysia, which advocates the imposition of

Shari'a. Secular nationalism remains in the ascendancy in Indonesia, where advances in democratic politics in the former dictatorship have been welcomed, but groupings oriented toward Islam are more vocal in the multiparty presidential system. These trends mean that the religion cannot be ignored by incumbent regimes and increasingly informs policies in many areas, including tourism.

Singapore is a secular republic with an elected parliament in which race-based parties are prohibited, yet the constitution does promise to protect the Malays who are almost exclusively Muslims. They are agreed to be the island's native inhabitants (Government of Singapore 2006), now out-numbered by the ethnic Chinese who make up about 75% of citizens. The stance on race is ostensibly aimed at averting social unrest, yet can be seen as a tool for frustrating challenges to the People's Action Party, which has been in power since 1968 and is renowned for its exercise of control (EIU 2008a). Official protestations about equality and equity have been questioned by critics who point to the influence of a Chinese political elite and comparative disadvantage of minorities (Rahim 1998). Therefore, race entwined with religion is a political question of some awkwardness in Singapore in spite of attempts at its depoliticization, which are reflected in destination marketing messages of harmonious multiculturalism.

Racial and religious divisions, reinforced by economic and political differences, are also a political issue in Malaysia and to a lesser extent in Indonesia (Crouch 2001). The relative wealth of the ethnic Chinese has inspired antagonism and sometimes physical attacks, especially in Indonesia where racial strife is recurrent (Jesudason 2001), while the affirmative action programs in Malaysia designed to raise the living standards of indigenous Malays, primarily Muslim, are a cause of discontent for those excluded. Non-Muslim Malaysians have been largely willing to tolerate sociocultural and political marginalization in return for the benefits of citizenship, but they are now more assertive in demanding their rights (The Economist 2007). The government thus has to reconcile its commitment to furthering the well-being of Malay Muslims with its obligations to Chinese and Indian residents and the political parties representing them on which it has historically depended for the retention of power.

Tourism is, however, a vehicle whereby countries can present themselves as they would like to be seen and this applies to race relations. Akin to other multicultural societies where there are stresses and fears of fragmentation, it is used to articulate officially sanctioned notions of national identity in Malaysia and Singapore. The sense of nationhood embraces and celebrates multiple cultural identities, which are presented as complementary and components of an overarching national identity, binding peoples together and fostering cohesion. Tourism can thereby be harnessed to social and political as well as economic ends, cultivating feelings of unity and consolidating the position of governments that portray themselves as creators and guardians of this happy state of affairs.

Nevertheless, realities sometimes contradict depictions of colorful cultural diversity circulated for internal and external consumption. Strains persist across Southeast Asia and are aggravated by religious intransigence with repercussions for states as destinations and generators of international tourists, whether Islamic or non-Islamic. Of major concern is the radicalization of Islam (Carpenter and Wienek 2004; Yunanto 2003) which has been a factor in ongoing and destabilizing ethnic disputes (Ganguly 2003) and it must be given due attention by tourists and the industry. Islamic militancy has found expression in terrorism, a topic of universal pertinence (Richter 1999; Pizam and Mansfeld 1996; Sonmez 1998) that has the capacity to disrupt tourism, although adverse repercussions depend upon the severity and frequency of outrages (Pizam and Fleischer 2002).

The actions of Islamic militants and terrorists and fears of attacks have harmed Southeast Asia's reputation and damaged its tourism, exemplified by the bombings in Bali (Pambudi, McCaughey and Smyth 2009). While Westerners are frequently targeted, violence perpetrated in the name of religion can be indiscriminate in its victims. Safety and security are the key foundations for destination development and the consequences of doubts about their existence are evident in parts of Indonesia. Brunei, Malaysia, and Singapore have been able to offer reassurances about low risks, but they too are tarnished by terrorist incidents and other sorts of regional instability.

Tourism and Islamic Tourism

Tourism plays a key role in the economies of the four countries, although they exhibit contrasting stages of tourism and general development (EIU 2008a–d) with Brunei and Singapore the most affluent (ASEAN 2009a). Singapore's government has allocated the industry a high priority for several decades and it is cited as a driver of economic growth in official strategies. In contrast, formal support for tourism in Brunei is relatively recent (Baum and Conlin 1997) and there are reservations about certain manifestations of Western-style mass tourism and attendant sociocultural disruption. Nevertheless, tourism is acknowledged as central to the economic diversification necessitated by the anticipated exhaustion of oil in 20 years and gas by 2040, sectors on which Brunei currently depends (Brunei Tourism 2008).

Indonesian and Malaysian national and provincial officials too have occasionally sought to limit international arrivals because of what are judged to be their damaging sociocultural impacts (Din 1989; Henderson 2003), but here also negative attitudes have been tempered by appreciation of tourism's actual and possible financial rewards. It is now Indonesia's third largest foreign exchange earner and a significant job provider and among Malaysia's most successful services and export industries, occupying a core place in federal long-term economic and physical planning (Henderson 2008a). International tourism thus tends to be regarded favorably within all four administrations and economic imperatives commonly underlie pro-tourism policies. There is an overall consensus that growth is desirable, the pursuit of which is the responsibility of formal agencies whose existence and work suggests the importance attached to tourism.

Brunei Tourism oversees this industry in the sultanate, and this function is exercised by the Ministry of Culture and Tourism in Indonesia where legislation approving the first full-fledged Tourism Board was passed at the end of 2008. Tourism Malaysia (which is the national tourism organization) reports to a Ministry of Tourism set up in 2004, and the Singapore Tourism Board is the statutory body that deals with planning, development, and promotion. Structures and processes differ, as do budgets and expertise, and the board is perhaps the most generously financed and influential of the organizations.

Table 1 provides details about total inbound tourists in 2008 and variations are attributable to different circumstances and tourism resource inventories (ASEAN 2009b). The underperformance of Indonesia is noteworthy, given its wealth of attractions and is partly the outcome of the instability and natural disasters to which the country is vulnerable. It also suffers from deficiencies in infrastructure, health and safety, and accommodation that led to a ranking of 80 out of 130 in a 2008 tourism competitive index, far below its neighbors (The Straits Times 2009a).

Table 1. International Tourist Arrivals (2008)

Country	Arrivals (in Thousands)
Brunei	226
Indonesia	6,234
Malaysia	22,052
Singapore	10,116

Table 2. International Arrivals from Muslim Countries and Singapore (2005)

Country of Origin	Brunei	Indonesia	Malaysia	Singapore
Bahrain	4	589	6,874	NA
Bangladesh	1,984	4,383	NA	54,352
Brunei	–	15,341	486,344	47,853
Indonesia	6,765	–	962,957	1,813,444
Iran	92	NA	NA	6,983
Jordan	46	NA	2,086	NA
Kuwait	75	NA	11,506	4,977
Malaysia	46,183	520,067	–	577,882
Pakistan	1,536	6,690	NA	15,945
Saudi Arabia	53	34,547	53,682	6,993
Singapore	7,947	1,359,755	9,634,506	–
United Arab Emirates	51	NA	29,606	28,062

Comprehensive and comparable data about the origin of tourists and the contribution of Islam are not available, but levels of Muslim travel are indicated in Table 2, which contains the latest figures published by ASEAN for a selection of Organisation of Islamic Conference (OIC) countries and Singapore (ASEAN 2008). The OIC has 56 members, which collectively are home to most of the world's estimated one and a half billion Muslims. OIC nationals are not exclusively adherents of Islam and information about religion is not collected, yet their visitation can be used as a measure of Islamic tourism. The contents of the table disclose the high degree of cross-border traffic between the Southeast Asian states and the relatively small numbers of international tourists from the others. Arrivals alone, however, can be misleading and authorities are equally interested in expenditure.

Islamic tourism initiatives usually concentrate on tourists from sections of the Middle East, who are especially welcome because of their high spending power, which compensates for small volumes. Other OIC members are much less prosperous and several have very large populations with low average incomes, those in sub-Saharan Africa among the most indigent in the world (UNDP 2008). Advantages of access, with many OIC countries located within six or seven hours flying time of Southeast Asia in contrast to longer haul flights that Europeans and Americans must undertake, may thus be negated. The more mature markets of the West also benefit from good communication links and a well-developed industry of tour operators and travel agents, as do prime Asian generating markets that additionally gain from being within comparatively easy reach.

Table 3. International Arrivals from Selected Non-Muslim Areas (2008)

Country of Origin	Brunei (in Thousands)	Indonesia (in Thousands)	Malaysia (in Thousands)	Singapore (in Thousands)
Australia	26	450	427	833
China	28	337	950	1,079
Europe	24	925	1,002	1,296
India	4	102	551	778
Japan	4	547	433	571
USA	3	174	223	397

Therefore, propensity and ability to engage in international travel is generally greater for advanced and rapidly emerging economies outside the OIC than those within. The statistics in Table 3 permit comparisons to be drawn between Islamic and non-Islamic demand and hints at the commercial power of the latter, a topic which discussed later (ASEAN 2009b). Looking ahead, the economic downturn, which commenced in 2008, and its reverberations must not be overlooked. A severe slump in global demand was apparent by 2009, but the duration and ultimate outcomes of both economic and tourism crises for individual markets and destinations are still unknown.

In terms of tourists from the Muslim world, Malaysia emerges as a leading destination and arrivals from the Middle East have been increasing since the turn of the century. The aftermath of the terrorist strikes in the United States in 2001 incited fears of a backlash against Muslims and practical barriers to their travel in the West, redirecting some tourism and prompting a doubling of Malaysia's Arab tourists that year and again in 2002 (The New Sunday Times 2004). The capital Kuala Lumpur with its numerous shopping malls attracts eager shoppers; coastal resorts Langkawi and Penang are also popular. Arabs are reported to be lavish spenders (averaging as much as RM10,000 or US$2,800 per person), and stay almost twice as long as other tourists, frequently journeying in large family parties. Most of the West Asian tourists come from Saudi Arabia, followed by the United Arab Emirates and Kuwait. Lebanon, Turkey, Jordan, Syria, and Oman are of some significance (The Straits Times 2005) and arrivals from Egypt have been rising steadily, staying over nine days on average and spending around RM7,000 (US $1,900) each (ITM 2008a).

Singapore too has seen an expansion in tourism from countries such as the United Arab Emirates, Qatar, and Saudi Arabia (AsiaTravelTips.com

2006). The United Arab Emirates, for example, recorded an average annual growth rate of almost 20% in 2007 (AME Info 2008a), which was maintained in 2008 and over 60% more Egyptians also visited Singapore that year compared to 2007 (STB 2009a). Iran is identified as a new market for all the destinations; 63,165 Iranians traveled to Malaysia in 2008, more than double the amount in 2007; those entering Singapore also rose by 50% in the same period. The first Iranian charter flights into Indonesia and Singapore commenced in 2009 and are expected to stimulate tourist flows further (TTG 2009b). The Middle Eastern market as a whole proved comparatively robust that year, despite the recession, and performed better than many others (The Straits Times 2009b).

Although outside the ambit of the chapter, it should be noted that domestic tourism is growing in tandem with economic progress across the region. The exception is Singapore where the city-state's small size and geography restricts vacationing at home and their prosperity enables residents to satisfy a preference for outbound travel. Internal movements can be deemed a type of Islamic tourism if those involved are from the Muslim communities. However, there is a paucity of information about the effects of religion on the decisions and behavior of such travelers that inhibits evaluation of domestic Islamic tourism.

The Development and Marketing of Islamic Tourism

Brunei, Indonesia, and Malaysia are members of the OIC, which favors Islamic tourism on the grounds that it can assist in "combating Islamophobia and rectifying the distorted images of Islam in non-Islamic countries." Cultural tourism overall is also praised for its capacity to help non-Muslims become "familiar with the input of Islamic civilisation and its legacy to human civilisation" (OIC 2008b:2). Tourism ministers have met six times for discussions and an announcement at the end of the 2008 gathering contains proposals for new Islamic tourism products, increased investment, and enhanced public knowledge of travel options. Greater direct contacts among relevant parties, the creation of appropriate machinery and public–private sector partnerships, better transport coordination, and exploitation of the Internet are also called for (OIC Journal 2008).

The three countries are signatories to the Damascus Declaration and presumably back the ideas espoused, but formal decisionmaking pertaining to Islamic tourism is not well documented. There are few signs of clearly articulated policies and strategies at a national level, although positions can be discerned from general and specialized media reporting and statements issued by governments and their agencies. Indonesia has shown little interest in cultivating the Islamic tourism market and no comments seem to have been made by the Ministry of Culture and Tourism. The exploration of possibilities in Brunei is indicated by a recent conference on the theme in which Brunei Tourism participated. Speakers concluded that Islamic tourism was a viable product, had strong appeal to niche markets and complemented the sultanate's natural attractions (Brunei Times 2008). However, schemes discussed have yet to be put into practice and there have been no official expressions of intent.

In contrast, Malaysia's Tourism Minister has spoken of the "huge potential for religious tourism" and talks between his Ministry and the Islamic Affairs Department in the Prime Minister's Office resulted in a joint committee devoted to the subject (ITM 2008b). Malaysia's hosting of the first OIC Global Islamic Tourism Conference and Exhibition, which Tourism Malaysia helped to organize, is a mark of that country's professed enthusiasm. Long-term objectives are the "expansion of tourism" worldwide by "developing new tourist destinations and strengthening institutional and governmental cooperation" and "adjustment of the tourist industries to the fundamental interpretations of Islam, including gender-segregated and alcohol-free venues as well as 'Islamically' financed and organised tourism" (The New Straits Times 2008a). An example of progress in this direction in Malaysia is the 2009 launch by a United Arab Emirates company of a "dry" three star business hotel in the capital, described as the first property to ban alcohol sales in the country and beginning of a chain (TTG 2009a). Kuala Lumpur was also the venue in 2008 for a World Islamic Conference and Expo, designed as a "ground breaking forum for the global Islamic tourism industry" to meet and do business, with ambitions to be the "leading travel and tourism trade fair dedicated to unlocking the potential of global Islamic tourism" (WITCX 2008).

Islamic tourism in Singapore tends to be conceived of in terms of a lucrative Middle East market and the setting up of two visa processing agencies in Dubai in 2008 was explained as a response to increasing demand from the Gulf States. A Singapore Tourism Board representative has said that "by continuing to honor and celebrate the links between our cultures ... we look forward to continuous growth in travelers from the region" (AME Info 2008b). In addition to Arab tourists, Indonesia and Malaysia together provide a sizeable proportion of Singapore's tourists and it could be considered an Islamic destination for some of them. Nevertheless, this type of tourism is not identified as a discrete product in the latest development programs where modern and purpose-built amenities without any religious connotations are at the forefront (STB 2007). The flagship multimillion dollar integrated resort complexes that are intended to transform the city-state's tourism do, however, include casinos and these will be out of bounds for Muslims who are forbidden from gambling.

With regard to marketing, authorities in Malaysia have tried to entice Middle Eastern tourists since the 1990s by presenting it as a Muslim-friendly destination (Timothy and Iverson 2006). Efforts intensified after 2001, and Tourism Malaysia has adopted campaign themes such as "Feel at Home." The Islamic culture in Malaysia and the ready availability of Arabic cuisine is stressed, but conventional urban and coastal attractions feature in advertising. The industry is encouraged to strive to meet the particular needs of Middle Eastern tourists and there are instances of shops and restaurants in the capital extending their opening hours for this reason. Hotels are also employing Arabic speaking staff and subscribing to Arabic television channels (The New Sunday Times 2004). Apart from promoting leisure and business travel, Malaysia positions itself as an education and healthcare destination both generally and with specific reference to Muslims (Islamic Tourism Media 2008b).

The Singapore Tourism Board too emphasizes the manner in which Singapore's Middle East tourists can enjoy travel "outside of their region in a comfortable, family-friendly environment that caters to their religious practices" (AME Info 2008b). The region, in combination with Africa, has its own Area Director for marketing and there is an Arabic version of the Visit Singapore website (AME Info 2008a). Tactical campaigns have been undertaken in Kuwait, the United Arab Emirates, and the Arab world as a whole. Selling points include shopping and healthcare alongside Muslim events such as those during the holy month of Ramadan when the Singapore Tourism Board sponsors illuminations in areas of the city with strong Muslim connections (STB 2009b). Appreciation of Muslim requirements is communicated in a brochure about *halal* food and a Muslim Visitor's Guide that date from 2006 (STB 2008b). Travel companies have been urged to offer packages for Muslim markets at festive occasions and other times of year, and those doing so in the past include Singapore Airlines, Thai Airways, Emirates Holidays, Qatar Airways, and Star Cruises (AME Info 2006).

Concerning Islamic tourism attractions, all the countries possess mosques and museums and heritage centers that tell aspects of the story of Islam and its place in society. They are also venues for the celebrations that accompany certain occasions in the Islamic calendar and for indulging in permitted food, both familiar and unfamiliar. However, a notable illustration of new product development is Taman Tamadun Islam in Malaysia, which is depicted by the operators as the "first and only Islamic Civilisation Park." It opened in early 2008 on a 33-hectare river island site near the capital of the northeastern state of Terengganu, which, together with Kelantan, is thought of as the traditional heartland of Malay Islamic culture. Although under the charge of the State Economic Development Corporation, the idea is attributed to Malaysia's Prime Minister and his desire to foster a moderate, plural, and progressive kind of Islam (Noor 2008).

The developers envisage an "intellectual center of Islamic art and civilization" which will "expose the glorious Islamic architecture; experience and inculcate the Islamic culture and way of life." Among the park's 21 scaled replicas of historic monuments are the Sacred Mosque of Saudi Arabia, the Al-Hambra Citadel of Spain, and the Indian Taj Mahal. The Crystal Glass Mosque, made of crystal shine glass and steel, is touted as another main attraction and the site boasts convention facilities, a commercial complex, and a children's playground (TTI 2009). Despite being officially hailed as a success, with 2 million tourists in its first year (Bernama 2009), the park has its detractors. Criticisms relate to the disappointing quality of the exhibits and experience, their limited appeal, confused purposes, inadequate marketing, and poor access (The New Straits Times 2008b; Noor 2008). Opponents censured the government for spending money on a "theme park" in a state, which is one of the poorest in the country, and for using the project for political advantage. General debate about the abuses of heritage by the tourism industry and politicians thus applies to Islamic heritage and Taman Tamadun Islam is also a reminder that issues of commercial viability are relevant to Islamic tourism.

Finally, it should be acknowledged that policies outside the tourism arena have repercussions for the development and marketing of Islamic tourism in Southeast Asia. An example is the free trade agreement signed in 2008 between Singapore and the Gulf Cooperation Council that comprises Bahrain, Kuwait, Qatar, Oman, Saudi Arabia, and the United Arab Emirates. One element is validation of Singapore's Muslim-compliant foodstuffs, which three of the Gulf Cooperation Council members agreed to accept as equivalent to their own standard, the remainder deliberating the question. The Islamic Council of Singapore contends that the move will have a positive effect on Muslim tourists from the Middle East and elsewhere, removing any fears about the acceptability of Singapore's food (Channel News Asia 2008). Business travel is also likely to be boosted by the forging of closer economic ties and trade links between Brunei, Indonesia, and Malaysia and other countries within the Muslim world, although whether such flows can be deemed Islamic tourism is a topic for conjecture.

CONCLUSION

This chapter reveals a growing appreciation of the size and value of Muslim tourism markets and interest in Islamic tourism on the part of tourists, private industry, and officials. It also hints at the need to ensure appropriate tangible and intangible provision to satisfy the multiple and varied demands of Muslim tourists, the difficulties of which vary according to the destination. Devising and delivering suitable products and services may be a more difficult task in multicultural societies and there are both contrasts and similarities in destination experiences as demonstrated by the four cases that are summarized below.

Malaysia appears the most active in the identification and exploitation of Islamic tourism opportunities, followed by Singapore. Involvement is at a nascent phase in Brunei and there is least activity in Indonesia. Levels of engagement are partly the outcome of wider development processes. Economic advances in Singapore have been very striking and facilitated the emergence of a thriving tourism industry with an aggressive national tourism organization that has the funding and expertise to conduct sophisticated marketing and strategic planning. Malaysia has evolved more slowly as an international destination, with an acceleration in pace during recent years, as growing prosperity has allowed investment in infrastructure and an administrative machinery. Indonesia continues to face formidable barriers to expansion, only now establishing a Tourism Board, and official encouragement of tourism in Brunei has a relatively short history.

Apart from economic determinants, sociocultural considerations embracing religion are especially apposite regarding possibilities for Islamic tourism and this is revealed by the differences between Singapore and its neighbors. Brunei, Indonesia, and Malaysia are predominantly Muslim societies directed by Islamic principles, which also influence government policymaking. Therefore, Muslims from overseas can be confident that their basic religious needs will be understood and met. Numerous sites and occasions associated with Islam also represent a fund of attractions. The presence of Malay Muslims in Singapore enables the authorities to reach out to Muslims elsewhere and offer some reassurances about certain essential religious requirements, but it is a secular state in which Muslims are a small minority. Islam does not permeate life to the extent it does among its neighbors and occupies confined physical, sociocultural, and political spaces. Islamic specific attributes are constrained, and more conservative Muslims looking for an environment that conforms closely to their home could be dissatisfied. Singapore thus offers its own version of Islamic tourism, which is less rigid and more pragmatic in conceptualization and operation than some depictions.

At the same time, Singapore and the other states have tourism assets unrelated directly to religion, which can enhance their appeal for Muslims. Facets of minority cultures of other religions such as festivals and the architecture of places of worship can also add novelty and variety to the tourist experience and Muslims are given a chance to safely combine the familiar and more exotic. Such experiences are also offered by the destinations to non-Muslim tourists who are generally greater in volume and value. Statistics quoted previously show that China and India are key emerging markets and Europe, Australia, Japan, and North America are still important, albeit mature, generators. These and other non-Muslim countries of origin are vital to the tourism industries of Southeast Asia which, in turn, have been seen to be central to economies. Overemphasis on Islamic tourism could erode demand for non-Islamic tourism with damaging economic outcomes. Therefore, an appropriate balance must be struck between the two, although securing this is not always easy in view of the chances of contradictions and conflicts.

Islam in assorted representations can be an attraction for non-Muslims, but Islamic tourism has certain qualities that could be at odds with that of a non-Islamic type. There is scope for tensions when Muslim and non-Muslim tourists meet at the same destination and share facilities; for example, those of another or no faith may expect access to alcohol and foodstuffs denied to Muslims and find segregation of the sexes unacceptable. Women's dress styles are likely to be very different, especially at seaside resorts where the scanty clothing worn by some could be deeply offensive to others. Commercial objectives of maximizing revenues and profits have also to be reconciled with the sociocultural and religious goals which underpin forms of Islamic tourism (Henderson 2008b).

Some observers might contend that non-Muslim tourists have been unfairly privileged in the past by an industry which focuses on their wants and that it is time to give equal attention, if not precedence, to Muslim markets for sociocultural, political, and economic reasons. Such an argument perhaps does not fully acknowledge commercial realities and the harmful repercussions of the alienation and exclusion of tourists from outside the Muslim world. The latter and the international tourism industry do, however, have obligations to respect the cultural norms of destinations visited and fellow tourists and avoid giving offence. Non-Islamic tourism may be compatible with Islamic tourism if properly managed and can be distinguished from an un-Islamic or anti-Islamic version, defined as tourism which fails to give due regard to the sensitivities and sensibilities of the religion and its followers.

Islamic tourism in Southeast Asia is thus best understood as a broad concept, which is open to interpretation and can extend to destinations that have minority, rather than majority, Muslim populations. Its development and operation suggests how religion can be a motivating and mediating factor and a tourism resource, which is utilized creatively by the industry. Islamic tourism is also shaped by the particular conditions in generating and receiving countries, giving rise to a diversity, which is illustrated by the examples discussed in the chapter. Destinations are not uniform and neither are markets that can be segmented on the basis of nationality as well as age and lifestyle and possibly religious orthodoxy.

Issues of tourism patterns among Muslims around the world and endeavors at provision are important avenues for further research in order to improve knowledge and understanding of the characteristics of demand and supply and underlying dynamics. Brunei, Indonesia, Malaysia, and Singapore are interesting laboratories for the study of Islamic tourism and their analysis illuminates some of the problems and opportunities when it is conceptualized and practiced outside more orthodox Muslim states. The cases thus merit monitoring in order to appreciate the ways in which Islamic tourism is evolving and how some of the challenges highlighted in the chapter are addressed, not least those of realizing untapped potential and ensuring a satisfactory relationship between tourists who are followers of Islam and those of other faiths or no religion.

Chapter 7

TOURISM IN SAUDI ARABIA

Deborah Joanne Johnson
Prince Sultan College for Tourism and Business, Saudi Arabia

Abridgement: The Kingdom of Saudi Arabia provides an interesting case study of a Middle Eastern country that has begun to exploit its potential as a destination. Tourism in the Kingdom interacts with a variety of sectors and all elements of the Saudi society, and involves individuals as well as organizations. The country is currently facing numerous economic challenges, emphasizing tourism training and education to provide the necessary skills to meet these challenges and to ensure the successful application and maintenance of sustainable tourism practices. This chapter discusses the current state of tourism in Saudi Arabia and its planned development initiatives, with a focus on responsible tourism planning.
Keywords: policy; religion; responsible tourism planning

INTRODUCTION

The Kingdom of Saudi Arabia (Figure 1) covers the majority of the Arabian Peninsula that has for centuries formed a natural bridge and axis for trade between different cultures. Jefri (personal communication) and Al-Jehani (personal communication) state that religious tourism has existed since ancient times and that many people have traveled for religious reasons. Je-Hani indicates that religious tourism in Saudi Arabia has been in existence for 1,430 years. This is evident from the many great cultures that have left their mark and the many pilgrims who have been coming to Makkah, the cradle of Islam, for nearly 1,400 years and continue to do so in increasing numbers.

Tourism in the Muslim World
Bridging Tourism Theory and Practice, Volume 2, 91–106
Copyright © 2010 by Emerald Group Publishing Limited
All rights of reproduction in any form reserved
ISSN: 2042-1443/doi:10.1108/S2042-1443(2010)0000002010

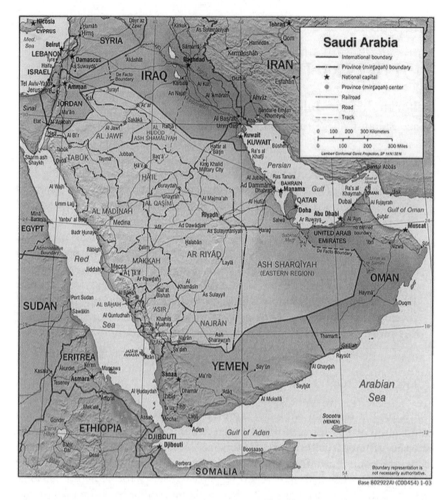

Figure 1. Map of Saudi Arabia
Source: http://en.wikipedia.org/wiki/File:Saudi_Arabia_2003_CIA_map.jpg

Saudi Arabia is an Islamic state based upon the principles prescribed by
the *Qur'an*, the Holy Book of Islam, and the *Shari'a* Islamic law. Jefri
(personal communication) posits that the path of tourism development in
the Kingdom is related to Islam and that travel and tourism are integral to
Islamic political, economic, legal, and social policies within the country.
Based on the Islamic worldview of God, man, and nature, tourism is part of

the *addin* (way of life) and travel is fundamental to Islam (*Qur'an*, Chapter 29: verse 20, Chapter 22: verse 46). Life is a journey in the way of God; thus, tourism in Islam indicates the sacred goal of submission to God's ways. The work of the Saudi Commission for Tourism and Antiquities (SCTA) conforms to the vision of Saudi Arabia for the tourism industry as it regards the Kingdom as the cradle of Islam, thus developing it in a sustainable manner set within the framework of Islamic values to ensure a sociocultural, environmental, and economic benefit for all. According to Al-Jehani (personal communication), tourism development is set within the framework of Islamic values and will not allow the use of alcohol, prostitution, or gambling. Revealing clothing for both men and women are also discouraged. Further it is encouraged that incoming tourists are treated with compassion and thoughtfulness.

Tourism can be used as an initiative for economic reform; however, it requires a sustainable focus and responsible planning, and set within the framework of Islamic values as the key driver of all activities and projects inclusive of effective leadership and strategic direction. Tourism is an information-intensive industry and the planning, development, marketing, and daily operations are dependent upon reliable and current information and data. Sadi and Henderson (2005) assert that Saudi Arabia originally devoted little attention to conventional international leisure tourism for a combination of social, political, and economic reasons. There were few financial incentives to do so in view of the wealth accruing from the discovery and exploitation of oil. However, there was a focus on the key role of religious tourism, with over a million traveling annually for the *Hajj* that requires a major organizational effort by the authorities (Sadi and Henderson 2005). This is a pilgrimage to Makkah that all Muslims are expected to make, if their circumstance permits, at least once in a lifetime. *Umrah* also involves a visit to the holy cities, but is not restricted to a specific date and can be done on various occasions but it is preferable during the Holy month of Ramadan. According to Al-Jehani (personal communication), those on the *Hajj* and *Umrah* accounted for almost 6 million arrivals in 2008 out of 14 million arrivals in 2008 in total. Approximately 7.5 million were business and event travelers. Leisure tourism is a new concept in Saudi Arabia and is classified as a new market area for development. Tourism is now Saudi Arabia's third largest industry after energy and manufacturing, and has recently emerged as the second most important in terms of foreign exchange (Sadi and Henderson 2005).

The body of knowledge regarding Saudi tourism is limited and needs to be developed. The literature on aspects related to tourism development within Saudi Arabia is restricted, with academics (Ahmed 1992; Bhardwaj 1998; Bogari, Crowther and Marr 2004; Seddon and Khoja 2003) focusing more on religious tourism and the *Hajj*. One of the first studies attempting to analyze Saudi Arabian tourism patterns and attitudes was conducted by Seddon and Khoja (2003). Their findings indicated that Saudi tourism had tended toward a mass market type and that infrastructure developments have proceeded without environmental impact assessments resulting in tourism activities degrading the natural resources upon which the industry depends. Further, their study revealed that vacationing Saudi families have the means and the interest to support future protected-area tourism development. Bogari et al (2004) conducted the first study on the motivation for domestic tourism in Saudi Arabia. They posit that tourism motivation in developing countries and Islamic culture has received scant attention and to understand tourism motivation is to see holiday travel as a satisfier of needs and wants.

Their study concentrated on the relationship between the motivation of Saudi tourists to travel in relation to push and pull factors set within the framework of Islamic and Arabic cultures as cultural variables play a significant role in this motivation. This study revealed nine push motivational categories as reasons for wanting to travel domestically: cultural value, utilitarian, knowledge, social, economical, family togetherness, interest, relaxation, and convenience of facilities (Bogari et al 2004). In terms of the pull motivational categories, the study reflected that safety, activity, beach sports/activities, nature/outdoor, historical/cultural, religious, budget, leisure, and upscale were aspects drawing Saudis to travel in their own country. The same study asserts that by far the most important push and pull factors for the Saudi tourists to travel domestically is the cultural and religious value of the tourism product. This provides one aspects of how tourism is perceived in Saudi Arabia; however, there remain a number of other market segments such as the international market and expatriate market that are significant but have not yet been analyzed.

In terms of the organization of tourism supply, Abdulaziz (2007) found that tourism in Saudi Arabia has lacked a unified structure and cohesion as there was no formal agency devoted to tourism prior to 1999. Its various sectors operated in isolation from one another and its systematic planning and development did not have the necessary leadership and strategic direction. Greater official interest has been expressed in tourism in recent years with the formation of specific policies and an administrative framework. To address tourism development within the Kingdom, the Supreme Commission for Tourism (SCT) (now renamed Saudi Commission for Tourism and Antiquities) was established in 2000 to promote tourism and to develop a solid framework for its development set within the framework of Islamic values. This required developing a framework for the country to ensure orderly growth and development and a guiding factor is the National Tourism Plan. The key focus of the plan is to develop, promote, and enhance the tourism industry of the country. Based on research conducted in 2007, it was estimated that approximately 57.5 million trips were taken by Saudi residents, inclusive of overnight stays with their expenditure estimated at about US$ 15 billion. It was further established that 36% of these trips were for leisure purposes, 26% for visiting friends and relatives, and 23% for religious purposes. This is indicative that the tourism industry in the Kingdom is substantial in terms of the commercial capacity. Further, tourism activity contributes approximately 4.6% to the GDP of the country.

It is estimated that 600,000 jobs are linked to the tourism industry but that only 10–15% of these are held by Saudis. Saudi Arabia possesses a rich natural and cultural heritage, which is of great interest to the domestic and to the foreign tourists. In addition, there is a varied and natural environment ranging from desert landscapes to scenic mountains. The Kingdom is also home to the two Holy Mosques, drawing many Muslim pilgrims. It is accepted that these tourism products have relevance, suitability, and value for tourism. However, the sites are not protected in a sustainable manner, and this requires a specific focus on responsible tourism planning. Saudi Arabia is an attraction for many Muslims globally but it is also appealing as a destination to a broader tourist audience that can assist in building bridges of cooperation and unity among countries. Bogari et al (2004) asserts that in this country there is a growing amount of free leisure time and a high disposable income that is being spent on various forms of tourism and as a result Saudis traveling domestically has increased.

In addition to domestic tourism, tourists arrive for many events and conferences that are held in the Kingdom. There is also a large expatriate community that indulges in tourism activities throughout the country. Sadi and Henderson (2005) assert that the main tourism markets are residents and expatriates living in the Kingdom, followed by Muslims worldwide interested in culture and heritage, ecotourism, and pursuits such as diving and trekking.

Tourism has been identified as an initiative for economic reform in Saudi Arabia. One of the major adopted initiatives is to develop tourism as a productive industry contributing to domestic tourism, the increase of investment opportunities, the development and promotion of national human resources, and the creation of new employment opportunities for Saudi citizens (SCT 2006). The Government has defined the development of sustainable tourism as a national economic project.

TOURISM IN SAUDI ARABIA

Tourism in the Kingdom has received official recognition and it is acknowledged that it can contribute significantly to the achievement of major national socioeconomic development objectives. The rationale for Saudi tourism is based upon the notion of sustainable development. Tourism is regarded as a service-based industry (SCT 2006). It is labor intensive which implies its potential for creating job and career opportunities for Saudis. As mentioned above, only 10–15% of positions in this industry are held by Saudis. Developing tourism positively can increase the job and career opportunities for Saudis and a key focus for development is education and training to prepare Saudis for the market. There is scope for the development of tourism education and training opportunities in the market. It can also make a contribution to the diversification of the economy, as it is a new, non-traditional, non-oil-based industry. Many of the provinces and rural localities have no major industrial activities with few alternative economic resources. Tourism can be a catalyst for regional development and assist in stemming the migration of rural populations to urban areas.

Tourism has inter-sectoral linkages and can create networking opportunities among them. There is scope for creating business and employment for Saudis in terms of small- and medium-sized enterprises (SMEs). In particular, there is now a focus for women entering the industry. Domestic tourism provides alternatives to outflows of Saudis to foreign destinations that keeps the currency in the country. There are many natural and cultural heritage sites within the country that provide an important base for the promotion of sustainable tourism development. The development of domestic tourism further provides opportunities for Saudis to better know their country and enhances the process of building the nation and making it a "Home for All."

Promotion of Saudi Arabia provides opportunities to improve the image of the Kingdom internationally. Tourism may also be developed to improve the quality of life of the people as it provides restorative opportunities and educational opportunities. The SCT (2006) further asserts that in order for domestic and inbound tourism to increase, development of tourism infrastructure such as accommodation and attractions will be required.

These are the key reasons and scope for the development of tourism in Saudi Arabia (SCT 2006).

Tourism, Policy, and Religion

One traditional intersection of tourism and religion in Saudi Arabia is pilgrimage to Makkah. There are policies in place set within the framework of Islam to take care of the Muslim participating in *Hajj* and *Umrah*. Each year there is much preparation for the *Hajj* and *Umrah* with regulations in force that forbid the use of alcohol at any time and other aspects that are in contradiction to Islam. The Kingdom develops and plans for tourism within the values of Islam (Al-Jehani personal communication). These are as prescribed by the *Qur'an* which is the constitution of the country and that SCT will not allow anything to contradict it. Possibilities of enhancing religious tourism have been acknowledged with initiatives such as "Umrah Plus" which aims to boost the movement of pilgrims outside the main centers of Makkah and Medina, exploiting a relaxation in visa regulations (AME Info 2002).

There are also opportunities for extended short break travel by the Gulf Cooperation Council nationals who do not require visas. Selling to non-Muslims internationally is more challenging due to matters of cultural sensitivity and security, with fears about the latter intensified by the terrorist bombings in Riyadh during 2003 and general regional instability (Sadi and Henderson 2005). This source further asserts that there are also problems related to mutual suspicions between the Islamic and Western worlds and political uncertainties that are likely to deter many tourists.

Although visa restrictions have been eased to some extent, the rules are still inconvenient for foreigners who wish to visit certain remote locations. The SCTA has accredited tour operators to work with regions that are interested to promote the Kingdom as a tourism destination. Non-Muslim tourists, who are interested in visiting the country, can organize trips through these accredited tour operators who liaise with travel agents in 65 countries including the United States, Europe, Asia, South Korea, Japan, China, Singapore, Malaysia, Australia, South Africa, among others.

Planned Initiatives

A key initiative for the Kingdom was the establishment of the SCT in 2000 (SCT 2006). Its purpose is to function as the national tourism administration for the Kingdom, to become the official agent of tourism development, and to drive development and growth of tourism within the country. Moreover, the SCT also had the role of establishing a tourism infrastructure. Saudi Arabia is rich in natural and cultural heritage sites. These sites have been evaluated and a national tourism structure plan has been formulated in respect to them. This further implies a recommended spatial strategy for long-term tourism development is in place for the Kingdom. The key focus of the strategy is on existing, emerging, and new areas across the country. The reason for this approach is to achieve a wider geographical distribution of tourism activity to contribute to regional development (SCT 2006). To cascade the development of tourism to a more local level, provincial plans are being compiled for the 13 provinces. The phasing is estimated over a 20-year period.

In terms of tourism products, the national plan prioritized the domestic leisure market, *Umrah* extensions, and specialized foreign niche markets based on the natural and cultural heritage of the destination. The target identified include the Gulf Cooperation Council states, Arab neighbors, Muslim countries, the Muslim community on a global scale, and international special interest niche markets, such as ecotourism, diving, and cultural tourism. To maintain an effective structure is important. It is contended that the nature and quality of the structure and organization of tourism is one of the preconditions of the success of a destination and the broader tourism industry. The SCT (2006) states that prior to its establishment there was no dedicated tourism entity in the Kingdom. However, with the formulation of the SCT and the compilation of the national tourism plan, formal structures are being set in place. From a governmental perspective, structures will be implemented from a national level to a local level.

Government can further encourage the private sector to organize and introduce a system of associations and accreditation methods to ensure a healthy competitive industry ascribing to a professional code of ethics and output. From the outset, as mentioned before, training and education was an important factor in the development of organizational structures for the industry. Aspects such as effective management and sustainable practices are key elements in training and education, preparing the prospective candidates to deal with the management and development of the industry. Quality is a main focus determining success and it is the responsibility of all the stakeholders to ascribe to quality and quality practices. The role of the SCT is to stimulate development of national tourism as an economically productive, socially, culturally, and environmentally positive industry by facilitating an environment conducive to achieving a balanced and sustainable development, while encouraging institutional support for tourism and its supplementary sectors and activities in the Kingdom (SCT 2006).

The role of the SCT can be regarded as threefold, namely that it will undertake certain activities for which it will have primary responsibility, while in respect of other activities it will share responsibility with other entities. Besides the role of national administration, the SCT will also be an advocate and supporter of the broader tourism structures being developed and set in place, in particular providing encouragement to the private sector. The notion is to create networking platforms for the "agents of tourism development": the private and public sectors. In terms of the national focus, there are 13 provincial tourism commissions, one for each province. These are separate legal entities with their own boards comprising private and public representatives. In terms of operation, they represent their provincial and local stakeholders. They will be supported by the national tourism policy and strategic direction from the SCT, which includes funding and technical support (SCT 2006). In terms of the private sector, it is proposed that independent tourism trade associations will be established as part of a gradual and evolutionary process, with priority given to hotels, travel agents, tour operators, and attractions.

The most vital elements of building Saudi's tourism currently are the requirements to have fullfledged organizational structures and to build capacity in the industry. In terms of these structures, the first priority is to further build the SCT in the terms of focused responsibility such as planning, policymaking, product development, marketing, research and information management, regulatory functions, and quality functions. The SCT established Ma'lomat wa Abhath Seyahiyah, a tourism information and research center in 2003, which provides an essential service to the industry (SCT 2006). It is the backbone of the industry and provides informative data that can assist any potential entrepreneur with tourism development. The development of the industry will be largely private sector driven, establishing facilities for the purpose of investment. It is contended that a key focus to drive the success of these initiatives will be the adequate training of Saudi manpower, both male and female.

Investment is also sought for SMEs to ensure survival of this segment. The availability of capital for large companies is not a challenge, but is for the SME segment, making support of investors necessary. Tourism is largely SME driven; thus, for planned growth and development of the industry, investment is required. If not provided, this can result in constraints for growth and development (SCT 2006). Structural initiatives of the SCT include a Tourism Business Service Centre to promote investment, and to advise current and future practitioners. Figure 2 illustrates the organization of tourism in Saudi Arabia (SCT 2006:22). In terms of project planning, the

Figure 2. Organization of Tourism in Saudi Arabia

SCT has created a project appraisal capability to determine the likely success of projects. Modalities of private participation in tourism development projects have been initiated, as well as the establishment of development corporations owned by the SCT, provincial commissions, municipalities, and interested public entities. The reasoning for these developments is to provide selected priority projects for private investment and development (SCT 2006). A national development fund has also been created to aid and facilitate selected projects, and in particular projects that fall under the responsibility of development corporations.

It is noted that the majority of the tourism workforce is from outside of Saudi Arabia from areas such as South and Southeast Asia. Specialists are also drawn on contractual basis from countries such as Australia, United Kingdom, United States, and South Africa. These specialists are brought over in an advisory capacity to provide insight and to engage in working on projects. As alluded to before, the proportion of Saudi nationals working in tourism is estimated at low and it is projected that by 2020 the industry will generate around 1.5 million jobs in direct and indirect employment. Therefore, there is a great opportunity to develop tourism employment opportunities for Saudi nationals as part of the policy of Saudization (SCT 2006). In view of the opportunities for development, it is noted that there is a significant expansion in terms of tourism products such as hotel developments. Caswell (2008) indicates that the government has made steps to attract greater foreign investment and well as easing visa requirements for tourists which has resulted in hotel chains and international airlines to evaluate the tourism potential of Saudi Arabia. Various international hotel brands such as Rotana, Rosewood, Rayhaan Hotels,

Accor, Sofitel, Crowne Plaza, and Park Hyatt have planned initiatives over the next five years.

Business travel remains largely male dominated in Saudi Arabia, but the government has relaxed the law that had previously prevented women from checking into hotels without being accompanied by their husband or male family member creating the platform for business women to network. Wolfgang O'Pachler (2008), managing director of the Rosewood's two properties in Riyadh indicates, "The Kingdom of Saudi Arabia is becoming more dynamic with the ongoing economic reforms, and the government has initiated multibillion dollar projects in various parts of the country for developing its infrastructure." As a result of the infrastructural development, the international traffic to the Kingdom has increased and the country is currently experiencing consistent demand for accommodation in the major cities, providing a unique platform for tourism development. An increase in flights to the Kingdom is also an indication that business tourism is operative. On the west coast of Saudi Arabia, a new city is being developed, namely the King Abdullah Economic City is a 14 km^2 Sea Port which includes a 300,000 passenger capacity *Hajj* terminal, an industrial zone, a central business district, residential area, educational zone, and sea resort. The focus of the resort is to attract tourists, adding favorably to the tourism infrastructure of Saudi Arabia.

In view of hospitality developments, the SCTA has established a separate body to construct, renovate, and develop hotels throughout the Kingdom to promote tourism. Prince Sultan Bin Salman, the SCTA President and Chairman indicated that private sector participation in developing tourism is necessary to increase the government revenue and provide employment opportunities for local youths. He further indicated that plans are under way to frame a charter to establish commercial and professional bodies to promote the Kingdom's tourism strategy, which will assist in developing the country as an important destination for global tourists (Rasooldeen 2009). Saudi Arabia is regarded as the Middle East's largest economy; and in terms of further development for tourism, the proposed plans include the attraction of 88 million tourists and to generate more than $ 30 billion in tourism revenue by 2020. The key focus is to be a major destination, to increase hotel room capacity and to increase capital investment in tourism and jobs (Bin Salman 2009). As already noted, the industry has also been urged to employ women. Prince Sultan Bin Salman has called on local travel and tourism organizations to offer employment to Saudi men and women alike, since the hospitality sector has been opened by the government for women's employment (Ali Khan 2009).

Responsible Planning

By evaluating the current plans and initiatives, it is evident that the STCA is attempting to conform to the principles of responsible planning. In view of the limited body of knowledge regarding Saudi tourism, the STCA through Ma'lomat wa Abhath Seyahiyah concentrates on research and to provide information in the areas of social, environmental, and the economic aspects of tourism. They have also established links with the Prince Sultan College for Tourism Business, one of the first educational institutions to offer tourism education in Saudi Arabia to males and females, as a training and a research partner. The key focus is to have a mutually beneficial relationship in offering education to Saudis and non-Saudis in tourism, business, and hospitality, in conducting research on related aspects, in building academic capacity, and in expanding on Saudi tourism literature.

Tourism in the context of Saudi social norms is a platform for further development, as STCA has indicated that opportunities for domestic tourism are currently inadequate, the social environment is unduly constrained, and travel to foreign destinations remains preferable (STC 2006). It is known that responsible tourism is a management strategy embracing planning, management, product development, and marketing to bring about positive economic, social, cultural, and environmental impacts. This is also referred to as the triple bottom-line approach of sustainable tourism development, namely the economic, social, and environmental bottom line. These elements are visible in the action plan as developed by the STCA and are articulated later (STC 2006:29). A five-year action plan as part of the broader National Tourism Plan provides the platform for the implementation of the first stage of the 20-year strategy. The objectives set within the framework of responsible tourism are to:

- Expand the industry in Saudi Arabia, based on its projected growth (economic bottom line);
- Assist in diversifying the economy through the development and strengthening of tourism as a new sector, boosting regional development and small and medium enterprises (economic bottom line);
- Aid in generating private investment for the required tourism facilities due to the projected growth volume (economic bottom line);
- Create new business and employment opportunities for Saudi nationals and in particular to contribute to the process of Saudization of the workforce (economic bottom line and social bottom line);

- Ensure that development of tourism takes place in a manner that is environmentally sustainable (environmental bottom line);
- Ensure that its development takes place in a manner that is socioculturally sustainable (social bottom line);
- Ensure that its development takes place in a manner that is economically sustainable (economic bottom line);
- Ensure that tourism structures are in place by providing planning assistance at a provincial and local level to introduce development standards and guidelines (economic, social, and environmental bottom line);
- Ensure that public lands with tourism development potential are identified, earmarked and planned, and made available for development by the private sector (economic and environmental bottom line); and
- Establish a national institutional and regulatory environment conducive for further growth and development, ensuring the maintaining of quality standards in the tourism industry (economic, social, and environmental bottom line).

The tourism institutional development and capacity focus of the STCA is to strengthen the capacity to coordinate the National Tourism Plan and to ensure the effective operation of the structure. The completion of the plan is the first essential step in tourism development for the Kingdom, followed by the preparation of provincial plans, as well as the planning of tourism development areas and selected project sites (STC 2006). The plan also incorporates destination marketing with key elements, such as product development focused on the packaging of the tourism product. Further marketing and promotion actions include the improvement of domestic travel and tourism distribution channels, promotional programs, facilitation and the development of an annual Saudi Tourism Convention and Travel Mart (STC 2006).

Saudi Arabia possesses unrealized potential and numerous outstanding cultural, heritage, and natural sites (Mintel 2002:3). According to Sadi and Henderson (2005), the cities of Riyadh, Jeddah, and Makkah are examples of such sites. Madain Salah is said to surpass the huge rock tombs of Petra, and Al-Jouf is home to antiquities linked to the origins of the Nabatean and Assyrian cultures. There are many parks and the Asir National Park covers over a million acres in the region that offers a comparatively green countryside, a mild climate, and many leisure facilities. Other nature-based amenities are those of the Red Sea and Gulf coasts and the SCTA has identified 10,000 attractions overall. However, it is noted with concern that many well-known landmarks have given way to development projects as part of the drive toward modernization, thereby reducing the attractiveness of the destination (Sadi and Henderson 2005).

To deal with this trend in association with the social and environmental bottom lines of responsible development, the National Tourism Plan (in terms of the cultural heritage development component) will preserve cultural resources and environments. Specific areas identified for development includes archaeology, built heritage, museums, handicrafts, traditional industries, and tangible and intangible heritage. It is also reflected that the employment of Saudis in tourism, as part of the policy of Saudization will be a key objective. Further, in line with the economic and social bottom line, the STC (2006) identified specific actions to ensure the Saudization process with such actions:

- An awareness campaign designed to counteract negative sociocultural perceptions and to encourage Saudi nationals to take up employment in tourism;
- Improvement of working conditions in the industry, coupled with incentives for both the employer and employees;
- The introduction of a national accreditation system based on agreed occupational skill standards and curricula that will lead to professional recognition of tourism jobs and that will enable career pathing;
- Ensuring that close cooperation and coordination take place with the Saudi Human Resources Development Fund, the General Organization for Technical Education and Vocational Training, and other stakeholders;
- Provision of education facilities and programs, geared to developing and providing a skilled workforce for the industry;
- Undertaking initiatives for effective recruitment, retention, and retraining of tourism personnel;
- Training frontline staff in customer service; and
- Setting up a national council for tourism education and training.

As a social bottom-line action step, the STCA has taken it upon itself to ensure that there is a positive position toward tourism by creating Saudi's awareness regarding the industry. The manner in which this position will be articulated to the Saudi population will be through the awareness campaigns, introducing codes of conducts for domestic tourists, introducing tourism into school curricula, reaching out to rural communities, and monitoring sociocultural impacts of tourism (STC 2006). George (2004) asserts that in the competitive tourism environment, customer care is important. Zeithaml and Bitner state, "People in the tourism industry are all human actors who play a part in service delivery and thus influence the buyer's perceptions, namely the organization's staff, the consumer, and other consumers in the service environment" (1996:26). It thus becomes essential that the quality of offerings is controlled and measured (George 2004). In view of the importance of service quality, the STCA as part of the National Tourism Plan will ensure that quality assurance measurements are in place. Proposed quality assurance measurements include the following (STC 2006:32):

- Establishing a legal framework and transferring relevant powers for the regulation of key tourism sectors in the STCA;
- Building up its institutional and technical capacity and in due course assist authorities and organizations on provincial and local levels to carry out regulatory and quality assurance functions;
- Updating, streamlining, and introducing licensing and, where appropriate, classification systems for the core tourism sectors;
- Introducing consumer protection measures for tourists within the Kingdom by combining statutory and voluntary regulations; and
- Introducing and implementing new tourist visa regulations.

To overcome the shortcomings in the tourism industry, the STCA was established as the leader for the development of sustainable tourism in the Kingdom. It will deal with obstacles impeding the growth of the industry and further integrating it within the economic base of the country. The STCA has developed a well-planned framework for the integration and organization of tourism in an orderly fashion and to further plan the growth and development within a framework of a clear vision and defined goals. The focus of the National Tourism Plan is to develop tourism throughout the country, including stakeholders within the government and the private sector. Its approach is in accordance with the government directive for reform and economic transformation, and it translates the identified charges into a tangible reality. It is evident that planned, orderly, and controlled development is feasible and that this goal is attainable within the framework of the fundamental values and tenets of Islam and the norms of traditional Saudi culture.

CONCLUSION

Modern tourism has expanded rapidly in the postwar growth era and a new age in tourism is being heralded for Saudi Arabia. The SCTA is the leader for establishing the foundation for tourism to flourish within the Kingdom. Tourism in Saudi Arabia is new and fresh with many opportunities for development in the years to come. The STCA has introduced the concept and the importance of a sustainable development strategy. This approach ensures that future generations will have sufficient resources to adequately sustain themselves and maintain a reasonable quality of life. It is contended, however, that careful planning and management of resources development will be the key to achieving sustainability. Sustainable tourism development is a positive approach intended to reduce the tension and friction created by the interaction among the industry, tourists, the environment, and host communities. Stakeholders will have to apply the principles of environmental sustainability to tourism and use it as a philosophy that the environment must be conserved if the industry is to be viable in the long term. It is contended that in terms of ensuring sustainable development, tourism training and education have become a segment that warrants special attention, as it will provide the necessary skills to meet the challenges of the new tourism era in Saudi Arabia and to ensure the successful application and maintenance of sustainable tourism practices.

Acknowledgments

The author wishes to acknowledge the help of both Yasin Jefri and Abdullah Al-Jehani, for providing information and guidance in writing the chapter; Khalid Khidr, highly acclaimed Saudi Arabian photographer, and the Saudi Commission for Tourism and Antiquities for assistance and providing information.

Chapter 8

MUSLIM TOURISM IN CHINA

Zhuo Wang
Peiyi Ding
Noel Scott
The University of Queensland, Australia
Yezheng Fan
Beijing International Studies University, China

Abridgement: China is primarily a nonreligious country with less than 10% of people following Buddhism, Taoism, Islam, Catholicism, or other religions. Two major communication paths, the land and sea Silk Roads, directly affected the distribution and development of Muslim tourism and attractions. The combination of Islam with local custom and culture is a unique feature in China, and contributes to its development as a form of ethnic rather than religious tourism. As a result, research in China focuses on ethnic product development, minority sports and anthropological tourism, themed events, and intangible cultural heritage. **Keywords:** Muslim tourism; China; ethnic tourism; Islam

INTRODUCTION

In Western countries, over 80% of people are religious, while in China around 90% are nonreligious, with a minority adherents to Buddhism, Taoism, Islam, and Catholicism (Tong 2005). When the term "religious tourism" is discussed, the two common forms referred to are Taoism and Buddhism, and Islam is seldom included. This is due to the geographic localization of the Muslim population, primarily in Western China. The

Tourism in the Muslim World
Bridging Tourism Theory and Practice, Volume 2, 107–119
Copyright © 2010 by Emerald Group Publishing Limited
All rights of reproduction in any form reserved
ISSN: 2042-1443/doi:10.1108/S2042-1443(2010)0000002011

introduction of Islam can be traced to around 1,300 years ago, and two major communication routes facilitated its adoption: the land Silk Road in the northwest of China and the sea Silk Road in the southeast, both of which played important roles as trade routes at that time. During its introduction, the religion was integrated into a number of local cultures along these routes and formed local subcultures. Over time, 10 ethnic minorities came into being. They adopted Islam as their faith and preserved Islamic customs, but also developed local ethnic folk customs and festivals, combining aspects of their ethnic minority beliefs and precepts of the Islamic religion.

Today, the Muslim population of China is around 22 million (The State Council of the Peoples Republic of China 2006); there are more than 30,000 mosques (Zhang, Song and Ma 1991) and over 40,000 imams (Islamic leaders) and *akhonds* (Islamic scholars) (State Administration for Religious Affairs 2009). These 10 ethnic minority groups constitute the majority of the Muslim population and are concentrated in the northwest regions. They are numbered among 56 minority groups whose ethnicity is emphasized, rather than their religiosity. Thus, the issue of religion is usually considered as an ethnic issue, especially in the tourism domain, and as a result, Muslim-related tourism is referred to as "ethnic tourism."

This chapter aims to outline the development of Islam in China and how its introduction has had a substantial influence on the location of related attractions and customer markets. The chapter emphasizes ethnic tourism, rather than religious tourism, and examines related developments and research as well as providing a perspective on the future.

ISLAM IN CHINA

Islam was introduced in 651 CE (the Tang Dynasty) during an official envoys' visit from Arabia to China (Bai 2000). In the subsequent 1,300 years of the Tang, Song Yuan, Ming, Qing dynasties and the Republic period, Islam was given a variety of names. Originally, it was called "Dashi Jiao," which translates as "religion of the Tazi"; this being a Farsi word used during the Tang Dynasty to refer to Arabs (Bai 2000:11–13). In the Ming Dynasty, it was called "Tianfang Jiao" (religion of Arabia) or "Hui Hui Jiao" (religion of the Hui Huis, or Hui teaching); the Hui are a Muslim ethnic group in China. During the late Ming Dynasty and the early years of the Qing Dynasty, "Qingzhen Jiao" (pure and true religion) was the general name, and during the Republic period the name reverted to a shortened form: "Hui Jiao" (Mi and You 2004). In 1956 CE, the State Council of

Table 1. Different Chinese Names for Islam

Period	Named as	Year	Translation
Tang Dynasty	Dashi Jiao	618–907 CE	Religion of Tazi
Ming Dynasty	Tianfang Jiao	1368–1644 CE	Religion of Arabia
	Hui Hui Jiao		Religion of Hui Huis
The transitional period between the Ming and the Qing dynasties	Qingzhen Jiao	1616–1911 CE	Pure and true religion
Republic Period	Hui Jiao	1912–1949 CE	Religion of the Huis
People's Republic of China	Islam	1949–present	Religion of Islam

Source: Developed for this research based on Mi and You (2004)

People's Republic of China (PRC) issued the "Notice concerning the name of Islam" which stated that on the mainland of China the term "Islam" was to be used as "the common name for this religion" (The Government Administration Council of PRC 1956). Islam is still called "Hui Jiao" in Hong Kong, Macao, and Taiwan (Table 1).

The eastward spread of Islam is primarily a result of trading activities between ancient China and Arab countries. Two major trading routes came into being and played important roles in this stage (Sha 2004). The earlier one started from the Persian Gulf, passing by India, the Malay Peninsula, and ended at southeast coastal cities such as Guangzhou in Guangdong Province and Quanzhou in Fujian Province (Bai 2000). This was called the sea route (Mi and You 2004). Subsequently, a land trade route was developed via Persia, Afghanistan, Central Asia, the Tianshan Mountain region and Hexi Corridor, to Chang'an (now Xi'an, Shaanxi Province). In addition to this trade mechanism, Islam was also introduced into the northwest by Arab and Persian diplomatic envoys and soldiers, and the intermarriage between foreign Muslims living in China and native Chinese accelerated its spread. Today, most of the Muslim groups and related places that tourists visit are distributed along these two routes. Besides these, there were two other trade routes, one from Arabia via India to Yunnan (China) and another sea route from Arabia via Annan (now Vietnam) to Yunnan

Province (Bai 2000). For this reason, there is also a presence of Muslims as well as Islamic buildings and mosques in the southwest.

Minorities and Distributions

As already indicated, Muslim tourism in China is different from that in other countries. The religion of Islam was able to preserve its major festivals; however, it also merged with local traditional folk customs during both its introduction and distribution into China (Xu and Yu 2009). A number of communities, who took Islam as their national religious belief, began to mix their native folk customs and culture into it, and in the process of localization and nationalization of Islam, formed into 10 major Muslim nationalities. They are the Hui, the Uyghur, the Kazakh, the Dongxiang, the Khalkhas, the Sala, the Tajik, the Uzbek, the Bao'an, and the Tartar (Zhou 2000). Besides these, there are a small portion of Muslims among such ethnic groups as the Mongolian, the Tibetan, the Bai, and the Dai (Mi and You 2004) who also live in a compact community.

In China, there are no exact statistics concerning the number of the Muslim population. Considering the majority of the population who take Islam as their faith is from the 10 nationalities, their numbers are usually considered as the total population, which according to the statistics of The State Council of the Peoples Republic of China (2006), constitutes over 22 million. Most of the Muslims in China live in the northwest of China, such as in Xinjiang, Ningxia, Gansu, Qinghai, Yunnan and Henan provinces, while there is also a considerable number in Shaanxi, Hebei, and Shandong (Mi and You 2004). The Hui is the largest of these minority groups, with a population of 8,602,978 in 1992. Muslims can be found in all of the cities and towns of China, with Ningxia Hui Autonomous Region being their biggest concentration. The Uyghurs are the second largest of these minorities with a population of 7,214,000, mainly living in the Xinjiang Uyghur Autonomous Region (Table 2).

A Niche Tourism Market

In contrast with a thousand years of development of Islam in China, Muslim tourism in this country only has a history of around 15 years. It consists of three segments: inbound and outbound Muslim markets, and a domestic Muslim ethnic-minority sector. The first was launched as a niche market in China and mainly comprises tourists from Islamic countries in Southeast Asia. The outbound segment is thriving, dominated by pilgrims to Makkah,

Table 2. Population of Islamic Minorities in China (1980 and 1992)

Minorities	Population		Location and Major Areas
	1980	1992	
Hui	6,400,000	8,602,978	Ningxia, Gansu, Qinghai, Henan,
Uyghur	5,400,000	7,214,431	Xinjiang
Kazakh	800,000	1,111,718	Xinjiang, Gansu, Qinghai
Dongxiang	190,000	373,872	Gansu
Khalkhas	90,000	141,549	Xinjiang
Sala	50,000	87,697	Qinghai, Gansu
Tajik	20,000	33,538	Xinjiang
Uzbek	70,000	14,502	Xinjiang
Baoan	6,000	12,212	Gansu
Tartar	2,000	4,873	Xinjiang

Source: Editorial Committee of Encyclopedia of China Islam (1995) and Li (2002)

and is steadily increasing each year. The domestic Muslim ethnic-minority tourism market is rising, but has fluctuated recently due to a number of internal problems.

The Muslim market first gained attention from the China National Tourism Administration in 1993. There were several motivations for its development; first, globally it has a population of over 1 billion (Xu 1993) and is an important potential market for niche tourism development; second, the Association of Southeast Asian Nations has around 160 million Muslims, with convenient access to China as well as a record of high inbound visitation; third, improvements in diplomatic relations has increased the visiting intentions of tourists from these nations (Xu 1993). Accordingly, a number of selected provinces in China, such as Guangxi, were considered as pilot sites to attract target tourists from Association of Southeast Asian Nations countries and the Middle East, and a set of Muslim tourism products and preferential strategies were developed and implemented. Focused marketing was used, and even in recent years, targeted exhibitions and events have been held in the key cities of these pilot provinces. For instance, Guilin Tourism Bureau organized a special exhibition in both Malaysia and Indonesia in 2008, promoting its Muslim hospitality facilities (Liuzhou Tourism Bureau 2008).

Identification of the potential of the inbound market triggered niche development in China, as well as the development of the outbound Muslim market. The latter has two major sectors: the pilgrimage segment and special

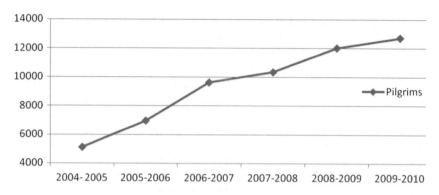

Figure 1. Summary of China Pilgrim Market Statistics (2004–2009)

groups who travel to other Muslim countries (Xu 1993). However, group travel, which is usually accompanied by activities such as communication of Islamic culture and business, is seldom included in official statistics. Instead, pilgrimage to Makkah is considered the main reason for travel. In China, Muslims of all nationalities enjoy the rights of ethnic equality as well as religious freedom (Mi and You 2004). They are permitted to travel freely on the *Hajj* to Makkah (Gladney 2003) organized by the China Islamic Association (The State Council 2006). Since the first 20 people went in 1955, pilgrims have traveled to Makkah each year, with the exception of the years of the Cultural Revolution (1966–1978). After travel resumed in 1979, numbers have increased each year and in 2007 reached 10,000, although this is a small proportion of the millions of pilgrims attending the *Hajj* each year (The State Council 2006) (Figure 1).

The domestic market has not developed as strongly; such travel may be considered as special interest and is comparatively a stable market dominated by Muslims. Timing of travel is closely related to traditional Islamic festivals and feast days. Participants are usually casual Muslim and general mass tourists, with ethnic-minority tourism attractions such as Islamic buildings, unique ethnic folk customs, and exotic landscape as their visit motivation.

Major Tourism Attractions

Muslim attractions can be divided into two categories: physical assets such as mosques and buildings, and intangible assets including feast days, events, customs, and culture. As already noted, there are more than 30,000 mosques (Zhang et al 1991) scattered throughout China (Table 3), and nearly every

Table 3. Location of Tangible Islamic Attractions

Location	Mosques	Famous Sites	Location	Mosques	Famous Sites
Beijing	10	0	Sichuan	9	0
Shanghai	1	0	Guizhou	2	0
Tianjin	4	0	Yunnan	9	2
Hebei	18	0	Tibet	2	0
Shanxi	4	0	Shandong	17	0
Liaoning	9	0	Hainan	1	0
Jilin	5	0	Zhejiang	3	0
Inner Mongolia	5	0	Anhui	8	0
Heilongjiang	13	0	Fujian	2	3
Jiangsu	8	1	Jiangxi	4	0
Hong Kong	2	0	Shaanxi	10	0
Henan	11	1	Gansu	19	0
Hubei	5	0	Qinghai	–	–
Hunan	6	0	Ningxia	10	0
Guangdong	3	2	Xinjiang	19	6
Guangxi	4	0	Taiwan	3	0

Source: Developed based on Ma (1997)

city and town has a number of Muslim buildings (Mi and You 2004). Muslim tourism attractions such as the Aitiduer mosque in Kashi (Xinjiang), Qingjing Temple in Quanzhou (Fujian), and Niujie in Beijing play important roles in local Muslim tourism. For instance, Aitiduer Mosque in Kashi (Xinjiang), built in 1442, is the largest and oldest mosque in China, with an attendance of more than 3,000 daily and more than 7,000 people at Friday prayers. Around 50,000 Muslims participate in the festival of Corban.

There are other notable features of Muslim attractions in China. As may be expected, they have a close dependant relationship with the distribution of Islam today along the land Silk Road in Xinjiang, Gansu, Ningxia, and Qinghai (Sha 2004). In the southwest, attractions are concentrated only in certain cities such as Quanzhou, the official starting point of the sea Silk Road, and where there are a number of UNESCO Islamic cultural heritage sites (Jing 1999). In other regions, mosques are scattered around the Muslim-dominated communities.

Customs and traditions among the minorities are the result of the inter-action of nationalization and localization and are classified by the Chinese

Government based on the 10 different ethnic groups that take Islam as their faith. Similarly, most studies focus on ethnic-minority rather than more general Muslim tourism. These 10 Islamic minorities were formed during the nationalization of Islam and have each developed their own unique folklore and local customs. For example, Zhang (2008) analyzes the relationship between the attractions of the Kazakhs and tourism development in the Yili area, and emphasizes that the unique folklore and cultural landscape of the Kazakhs is the core competitiveness that could distinguish it from other similar cities.

In non-Muslim regions, buildings have survived more easily than the intangible assets of customs and culture, and play an important role in local tourism (Table 4). In the southeast of China, the "Four Ancient Mosques"

Table 4. List of Major Intangible Ethnic Attractions

Name	Nationality	Descriptions
Aites	Kazakh	A competitive musical dialogue with the content of history, culture, and affection of the Kazakh
Dawaz Art	Uyghur	A traditional upper tightrope art with a history of over thousand years in Uyghur
Dolan Maxrap	Uyghur	Folk singing and dancing art, with the content of hunting, harvest celebration, and happy life showing
Handicraft	Uyghur	Traditional ceramics, colorful felt, weaving, and dying skills on printing fabric, mulberry paper making, etc.
Hawk Dance	Tajik	A dance form that represents a hawk worship of the Tajik minority by simulating hawk habit and movement
Hua-er	Hui, Sala, Bao-an, Dongxiang	A traditional annual singing festival of mountain airs
Hui Art	Hui	Embroidery, traditional costume, musical instruments
Manasi	Khalkhas	An epic of the Khalkhas in a singing form
Muqam	Uyghur	A folk music, with representatives of 12 Muqam, Turpan Muqam, Hami Muqum, Dolan Muqam,
Sala Wedding	Sala	A winter wedding ceremony inc. wedding dancing, and customs
Tajik Festivals	Tajik	A series of traditional farming festivals and ceremony, including water diversion festival, and sowing festival

Source: Developed for this research based on Anonymous (2009)

are important attractions. These are the Huaisheng Mosque in Guangzhou (constructed in the Tang Dynasty), the Qingjing Mosque in Quanzhou (constructed in the Northern Song Dynasty), the Xianhe Mosque in Yangzhou (constructed in the Southern Song Dynasty), and the Fenghuang Mosque in Hangzhou (constructed in the Yuan Dynasty) (Mi and You 2004). However, traditional customs and events, such as Corban and Hari Raya Puasa, do not attract tourists in these non-Muslim regions as they do in Xinxiang, Ningxia, and Gansu. Intangible Muslim tourism attractions, such as customs, events, and festivals, are instead found in the northwest regions, and when merged with native ethnic culture and folk customs, make attractive products. Importantly, as a form of religious tourism, the use of sites is usually by the followers themselves. Compared with other types of tourism that have received a great deal of investment and policy priority from local governments, most of the investment in Muslim tourism sites is from private sources.

Relevant Tourism Research

In China, the terms "Muslim tourism" or "Islamic tourism" are sensitive words and, as stated earlier, researchers are inclined to study this phenomenon from the perspective of ethnic rather than religious tourism. Thus, the term "ethnic tourism" is preferable to describe various ethnic groups, rather than the term "Muslim tourism" or "Islamic cultural tourism." There are only five studies on Muslim or Islamic tourism and less than 30 journal papers taking an ethnic tourism perspective that focus on the customs or cultural tourism of minority groups who take Islam as their faith. Minority groups such as the Hui, the Uyghur, and the Kazakh have received attention as the subject of case studies; research on the other ethnic minorities would be advantageous (Table 5).

There are 14 journal papers on ethnic tourism of the Hui, and 11 of these focus on the development of ethnic attractions, primarily using a qualitative research approach. The other three papers are from the perspective of community participation (Bai 2009; Yang 2008b). Yang (2008a) examined the local residents' perceptions of tourism, while Yang (2008b) found that in the development stage of tourism, residents have an ambivalent attitude to its effect. On the one hand, they are positive about the increased employment prospects and the opportunity for the propagation of their religion; on the other hand, they worried about the threat of tourism development on traditional culture and religious beliefs (Yang 2008a). Bai (2009) analyzed the external identity of the Hui ethnic community in Xi'an

Table 5. Islamic Ethnic Tourism Studies

Minority	Topic	Number
Hui	Ethnic tourism attraction	11
	Community participation	3
Uyghur	Ethnic tourism development	4
	Ethnic sport tourism development	1
	Uyghur food tourism development	1
	Anthropological perspective	2
Kazakh	Ethnic tourism development	3
	Kazakh food tourism development	1
	Ethnic festival and event	1
	Community participation	3

Source: Developed for this research based on CNKI Database (2009)

and found that tourists' recognition had a positive correlation with the perceptions of the attractiveness of the community, the safety of the environment, and the extent of cross-cultural communication.

There are eight journal papers and theses on the Uyghur-related ethnic tourism. Two papers and four master degree theses focus on cultural or ethnic tourism development, with four of them examining the relationship between the development and conservation of Uyghur attractions, one on Uyghur food as an attraction (Ma 2009), and one on ethnic sport attractions (Zhang 2008). The unique Uyghur folk customs and culture are more attractive to tourists than the natural landscape (Yimamu 2008). However, these papers indicate that the development of intangible attractions is still in its initial stage, only meeting the superficial demands of the tourists and requiring improvement (Dou 2006). In addition, one thesis (Silayi 2008) and one journal paper (Li 2008) examine these ethnic groups from an anthropological perspective, choosing an Uyghur community as a case study. These indicate that threats to traditional folk customs have gained the attention of the local community (Li 2008).

There are eight journal papers on the Kazakhs. A large proportion are development studies, including four pieces on the importance of cultural factors (Zhang and Hanaiti 2009; Zhang and Wang 2007), one on food (Zhang and Hanaiti 2008), and one on ethnic event and festival development (Wupur 2006). Ethnic-community participation is another focus for tourism researchers. Sha (2009) focused his research on the people involved in Kazakh tourism and noticed that among these traditional nomadic minority people, participation in business was somewhat shameful. However, through participation, the local Kazakh community's attitudes to tourism had changed to more active engagement.

As may be seen, research is dominated by ethnic tourism product development, rather than religious issues. Qualitative assessment of ethnic attractions and their exploitation perspectives are the major research area, consistent with the current methods for studies of tourism development. Recently, intangible cultural heritage has begun to gain attention, and a number of papers from the perspectives of anthropology and community participation (Li 2008; Yimamu 2008) have appeared.

The major research strategy used in Muslim-tourism-related research is the use of case studies focusing on ethnic minorities in a given area (Ran and Lu 2005; Yang, Xie and Li 2001) or a given feature of a minority. Qualitative methods are used more in the study of tourism development, although quantitative approaches such as descriptive analysis (Yang 2008a, 2008b) and structural equation modeling (Bai 2009) are also used in other papers.

Government-led Niche Tourism

The State Administration for Religious Affairs is the department of the State Council in charge of religious affairs. The China Islamic Association, established in Beijing in May 1953, is the only Islamic organization subordinate to the State Administration for Religious Affairs. The major roles of the association and its subchapters, in terms of tourism, are to organize Muslims across the country in their pilgrimage to Makkah, and to form Muslim groups for cultural and religious travel. Since Deng Xiaoping's post-1978 reforms, Muslims have sought to take advantage of the liberalized economic and religious policies (Gladney 2003). A policy of China is that religious venues must be independently managed by religious groups authorized by the local government (Cao 2002). Accordingly, Muslim tourism venues and attractions must be supervised by Muslim groups, which are generally the local branch of State Administration for Religious Affairs.

Similar to the management mode in Buddhist and Taoist tourism, local Islamic associations, which are subordinate to State Administration for Religious Affairs, are the only legal administrative departments directly in charge of religious-based tourism. The venues are managed and operated by locals with the profits distributed by their Islamic association. Tourism corporations or administrative departments can be partly involved in religious tourism development and event management, but cannot directly benefit from religious tourism.

The development of Muslim tourism is a result of government-led initiatives. The government and its relevant departments have played an important role at various stages. In the emergence stage, the China National Tourism Administration realized the potential opportunities for an inbound niche tourism market, and initiated a series of pilot Muslim tourism products in several selected provinces (Xu 1993). In the development stage, China National Tourism Administration developed preferential policies encouraging the growth of tourism in ethnic regions and for religious minorities. For example, a new enterprise set up by an ethnic group can enjoy a tax deduction for three years; tourism in such regions receives investment and credit aid; and ethnic businesses receive discount-interest loans for some types of buildings and technology (Zhang 2008). The central government has also established a number of ethnic institutes and schools, including 15 universities (Li and Jia 2009), 59 teachers' colleges, and 158 vocational secondary schools to foster ethnic elites to the advantage of such sectors as tourism.

CONCLUSION

Islam was introduced in China as a result of conflicts as well as trade, and by blending with the local community acquired a distinctive tradition. However, tourists' interest in Muslim ethnic-minority tourism is significantly less than that in more mainstream forms. Tourism in ethnic-minority regions such as Gansu and Xinjiang has developed slowly. The watershed events of the September 11 terrorist attacks and the subsequent worldwide "war on terrorism" have exacerbated an already distorted attitude toward Muslims and the Islamic religion. In addition, the threat from Eastern-Tuki terrorism has led to concerns about security in ethnic-minority areas (Xu and Yu 2009) as well as damaging tourism. In China, tourism to these areas is erratic, and any international or domestic ethnic unrest can cause disquiet among tourists dissuading them from traveling. After the July 2009 riots in Urumqi, the capital city of Xinjiang, tourism in the Xinjiang region suffered an unprecedented decline. Around 4,600 tourist groups (approximately 280,000 tourists) canceled their booked package within a period of only eight days after this event (Wang, Xu and Liu 2009). Afterwards, the relevant tourism administrations have attempted various promotional approaches and concession measures, and tourism, although depressed, is beginning to recover.

There are other obstacles for Muslim tourism in China. For instance, the remote location of the Muslim attractions means that the cost of long-haul travel to domestic Muslim destinations is higher than that for outbound tourism to traditional Southeast Asian destinations such as Singapore, Malaysia, and Indonesia. The large distances between different iconic sites are another obstacle; this means more transport is needed and results in an increase in the total travel time and cost. Further, restricted availability of accommodation, lack of investment, and backward tourism practices are other problems that restrict the development of ethnic-minority tourism in the Muslim regions (Sha 2009; Wang 2007).

These temporary crises and restrictions, however, cannot hide a positive trend in the development of Islamic tourism. The younger generations in ethnic minorities are realizing that the intangible aspects of their heritage can play an important role in tourism, and are beginning to learn their traditions from the older generations in order to preserve them. From the aspect of the tourism market, the unique folk customs and exotic landscape in the northwest of China are proving to be attractive, and many tourists, either serious or casual, intend to visit. It is anticipated that Muslim tourism and Muslim ethnic-minority tourism, as a niche market, will increase. It has been stimulated by the strategy of the central government of China to develop western parts of China (Xie 2005), resulting in increased availability of investment environment, improved accessibility, and preferential policies. This will help to broaden the experience from sightseeing to include folk customs, special sport entertainment, ethnic vacations, and souvenir shopping. Local folk customs featuring hospitality facilities, religious catering (Xu 1993), festival activities, and theme parks and villages will need to be improved or built (Yang 1997).

The future priorities in terms of the Muslim tourism market in China will target both general ethnic-minority tourism and religious tourism. The former, which integrates the local landscape, the unique food, and the exotic local customs, will interest both the casual Muslim tourist and the mass tourism segments. The latter that integrates Islamic communication, religious events, and festivals, will interest the more devout Muslim tourists.

Chapter 9

TOURISM IN TURKMENISTAN

Jonathan Edwards
Bournemouth University, UK

Abridgement: This chapter reviews the factors determining the characteristics of the tourism sector of Turkmenistan. Particular attention is given to the adoption of Islam resulting from Arabic, Seljuk, and Sufic cultural influences. The resulting distinctive form of Islam, incorporating pre-Islamic traditions and beliefs together with the persistence of tribalism, Soviet and post-Soviet governance, and the sociopolitical and economic characteristics of contemporary Turkmen society are considered in order to underpin an analysis of its underdeveloped and little-known tourism industry. An outline of the results of a small-scale preliminary case study of tourists in one of Turkmenistan's World Heritage Sites is presented as an illustration of current tourism activity and the future opportunities in its development. **Keywords:** Turkmenistan; Silk Road; Avaza tourism project; World Heritage

INTRODUCTION

The intention of this chapter is to reflect upon the practice and development of tourism in a little-known and poorly documented country located in a region that is equally little known and only rarely considered either in terms of the practice of Islam or as a venue for international tourism and where patterns of domestic tourism are even less well reported and analyzed. The chapter begins by providing a brief introduction to the country, followed with an overview of the waves of migrations and invasions that have impacted upon Central Asia. These waves of migration of different cultures with

Tourism in the Muslim World
Bridging Tourism Theory and Practice, Volume 2, 121–139
Copyright © 2010 by Emerald Group Publishing Limited
All rights of reproduction in any form reserved
ISSN: 2042-1443/doi:10.1108/S2042-1443(2010)0000002012

different origins have, over time, resulted not only in the establishment of a resilient tribal/clan society but also the embedding of the Islamic faith that has evolved along a particular and distinct path. The tribal nature of Turkmen society and its particular form of Islam had been entrenched for thousand years prior to the century of Russian/Soviet domination that came to an end in 1991, since then Turkmenistan has sought to define and establish itself as a truly independent state.

The sociopolitical characteristics of this last period of Turkmenistan's history are analyzed together with a brief review of the legacy of Soviet policy and the potential and actual economic benefits of the exploitation of major reserves of oil and particularly natural gas. The resulting economic, social, and environmental consequences are assessed both in relation to the hitherto underdeveloped tourism of the economy and in terms of recent proposals for major investments in the industry. A synopsis of current patterns of international and domestic tourism, primarily based upon personal observation (as there is little if any documentary material), is provided, together with a preliminary case study of tourists to the designated World Heritage Site of Merv where Islamic beliefs and practices are a key consideration for tourists and site management.

Similar in size to Spain, Turkmenistan borders the Caspian Sea on the west, Afghanistan on the southeast, Iran on the south, Kazakhstan on the north, and Uzbekistan on the northeast (Figure 1). The Karakum or Black Sands desert comprises in excess of 80% of the country. The climate demonstrates clear seasonality with very hot (50°C) dry summers, cool winters often with snow, mild springs with some rain (8–30 cm), and warm pleasant autumns. The Amu Darya (Oxus) river, which forms much of the border with Uzbekistan, is the principal source of fresh water and now feeds the Karakum Canal, which was completed in 1988 during the Soviet period, partly to supply water to Ashgabat, the capital, but primarily to supply water to irrigate wheat and cotton crops. Diverting water to this 1,400 km long canal is one of the principal causes of the drying out of the Aral Sea.

The country is at risk from violent seismic activity and, while underreported at the time outside the Soviet Union, a violent earthquake (7.3 Mw) in 1948 devastated Ashgabat, and an initial estimate death toll of 10,000 was officially revised in 2007 to 176,000 killed (State News Agency of Turkmenistan 2007). The majority of the population, estimated by varying international agencies as a little under 5 million (UNESCO 2006; Central Intelligence Agency 2009b), lives around the edges of the Karakum relatively close to the borders of the country; consequently, many journeys in Turkmenistan involve crossing the desert. Today the choice is between road,

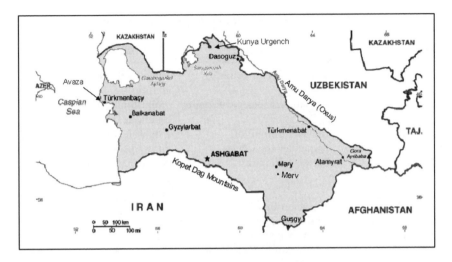

Figure 1. Map of Turkmenistan
Source: Based on http://www.national-anthems.net/images/maps_grey/tx-map.gif

rail, and air. The latter is the transport of choice for anyone who can afford tickets, which were until recently heavily subsidized; the trains are slow, the roads generally in a poor state of repair, and both roads and rail lines face the ever present problem of inundation by the desert sands.

The first inhabitants of this region were Indo-European tribes having a horse-based herding culture who arrived around 2000 BCE. Table 1 summarizes the subsequent history of the region that became part of, and on occasions the center of, major empires. Two features emerge from this rich and troubled history, one is the adoption of Islam and the other is the resilience of a tribal society, which is still evident in the 21st century.

The Adoption of Islam

While the sedentary agriculturalists of Central Asia accepted Islam relatively quickly, acceptance was much slower by the nomadic livestock herders of the area. These nomadic cultures did not accommodate the establishment of the urban text-based ecclesiastical structures of Islam rather the nomadic culture facilitated the development of Sufism. Sufi *shaykhs* (holy men) were key players in converting the tribal societies, in part due to their knowledge of Inner Asian pre-Islamic religious traditions and their ability to convey Islam's power and meaning to local populations.

Table 1. Summary of the History of Turkmenistan

Date	Society	Cultural Legacy
2000 BCE	Indo-European Tribes	Horse centered nomadic culture
500 BCE	Persian Achaemenid Empire	"Silk Road" trade route well established
356–323 BCE	Hellenic Empire of Alexander the Great	Established the city now known as Merv
238 BCE–224 CE	Parthian Empire	Nisa one of the capitals located near the current capital Ashgabat
224–651 CE	Sassanian Empire	
From 650 CE	Arabic Invasion	Islam introduced
750 CE	Abbasid Empire	
1040 CE	Seljuk clan of Oguz tribe established Seljuk Empire—capital at Merv	Cities of Merv and Kunya Urgench major trading cities on the "Silk Road" and important centers of religion, culture, and learning
1219–1222 CE	Mongol Invasion Ghenghis Khan	
1370 CE	Timur (Tamerlane) reestablished empire of Genghis Khan	"Silk Road" trade effectively concluded
1400–1880 CE	Loose affiliation of several tribes	Reversion to horse-centered nomadic culture
1881–1923 CE	Tsarist Russia	Tribes caught up in the "Great Game," a geopolitical conflict between Russia and Great Britain
1924–1990 CE	Soviet Empire	Imposition of the ideal "Soviet Society" Tribal groups settled, an expansion of agriculture notably cotton production
From 1991 CE	Independent Turkmenistan	

As a result, a version of Islam that incorporated pre-Islamic beliefs, most notably ancestor worship, evolved. These "beliefs" are manifest in that these *shaykhs* were frequently adopted as "patron saints" or progenitors of particular clans or tribal groups, thereby becoming their "founders," echoing the existing prominence of ancestor worship in Turkmen religious traditions (Walker 2003).

The burial sites of these Muslim founding fathers then became a focal point of veneration, and the sites, real or imagined, took on the qualities of shrines where vital concerns (both spiritual and otherwise) could be addressed. These shrines thus emerged not only as sites where sacred power was localized but as points where Islam and the traditions of pre-Islamic times joined and developed (Kuru 2002; Levin 2006; Tyson 1997). The Russian colonization under the Tsars sought to accommodate these practices, but the Soviet period post-1924 saw all religious beliefs attacked by the communist authorities as superstition and "vestiges of the past." Most forms of religious schooling and religious observance were banned, and the vast majority of mosques closed. Atheist indoctrination stifled religious development and contributed to the isolation of the Turkmen from the international Muslim community. Some religious customs, such as Muslim burial and male circumcision, continued to be practiced throughout the Soviet period, but most religious belief, knowledge, and customs were preserved only in rural areas in "folk form" as a kind of unofficial Islam (Bennigsen and Wimbush 1985).

While the major Turkmen tribes lay claim to the same mythical ancestor Oghuz Khan, there are other "tribes" who lay claim to a different earlier ancestry. One group of these tribes, the "Owlat," are variously referred to as the "holy" or "honor" groups, each of which traces its ancestry to one of three of the first four caliphs of Islam. These claims appear to be recognized by all the other tribes who show particular respect to Owlat peoples, irrespective of age or gender. The fact that the Owlat groups were "Non-Turkmen" enabled them to stand aside from tribal quarrels and act as mediators and their blessing would be sought for a range of important events such as harvest and childbirth. Owlat members were also deemed to have powers of healing and spirituality and this "holy" or honored status was and is reflected in the sacredness ascribed in many cases to their burial places (Brummell 2005; Centre for Asian Studies Michigan State University (n.d.); Tyson 1997). Again there is evidence that this ancient belief/tradition survived the Soviet disdain for "folk religion" and may be discerned in contemporary Turkmen society.

Tribes and Clans

Turkmenistan is said to possess one of the most well-defined tribal structures in Central Asia (Edgar 2004; Tyson 1997). During the Soviet period, there were conscious efforts and active policies to overcome tribalism (Edgar 2004), both because the Soviet system and officials were being drawn into intertribal conflicts and because the strong genealogical identities and kinship loyalties were perceived as hindering the socialist perception of society. It is undoubtedly the case that the forced settlement of the nomadic populations during the Soviet period and other Soviet policies over time, such as the introduction of a countrywide education system with a standard curriculum and language of instruction, Russian (in the majority of schools), eroded the significance of tribal structures.

Nevertheless, the tribal ancestry appears to have survived the Soviet Period. It is currently asserted that there are still at least six identifiable tribal groups, each divided into clans; the Tekke, the Ersari, the Yomud (Yomuts), the Goklens, the Sarik, and the Salor (Salir) (Brummell 2005). These tribal groups can be identified with different regions of the country; for example, one branch of the Yomut tribe is associated with the northern province of Dashoguz while the other is concentrated inland from the Caspian (Akbarzadeh 1999; Edgar 2004; Kadyrov 1996).

The tourist is most likely to encounter the tribal influence when viewing carpets, a classic Turkmen souvenir, as it is claimed that the different tribes/clans are associated with particular *guls* (motifs) that are incorporated into the designs. The particularly observant tourist may discern the motifs of what were at the time, 1991, regarded as the five principal tribes in the flag that was designed to celebrate the creation of the independent state of Turkmenistan (the Goklen are not represented on the national flag). The flag, has from the outset, included the Islamic Crescent, and with its more recent editions depicting crossed olive branches to signify the recognition of "neutrality" accorded to Turkmenistan by the United Nations in 1995.

In terms of society, Akbarzadeh (1999) argues that the choice of a marriage partner continues to be influenced by tribal affiliation and that in the realm of politics; the Tekke tribe was, and probably remains, the most powerful of the tribal groups following the collapse of the Soviet Union. Sapamurat Niyazov, was a member of the branch of the Akhal Tekke tribe that associates itself with the Akhal province, home to the capital Ashgabat.

TURKMENISTAN TODAY

In 1924, in the wake of the Bolshevik revolution, present day Turkmenistan was designated the Turkmen Soviet Socialist Republic. This domination ended in October 1991. However, the available evidence suggests that there was little support for Glasnost (or the reforms of Gorbachev or Yeltsin) in Central Asia generally and in Turkmenistan in particular, and that the rapid disintegration of the Soviet system came as an unexpected and unwelcome surprise to the ruling elite. Nevertheless, this small privileged group moved quickly to retain power. While initially having to address some lawlessness and acute food shortages (the country is, e.g., heavily dependent on imports of wheat for bread, an important staple at most meals), they rapidly achieved control. In Turkmenistan, the Communist Party was renamed the Democratic Party of Turkmenistan. Niyazov, who had been elected First Secretary of the Communist Party in 1985, assumed the role of Executive President of Turkmenistan in 1991. Following his death in December 2006, he was succeeded by Gurbanguly Berdymukhamedov.

Niyazov has had a significant impact upon the development of his country, early in his presidency he began to refer to Turkmenistan as the mother country of the Turkic peoples and chose to refer to himself as Sapamurat Turkmenbashi (Kiepenheuer-Drechsler 2006), or "father of the Turkmen people," a father who expected loyalty from all the different groups in the country. This father figure was prevalent everywhere in photos and placards adorning the exterior of many buildings and hanging in many rooms and in the passenger cabins of the state airline. The country's international airport in Ashgabat bears his adopted name, as does the main port on the Caspian coast. Early indications are that his successor Gurbanguly Berdymukhamedov is pursuing his own personality cult (Horak and Sir 2009).

Few decisions are made by anyone other than the President and appointments to and dismissals from office are frequent with few exceptions. Purportedly democratic elections are all reported to have secured in excess of 90% of the popular vote, but their legitimacy has been challenged by the international community (US Mission to OSCE 2008). A People's Council (The Khalk Maslahaty), a supposedly democratic institution, created in 1991–1992 was abolished in 2008 and replaced by the Council of the Elders (Yashularynyn Maslahaty). This body, which is known to have characterized the Seljuk dynasties, is again of variable composition, claimed to be another opportunity for the populace to engage in, discuss, and influence national policy. It is almost certainly relevant that the first meeting of the Elders in spring 2009 focused upon agriculture production, food security, and drug addiction. The latter is believed to be a more serious issue in the agricultural rural areas than in the marginally more prosperous cities (News Central Asia 2009).

Society and Religion

In the early years of independence, there was a shared vision of building the nation of Turkmenistan, which could define itself anew rather than being perceived as one of the more backward Soviet Republics. To do this, special attention was given to promoting the Turkmen language and to accentuating the history of its people. Consequently events and historical figures were reviewed as to their suitability for defining and reinforcing Turkmen identity. One proposal was to accentuate the Parthian Heritage as Nisa, one of the ancient capitals, which is a few kilometers from Ashgabat. While the Parthian heritage is recognized, attention was finally focused on celebrating the Seljuk legacy (Akbarzadeh 1999). The Seljuks were a branch of the Oguz Turks and their empire and Islamic civilization reached its zenith in the 12th and 13th centuries when the cities of Merv in the southeast and Kunya Urgench in the north were major centers of culture and learning, as well as being key trading cities on the Silk Road. Consequently although the ruling elite in Turkmenistan has shown little inclination to engage with many of the international agencies, they have actively pursued the accolade of World Heritage status for Merv (UNESCO 1999), Kunya Urgench (UNESCO 2005), and most recently Nisa, one of the capitals of the Parthian Empire (UNESCO 2007).

While the desire to supplant tribalism with nationalism was a continuation of Soviet policy, Niyazov appeared initially to wish to reestablish Islam as the national religion in a secular state and he was the first Central Asian Head of State to undertake a pilgrimage visit to Makkah. His successor, Berdymukhamedov, shortly after assuming the presidency also undertook an *Umrah* as a demonstration of his Islamic piety, a visit that received extensive coverage in the state controlled media in Turkmenistan (Boucek 2007b). A number of donors, including the United Arab Emirates and Turkey moved quickly to donate funds and skills for the construction of a number of Mosques in Ashgabat and generally to encourage the resurgence of Islam.

During the 1990s, public pronouncements by Niyazov appeared to support a clear role for Islamic teaching, as he stated:

> The history of our civilization and our people has been combined with Islam for centuries and it is impossible to analyze and understand the history, civilization, and politics of the Turkmen nation without knowing the history of Islam and the Holy Qur'an. I therefore, propose that lessons on Qur'anic wisdom and the history of Islam be taught in our schools.

In the first decade of his presidency, a Council for Religious Affairs headed by the President was established to provide a forum for an Islamic input into government policy and a leading Islamic authority was officially recognized. The incumbent in the mid-1990s was Kazi Nasrulla ibn Ibadulla who at first appeared able to work within the presidential circle. As a further sign of its support for Islam, the Islamic feast day (Kurbam Bairam) was declared a national holiday as it "would help to restore the representation of our culture and customs that have accumulated over many centuries of history" and that "the awakening of the national self awareness is characterised by the revival of popular interest in the religion of Islam" (Kazi Nasrulla Ibn Ibadulla, the then highest Islamic Authority in Turkmenistan, cited in Akbarzadeh 1999). The creation of this Turkmen "authority" required separation of the country's Islamic clerical establishment from the Central Asian Muftiyat in Tashkent. This breakup of the Central Asian Muftiyat is of course contrary to the Islamic teaching of Unity and Niyazov's insistence upon a separation from the Islamic Central Asian authorities may well have been motivated by a desire to minimize the universalist message of Islam.

Traditionally, the Turkmen of Turkmenistan are Sunni Muslims (Hanafi School) (Bennigsen and Wimbush 1985), although some minority groups such as the Azerbaijani and Kurds adopt Shia Muslim practices. Curtis (1996) suggests that, in terms of the population at large, while a majority of Turkmen identify themselves as Muslims and acknowledge that Islam is an integral part of their cultural heritage, many others are nonfollowers and support a revival of the religion's status only as an element of national revival. Calls to prayer are rarely heard and few attend services at the mosque or demonstrate their adherence publicly, except through participation in officially sanctioned national traditions associated with Islam on a popular level, including lifecycle events such as weddings, burials, and pilgrimages. This attitude to Islam is equally evident in the dress adopted by the women. It is extremely rare to see the traditional Islamic dress codes being observed; conversely, it is extremely common to see women of all ages dressed in long traditional Turkmen dresses with a collar the pattern of which may well have some reference to tribal affiliation. Again many women wear a headdress, but this is rarely a black head covering; it is far more likely that a colorful scarf will be worn.

By the late 1990s, Niyazov seems to have come to the conclusion, shared by leaders of other Central Asian states that Islamic extremism represented a potential threat to the regime, and this continues today (ICG 2009). As a result, the Islamic authorities were subjected to severe restrictions: the madrassah (school) in Dashoguz, opened shortly after independence and largely staffed by Uzbek Mullahs and teachers, was forcibly closed in 2001. Following on from this, Niyazov is said to have personally ordered the arrest and imprisonment of Kazi Nasrulla Ibn Ibadulla in 2003, for casting doubt upon the claim of divinity for the Ruhmana, the book the president asserted he was inspired to write (Kuru 2002; Human Rights Watch 2004). Niyazov subsequently removed Ibn Ibadulla's successor in 2004. The activities of the Faculty of Muslim Theology at the Magtymguly State University were drastically scaled down in 2005. President Niyazov allegedly gave as the reason, "we have one religion and unique traditions and customs, and there is no need for people to look beyond these." "Otherwise," he continued, "there will be self-styled mullahs, each one of whom will interpret religious rituals in his own way, which could in the end lead to feuds" (Rotar 2005).

To address what Niyazov claimed were shortcomings in the *Qur'an*, he published in 2001 the first volume of the Ruhnama (*The Book of the Soul*), which he claimed to have written with divine guidance. Niyazov compares the gift of the Ruhnama which he received to the gift of the law to Moses and the Israelites. This was followed in 2004 by the publication of a second volume (Morgunov 2003). Considerable doubts exist as to the originality of all the text of this new holy book, according to Horak (2005) the Ruhnama is "an aggregation of disparate facts, which finds its inspiration in the *Qur'an*, communist brochures, Turkmen traditions (or pseudotraditions) and the Turkmen interpretation of history." It contains, for example, some of the poetry of Magtymguly Pyragy an 18th century Turkmen poet who sought to overcome tribal factionalism and to unite the Turkmen peoples (Levin 2006), very much an apparent aspiration of President Niyazov who in his earlier pro-Islamic period had argued that just as Magtymguly had valued the *Qur'an* so should the people of Turkmenistan in the 20th century. During the final years of Niyazov's presidency, the Ruhnama was compulsory reading in schools and colleges with "entry" examinations allegedly dependent upon knowledge of the book—a situation that apparently continues in part at least under the auspices of his successor.

The Economy

In his day, President Niyazov would frequently talk of the coming "Golden Century"—a time of peace, plenty, and prosperity for his subjects, and he had good reason to portray such a dream. While analysts' opinions vary, it is widely believed that Turkmenistan is in the top 10, possibly the top 5, of countries with the largest reserves of natural gas together with not inconsiderable oil reserves, this is an enviable situation for any country. There are ongoing proposals to bring a pipeline under the Caspian to export gas directly to the European market, thereby reducing Turkmenistan's dependency on the existing Russian-controlled distribution system. Oil production and exports continue to increase. In 2007, these exports, together with natural gas and other petroleum products, account for over 80% of the export revenue (Boucek 2007a). Cotton was an important product and it was to increase cotton production and thereby lessen dependence upon imports from outside the Soviet Union that the Karakum Canal project was undertaken. However, this canal has had a range of unforeseen destructive environmental effects.

Compared with agriculture and the energy sectors in Turkmenistan, the service sector economy is very underdeveloped and is currently largely under the direct control of the State. Prior to and during the first years of Russian domination, pilgrimage to holy sites was the principal form of tourism and included visits to sites in northern Iran. As the Soviet system took hold, two forms of tourism developed, both essentially domestic. For the majority of the Russian population of Turkmenistan and the Soviet Union, this revolved around visits to "successful" agricultural and industrial enterprises, while Turkmen nationals endeavored to continue with their visits to holy sites. More prosperous Russians and Turkmens were also able to avail themselves of cheap air travel to go to resorts in southern Russia, to escape the extremes of the heat of summer in Turkmenistan.

In the late 1930s, some discussion took place regarding the "wider" tourism potential of the country. However, the advent of the Second World War, in which many Turkmen fought and died, followed by the disastrous earthquake of 1948, led to a 7–10 year period of rebuilding. Some of the first hotels built catered to business people and government officials. In the 1960s, tourism developed slightly more rapidly, the main forms being tours of the country's archaeological sites and health tourism, most notably to the Sanatorium at Bairam-Ali near the ancient city of Merv. Gradually other hotels were built in other cities and offices of Intourist and Sputnik were opened.

About the end of this decade, Hotel Ashkabad opened and was the first property to cater for international tourists, mainly coming from "fraternal socialist countries," together with a few from nonsocialist countries in escorted groups. During this time, the commercial accommodation sector was characterized by very poor standards of catering and food preparation. In terms of attractions, one or two theaters were opened in Ashgabat, as was a Museum of Local History and Geography. Outside the main cities, the other major development in Turkmen tourism in the past 40 years of Soviet domination was sport related, particularly mountaineering and hiking.

Tourism Activities in Turkmenistan Today

The first two decades since Independence have seen major investments in tourism-related infrastructure, confined in the first decade to Ashgabat, as with many investment decisions, these were largely related to the vision of President Saparmurat Niyazov. These developments have included an Earthquake Monument, the Arch of Neutrality, National, Carpet and Fine Art museums, an amusement park, the "World of Turkmen Fairy Tales," a Race Course, an Ice Palace, and a Water Sports complex, an "Olympic" Stadium, and a cable car in the nearby foothills of the Kopet Dag. As part of these developments, many of the older urban areas have been leveled to make way for a series of parks containing exotic statues and water features. Imported white marble has been used to face many of these structures reflecting Niyazov's dream of Ashgabat as the "White City." The new marble-clad buildings are to be interpreted according to Kiepenheuer-Drechsler (2006) as symbolizing presidential ideas in that they represent the realization of the Architecture of the golden age and that this outer transformation of Ashgabat demands an internal transformation of society toward an ideal, heavenly, and golden future.

One of the most exotic of President Niyazov's initiatives was the construction of the "Spirit of Turkmenbashi" Mosque that can accommodate 10,000 worshippers; it is situated a few miles from the center of Ashgabat at Kipchak where Niyazov was born. The Mosque, which is suggested to have benefited from a major bequest from Saudi Arabia (Boucek 2007b), was built by the French construction company Bouygues responsible for many of the presidential projects. Adjacent to the mosque is a mausoleum, which when the complex was inaugurated in 2004 contained the remains of the President Niyazov's family, and it is where he was interred following his death in 2006. Many Muslims are disturbed by the internal decoration of the Mosque, which incorporates quotations from the Ruhnama, alongside quotations from the *Qur'an*.

It is undeniable that Ashgabat comes as a very considerable surprise to many first-time Western tourists. Those arriving with the image of Ashgabat as a small- to medium-sized unprepossessing town in the desert encounter in the central area of Ashgabat wide streets linking the relatively new aforementioned modern buildings and parks. The older, not unattractive suburbs of single- or two-storey properties, restricted in height during the reconstruction following the 1948 earthquake, are perhaps a better reflection of the image many may have had prior to their arrival. To host potential tourists up to 20 hotels have opened. Several of these were initially managed by international management companies, but many have now reverted to being managed by appointees of the various government ministries to which most hotels are linked. Perhaps unsurprisingly, the most luxurious hotels are linked to the Ministry of Oil and Gas.

Set against the extravagance of these developments in Ashgabat, minimal investment was made in the regional population centers. This was largely restricted to the building or renovation of hotels managed by the State Committee for Sport and Tourism, which provided little recreational or leisure facilities for residents. Similarly, low levels of investment characterize the country's infrastructure. An international airport, sponsored by international donors, was constructed in Ashgabat in the early 1990s, supporting domestic and international services of the national airline and a small number of carriers from other countries. A rail line to Iran now exists and there has been some but limited improvement in the internal road network.

International Tourism to Independent Turkmenistan

The image and attractions of Turkmenistan for international tourists at the present time, if indeed they exist at all, are likely to focus upon historical sites, particularly those linked to the fabled Silk Road. Tours of these sites, often coupled with visits to historical sites in neighboring Uzbekistan, are the principal offer of the three or four Turkmen tour operators active within the international market. Additional reasons may include an interest in the native Akhal Tekke horses and the possibility of horseback trekking in the Karakum.

One of the key obstacles faced by would-be tourists in recent years has been obtaining a visa, which is not a simple matter (Brummell 2005). Contact has to be established with one of the few national Tour Operators or Tour Agencies, the majority of whom are linked to the national government. A legacy of Soviet times remains evident as its bureaucracy centralized the administration of travel and many other services in Central Asia in Tashkent (Uzbekistan) and this network still underpins the systems operating today.

Currently there are few international tourists, and in recent years arriving on an international flight in Ashgabat in the company of more than 10 other tourists has been an experience to be remarked upon. Accurate tourism statistics, indeed any statistics, are simply not available, despite the fact that those regarded as business tourists, principally visiting at the invitation of government ministries, are upon arrival and departure channeled through the airport as commercially important tourists. In regard to leisure tourists, one tour operator suggested in 2007 that increasing the number of leisure tourists to between 10 and 15,000 by 2010 was an appropriate aspiration.

The Turkmen government states, however, that this is about to change, driven by a very ambitious tourism development planned for Avaza, on the shores of the Caspian Sea near the port of Turkmenbashi (formerly Krasnovodsk), the center of Turkmenistan's oil and gas industry. The area around Avaza has been designated as a Tourism Development Zone, apparently with an international clientele in mind. Historically the Avaza area was a favored location for Turkmen families who rented temporary accommodation along the shoreline, when seeking a coastal location in the hot dry summer months. However, these "summer houses," often temporary structures, have now gone and the first hotels were opened in summer 2009 by the Turkmen President in the company of national figures and representatives of international energy companies. President Berdymukhamedov has continued the enthusiasm for the project shown by his predecessor and has apparently committed the government to contribute US$1 billion to complement the estimated $5 billion being sought from international investment groups (News Central Asia 2009). The state news service states that in the near future, Avaza will comprise some 60 hotels and apartment complexes, together with an appropriate infrastructure (ECOTimes 2009).

This desire to encourage international investors is reflected in the new constitution of 2008, which incorporates clauses designed to facilitate international investment in Turkmenistan. While it is apparent that there are investors who are interested in financing the oil and gas industries, whether there is readiness to invest in the Avaza tourism project remains to be seen. President Berdymukhamedov, early in his term, encouraged Saudi Arabians to consider investing not only in the energy sector but also specifically at Avaza (Boucek 2007b). The new constitution also specifies that small- and medium-sized enterprises should be encouraged and supported. At first reading, this may appear a very positive development for the tourism industry, which is almost universally characterized by small- and medium-sized enterprises. Perhaps in anticipation of these developments, some of the international development agencies have been providing short tourism-business-related courses, such as the potential for developing home-stay style accommodation enterprises in rural agricultural communities. To attract non-Turkmen tourists, many of the restrictions on their movements would have to be lifted. Equally, if such enterprises were to develop, they would compete with a traditional friends and relatives supply of accommodation for the domestic market.

Historical Sites and Shrine Pilgrimage

While the rich diverse historical sites in Turkmenistan receive very few international tourists, many are visited and frequented regularly by the Turkmen population. This is particularly true of sites of religious significance, including those that are internationally known, as well as many other sites recognized and revered locally (Levin 2006). The numerous pilgrims include many women and childless couples who undertake various ceremonies associated with matrimony and fertility.

Domestic tourists are much in evidence at Kunya Urgench in the north of Turkmenistan and more particularly at Merv, 360 km (225 miles) east of Ashgabat. The designation of the UNESCO (2005) inscription identifying Kunya Urgench as a World Heritage Site notes, "The old town contains a series of monuments mainly from the 11th to 16th centuries" and that "most of the visitors are in fact pilgrims from the region." Onsite observations suggest that the majority of domestic tourists to Kunya Urgench are indeed pilgrims drawn there to visit the remains of more than 10 mausoleums, which can still be identified, a number of them in a remarkably good state of repair. Again, the focus of the pilgrimage to these ancestral shrines appears to have a significant focus on fertility, child bearing, and child welfare. Such is the conviction of these pilgrims that archaeological excavation pits will quickly become "sacred" with dolls, toy cots, and a range of child-related materials being placed in the vicinity of the different mausoleums.

Merv was the first of the World Heritage Sites in Turkmenistan to be designated by UNESCO (1999) having been nationally designated in 1987 as "Ancient Merv" a State Historical and Cultural reserve. This Archaeological Park contains early city-sites including the imposing Great and Small Kyz-Kalas erected in the 6th and 7th centuries from mud brick. The extant religious or sacred buildings include the Mausoleum of Sultan Sanjar dating from the 12th century; and buildings erected in the 16th century to honor the eminent 12th century Sufi scholar Hodja Yusup Hamadani. The Hamadini shrine is a particularly notable focus of pilgrimage and has associated with it a series of buildings for religious observance and sacrifice. International tourists to Merv quickly recognize the significance of these mausoleums for many of the Turkmen tourists. They also realize that despite the efforts of the Park authorities, many strive to bury family members as close to some of the mausoleums as possible, although the ancient graveyards are regarded as important archaeological sites and should not be disturbed by the interment of today's family members.

Tourists to the Merv World Heritage Site

A survey of tourists to Merv in 2007 and 2008 indicated that the overwhelming majority of them are domestic. There was only one international respondent to this survey; an Uzbek national. Over 90% of the respondents either came from the Mary province where Merv is situated or from the Ahal province that includes the capital Ashgabat, both of which are the traditional home of the Tekke tribe. The respondents were predominantly male (70%), one-third of whom were making return trips of over 400 km largely from the vicinity of Ashgabad; conversely the majority of the female respondents (83%) came from nearby locations around Merv. Over one-quarter of all female respondents were in the 17–24 age range compared to the 7% of male who were in this age range. Over half (54%) of the respondents were over 45 years old and half of all respondents stated that they had first visited Merv when they were under the age of 16.

When asked the purpose of their visit, the most frequent (33%) first reason given was to see historical monuments, with visiting holy places given as the second most important reason by a quarter of all respondents. While 10% claimed they timed their visit to coincide with religious events, the majority stated that the availability of free time determined the timing of their visit. Two-thirds (68%) stated that their parents had visited the site, of these slightly less than half (45%) said their parents visited as "pilgrims," the remainder used the term "for outings." All respondents indicated that they had knowledge of Merv before their visit, with parents and school being the principal sources and for the majority (75%), park staff were seen as the obvious source of additional information. Pre-visit preparation also characterized respondent's attitude to food and drink as they brought items from home or from the home of the relative with whom they were staying, this included the respondents who brought animals to sacrifice.

Tourists to sites such as Merv currently find relatively few if any onsite facilities (such as restaurants, restrooms or retail outlet), however, there are in some instances facilities for pilgrims. Nevertheless, when respondents were asked how their visit could be improved or if any further facilities were required, two-fifths (39%) stated that everything was fine as it was. The greatest demand (27%) was for guides and literature, while 13% suggested additional rest places/restaurants, 9% suggested transport around the site (area of 1,500 ha), and a small minority 3% suggested a hotel near the site (the nearest overnight accommodation available is in Mary some 20 km away).

The findings of the survey have to be treated with considerable caution as there were practical constraints in terms of sampling and only Russian was used as the language of communication. Nevertheless, these findings taken together with onsite observations and conversations with archaeologists familiar with the site indicate very clearly that both pride of and interest in their ancestors is a motivation for domestic tourists; this would presumably provide encouragement to those who seek to embed in Turkmen identity a legacy of the Seljuk civilization, which is renowned for its philosophers, artists, and scientists. Equally, the status ascribed to and worship of ancestral figures remains a powerful attraction for many. This is apparent in the upkeep and management of the shrine complex of the Sufi scholar Hodja Yusup Hamadani, as well as in the demand to inter-family members adjacent to revered mausoleums and the many indications of prayers and supplications relating to marriage, child bearing, and child health. These observations at Merv and at other sites in Turkmenistan clearly demonstrate that the Turkmen Sufi-inspired form of Islam that accommodates older pre-Islamic beliefs and customs, integrated into a tribal society remains vibrant for an as yet, undetermined percentage of the Turkmen nation. This is despite 65 years of Soviet policies, which sought to portray any form of religious belief and practice as a sign of ignorance.

CONCLUSION

Turkmenistan emerged as an independent state in which Islam is one of the two religions that are officially recognized, the other being the Russian Orthodox Church. Unlike many of the other former Soviet Islamic states, Islam has not to date been a focus for politically inspired violent opposition to the former communist party elites, which assumed control through supposed democratic means. Initially Islam was seen as a tool to support nation building, second only in importance to the promotion of the Turkmen language. But its actions and influence has in the past 10 years been severely curtailed. In the population at large, there are few signs of orthodox Islamic practices. It appears that for many Islam is just one of the components of Turkmen culture. Thubron (1994) records that when traveling in Central Asia in the early 1990s, he was told on a number of occasions that the population sought to emulate the Turkish (Sunni) rather than Iranian model of Islam and the beliefs that have endured appear to be rooted in certain pre-Islamic traditions that have been embraced by a Sufi-infused Sunni branch of Islam.

Whatever might motivate international tourists to visit Turkmenistan, the reality is that until now politically inspired restrictions have curtailed international arrivals. Domestic tourism has also been restricted. Limits on internal travel and on access to the Caspian shore are now being curtailed by the designation of the Awaza tourism zone. Other restrictions limit access to the mountainous areas, another traditional venue for those wishing to escape from the high summer temperatures. These restrictions may result in excessive emphasis being attributed to cultural/historic/shrine-based domestic tourism, although travel restrictions may well also reduce visitation.

The enigmatic, environmentally challenged Awaza scheme has been compared to Las Vegas, which raises the issue of the legitimization of gambling in an Islamic society, if there is sufficient demand from the implied target markets of Russia, Iran, and the Middle East. It is unlikely that domestic demand will be significant, as only a very small percentage of the Turkmen population can afford the published preopening room rates ($50/room, 2007 prices), unless there is to be a massive state subsidy.

In summary, the future for tourism in Turkmenistan is uncertain for a number of reasons. In resource terms there are limits to the ability of the existing historic and cultural sites to support a vibrant tourism industry. The cultural potential of the "Silk Road" as a Trans-Asian tourism product has been recognized by UNWTO. However, despite a published series of reports and recommendations promoting this over more than a decade, the central Asian sections of the Silk Road have yet to realize their potential (UNWTO 1999; UNWTO 2001a). The extraordinary proposed multibillion investment on the Caspian at Awaza raises many questions, while other resources, not least a rich and diverse natural environment around the margins of the Karakum and in the mountainous regions, are almost totally ignored. Equally, it is a legitimate question as to whether the extravagant buildings and parks in Ashgabat will attract increasing numbers of domestic and international tourists. Evidence suggests that shrine pilgrimage retains its appeal. But it remains to be seen if this thousand-year-old tradition can survive the continuing repression of Islamic beliefs and traditions that are currently adopted by Turkmenistan's presidential style of government. Although its first president invested many millions of dollars in constructing his family's mausoleum, it is a matter of speculation if at any point in the future this will become a focus of shrine pilgrimage.

It is perhaps too simplistic to think that a change of philosophy and approach to social development by the current ruling elite is all that is required for the advancement of Turkmenistan. However, this change of philosophy is a very necessary first step both in allowing an unfettered expression of Islam, in what is currently a repressed and secular society, and of the subsequent impacts of this upon the development of the country's tourism potential.

Chapter 10

ISLAMIC TOURISM IN JORDAN
Sacred Topography and State Ambitions

Norig Neveu
Ecole des Hautes Etudes en Sciences Sociales, France

Abridgement: Islamic tourism has developed rapidly since 2001, and Jordan has embraced this movement and encouraged the construction of important infrastructure around mausoleums. Based on an analysis of official speeches and on fieldwork with tourism specialists, the impact of Islamic tourism on political and geopolitical matters in Jordan will be considered. Leaning on different scopes and levels of analysis, it will be shown that the promotion of Islamic tourism in Jordan not only bears a major economic impact on the country, but also permits it to rewrite its national history for internal and international political purpose. Further, the discussion considers how other countries are being targeted by this new kind of tourism, and the limits of its potential development.
Keywords: sacred topography; promotion; geopolitics; representation; Jordan

INTRODUCTION

For Muslims, Jordan is a blessed landscape marked with many holy shrines and tombs. Visiting these sites is approved behavior in Islam for both men and women. Here the faithful will learn, better understand and enhance their faith (Jordan Tourism Board 2002:1).

Tourism in the Muslim World
Bridging Tourism Theory and Practice, Volume 2, 141–157
Copyright © 2010 by Emerald Group Publishing Limited
All rights of reproduction in any form reserved
ISSN: 2042-1443/doi:10.1108/S2042-1443(2010)0000002013

The UN World Tourism Organization defines tourists as "all people traveling for holidays, leisure, business, and religious purposes" (Burns 2007). In accordance with the definition, this chapter describes the development of Islamic tourism—the phenomenon of tourist attendance to the shrines and mausoleums of *Qur'anic* prophets and Companions of Prophet Muhammad—between 1990 and 2009 in Jordan. Developing Islamic tourism has been a goal of the government since 2000. This objective is central to the Ministry of *Awqâf*, which is in charge of religious affairs and properties. A promotional campaign is launched following important renovations or reconstructions of shrines and mausoleums (Figure 1). The development is supported by further state investment in local holy sites for national and international purposes. Beginning in 2004, many Jordanian tourism agencies started to propose Islamic tours targeting new markets, especially from East Asia.

Religious issues play an important political role for Jordan with regard to local legitimacy and international standing. It is for this purpose that the members of the Hashemite royal family strongly promote their prophetic ascendancy. In fact, the members of the royal family descended from Prophet Muhammad. King Abdullah II represents the 43rd generation of descent from the Prophet. In addition, the recent expansion of Islamic tourism follows the successful development of Christian tourism in Jordan beginning in the 1950s (Katz 2003), and is encouraged by two major factors: the three papal pilgrimages (Paul VI in 1964, John-Paul II in 2000, and Benedict XVI in 2009) and key archaeological discoveries (Mont Nebo, site of Christ's baptism). These events encouraged the recognition and the redefinition of Jordan as part of the Christian Holy Land. The development of Christian tourism was followed by the promotion of interreligious dialogue launched by Prince Hassan (brother of late King Hussein) in the 1980s. This chapter will show that the official promotion of Islamic tourism since 2000 followed a very similar pattern to that of Christian tourism, but carries the unique imprint of the Monarchy.

The chapter is based on an analysis of the different steps and methods used in the reconstruction program of Islamic holy places, as well as an evaluation of official literature published by the Ministry of *Awqâf* and the Ministry of Tourism and Antiquities. In addition, interviews with architects, managers of tourism agencies, and members of the Ministry of Tourism and Antiquities were conducted between 2006 and 2009. Fieldwork (observation, conferences attendance, interviews) was carried out between 2006 and 2009 around the holy sites, and with the Royal Committee, which was responsible for their reconstruction. The chapter will at first focus on the local level,

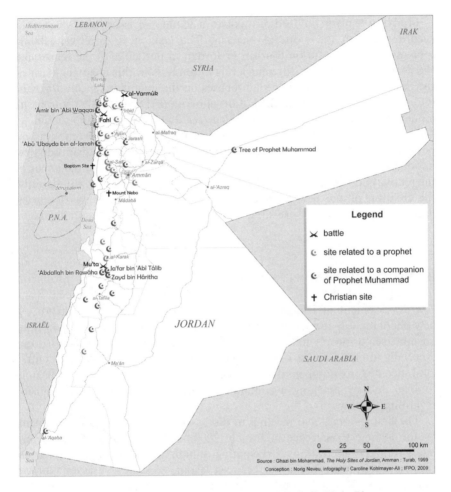

Figure 1. Location of the Renovated and Rebuilt Holy Places
Source: Bin Muhammad (1999)

cities, or villages surrounding the mausoleums and shrines. It will then broaden its analysis to the national and international levels. Two questions will be addressed at all three levels: How has the tourism industry changed due to the sacralization of the Jordanian territory, as well as the shift of Islamic tourism from a local and national issue to a regional and international geopolitical one? What were targeted by the travel agencies, and how has Islamic tourism been developed?

Studying tourism in Jordan involves a variety of issues that change in accordance with the scope of analysis. The lack of research on Islamic tourism in general and on tourism in Jordan in particular is the reason for the decision to consider different levels of analysis in this chapter. Most of the research on tourism in Jordan focuses on the potential for development (Gray 2002; Kelly 1998), on the notion of heritage (Daher 2007a), and on its influence on the local communities (Hejazeen 2007) or in Jordan as a whole. There has been little analysis of the impact of touristic promotion on political and geopolitical matters, especially as this trend introduces new nationalities to Jordan. The focus will remain on an analysis of the issues of the renovations in the context of Islamic tourism promotion. It will describe the creation of the new Islamic tourism industry and will also focus on touristic attendance at these sites.

ISLAMIC TOURISM IN JORDAN

The development of Islamic tourism (al-Hamarneh and Steiner 2004) is a new phenomenon and has emerged from the observation that tourism is an unstable sector deeply influenced by the international geopolitical situation, especially after the events of September 11 (or 9/11). Muslim countries after 2001 decided to compensate for this uncertainty by developing Islamic tourism and by reaching a common declaration and regional agreement regarding tourism.

The first international meeting to discuss Islamic tourism was organized by the Islamic Conference in Iran in 2000, with 23 countries and several international organizations participating. It highlighted the need for a deeper cooperation in touristic matters between Islamic countries. A second session took place in Kuala Lumpur in 2001. For the first time a document was published, which clearly mentioned the will to develop tourism. After the third meeting in Riyadh in October 2002 (attended by 45 countries), the role of the conference in the tourism industry was acknowledged and a cooperation treaty was signed with the UNWTO. The conference estimated the touristic attendance in the Middle East and Maghreb in 2020 at 60 million per year. The Islamic Conferences in 2005 and 2008 did not lead to significant change in the definition of Islamic tourism. The most recent Global Islamic Tourism Conference and Exhibition took place in Kuala Lumpur in July 2009 and included a trade show. Islamic tourism is a growing industry and one in which Jordan is seeking to play an active role.

The Jordanian Ministry of *Awqâf* has been trying to promote and develop Islamic tourism since 2004. A brochure published in that year by the Ministry titled "The Sites of the Religious Tourism in the Hashemite Kingdom of Jordan" clearly expresses the intention to renovate or rebuild Islamic sites in order to allow the development of tourism:

> Jordan is an open air museum where antiquities from different ages can be found, there is an important diversity of Islamic antiquities: citadels, historical sites, old mosques shrines of prophets and companions of the Prophet. The major part of these sites needs important funds for their promotion and tourism marketing in order to attract tourists from all over the world. This tourism would contribute in building the national economy of this country (Ministry of *Awqâf* 2004:2).

There are two major sources for the definition of Islamic or religious tourism in Jordan. The first can be found in the literature provided by Jordanian scholars, such as archeologists Muhammad Âbed al-Qa'îd (2002) and Muhammad Wahîb (2004). They consider this tourism to concern Islamic historical sites (mosques, castles, or shrines) and mainly focus on the sites and their history. Tourism is thus considered as a way to discover the places of Islamic history. The second definition, provided by the Ministry of *Awqâf* in its promotion of religious tourism, focuses on the reconstruction of the *maqâmât* (shrines or mausoleums) and *darâ'ih* (sanctuaries) in relation with developing tourism. Here, the definition of Islamic or religious tourism used by the Ministry focuses on visits to the sanctuaries. According to this definition, visiting Islamic sites is a major part of cultural tourism and a way to acquire better knowledge of Islamic history.

Creating a Sacred Topography

As early as the 1980s, the late King Hussein expressed a will to rebuild the shrines of *Qur'anic* prophets and Companions of the Prophet in Jordan. The impetus for this came from the Monarchy's desire to show that Jordan was fully integrated with Islamic history, and to recreate an architecture that would correspond to the inhabitants' religious behavior. It followed an Islamization of Jordanian urban architecture (Rogan 1986), especially in the city of Amman. A large number of mosques were built in Amman between 1980 and 1982, deeply affecting the urban landscape. The current renovation of shrines and mausoleums, which started in the 1990s, also contributed to the Islamization of the Jordanian landscape and has been a way to spread this movement all over the country.

At the beginning of the reconstruction process, the sites complemented a national political will to create memorial places (Nora 1984). An example of this is that in 1995 the Ministry of Youth asked Yussef Ghawânmeh, an eminent medieval historian, to write a book about the shrines and mausoleums in order to enlighten the population about the history of these holy sites—see Ghawânmeh (1995). The initial intention was that these mausoleums would be used by the local population, but this function was redefined. Since 2001, the use of these sanctuaries has changed to touristic purposes. In the Jordan National Tourism Strategy for 2004 to 2010, religious touristic development appears as one of the priority niche markets (Ministry of Tourism and Antiquities 2004a). The strategy aims to double Jordanian tourism revenues by 2010. The program, developed in collaboration with USAID experts, considers these sites as a way to offer a greater touristic diversity. The evolution of the function of the sites, from the local to the international level, is relevant in the study of the renovation projects and of their architecture. Indeed, the size of the initial mausoleums increased after each project and numerous services were added.

In 1994, the Royal Committee for the construction of mosques and mausoleums of prophets, Companions of the Prophet and Martyrdom was established. This committee was composed of approximately 10 members under the authority of the princes Ra'îd b. Hussein and Ghazi b. Muhammad. The latter was entrusted by King Abdullah II with the role of dealing with religious affairs in the name of the Hashemite Monarchy. He welcomed Pope Benedict XVI in Jordan in April 2009 and has promoted Muslim–Christian dialogue. The committee depends on the Ministry of *Awqâf*. Its director is the advisor to the minister, and members of the Ministry of Tourism and Antiquities are also part of it. One of its functions has been to select a number of sanctuaries to be renovated, and to appoint architects for these projects. Many well-known Jordanian architects, such as Rasem Badran and Ayman Zuayter, have participated in this movement.

The first step of the reconstruction campaigns concerned the mausoleums of the three Companions of the Prophet who died in the Battle of Mu'ta (629 CE) in Mazar (south of al-Karak). The first campaign started under the reign of the late King Hussein and led to the renovation of the three mausoleums of Ja'far, Zayd b. Hâritha, and Abdullah b. Rawâha. A second project was launched at the beginning of the reign of King Abdullah II in 1999 and resulted in an incorporation of two of the mausoleums (Ja'far's and Zayd b. Hâritha's) within a single wall. During this second project, various services were added to increase touristic attendance. This site was devoted to tourism at an early stage because of the high level of Shi'a attendance that started in the 1990s.

The evolution of the architecture of the site reveals a reorientation of the function of the sanctuary:

> As it is the case in Cairo, Aleppo or other Islamic cities, it was essential to connect the life elements and the daily functions with the project. (...). The commercial market is the essential element connecting the spiritual religious activities and commercial activities. Furthermore, it is the element which absorbs the noise represented by the car movement, expected to increase in the future. Activities to be practiced in the market were specified so that they do not come into contradiction with the spiritual and religious importance of the place, limited to the following works: library, souvenirs selling, *Qur'an* copies and rosaries selling, a tourism office, etc.... . The commercial market contains 16 commercial shops (Royal Committee 1996:7).

The site's development has sought a compromise between religious and commercial activities, although the shops around the mausoleums are not currently active. This could change with the third project in 2010, which is expected to assimilate a third mausoleum within the religious complex. As a result, new tourism activities will be created, such as horse rides to the site of the battle (located about 2 miles out of town). Between 1994 and 2010, the architects in charge of these three developments were replaced, as the vision for the site evolved. Originally, the project was commissioned to reflect the personality of the Mu'ta commanders. The current project, however, is more directly related to the development of tourism policy. Incidentally, one of the architects of the project said that the touristic attendance of Shi'a pilgrims to the site had a direct influence upon its architecture. As explained, the exceptional size of the site responded to Shi'a architectural conceptions concerning the mausoleums.

The site of the mausoleum of Abû 'Ubayda b. al-Jarrah (an important military leader who participated in the Battle of Fahl in 635 CE and Yarmûk in 636 CE) has been under reconstruction since 1994 following a similar plan and strategy. A *Qur'anic* school, a library, and some facilities for tourists, such as shops and cafeterias, were built around the mausoleum. This site also comprises a VIP hall and infrastructures for a souk (which is not yet in service). In an interview in 2009, Rasem Badran, architect of the site, explained that this souk was first considered as a site for use by the local communities. It was developed in 1994 in order to be a local market where the local community (and farmers especially) could sell their produce. It is now, however, considered by the Ministry of *Awqâf* as a keystone of the Islamic tourism development strategy, and fully dedicated to this purpose.

In size, these two religious complexes, the mausoleum of Abû 'Ubayda b. al-Jarrah and the site of Mu'ta, are the most important of the projects, as they have the greatest attraction and touristic potential. More than 32 shrines and mausoleums have been rebuilt since 1994, and the committee continues to launch projects all over the country. For reasons seemingly related to the geopolitical situation and to the competition over the promotion of holy places, most of these sites are located in the Jordan Valley and are along the Israeli border. Building religious monuments along the border may be for Jordan a symbolic response to Israel's assertion of its land as a Jewish Holy Land. Most of the rebuilt complexes share a common scheme. The sites initially had modest dimensions and often consisted only of the mausoleum. The rebuilt sites are organized around the shrine with a mosque, a prayer hall for women, gardens, and facilities for tourists such as cafeteria and shops.

The ambition of this movement is not to renovate the old monuments (most of the time from the Mameluke or Ottoman periods) but to rebuild them, and the works were carried out, without reference to the notion of heritage. Some specific local architectural features have disappeared. This is particularly obvious in the case of the mausoleum of Âmir b. Abî Waqqas located in the North of the Jordan Valley. This mausoleum was small and dominated by its original *qubba* (dome). It was rebuilt by the Royal Committee with completely different architectural plans, based upon contemporary architectural conceptions and rules. The old *qubba* was replaced by another one, which fitted in with contemporary standards. The same approach can be found at most sites. As explained by the architects of these sites, the old monuments disappeared in order for the shrines to be more representative of the "greatness" of the prophets and of the Companions of the Prophet.

This is also a way to erase the former architectural forms and to reoccupy local sites of piety. Virginie Prevost (2009) describes a similar phenomenon in the disappearance of Ibadite mosques in Algeria, Libya, and Tunisia. These have disappeared because they were not frequented anymore, or were destroyed in order to be rebuilt in accordance with modern architectural norms. This researcher explained that Ibadites art is representative of the particularities of religious conception of the Ibadite Bedouin society. In the Jordanian case, the new architectural tradition supports the social redefinition wished for by the Monarchy. Official art and architecture tend to give a new definition of tradition, culture, and national community. This new definition is spread by a rewriting of the national history, largely promoted by the Ministry of *Awqâf*.

Promotion and Ambitions

A section dedicated to the promotion of Islamic tourism has been created within the Ministry of *Awqâf*. The most important project of this department, regarding these mausoleums, is to encourage a visit to them in the *Hajj* month (the pilgrimage month). The strategy focuses on the promotion of a tour that would include the pilgrimage to the holy cities of Mecca and Medina, a visit to Jordanian holy sites, and a visit to the holy places of Jerusalem. For this purpose, the Ministry emphasizes on the geographical position of Jordan:

> It is situated in the middle of the Arab and Islamic World, the route leading to *Hajj* and *Umra* (minor pilgrimage) to Mecca, the bridge stretching between the first of the two kiblahs, Jerusalem (...) and the Holy Mosque, which is the first house erected to worship God on Earth. It is the route followed by the Arab Hashemite Prophet in his journey to Jerusalem (Ministry of *Awqâf* 2000:7).

This extract highlights the geographical position of Jordan between the holy sites of Hedjaz and Jerusalem and also directly links the region to the life of the Prophet. Jordan is thus assimilated into the land of the Prophet, and many *hadiths* and *Qur'anic* verses are used to prove this assimilation. Similarly, the Royal Committee built a wall and a small house for a guardian around the tree, where Islamic tradition says that Monk Bahira recognized Prophet Muhammad as carrying the prophecy while he was a child, and was following the caravan of his uncle between Mecca and *al-Shâm* (Damascus) (Abel 1960:950). This tree, located in the region of al-Azraq, is of a great importance because it demonstrates the link between the national territory and the life of the Prophet.

According to Islamic tradition and the literature, there are two definitions of the Islamic Holy Land (Aubin-Boltanski 2004:32). The first one considers

Jerusalem as the Holy Land, while the other mentions the full *Bilad al-Shâm,*
or even a territory from the Hedjaz to the Euphrates and from the desert to
the Mediterranean Sea, as the Holy Land. As a result of the first definition of
the Holy Land, some tour operators are proposing Islamic tours to *Bayt
al-Maqdas.* This term, originally used for Jerusalem, is now applied to the
city and surrounding region. According to the second definition, Jordan is
described in the promotion brochures as belonging to the Islamic Holy
Land. In fact, for over five years, the emphasis of this definition of Jordan as
the Holy Land has found some echoes in the Islamic tours proposed by the
national and international tour operators.

Since 2004–2005, the number of travel agencies proposing Islamic tours
has increased. Today, about 15 of them offer this kind of tour. Most of them
are national or multinational businesses, with offices in Amman or Petra.
The majority offers a large range of tours (religious, adventure, cultural, and
medical) with the exception of the specialist English tour operator, Islamic
Tours. According to the directors of these tourism companies (personal
communication in 2009), Islamic tours appeared due to tourist-led demand
and the development of this industry in neighboring countries. The majority
of these actors explained that their companies were working in Islamic
tourism prior to 2004, as during the *Hajj* month many pilgrims traveled via
Jordan. The creation of Islamic tours, however, highlights a lack of
communication between these companies and the Ministry of *Awqâf.* In the
majority of cases, the literature, printed by the Ministry of *Awqâf* since 2001,
was unfamiliar to the travel agencies' managers; nor did they know about
most of the renovated sites.

Different types of tours have been proposed, with length ranging from
one to four days. The tours can be divided into two categories: those mixing
visit to the shrines and mausoleums, with visit to archaeological sites, and
those strictly religious tours. The typical trip includes a visit to the shrines of
prophets in the cities of al-Salt and Jarash, to the shrines of Companions of
the Prophet in the Jordan Valley, and to the site of the battle of Mu'ta in
al-Karak. The majority of tourists visit Jordan during the *Hajj* month or
around their Umrah before going to Jerusalem. This is particularly obvious
from Figure 2, which shows that the attendance of Turkish tourists, for
instance, greatly increased in November and December 2008 (the *Hajj*
month this year). The other groups of tourists generally come to Jordan for
one or two days, after visiting the holy places of Syria or Palestine.

Attendance at the sites is difficult to estimate, as no official statistics
are furnished by the Ministry of Tourism and Antiquities. According
to the managers of travel agencies and the records at the entrance to each of

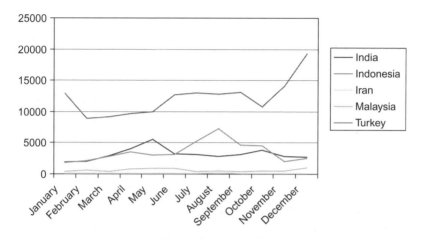

Figure 2. Arrivals of Tourists by Month (2008)
Source: Ministry of Tourism and Antiquities (2009)

the shrines, the majority of Islamic tourists originate from Malaysia, Indonesia, and Turkey, and are traveling as part of a group for a one- or two-day transit in Jordan. The statistics provided by the Ministry of Tourism and Antiquities reveal an increase in the number of tourists coming from countries such as Malaysia and Indonesia. This attendance is nevertheless low in comparison to other nationalities such as Saudis and Kuwaitis. This highlights an increasing potential in the attendance of the religious complexes. Targeting the East Asian market is a goal of travel agencies.

Entry statistics by nationality from the Ministry of Tourism and Antiquities (Figure 3) includes East Asian workers, mostly from Indonesia and the Philippines, who travel to Jordan to find work. Therefore, it is difficult to evaluate the tourist attendance at the Islamic sites. The tourism agencies claim that between 200 and 2,000 clients attend the Islamic holy sites every year, whereas the records at the entrance to the shrines show an average attendance between 10 and 30 tourists per month, although this indicator should be treated with caution, because many tourists do not sign the records. Islamic tourism continues to be marginal. Regional tourists, such as Saudi Arabians, who every summer visit Jordan in large numbers (more than 1 million in 2008, according to the Ministry of Tourism and Antiquities), do not visit these complexes during their stay, as they consider them to be of little religious significance.

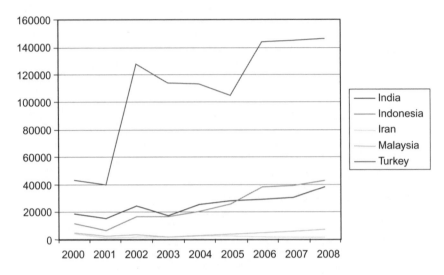

Figure 3. Arrivals of Tourists by Year (2000, 2001, 2002, 2003, 2004b, 2005, 2006, 2007, 2008)
Source: Ministry of Tourism and Antiquities (2001, 2002, 2003, 2004a, 2004b, 2005, 2006, 2007, 2008)

The site of Mu'ta has great potential due to the relatively high level of development of its reception infrastructures. Tourists can find signs translated into many foreign languages, including English, Farsi, Arabic, and Urdu. The mausoleum is particularly important for Shi'a Muslims because Ja'far was the brother of Imam Ali. Moreover, in 1980, after the beginning of the Iran–Iraq war, the Shi'a holy sites of Najaf and Karbala were closed until 2003, and the Kingdom of Saudi Arabia imposed a cap on the number of pilgrims allowed entry. The difficulty faced by the Shi'as for access to their holy places has created a new map for pilgrimage sites, including Mu'ta and many Syrian holy sites (Ababsa 2001). Since 2003 and the fall of the Iraqi regime, the pilgrimage to Karbala has resumed, with attendance peaking during the Ashura (the annual commemoration of the martyrdom of Hussein in the battle of Karbala).

Since the 1990s and the Gulf War, the mausoleum has been visited by Iraqi migrants living in Jordan. As a way to keep in touch with their Iraqi cultural heritage, many of these migrants formed a social support group based around the mausoleum which drew upon the attendance of pilgrims (Chatelard 2005a:3). In 2004 and 2005, agreements between Jordan and Iran were enacted to boost the development of religious tourism, which resulted in increased attendance. "More than 3,000 pilgrims visited the shrines of martyrs of the Battle of Mu'ta in the first half of 2005. The director of the *Awqâf* Department in south Mazar said that the Iranian pilgrims would soon visit this site in accordance to the Iranian–Jordanian agreements on religious tourism" (Hijawî 2005). Most of these Shi'a pilgrims visited the site of Mu'ta in 2005 and 2006.

By 2006, the political situation in the region (especially the death of Sadam Hussein) caused these celebrations to be banned, and restrictions were placed on Iranian tourism. One can infer that the significance of this site for the Iraqi migrants was the primary reason for its closure. Some of travel agency managers resent this decision and show a desire to develop Iranian and Indian Shi'a tourism in Jordan. Syria is a particularly alluring destination for Shi'a Islamic tourism. Many scholars have studied the significant influence of tourism on the urban geography and social organization of Syria (Ababsa 2001; Adelkhah 2007; Mervin 1996; Pinto 2007). The adoption of changing tourism strategies can be traced to the geopolitical role that Syria and Jordan wish to play in the region. A visit to the shrine by Iranians bears political significance, especially considering the favorable diplomatic relationship between Syria and Iran. Islamic tourism in Jordan is also guided by a complex geopolitical strategy based on the Companions of the Prophet.

In her book published in 2004, Irene Maffi discusses patrimonial politics in Jordan and explains how the Monarchy used historical continuity with the original local civilizations (especially the Nabataean one) to give legitimacy to the state (Maffi 2004). In the same way, the sites discussed here are a way to stimulate discussion regarding Jordanian Islamic history. The shrine of Abû 'Ubayda b. al-Jarrah and the mausoleums dedicated to the Mu'ta commanders are the keystone of this policy. They are considered a bridge linking the history of Islamic conquest of *Bilad al-Shâm* and the history of contemporary Jordan. Thus, this movement of renovation focuses on the role of the Companions of the Prophet and their bravery, but also on the importance of Jordan in Islamic history and conquest.

Special attention is given by the Ministry of *Awqâf* to Ja'far, a distinguished figure of Islamic history who was a member of the Hashemite family (his father was the brother of Prophet Muhammad's father and the chief of the Hashem clan). He is thus described in *The Holy Sites in Jordan* as a person bearing a resemblance to the Prophet "physically and morally" (1999:7). Abû 'Ubayda b. al-Jarrah is a recurrent figure as well. He was the *amîn al-umma*, or the Trustee of the Nation. He represents piety and fidelity. The historical relation of the companions with the Royal Family or the

Prophet is particularly significant through these two figures. The Prophet is also described by the Ministry of *Awqâf* (2000) as an "Arab Hashemite." Thus, a common familial relationship to the Hashem family unites the history of Prophet Muhammad and the history of the Royal Family.

Through this reconstruction program, Jordan has been designated as the land of the Prophet's journey and the land of the Companions of the Prophet, and consequently, the land of the Hashem family. A historical depth is given to Jordanian history, which allows not only a direct link between the time of the golden age of the Islamic conquest of *Bilâd al-Shâm* and the contemporary Islamic history of Jordan, but also between the history of the leaders of the conquest with that of the Hashemite kings. This can also be considered as an attempt to create memorial sites common to all Jordanians based on the pre-eminence of a prestigious past to which the entire population can relate. This newly written history is disseminated at the local level by the educational system and the national institutions. This elaboration is also important at the international level, since tourism is a way of diffusing the message beyond national boundaries.

The development of Islamic tourism is a geostrategic tool, because tourists bring impressions of Jordan to their own countries, which impacts how that country views Jordan. The tourism industry is in fact linked to the topic of representation. In their book about tourism in the Third World, Mowforth and Munt state, "tourism is a way to represent ourselves to the world and to represent it to others" (2003:24). The promotion of Islamic tourism is a way to present to the Islamic world the image of Jordan carrying the prophetic heritage. The late King Hussein and his son, King Abdullah II, helped to imbue an atmosphere of tolerance and religious dialogue between different components of Islam by using their ability to organize international conferences on this topic (as the Muslim–Christian consultation organized by Prince Hassan between 1985 and 1997). This dialogue presents Jordan as a space of mediation between the different components of Islam. Thus, developing Islamic tourism is a way for the Jordanian kings to assert themselves as spokespersons of a tolerant and modern Islam.

Furthermore, the mausoleum of Abû 'Ubayda b. al-Jarrah has become a place that provides an official representation of the Monarchy. A VIP hall was built there, where King Abdullah II welcomed most of the leaders of Islamic countries and foreign ministers of *Awqâf*. Through these official ceremonies, the mausoleum was used to symbolize the importance of Jordan in Islamic history. It also symbolized the integration of Jordan to the Islamic Holy Land. As descendants of Prophet Muhammad and rulers of the country, the late King Hussein and Abdullah II appeared as fundamental players in the Islamic world. On a larger scale, tourism is also a way to spread the national message and to portray Jordan as the land of the Islamic conquest that preserves the Islamic traditions. Thus, matters of representation are fundamental in the promotion of Islamic tourism.

CONCLUSION

Islamic tourism is a new government strategy, which has been elaborated around rebuilt holy sites all over Jordan. Since the 1990s, the Ministry of *Awqâf* has published literature concerning these sites, which has helped promote Islamic tourism. Since 2004, many tourism agencies have started to provide Islamic tours, targeting the East Asian market. However, since 2006 the closure of the mausoleum of Ja'far to Shi'a tourists (mostly from Iran and Iraq) has decreased the attendance to the Islamic sites. They are mostly now attended by Malaysian, Indonesian, and Turkish tourists who visit the country during the *Hajj* or *Umra*. An important gap then exists between the intentions of the government and the real attendance at these sites.

This chapter has discussed how a new tourism sector was created in Jordan, and its significance on different levels of analysis. At a national level, it is considered as a way to augment historical depth and continuity between contemporary Jordan and Jordan as represented by the Islamic conquest of the *Bilad al-Shâm*. These sanctuaries are the tools for rewriting Jordanian history with the help of the "Angel of History," as Benedict Anderson (2002:159) terms it. Additionally, they have also stimulated artistic and architectural movements in Jordan. Furthermore, the concept of perception plays a central role in this kind of tourism. At a regional and international level, tourism is a way to spread the image of Jordan and King Abdullah II as spokespersons of a tolerant and modern Islam throughout the entire Islamic world. However, the lack of cooperation between the Ministry of *Awqâf* and tourism professionals has limited the appeal of tourism for foreigners and consequently decreased accurate foreign perceptions of the country.

As demonstrated, Islamic tourism is linked with geopolitical matters. This was also the case with Christian tourism in Jordan. Tourism matters were an important part of the discussions during the treaty between Israel and Jordan in 1994, especially for economic reasons (Hazbun 2002). One of the main roles of tourism concerns the promotion of interreligious dialogue. In fact, the Christian tourism development occurred at the same time as an increased Muslim–Christian dialogue. The restoration of the cave of the

Seven Sleepers (South Amman) exemplifies the peaceful historical relationship between Christians and Muslims in Jordan. But above all, the promotion of dialogue between the different components of Islam plays an essential role. This dialogue followed the development of Shi'a visitation. Nevertheless, the closure of the mausoleum of Mu'ta revealed a wish to limit the Shia pilgrimages. Furthermore, in a similar process of peace building and dialogue (at least symbolically), Jordan wished to play a unifying role in terms of religious matters.

On a local perspective, the development of Islamic tourism can be seen as a way to control the habits of the local populations living around these sites. Local and regional pilgrimages existed until the 1970s for most of these sites. These pilgrimages mainly stopped because of new religious education that considers pilgrimage as being a *bida'* (innovation) and criticizes this behavior. Pilgrimages were representative of "popular Islam," which is not valorized in the constructions of the Royal Committee. These constructions allowed diffusion of a particular representation of the territory. The promotion of Islamic tourism in Jordan seems to bear the wish of a restriction of the historical visibility of certain populations (the local populations). The new architectural monuments built on the ancient mausoleums can be seen as a way to erase local beliefs and local particularities.

Studying the perceptions of foreigners in the touristic context highlights some questions about the self-perception of local communities. Although these sanctuaries have retained some symbolic significance, they are less well attended by the local communities since their reconstructions. Géraldine Chatelard (2005b) showed that tourism in the Desert of Wadi Rum in Jordan was based on power relations between the Western tourists and Bedouin inhabitants on one side, and Jordanian public institutions and transnational agencies on the other. Those relations have put the Bedouin inhabitants in a state of dependency and enclosed them in an authentic and exotic state. It would be interesting to question in further studies how Islamic tourism could affect local self-perceptions. The concept of perception and self-perception is extremely complicated, but nonetheless important in developing a conceptual understanding of tourism.

This case study reveals the role that the local populations play in developing the tourism industry and how they potentially impact its development in rural areas of the country. In fact, the development of this new type of tourism could face many limits that need to be considered. An analysis of such parameters as infrastructural development, tourism habits, transportation, and accommodation would be necessary to understand the relative failure of Islamic tourism in Jordan. This failure would also have to be analyzed in a regional context, answering the question of whether the same kind of Islamic tourism promotion is more efficient in the neighboring countries among the Sunni populations. A study comparing Syrian and the Jordanian Islamic touristic policy would be an interesting way to understand all of the issues present in the development of Islamic tourism.

Chapter 11

JAPANESE TOURISM IN IRAN

Kazem Vafadari
United Nations University, Japan
Malcolm Cooper
Ritsumeikan Asia Pacific University, Japan

Abridgement: Iran has significant potential for an international tourism industry based on culture and heritage. However, the rich fusion of Persian and Islamic cultures that distinguishes Iran from the rest of the Middle East is not easily promoted for tourism internationally, mainly as a result of successive American and European attempts at forcing Iran's isolation since 1979. Given that Japan was a significant inbound and outbound market for Iranian tourism in the 1980s and is a close trading partner of the group of countries aligned against Iran at present, this chapter focuses on the recent development of the Iranian inbound tourism industry with the history and current status of the Japan–Iran tourism connection. **Keywords:** Persian and Islamic culture; international relations; Iran's National Tourism Development Plan

INTRODUCTION

Iran is one of the world's most important countries in terms of the sheer age and volume of its historical and cultural sites (Mashai 2005; Vafadari and Cooper 2007), and as a result has significant potential for an international tourism industry based on these resources. Unfortunately, while Iran has generally experienced stable official relations with countries like Japan, Turkey, Russia and the Central Asian Republics, and Islamic (Shia)

Tourism in the Muslim World
Bridging Tourism Theory and Practice, Volume 2, 159–179
Copyright © 2010 by Emerald Group Publishing Limited
All rights of reproduction in any form reserved
ISSN: 2042-1443/doi:10.1108/S2042-1443(2010)0000002014

countries, European countries and the United States have made attempts at forcing Iran's isolation, causing problems for inbound tourism. The "sanctions" situation has, for example, had adverse consequences for the ability of the national airline to service its markets (sanctions supposedly concerned with nuclear weapons material extend to civilian aircraft and especially spare parts in the United States' view). Despite these problems, the country has seen and continues to see growth in inbound tourism. This chapter discusses factors that have influenced this industry and outlines the state of Iran's tourism industry today and the status of the Japan–Iran tourism relationship. In this context, the early 1990s suspension of the visa waiver program between Japan and Iran and its effect on tourism relations of the two countries is discussed as a case study. Recent interviews conducted with Japanese tourists in Iran and Iranian tourists in Japan bring further insights to this relationship and help clarify the needs and expectations of tourists in each country. It is suggested that both countries could help offset current international tensions and even benefit economically and socially if the movement between them for tourist purposes was redeveloped and expanded.

Governments in the 21st century cannot be indifferent to the importance of the continued economic expansion of the global tourism industry and to increased competition in the international tourism market. However, competition in this field is different from other industries as its main product (destination) cannot be exported and tourists are forced to move to it as consumers (Cooper, Abubakar and Erfurt 2001; Goeldner and Ritchie 2006; Laws 2006; Kozak 2002). In this situation both the quality and price of the product as well as its image in a target market play key roles in determining the flow of tourists to any particular destination (Andreu, Bigne and Cooper 2000; Andreu, Kozak, Avci and Cifter 2005; Crompton 1979; Kozak 2002). This chapter analyzes the image of Iran as an international destination, describing how the Iranian tourism industry is suffering from an image problem despite being able to offer rich cultural heritage and safe and cost-effective travel to tourists. The internal political environment of Iran and its international relations, the geopolitical situation of the region that Iran is a part of, and unfamiliarity with Iran as a country or destination are the main challenges for the Iranian tourism industry in reaching the overseas tourism markets, especially Japan. While the possibility for a change in the political situation exists, it will take time and effort to remove the wall of unfamiliarity and prejudice and change the image of Iran among world tourists.

Success in a particular target market depends on many factors (Bitner 1995; Linhart and Frühstuck 1998; Moscardo, Morrison, Pearce, Lang and

O'Leary 1996; Pearce and Benckendorff 2006), and is doubtful where adverse images can be constructed by third parties. People from one society have many reasons to want to experience another one, but to want to leave their own familiar environment in order to visit an unfamiliar or even a strange one that is at the same time being painted in an adverse way takes courage and not a little faith (Adams 2003; Harrison 2007; Kotler, Bowen and Makens 1999). Thus, for overseas tourists to Iran, given that the main (or perhaps only) reason to visit is to experience the cultural heritage of Persia and Islamic Iran, the image of the country as a radical Muslim (and hence dangerous) society so assiduously promoted by the United States and its allies (Alavi and Yasin 2000; Vafadari and Cooper 2007; World Factbook 2007) serves to undermine the very reason for visiting the country. Nevertheless, cultural tourism makes up a major part of the international tourism market (Cooper, Ogata and Eades 2008; Crouch and Lubbren 2003; Richards and Wilson 2007), which makes tourism at least theoretically attractive between Iran and other countries. This chapter shows that a pragmatic path for tourism promotion for Iran in the Japanese and other international markets in the face of the barrage of adverse images from Europe and the United States would be to start with the cultural promotion of Persia/Iran to the wider society in each international target market instead of trying to develop actual visits to Iran from the beginning.

THE TOURISM INDUSTRY OF IRAN

Tourism is not new to Iran as a country through which, for thousands of years, the Silk Road connected East and West and the march of empires played across its landscape (Bonavia 2004; Middleton 2005), but is only quite recently that effective tourism planning and management has once more been practiced (Mashai 2005). The tourism industry provides 9% of total employment in the high job-demanding youthful society of Iran, which has highlighted the importance of tourism to the Iranian government. The country achieved an unprecedented number of arrivals by 2005–2006 with over 2 million inbound tourists. However, the industry is negatively affected by the political environment within Iran and its difficult international relations (Euromonitor 2007). To offset this problem, the importance of the history of Iran and its cultural heritage in tourism promotion has been considered more seriously by the Iranian government in recent times. For instance, the recent merging of the Iran Touring and Tourism Organization and the Iran Cultural Heritage Organization in 2004, which created the Iran

Cultural Heritage and Tourism Organization, is evidence of emphasis on the role of Iran's cultural heritage in tourism promotion by the government (Naghi 2000; Vafadari and Cooper 2007). Furthermore, Iranian tourism officials admit that effective promotion at the moment for Iran must be based on small-scale cultural tourism, because Iran is not yet socially ready to develop mass tourism (personal communication 2008).

Changing the world's attitude toward Iran as a destination is included in the marketing strategies of Iran Cultural Heritage and Tourism Organization as an aggressive advertising campaign on international TV channels (IRIB 2006). An amount of US$10 million was allocated in 2006–2007 by Iran Cultural Heritage Organization to advertise Iranian tourism in the international media, and has since been expanded. The BBC, EuroNews TV, Al-Arabia, Al-Jazeera, and MBC are TV channels that have already started broadcasting such advertisements. In an effort to counter the propaganda peddled by the Western news media and provide the world with the truth (as Iranian officials see it), an English speaking Iranian TV channel called "PressTV" was launched in July 2007. The channel is available internationally and will advertise Iran's attractions, as well as broadcast news (IRIB 2006). Unfortunately, this news channel is addressed mainly to Europe and America, not to Japan, and similarly, Iranian attractions are yet to be advertised on Japanese TV channels.

In addition to attractions marketing, in cooperation with Iran's Ministry of Foreign Affairs, in 2008 Iran Cultural Heritage and Tourism Organization implemented a weeklong entry visa facility in order to facilitate inbound tourism, which is currently issued to foreign tourists at Iran's main airports. Tourists from all countries (except Israel) are eligible to receive their visa to enter the country at the airport. This policy of opening the doors also shows the government's willingness to promote tourism, but may not be attractive to the Japanese market that relies on long-term considerations of stability and safety before it will commit to travel.

Religious Tourism to Iran

As a result of the political situation, religious tourism and pilgrimage make up much of the inbound trade and are thus inseparable parts of the modern industry of Iran. The holy sites of Iran are important landmarks in attracting domestic religious tourists, as well as Arab and other Muslim tourists from across the world. Over 5 million domestic tourists per year now visit these holy sites, among which the shrine of Imam Reza in Mashhad, Iran's Shia holiest city, is the greatest attraction. Most foreign religious tourists are from Bahrain, Iraq, and Lebanon. Although Mashhad is their main destination, they also show interest in other cities. Tourists from Saudi Arabia and the United Arab Emirates who are relatively high spenders are targeted currently by Iranian tourism promotional activities. The relationship between Iran and Saudi Arabia is bilateral, in which Saudi tourists rank highest among the international arrivals in Iran, and Iran provides more than 20% of the 3 million religious tourists on *Umrah* (minor *Hajj*) to Saudi Arabia in return (IQNA 2007).

Religious tourism between Iran and its neighbors is not easily sustainable and affected negatively by the political situation. Continuation of the civil war in Iraq recently has led to conflicts between Shia and Sunni Muslims, for instance. Though initiated by the American invasion, a new wave of Shia–Sunni conflicts seems to be spreading out through the region, bringing up new political problems for the Shia state of Iran with its neighboring Sunni States of Saudi Arabia and Dubai. Accordingly, Iranian Shia pilgrims have found it uncomfortable to visit Makkah recently, and Iranian tourists are complaining about not being treated respectfully by the Dubai airport staff. In commenting on the aggressive manner of Saudi officials to Iranians in June 2007, Ayatollah Makarem Shirazi, a senior Shia cleric, declared: "Going on minor *Hajj* in such conditions undermines Shia Muslims' dignity and if the Saudi *Hajj* officials do not change their attitude toward Iranian pilgrims, the Shia leadership will boycott minor *Hajj*" (IQNA 2007). Thus, the ongoing situation in Iraq is negatively affecting the regional political and social situation for religious tourism. This will not change without a reliable solution to that problem.

Inbound Tourism and Marketing Opportunities

According to the UN World Tourism Organization, 922 million people traveled abroad during 2008–2009, including 55 million to the Middle East (UNWTO 2008, 2009). The sheer weight of numbers of tourists may in fact force changes in the flows to Iran in a positive way if the adverse imagery can be counteracted effectively. In this context, Japanese tourists are distinguished as being very important on a worldwide basis, especially for cultural and heritage tourism (Carlile 1996; Cha, McCleary and Usal 1995; Keown 1989; Schumann 2006; Shono, Fisher and McIntosh 2005). While there has been a decline in the number of Japanese outbound tourists in the past year (from 17.3 to 15.3 million), a new marketing opportunity for Iran in the form of Japanese senior tourists may significantly increase in future years. This group is the beginning of retirement of the Japanese baby boomer generation with a strong interest both in domestic and foreign travel (Nitta 2006).

The share of different countries and regions of the Japanese international travel market does vary according to the preferences of Japanese tourists (Ahmed and Krohn 1992; Mok and Lam 2000). East Asian countries are now the most preferred destinations, with North America, Italy, Germany, Thailand, France, and Hawaii remaining strong contenders (JTMC 2009). As a result, the share of the Middle East region in Japan's tourism market is inconsistent with the potential of the Middle East countries to attract Japanese tourists. The region, which has been referred to by historians as the Fertile Crescent, is the cradle of civilizations and the birthplace of many of the world's main religions. However, only some countries in the region have been relatively successful in attracting Japanese tourists. For example, 80,000–100,000 Japanese tourists travel to Turkey per year, but tourism to many of the countries of the region, such as Iran, Syria, Jordan, and Lebanon, has not even reached this low level.

Iran's unattractiveness to Japanese tourists is an unfortunate example of this pattern. According to UNESCO, Iran is ranked as one of the top 10 countries in the world in terms of its ancient and historical sites. There are a million historical monuments in Iran, with more than 12,000 of them registered officially (Mashai 2005). However, the Islamic revolution in 1979 and subsequent media distortions of reality has led to a dramatic change in Iran's social and economic situation and the state of the tourism industry is no exception. In the 1970s, some 60% of all tourists to Iran were Americans, for example, spending an estimated one billion dollars each year, but this trade almost disappeared after the revolution (Mideast Mirror 1998). In the case of Japanese tourists, while 24,106 Japanese traveled to Iran each year before the Islamic revolution, a share of almost 0.6% of the then overall Japanese international market, this market segment rapidly declined during the years after the revolution. Today, the number of Japanese tourists in Iran is only 3,000 a year.

Nevertheless, Japanese tourists have a good chance of becoming interested in Iran as a destination once more because of their curiosity about cultural and heritage tourism. The constraints which exist in the current Iranian society, making it different to many other cultural destinations in the region (even Islamic ones like Dubai), are the absence of developed sea and sand destinations and also the religious attitude to sex outside marriage and the serving of alcohol. However, Japanese senior tourists at least seem not to be worried about this as much as other tourists. Though sea and sand holidays are not expected to disappear from the Japanese's motivational framework, they have declined in relative importance among all age groups, as more and more tourists seek challenging educational and/or relatively unique experiences (NWHO 1999). Further, in the case of Iran, while the recent decline of the tourism industry can be attributed to many factors, the most important are political relations with the rest of the world and the negative images promoted in the mass media about Iran by its adversaries. There have, however, been almost no political problems between Iran and Japan, and in this context the fact that Japan remained the major customer of Iranian oil after the Iranian revolution brings a comparative advantage as well as allowing Iranian tourism policymakers to focus on Japan as a target market, should it choose to do so.

Facilities for Tourism

In relation to such sophisticated markets as Japan, there is no doubt that attractions, accommodation, transportation, and retail infrastructures need to be further developed in order to develop inbound tourism. However, inadequate facilities in Iran cannot be the only factor responsible for the gap between potential and market realities, because the existing capacity of such facilities is in fact not properly used by the tourism industry. For example, overall hotel occupancy rates in the country stood at a low 39% in 2007 (personal communication 2008). A particular problem though is that the size of the country necessitates the use of domestic flights in Iran in addition to other means of travel. There are 30 airports in active use across Iran, 8 of which have international terminals, and the completion of Tehran's new airport (Imam Khomeini International Airport) is an additional major accomplishment, with a capacity of 7 million passengers per year. However, there is little hope for serious development at present in the internal aviation industry of Iran, as a result of sanctions that restrict the purchase of planes to those with less than 10% of US-made components and restrict the purchase of spare parts (except on the black market; personal communication 2009).

The most important dilemma facing the tourism market of Iran is the large number of travel agencies that have appeared around the country during the past few years. Though the existence of a travel agency itself is to help the industry and tourists, their recent rapid growth has resulted in a different scenario. The majority of them that have mushroomed throughout the country cannot even afford their internal expenses and have turned into loss-making entities (Euromonitor 2007). While the travel agencies that dominate Iran's inbound market are handful with their roots in governmental foundations, the rest are limited to functioning as dealers in obtaining tourist visas for Iranians, mainly pilgrims. As a result, there is no room for the majority of travel agencies to undertake international marketing and make the contacts that they need to assist in attracting inbound tourists, and thereby grow themselves while diversifying the industry and creating more opportunities for tourism in and outside of Iran.

Cultural Heritage

Despite these problems, what does the country have to offer to effectively promote it as a destination to the Japanese market? Iran has a long history that is important both to the country and to the rest of the world, to which it has made significant contributions in the past. Its recorded history commenced in 559 BCE with the Achaemenid Dynasty (ITTO 2001), but has much earlier roots. There is no lack of world literature on different aspects of Persian civilization and history such as architecture, administrative knowledge, art, and religion. The difficulty lies more in the fact that this history is not identified with modern Iran, although Persian culture has been preserved throughout its long history in spite of changes in the political boundaries and ethnic diversity of the country. Authentic cultural elements of ancient Persia are still alive in modern Iran, which makes the place highly qualified to attract many cultural tourists.

The land of Iran has experienced the flow of many different nations in the form of migration, invasion, and war. Different races and tribes including Turks, Mongols, Afghans, and Arabs have ruled the country, as well as the Persians themselves. The rich secular and religious environment of Iranian/Persian history represents a remarkable sense of tolerance combined with a strong religious life. Persia has been a haven for religious minorities over time and they have been free to practice their religious life in Persia within its confines. Nestorians, for example, who had separated from the main Christian church over doctrinal questions, were allowed to establish their churches in Persia, along with Jewish communities. Buddhism appeared in the eastern lands of the Persian Empire, and through these areas the message of Buddha traveled to China. However, Persian culture has remained dominant in its role of imposing unity upon the variety of ideas, forms, and ideologies entering its borders from the East and the West each time and has succeeded in creating a new and profound Persian identity (Benny and Nasr 1975).

Known as Persia until 1935, Iran has inherited the civilizations that have occupied its land area since 550 BCE, as shown in Figure 1 (Briant 2002).

Figure 1. Map of the Persian Empire 500 BCE
Source: Wikimedia Commons (2010)

Iranian/Persian culture and civilization has strongly contributed to the world's art and civilization over the centuries. The peoples who have lived in Iran are many and diversified, but at the same time have been unified under the Persian language (Farsi) and culture. Over the centuries the land of Iran has experienced many invasions by different people from the West, Middle East, and Central Asia, such as the Greeks accompanying Alexander, the Arabs, the Turks, and the Mongols. However, the conquerors, if they stayed, lived in Iran without bringing about appreciable racial and ethnic transformation. Furthermore, they were assimilated into the composite Iranian/Persian culture. Maintenance of the Persian identity and language over time is the evidence for the proposition that it has been the culture that has unified people in Iran, not ethnic identity (Benny and Nasr 1975). In this context, the culture and civilization of traditional Persia survived until the time of the Sassanids (224–651 CE), the last native Persian rulers. The civilization bequeathed by the Sassanids to later cultures was based on two elements: Zoroastrianism and the ancient culture of the Achaemenids—the culture of *Shah* (the king) and *Shahanshah* (king of kings). This culture provided Iran with a foundation that has survived many identity crises from the Seleucid (330–328 BCE), Parthian (328 BCE–224 CE), and medieval periods to the present, in spite of insecurity, poverty, war, and invasion (Khodadadian 1999).

The spread of Islam into Persia subsequent to the Sassanids was a gradual process that took almost a hundred years. Persia did not convert to Islam because of the fear of the Arab forces, but a profound spiritual need (Iqbal 2003). The new religion enabled Persians to contribute to Islamic civilization as well as to preserve their own cultural identity. For all that the Islamic Iran was not in contrast with the ancient Persian civilization, but rather the combination of Persian culture and Islam has gifted Persia a distinctive identity among the other Islamic Arab countries in the region. In the Islamic period, Persian culture had such a deep influence on the Arabs that it was adopted by the Court of Umayyah and the Abbasids in Baghdad and Damascus (Iqbal 2003).

A number of dynasties ruled Iran/Persia in various forms during the subsequent centuries. Of these, perhaps the most important from the point of view of continuity with the traditional Persia was that of the Safavids (1501–1722 CE), a native dynasty. It was the Safavids who made Iran the spiritual bastion of Shi'ism against orthodox Sunni Islam, and the repository of Persian cultural traditions and self-awareness as part of the Iranian Nation (Hillenbrand 1999) acting as a bridge to modern Persia. The founder of the dynasty, Shah Ismail, adopted the title of *Pādišah-i Irān*

(Persian Emperor) with its implicit notion of an Iranian state stretching from Khorasan as far as the Euphrates, and from the Oxus to the southern Territories of the Persian Gulf. According to Savory:

> In a number of ways the Safavids affected the development of the modern Iranian state: first, they ensured the continuance of various ancient and traditional Persian institutions, and transmitted these in a strengthened, or more 'national', form; second, by imposing Ithna 'Ashari Shi'a Islam on Iran as the official religion of the Safavid state, they enhanced the power of religious officials. The Safavids thus set in train a struggle for power between the urban and the crown, that is to say, between the proponents of secular government and the proponents of a theoretic government; third, they laid the foundation of alliance between the religious classes (Ulama) and the bazaar which played an important role both in the Persian Constitutional Revolution of 1905–1906, and again in the Islamic Revolution of 1979; fourth the policies introduced by Shah Abbas I conduced to a more centralized administrative system (2008:268).

In 1925, Reza Shah overthrew Ahmad Shah Qajar, the last Shah of the Qajar dynasty (1794–1925), and founded the Pahlavi Dynasty. He established an authoritarian government that valued nationalism, secularism, and anticommunism, combined with strict censorship and state propaganda (Zirinsky 1992). Reza Shah introduced many socioeconomic reforms, reorganizing the army, government administration, and finances. To his supporters his reign brought "law and order, discipline, central authority, and modern amenities—schools, trains, buses, radios, cinemas, and telephones" (Abrahamian 2008). However, his attempts of modernization have been criticized for being "too fast" and "superficial," and his reign a time of "oppression, corruption, taxation, and lack of authenticity" with "security typical of police states" (Abrahamian 2008). For many Iranian nationalists, he is considered the father of modern Iran. Under Reza Shah and his son, Iran became a constitutional monarchy for a brief period, though interference from the United Kingdom, the United States, and Russia in furthering their oil and other interests periodically destabilized it. It was during this period that inbound tourism from Europe and the Americas flourished.

Iran's political landscape changed radically in 1979, from a monarchy to an Islamic Republic through the overthrow of the Shah. Although the polity of Iran/Persia has not been separate from its religion throughout history, changing the monarchy or *Shahanshah* to the Islamic Republic was a turning point for the country. For Iran, it was the second time its name was to be changed within 40 years when the term "The Islamic Republic of" was added by the revolutionary regime in 1979 to that of Iran. The first change was in 1935 when Reza Shah requested other countries to use Iran in official matters instead of "Persia." Today, Persia does not exist as a country name, with the relationship between Iran and Persia is very tenuous in the minds of the international community and especially in Japan. The authors' experience when conducting ad hoc interviews with Japanese people at travel agencies in Oita and Tokyo for this discussion revealed that for many Persia is a part of the Arab world and does not have any relationship with modern Iran.

Tourism and Politics in Present-Day Iran

Government involvement is a fact in tourism and the industry cannot survive without it, especially in the modern world. It is generally only governments within the political boundaries of each country who are able to bring the stability, safety, and the legal and financial bases that tourism requires (Elliot 1997). In the case of Iran, external political issues and international relations have been playing a fundamental role in the modern tourism industry since the overthrow of the Shah in 1979. In this regard, the Iran–America conflict, which has also been influencing Iran's international relations, especially with American allies including Japan, is the main issue. In this context the Islamic revolution brought about a fundamental change in its international relations with Europe and America as well as a revolution in ideologies and cultural values inside the country (Mahdavi 2004). In subsequent years, there have been few efforts from the Iran side to introduce and explain the Islamic revolution to the world, and as a result the way that European and American media have been misrepresenting Islamic Iran to the international community has brought an image problem for the country, especially as a destination that has not been countered effectively. It is, however, true that Iran's tourism industry would have experienced turbulent times during the past three decades anyway. The Islamic revolution in 1979, the tragic eight years of war with Iraq (Iraq assisted by the Americans, 1980–1988), wars in Iran's neighboring countries of Kuwait, Afghanistan, and Iraq, and recently the nuclear issue of Iran and the story of the United Nations sanctions which are ongoing, are among the political problems and challenges for the country and its tourism industry. From the time when the Islamic Revolution ended the cozy relations between the United States and the Pahlavi regime, the US government has not hesitated to go to any lengths in order to limit Iran's international relations. This has obviously been negatively effecting Iran's tourism industry as well (Fayazmanesh 2003).

The United States' policy of confrontation is still in effect with many of the Muslim countries of the Middle East and North Africa, including Iran that is waged through sanctions, coups, invasions, bombing and/or sabotage, and the actions of its client states. However, the number of international arrivals in Iran recently has been growing from the Islamic world and other neighboring countries. Iran is finding a new position in the Islamic world. Furthermore, the country has experienced relatively stable relations with Japan and other Asian countries, compared to those with Europe and America in the past two decades, even though Japanese tourists are missing in Iran compared with the years before the Islamic revolution. Finally, it should be understood that the issues discussed in this chapter are selected more in order to provide the reader with a background to the political environment, in which the Iranian tourism industry must perform, than to discuss the political events themselves.

The International Media, the Real Iran, and its Tourism Plan

The real Iran today is different from its image presented in the international media. What Iranians have achieved through the revolution is rarely mentioned. According to the World Bank, Iran has made the greatest progress in eliminating gender disparities in education among countries in the region. An Iranian doctor received the UN Population Award in 2007 for human progress and development and improvement of heath procedures, particularly in respect of adolescent health, reproductive health, and family planning (UN News Center 2007). The number of university students in 2004 was six times more than in 1979. Thousands of scientists, engineers, technicians, administrators, military officers, teachers, civil servants, and doctors have been trained. There are currently 2.2 million college students in Iran. Today, 55 Iranian pharmaceutical companies produce 96% of the medicines on the market in Iran, which allows a national insurance system to reimburse drug expenses without paying exorbitant fees to European and American suppliers (Flounders 2006).

The social situation of women in Iran after the Islamic revolution has also been in focus recently, which has much contributed to the image problem for the country. In this context, there has been a full coverage about implementing the law of Islamic veil by the media, which is compulsory for all women in Iran, including foreigners according to the Islamic Republic Constitution (BBC News 2004; MSNBC 2007). However, it is never mentioned that more than half the university students in Iran are women, or that more than a third of the doctors, 60% of civil servants, and 80% of all teachers are women (Flounders 2006). In addition, while 63,000 of Iran's 66,000 villages in 1979 had no piped water and the country was dependent on importing agricultural products to feed its people, it has been exporting a surplus of wheat from 2007 (Iran News Agency 2007). Although the revolution made all these outcomes possible, the focus of media coverage on Iran is to describe it as a radical religious country in a state of medieval backwardness. This is the way that the country is made to appear to the world and to potential tourists.

In an attempt to counter these problems, Iran has recently developed a National Tourism Plan in order to explain the government's attitude toward tourism, which aspects the country expects to benefit from tourism, and how the country is willing to support the industry and develop it in the face of the pressures outlined above. The first draft of Iran's Tourism Development Master Plan was prepared in 2001. It was formulated under the sponsorship of Iran's Tourism Supreme Council with the support of the UNDP and the UNWTO (ITTO 2001). While to discuss all aspects of this Plan is out of the scope of this chapter, it does provide in summary a window on the attitude of the Iranian government toward the tourism industry. Furthermore, the extent to which Iran's tourism planning will be able to attract overseas tourists to Iranian heritage depends on the plan. The plan itself takes the form of a Master Plan developed a decade after the turbulent times of the 1980s, as a national project. This implies both economic and social stability in the country and the fact that Iran is prepared to host foreign tourists. As a precursor, the infrastructure that was damaged by the Iran–Iraq war in the 1980s was reconstructed in the 1990s and allowed the country to revive its tourism and hospitality industry.

The overall development objectives of the tourism industry are to contribute to the strengthening of Iran's ties with other countries as part of its "dialogue of nations" strategy, to generate much needed employment for the youth and unemployed, to provide economic opportunities in rural areas, to increase the country's foreign exchange earnings, to help to raise the level of social welfare, and, most importantly to ensure that the development of tourism is sustainable from an environmental and socio-cultural point of view (ITTO 2001). To improve Iran's international relations as mentioned above is considered as the first development objective of the tourism industry as a part of the so-called policy of a "dialogue of nations." The dialogue among civilizations, which is called a strategy in Iran's tourism plan, is a theory of international relations proposed by Mohammad Khatami, a former President of Iran. It became famous when the term "the Dialogue among Civilizations" was adopted by United Nations to name the International Year of 2001. However, while stable international relations are considered as a precondition in order that tourism can grow, it is questionable if tourism itself can contribute to the strengthening of Iran's ties with other countries and solve the problems in Iran's international relations given the implacable opposition from the United States to this happening (Flounders 2006).

Studies of the impact of tourism on Iran's economy indicate that its total effects are still relatively modest. For example, the contribution of tourism to GDP and employment was estimated at around 3.3%, to imports about 14%, to government revenue about 0.15%, and to non-oil exports about 14.58% in 2000 (ITTO 2001). These numbers reflect the small scale of the industry, its weak backward and forward linkages with other industries, and a governance structure that is in transition from the public to the private sector. Although data on the concentration of the economic impact of tourism are not available, a review of the concentration of where tourists go in the country suggests that these impacts are highly concentrated in a handful of locations (the cities of Tehran, Isfahan, Yadz, and Mershad). Overall, however, tourism is on a path of positive development even though the industry is facing serious challenges as outlined above. In this context, political stability plays a fundamental role in tourism development. All the attractions in the world will not bring tourists to Iran without political peace.

The tourism plan for Iran examines the current situation of the industry in detail. Through an interdisciplinary approach, its authors reviewed many tourism-related documents, mounted field trips to virtually all parts of Iran to survey and evaluate tourism resources, facilities, services, infrastructure, human resources, and education and training institutions (ITTO 2001). The final outcome of this process was that cultural and heritage tourism is undoubtedly Iran's major potential. The historical monuments, including the world heritage sites from Persia and Islamic Iran, the Silk Road, the diverse ethnic communities and villages, and the rich intangible living culture are seen as Iran's main potentials. In addition to its rich cultural heritage, Iran also possesses a rich and diverse set of natural assets. The range of climates, protected areas and national parks, hot and cold mineral springs, and therapeutic mud are the potential resources for ecotourism in

Iran. However, according to the Tourism Master Plan, the use of sustainable management practices, including effective conservation practices, interpretation, and signage, is limited and overall management capabilities remain weak (Vafadari and Cooper 2007).

The Japanese Market

Japanese overseas travel is considered in Iran's current tourism plan as the largest potential market for the country in Asia. The plan accepts that the negative influence of the Western media coverage of Iran over the past 25 years has impacted to a degree on the consumers of all major markets. However, it is suggested that this impact has not been as damaging in Asia as it has in respect of European and North American markets. The first draft of the tourism plan was prepared in the Khatami administration, and according to its preamble "there is more 'openness' among Asians than Europeans to the reformist changes now underway, particularly in Japan where there is an assiduous appetite both on the part of the travel trade and the traveling public for information on Iran's attractions and facilities" (ITTO 2001). Having said that, it is unfortunate that the current political problems are producing a very different situation.

The marketing strategies that should be implemented in markets like Japan to take advantage of the cultural resources are categorized in the plan. However in the experience of the authors, the Japanese who are supposed to be aware of Iranian tourism marketing activities are not, and this reveals that unlike other countries in the Middle East and Europe, none of the marketing strategies for Japan have actually been implemented (Vafadari and Cooper 2007). Nevertheless, the plan does note a potential for short-term cultural relationships between Japan and Iran and emphasizes concentration on marketing and promotional activities in Japan to take advantage of this. For tourism promotion in the long term, the plan proposes the establishment of a market representation system in Japan, but contains no detailed explanation about the actual system to be made available, nor has any progress been made in implementing such a system since the plan was formalized.

Japan experienced a dramatic increase in the number of Iranians to the country from 1985 to 1992, coincided with the Japanese "Bubble Economy" (Vafadari and Cooper 2008). However, the real situation of Iranians in Japan involved a combination of work and tourism activity. As a result, the many Iranians who overstayed their three-month tourist visas were in fact more interested in seeking work, than in sightseeing in Japan from the start.

Consequently, the accelerating trend of Iranian tourists to Japan in the early 1990s led to a suspension of the visa waiver agreement between the two countries. Unfortunately, the outcome of this change has been a reduction in the likelihood of Japanese traveling to Iran as much as that of Iranians traveling to Japan. Today, more than 15 million Japanese travel overseas and only about 3,000 visit Iran, while the number of Japanese visiting Turkey is about 80,000 (more than 25 times larger than the share of Iran in Japanese overseas travel).

As a result, Iran now has almost no place in the Japanese consciousness as a destination, as the majority of the population has almost no knowledge about the country and its various attractions. More importantly, the absence of a direct source of information from Iran leads to misinformation and even disinformation about Iran from other countries being accepted in Japan. At a minimum, Iran is misclassified with its neighboring Arab nations, especially Iraq. Present-day Iran is not representing its long historical background to offset the negative publicity it receives from European and North American sources, and the idea of traveling to Persia is more to an imaginary than a real destination to be traced on the map. In other words, in the Japanese perception, Iran and Persia are totally different countries and the advantages of Persian unique cultural elements such as Persian carpets, cannot be used in promoting the Iranian tourism industry (Vafadari and Cooper 2007).

The security and safety concerns in the Japanese people's popular image of Iran can be considered as the major problem hindering tourism between the two countries, but this is externally created by a third party. As a part of the region in which the world's most serious conflicts are ongoing, the Iranian tourism industry is suffering from the wars on Iraq and Afghanistan. For the majority of people in Japan, it is not clear whether the wars in Middle East are also inside the borders of Iran, like its neighbors of Afghanistan and Iraq. In this context, Iran's nuclear issue with primarily the United States is an added burden for its tourism industry. In addition, there has been no attempt to provide Japanese people with information on the real situation of Iran for years by the Iranian authorities. In this climate Japan's international tourism market is neglected by the Iranian authorities themselves. While the United States and European media remain the main source of information about Iran, there will be no serious development in tourism relations between Iran and Japan in the short term.

Thus, the road to promote Iranian tourism in Japan is not without serious challenges. Tremendous opportunities also exist. The country has achieved impressive change since the Islamic revolution and Iran has found a good market in Japan for its oil. The fact that Japan is the main customer of Iranian Oil implies that there could be success in reaching Japan's markets in a more general way by Iranians. As a marketing policy, Iranian tourism officials should take advantage of existing business contacts between the two countries to promote Iran both as a safe source of energy for the Japanese economy and as a destination with rich history and culture that can attract Japanese tourists having heritage and cultural interests. However, Iran is not improving tourism relations with Japan using these connections presently, but is also losing its share of Japanese energy supplies under the new political crises framed as Iran's nuclear weapons ambitions.

Within tourism itself, Iran should capitalize on its rich history and tradition in Japan's market. Japanese senior tourists seem not to be worried about the absence of sea, sand, and alcohol in destinations like Iran, as many European tourists are. Therefore, focusing on cultural and heritage tourism in Japan is the key to the promotion of Iran in this market. In fact, the chance to succeed has begun to increase from 2007 at the start of the retirement of a notable number of Japanese baby boomers with interest in heritage tourism. However, only few travel agencies in Japan have experience of tourism business relations with Iran. They specialize in Middle East and Silk Road destinations, among which Iran is highly recommended. Such tour operators agree that Iran has exceptional potential to attract Japanese tourists, which is not yet reached. It is to be concluded that to gain a better share of Japanese market as a Middle Eastern destination, the Iranian tourism industry should take advantage of cooperation with the experienced travel agencies as the cultural brokers in this field.

A personal recommendation is an important factor in triggering a Japanese tourist's decision to visit a destination (Chon, Inagaki and Ohashi 2000). Thus, in order to market Iran tourism in Japan, Japanese tourists should be thought of less as consumers and more as opportunities to spread knowledge, and less as economic opportunities and more as potential cultural ambassadors. In this sense, the time spent by the few current Japanese tourists in Iran should be considered by Iranian tourism policymakers as a training period for these cultural ambassadors. However, the typical Iranian package tour is fully planned for sightseeing, but too isolated to provide a chance for "life-seeing" (personal communication 2008). Although visiting Persian historical sites is the main activity for Japanese tourists, they are also interested in cultural activities through which they can meet local people. Therefore, to prepare opportunities for interested tourists to experience the Iranian lifestyle is the critical challenge for local tour operators in the process of obtaining higher tourist satisfaction in the existing market and in expanding into potential markets.

Finally, the key point in the promotion of Iran as a destination in Japan is to bring more awareness and knowledge about the real Iran to the Japanese population. In this context, public investment is necessary to introduce attractions and to change Japanese people's attitude toward Iran. In this way, even though the current image problem of Iran among the Japanese population is an obvious fact that one cannot expect to be changed quickly, its worst aspect of the Europeans and Americans trading on ignorance can be offset with some effective countervailing efforts.

CONCLUSION

Because tourism and the desire to travel are contingent social behaviors, it is difficult to provide absolutely clear solutions to the difficulties of promoting a certain destination, or developing interest among people to pay a visit to a particular place without complete knowledge of the social situations in question. However, it is possible to help in narrowing the gap between market potential and realities for Iranian inbound tourism given. This chapter has suggested the following conclusions and recommendations.

A lack of attractions, poor tourism infrastructure such as accommodation and transportation, security problems, difficulties in getting visas, and a policy of closed doors might be the reason for some destinations failing in the international travel business, but few of these apply in the case of Iran. Nevertheless, the country has not succeeded in the Japanese market and there would appear to be no desire on the part of Japanese tourists to visit Iran. When Japanese people are asked to explain the reason for their negative attitude toward visiting Iran as a destination, it is likely to be its image as an Islamic Arab country with a social situation back in the medieval ages with respect to religious restrictions on women and civil war, and as a country very far from 21st century civilization, not even related to Persian civilization (Vafadari and Cooper 2007).

This image is something similar to what the Western media represent as Iran, which has roots in the political conflict between Iran and the international community, especially with the United States. So, while the image of Persia, which is the former/second name of Iran is positive generally in Japan, Persia does not represent more than a myth for the Japanese, being thought of as the land of flying carpets or a bazaar, except for those who are interested in world history. The real questions are many. Is it really safe to visit Iran? Does the country have anything to offer as attractions to Japanese and other tourists? The answer to these questions from Japanese sources is perhaps unsurprisingly much more negative compared with the viewpoint of the Arab Muslims of the Middle East, for example. It is also highly dependent on the source of information about Iran available to the majority of potential tourists. In the case of the Middle East, it is true that the whole region is facing an image problem because of the ongoing conflicts in Iraq and Afghanistan, but the image of Iran as a destination is damaged in Japan much more than its neighboring Turkey or Dubai, for example, which are relatively successful in attracting Japanese tourists.

The current image of Iran as a destination in Japan is the result of this market being neglected by Iranian officials for almost three decades, as well as a result of the adverse publicity from American and other sources, in spite of the fact that the Japanese market used to be a main source of tourists to Iran. The loss of that market happened while Iran experienced more stable political relations with Japan than with European countries, The Iranian Embassy in Tokyo did not close because of the change of government and Iran Air flights between Tokyo and Tehran have not been stopped even for a single week. There have been enough opportunities for Iranian officials to provide basic information about the country in Japan in the past 30 years in order not to be mistaken for Iraq. Furthermore, the strong oil business between Iran and Japan provided enough room for the Iranian government to undertake cultural marketing if it had desired during the past decades.

The problem of promoting Iran in the Japanese and other markets thus not only goes back to the political issues and its international relations, but is also related to the desire to accept foreign tourists, including Japanese. It took years for the Iranian government to rethink the policy of "Neither East, Nor West" that was one of the strongest slogans of the Islamic revolution (Vafadari and Cooper 2007). International tourists (or at least foreign cultural tourists) are not regarded anymore as the representatives of cultures that may destroy the values of the Islamic revolution, as was the case during the 1980s. However, the cost that Iranian society has paid to learn how to change attitudes toward foreign tourists is the loss of Iran's share of international travel, among which the Japanese market is no exception. Today, the Iranian population, which is more than double that when the Islamic revolution took place, is willing to host international tourists. The government is also looking for foreign tourists to provide jobs for the young generation. The fact that both Iranian people and the government are culturally prepared to value the benefits of tourism, instead of relying on oil revenue, can be seen in the new tourism promotion policy. The exhibition "Glory of Persia" in the major cities of Japan in 2007, for example, was a symbolic action of the new policy and resulted in a 20%

increase in the total number of Japanese tourists to Iran in the first half of 2007, compared with the previous year.

The demand for learning about other countries and cultures is high in Japanese society. The authors' experiences of living and conducting research in Japan have proved the demand for learning about Iranian culture among the Japanese people in different groups, from high school students to retired people. However, in meeting with a group of Japanese, it is enough to surprise almost every one of them by saying that Iranian people do not speak Arabic, they grow rice, and polygamy is not culturally accepted, because they generally hold a totally different image of Iran as a nation and a destination. So, while the rich culture and long history of Iran might increase the possibility of success in promoting its cultural tourism in the Japanese market, it is currently not able to be effectively used.

In order to get around the problem of ignorance and the distortions of reality fostered by European and North American media, the remains of Persian art and architecture that are still flourishing in other countries like India, Uzbekistan, and Egypt might be used as proxies to attract Japanese and other foreigners by advertising their intimate connection with Iranian culture and civilization. Visiting the Islamic section in the Louvre museum in Paris, where more than 50% of items are from Iran, has also triggered the decision for some Japanese tourists to visit Iran according to Iranian tour operators. In this way, people who have visited the cultural borders of the ancient Persian Empire, which are much wider than the land of modern Iran, may be more willing to visit the core landscape of Persian civilization later. New marketing opportunities are also provided from 2007 on in Japan and other countries with the retirement of a high number of the baby boomer generation.

Nevertheless, an effective tourism promotion plan to target the Japanese and other overseas markets must be realistic and patient enough not to expect a big change in the number of actual tourists in a short period of time. The long period that most countries have been neglected by Iranian tourism officials, coupled with the negative publicity the modern state receives, must be considered in order to understand the level of unfamiliarity that exists about Iran among most markets. However, a change in the political environment of Iran, especially in Iran–America relations, could bring about a completely different situation.

Chapter 12

IMPACTS OF SEPTEMBER 11
A Two-Sided Neighborhood Effect?

Christian Steiner

Johannes Gutenberg University, Germany

Abridgement: After the September 11 event in the United States, some Muslim destinations faced a severe decline in tourist arrivals because of the so-called neighborhood effect. Concurrently, other destinations performed extremely well. This chapter addresses the question of how the emergence of inconsistent tourism patterns within the same region can be explained. The analysis demonstrates that whereas arrivals from the Western countries decreased, intraregional tourism boomed and Muslim tourists avoided traveling to the Western destinations. This regionalization of travel behavior is explained by the rise of confrontational geopolitical world pictures in the Western and the Muslim worlds. This has created a new two-sided neighborhood effect, which has stabilized destinations in the Muslim world with a strong intraregional orientation.
Keywords: crisis; neighborhood effect; September 11; violent political unrest; Muslim world

INTRODUCTION

Following the 11 September 2001 events (hereafter 9/11), commentators declared that the world had changed. Although this assumption could be questioned in general, the attacks themselves, the ensuing wave of Islamist terrorism that was propagated by Al-Qa'ida, and the "War on Terror" have undoubtedly impacted world tourism. Recurring terrorism-induced security

Tourism in the Muslim World
Bridging Tourism Theory and Practice, Volume 2, 181–204
Copyright © 2010 by Emerald Group Publishing Limited
ISSN: 2042-1443/doi:10.1108/S2042-1443(2010)0000002015

crises have disrupted global travel and mobility seriously in the beginning of the new millennium. This disruption was evident both on the global stage and in Muslim countries where it became a particular problem.

Although the impact of violent political unrest on international tourism is a well-known phenomenon (Brunt and Cousins 2000; Enders, Sandler and Parise 1992; Sonmez 1998), the magnitude of the repercussions following 9/11 was extraordinary. According to the UN World Tourism Organization (UNWTO), global tourist arrivals decreased in 2001 by 0.6% (UNWTO 2002b) because of an increased fear of traveling, and heightened air traffic and travel restrictions (UNWTO 2001b). Although this decrease may not seem significant at the first glance, it is unique in that it represents only the second decline in international arrivals since 1982 (UNWTO 2002b). In addition, because the attacks occurred late in 2001, their negative effects were spread over the 2001 and 2002 calendar years and are not adequately captured by annual statistics.

Nevertheless, the effects of 9/11 and the following events were tremendous. In October 2001 alone, the globally flown passenger kilometers declined by 23%, according to the International Air Transport Association (IATA 2007). The American Office of Travel and Tourism Industries recorded a 33% decrease in international arrivals in the United States in September 2001 compared to the same period in the previous year; the decrease was 39% in October, 35% in November, and 26% in December 2001 (OTTI 2007).

In addition to the US-related inbound and outbound tourism markets, long-haul travel and Muslim destinations also suffered from the crisis. The destinations in the Muslim world, particularly the well-established destinations in the Middle East, were staring into the abyss (UNWTO 2002b). Remarkably, Muslim destinations were even more affected by the terrorist attacks of 9/11 than the United States itself. The Middle East saw a 30% decline in international arrivals, whereas North America experienced a 27% loss from September until December 2001 (UNWTO 2002b). Obviously, the terrorist attacks have been attributed to the Muslim world in general and to the Arab world in particular, which has caused declines in arrivals at destinations that are more than 10,000 km away from the places of aggression. This redistribution of traffic flows following 9/11 can be explained by the so-called "neighborhood effect" (Hollier 1991). This well-studied phenomenon describes the decline of arrivals in destinations that are perceived to be "neighboring" places where security problems occur.

Given these circumstances, it is astonishing that not all Muslim destinations did experience a decrease in tourism. Whereas some such as

Egypt, Morocco, Indonesia, and Tunisia faced severe crises with substantial declines in arrivals between 2000 and 2002, the tourism in other destinations in the region such as Turkey, Lebanon, Jordan, Syria, the United Arab Emirates, and Malaysia was booming (UNWTO 2007b). Thus, it is apparent that the neighborhood effect is not identifiable in all Muslim countries. This diagnosis inspires the question of how can one explain the varying emergence of neighborhood effects and the varying development paths of different destinations in the Muslim world after 9/11?

In addressing this question, this chapter aims to contribute to the body of theoretical knowledge by explaining the varying emergence of neighborhood effects. It compares various Muslim destinations, analyzes the quantitative changes in the structures of inbound and outbound flows from a cultural geographic perspective, and evaluates whether 9/11 caused a long-lasting tourism crisis or was just a short-lived hiccup within an ongoing story of success and long-term growth.

This analysis demonstrates that the neighborhood effect is not measurable in the group of intraregional Muslim tourists. Therefore, destinations with a significant share of intraregional travel did not suffer as much under the effects of 9/11 as those with a strong focus on the Western industrialized markets did. On the contrary, the changing patterns in travel behavior of Muslim tourists, which was partially driven by the rise of confrontational geopolitical world pictures in the Western industrialized and the Muslim worlds that resulted in an increasing regionalization of tourism demand, caused intraregional traffic to boom.

The conclusions presented in this chapter result from the interpretation of an empirical, descriptive analysis of statistical data, which were gathered from various international and national organizations and institutions. The statistical analysis focuses on the top 10 Muslim tourist destinations. Furthermore, because these 10 sites account for 81% of all international tourist arrivals in the Muslim world (UNWTO 2007a; author's calculation), they offer a good overview of developments in the region. The resulting picture is complemented by personal research experience in numerous Arab and Asian countries. Insights into the intraindustrial perspective were derived from interviews with regional representatives of the leading international hotel chains in the Middle East and North Africa, which are predominantly based in Tunisia, Egypt, and the United Arab Emirates. In addition to the interviews, conversations were recorded with representatives of tourism-related governmental organizations between 2003 and 2005.

The findings are interpreted according to a "postdisciplinary perspective" (Coles, Hall, and Duval 2006) that merge various theoretical approaches.

The perspective of a tourism study regarding (a) the impact of insecurity on travel behavior in general and (b) on the occurrence of neighborhood effects in particular is combined with the perspective of a cultural geographical study regarding (c) the way people construct their everyday geographies and (d) the impact of these geographical world views on their behavior. Moreover, these perspectives are embedded (e) within the framework of a specific regional studies focus. The goal is to develop an empirically informed in-depth understanding of contextualized motives and patterns of individual behavior (Stake 1995). Therefore, the presented results are focused on demonstrating *how* (potential) tourists reacted to 9/11 by analyzing quantitative data and also on interpretatively explaining from a social and cultural science perspective *why* they behaved in a given situation in a particular way.

POLITICAL UNREST AND CONFRONTATIONAL WORLDVIEWS

Most scholars agree that peace, security, and stability are necessary prerequisites for the development of tourism (Cavlek 2002; Hall 1994; Santana 2001). Indeed, it is commonly accepted that violent political unrest such as interstate wars, civil wars, terrorism, and crime has a particularly negative effect on tourism demand. Many studies have explored this relationship (Brunt and Cousins 2000; Cavlek 2002; Enders and Sandler 1991; Enders et al 1992; Hall and O'Sullivan 1996; Pizam and Fleischer 2002; Richter and Waugh 1986; Sonmez 1998; Sönmez, Apostopoulos and Tarlow 1999; Sönmez and Graefe 1998). Case studies in the Muslim world and especially in the Middle East have made important contributions to this field of knowledge (Al-Hamarneh and Steiner 2004; Aziz 1995; Bar-On 1996; Hollier 1991; Issa and Altinay 2006; Meyer 1996; Steiner 2007, 2009a; Wahab 1996).

Indeed, tourism is vulnerable to violent political unrest because of the nature of the product. Unlike the manufacturing sector, tourism is often directly hit by violence and serves as a strategic target for terrorists (Poirier 1997). In addition, it offers services that can only be consumed on site. Security is therefore of "special consequence to tourism because of what is being sold: serenity, leisure, fun, and comfort. These can only be marketed under stable conditions" (Richter 1994:227).

The literature also demonstrates that tourists are very sensitive to any kind of violent political unrest and change their vacation destinations very quickly (Brunt and Cousins 2000; Sönmez and Graefe 1998). The considerable fluctuation in the number of tourist arrivals in most Muslim countries during the last few decades can be traced to security-related problems. Muslim destinations extensively depend on the generating markets of the Western industrialized world whose tourists seem to be particularly sensitive to violent political unrest (Steiner 2009a). Furthermore, Hollier (1991) demonstrates that it is not important whether any kind of violent political unrest takes place in a particular country itself or in a different country in the region. According to his findings, security problems in the Persian Gulf have led to decreasing tourist arrivals in North Africa. In this regard, the study indicates that many tourists seem to perceive the Muslim world in general and the Arab world in particular as a homogeneous area, and that they associate a perception of negative risk in one destination with an entire region (Santana 2001:226). Consequently, tourists refrain from traveling to these countries. In reference to these findings, Santana (2001:225) concludes that travel decisions are not based on any kind of objective risk assessment, but on the individual's level of perceived safety. The result is often a disastrous decrease in tourist numbers, even in countries that are not directly hit by a crisis situation, hence the "neighborhood effect" (Hollier 1991).

Whereas the quantitative occurrence of this effect has been documented in several studies (Bar-On 1996; Brunt and Cousins 2000; Enders et al 1992; Hollier 1991; Sönmez and Graefe 1998), its explanations remain rare. Moreover, none of the studies analyze disaggregated data. Therefore, neither the variations in the behavior and reactions of different tourist groups on security problems nor an interpretative explanation for the occurrence of potential differences are discussed in-depth in the existing literature. However, a very interesting explanation for the general emergence of the neighborhood effect is presented by Weimann and Winn (1994) and Sonmez (1998). They suggest that its occurrence is highly dependent upon the extent and duration of the media representation of a given incident of violent political unrest, because potential tourists depend heavily on the information, interpretations, and images about a particular destination that are provided by the media.

Although it appears nearly impossible to empirically and exactly assess the role of the media in the emergence of neighborhood effects because of methodological problems, its influence on travel decisions is undoubted. Rojek (2000:53) explains that mediatized destination images are important because of the distance of tourism sites from one's home; travel to the site "invokes the unfamiliar," which is nothing less than a kind of uncertainty. This uncertainty about what will be found at a site invites speculation and information; images, tales, symbols, myths, and fantasies about the site merge into these speculations. Referring to Dewey's work (2001, 2002), one could say that by internalizing mediatized images and information people try to eliminate uncertainty to be able to (re-)act in a given situation. Within this process, global mass media is increasingly influential, and it serves as a central means of mass communication to provide the information and interpretations needed by an individual (Rojek and Urry 2000). Therefore, media can play an important role in shaping one's images and risk perceptions of a given destination (Santana 2001; Taylor 2006) and in influencing travel decisions (Um and Crompton 1992).

The result of this process is a generalized image of the unfamiliar "other" and an individual landscape of travel risk that is sculpted by media information, cultural interpretation schemes, and personal experience. This internal landscape, like any other part of one's individual reality construction, is socially produced and reproduced in a circular process of communication and internalization (Berger and Luckmann 1966). This creative process can be conceptualized as an infinite form of bargaining about the objectivity of one's own constructions, which are then corroborated or challenged by others. This natural characteristic of the perception of the world one lives in is the reason that images of spaces and places are constantly on the move.

Therefore, these internal landscapes—or geographies—of our everyday lives are both permanently (re)produced by actions of people and also serve themselves as a basis and orientation for individual action (Werlen 1993, 2009). This fundamental reciprocal relationship among society, action, and space explains from a theoretical, cultural, and geographical perspective why destination images influence the behavior of potential tourists.

Tourism in the Muslim World

Regardless of economic and political turmoil, world tourism has been one of the most robust economic sectors in the last 20 years. According to the UNWTO, international arrivals more than doubled from 286 million to 699 million between 1980 and 2000 (United Nation World Tourism Organization (UNWTO) 2006b, 2006c). In the same period, international tourism receipts increased nearly fivefold from US$104 billion to $482 billion (UNWTO 2006c). Tourism development in the Muslim world made a significant contribution to this success story. Growth rates in this area consistently exceeded the world average, and member states of the Organization of the Islamic Conference (OIC) increased their world market share of international arrivals from 7.8% in 1990 to 13% in 2005. In 2005, the OIC states welcomed 103.9 million tourists who generated more than $70 billion in receipts (OIC 2008a:8). Even though these results are worth recognizing, the benefits of tourism development are not equally distributed. The top 10 Muslim tourism markets accounted for more than 81% of all international arrivals in the OIC countries in 2005 (UNWTO 2007a; author's calculation). The largest market by far is Turkey, where more than 20 million international tourists arrived in 2005, followed by Malaysia, Egypt, Saudi Arabia, United Arab Emirates, Tunisia, Morocco, Indonesia, Bahrain, and Syria (OIC 2008a:76, 82; own calculation) (Figure 1).

When those 10 countries are considered, the highly globalized character of the tourism industry in the Muslim world becomes obvious. Whereas Saudi Arabia, Bahrain, and Syria represent classic examples of pilgrimage-related and intraregional tourism, in general intraregional tourist activities are limited in the top 10 nations. Tourists from other Muslim countries are usually only a minority of all arrivals. The main Mediterranean destinations such as Morocco, Tunisia, Egypt, and Turkey are particularly dependent on tourists from the Western industrialized countries.

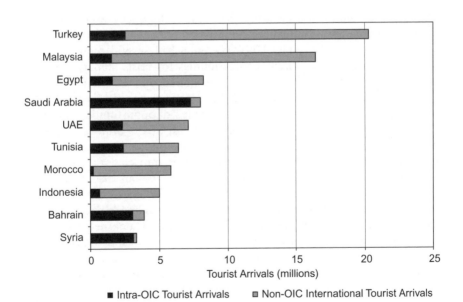

Figure 1. Top 10 International Tourism Markets in the Muslim World (2005)
Source: OIC (2008a:76,82)

The British Department for International Development (DFID 1999) states that tourism significantly contributes to a national economy when the income from it equals more than 5% of all exports or more than 2% of the GDP. Using these criteria, tourism is a strategically important sector for more than 60% of the OIC member states for whom data is available (OIC 2008a:81). Of the top 10 markets in the Muslim world, only Saudi Arabia and the United Arab Emirates, which are large, oil-exporting countries, do not meet these criteria. The major oil producer in the latter country is Abu Dhabi. However, an analysis of the national economy of Dubai, which is its major destination, reveals that tourism contributes directly to 14% of its GDP (Government of the UAE 2004). This means that out of the top 10 Muslim destinations, tourism is not a significant and strategic economic sector only in Saudi Arabia. Under these circumstances—the high economic significance of tourism and the strong dependence on extraregional volatile tourist inflows—the national economies of most Muslim countries are quite vulnerable to disturbances in the tourism sector.

Effects of 9/11 on Tourism in the Muslim World

Although the terrorist attacks of 9/11 and subsequent events severely impacted international tourism, research-based publications thematizing the effects are quite limited. The UNWTO published several reports on the immediate situation and discussed possibilities for crisis management and recovery (2001, 2002a). Hall (2002), Kagelmann and Rösch (2002), and Ulmann (2002) tackled the impact of the attacks on tourism in the United States, while Fall and Massey (2005) analyzed opportunities for crisis communication and marketing in the aftermath of the attacks. Edmonds and Mak (2006) analyzed the effects of 9/11 on tourism in the Asia-Pacific area, and Anderson (2006) investigated how it impacted the Australian tourism industry. Although Edmonds and Mak (2006) also focused on Malaysia, and Henderson (2003) and Putra and Hitchcock (2006) examined the impact of the Bali bombings, research in the Arab and Muslim worlds is very limited. Seminal work has been completed by Al-Hamarneh and Steiner (2004), who discuss the impact of 9/11 on the Arab world in the context of a shift toward a new trend of Islamic tourism and a strengthening of intra-Arab travel. In addition, Steiner (2007, 2009a, 2010) examines how the transnational hotel industry in the Arab world has responded to the events following 9/11; these works examine the organizational learning processes within the industry and the effects of the attacks on tourism-related foreign direct investment in the region.

Nevertheless, none of the existing studies comprehensively assess the impact of 9/11 on tourism flows and structures in the Muslim world. This fact is even more astonishing, considering the increased attention to Islamic area studies in the United States and Western Europe after the 2001 attacks. Building on the work of Al-Hamarneh and Steiner, this chapter broadens the focus from Arab to Muslim destinations and provides a more comprehensive overview of the impacts of 9/11 on inbound and outbound tourism to and from the Muslim world. Toward that end, the chapter aims to contribute to the theoretical state of knowledge by explaining the varying emergence of neighborhood effects within the region.

Perhaps surprisingly, Muslim destinations have been more affected by the terrorist attacks in New York and Washington DC than the United States itself. While North America confronted a 27% decline in international tourist arrivals from September until December 2001 (Figure 2), the loss of the Middle East was 30% (UNWTO 2002a:15). Egypt has been the most affected destination around the world. Arrivals declined by more than 55% in October 2001 (UNWTO 2002b). However, Muslim destinations in Asia also suffered as a result of 9/11. According to the country's Ministry of

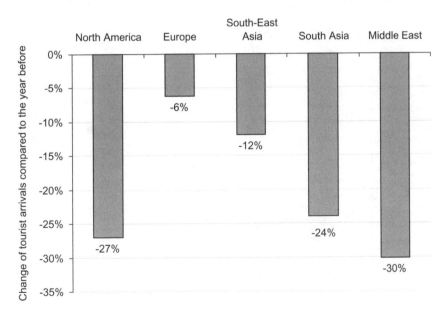

Figure 2. Decline of International Tourist Arrivals by Region (Sep.–Dec. 2001)
Source: UNWTO (2002a:15)

Culture and Tourism, Indonesia faced a 13% drop in international arrivals in October 2001 alone (MCT 2005).

Obviously, the terrorist attacks have been attributed to the Muslim world in general and to the Arab world in particular, and this has caused a neighborhood effect more than 10,000 km away from the places of aggression. Indeed, Arab and Muslim destinations suffer from being perceived as close to the conflict (2001) and that the "redistribution of traffic flows post September 11th has been partially driven by ignorant cultural stereotypes" (UNWTO 2002a:8). Tourists from Western Europe avoided traveling to the United States and to the Muslim world, and instead chose domestic holidays or destinations in their close neighborhoods, which were perceived to be safer (Frangialli 2002; UNWTO 2002a) (Figure 3).

Given these circumstances, it is astonishing that only 14 of the 50 member states of the OIC faced a decline in arrivals in 2002 compared to the precrisis year 2000 (OIC 2008a). More specifically, only 2 of the top 10 Muslim destinations, Egypt and Indonesia, faced tourism decreases between 2000 and 2002, and Tunisia's development stagnated after a long period of constant growth. However, official data on tourists visiting Morocco is a bit misleading because it includes the arrivals of nationals residing abroad.

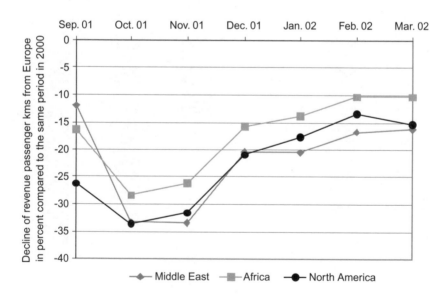

Figure 3. European Outbound Tourism by Destination Region (Sep. 2001–Mar. 2002)
Source: UNWTO (2002a)

Table 1. Top International Muslim Tourism Destinations in Millions (2000–2005)

	2000	2001	2002	2003	2004	2005
Turkey	9.586	10.783	12.790	13.341	16.826	20.273
Malaysia	10.222	12.775	13.292	10.577	15.703	16.431
Egypt	5.116	4.357	4.906	5.746	7.795	8.244
Saudi Arabia	6.585	6.727	7.511	7.332	8.599	8.037
UAE	3.907	4.134	5.445	5.871	6.195	7.126
Tunisia	5.058	5.387	5.064	5.114	5.998	6.378
Morocco	4.278	4.380	4.453	4.761	5.477	5.843
Morocco without nationals residing abroad	2.325	2.249	2.222	2.223	2.707	3.055
Indonesia	5.064	5.153	5.033	4.467	5.321	5.002
Bahrain	2.420	2.789	3.167	2.955	3.514	3.914
Syria	1.416	1.801	2.186	2.085	3.033	3.368

Source: OIC (2008a) and UNWTO (2007); own calculation

If these nationals are subtracted from the official data, it is obvious that Morocco was also seriously suffering (OIC 2008a; UNWTO 2007b; own calculation) (Table 1). It received 40% fewer Americans, 25% fewer Italians, 19% fewer British, and 17% fewer Germans (Al-Hamarneh and Steiner 2004). It was only spared from being hit harder because of a stable number of tourists from France. Many French citizens visiting Morocco are of Maghreb descent, and their plans to visit friends and relatives are not as strongly affected by other events.

Whereas the above-mentioned destinations experienced a crisis, other Muslim destinations such as Turkey, Lebanon, Jordan, Syria, the United Arab Emirates, and Malaysia were booming (UNWTO 2007a). The Emirates reported a 43% increase in arrivals between 2000 and 2002. In the same time period, Syria reported a 42% increase, Malaysia 30%, Bahrain 25%, and Saudi Arabia 14% (UNWTO 2007; author's calculation).

Unfortunately, global security did not improve in the following years. The violent incidents in the aftermath of 9/11, which ranged from the wars and the occupation of Afghanistan and Iraq to the recurring Islamist terrorist attacks against tourists, citizens, and institutions of the Western industrialized countries (FAZ 2005; Spiegel Online 2006a, 2006b; SZ 2005) (Table 2), repeatedly and negatively impacted tourism in the Muslim world (Al-Hamarneh and Steiner 2004; Henderson 2003; Putra and Hitchcock 2006; Steiner 2009a).

Table 2. Terrorist Attacks Targeting Western Citizens and Institutions[a,b]

Date	Place[c]	Target	No. of Victims	
			Dead	Injured
11.09.01	New York & Washington (USA)	World Trade Centre, Pentagon	~3000	n.s.
11.04.02	Djerba (TN)	Synagogue	21	n.s.
08.05.02	Karachi (PK)	Hotel	14	23
14.06.02	Karachi (PK)	US-Consulate	12	50
12.10.02	Bali (ID)	Clubs, bars, restaurants	202	303
28.11.02	Mombasa (KE)	Hotel with predominant Israeli customers	18	n.s.
12.05.03	Riyadh (SA)	Gated communities of Western expatriates	35	194
16.05.03	Casablanca (M)	Western and Jewish institutions	45	>100
05.08.03	Jakarta (ID)	Marriott Hotel	12	149
08.11.03	Riyadh (SA)	Gated communities of Western expatriates	10	100
16.11.03	Istanbul (TR)	Two synagogues	24	300
20.11.03	Istanbul (TR)	British Consulate	25	390
11.03.04	Madrid (ESP)	Trains	191	n.s.
20.04.04	Riyadh (SA)	Gated communities of Western expatriates	17	100
01.05.04	Janbu (SA)	Harbour	25	n.s.
29.05.04	El Khobar (SA)	Gated communities of Western expatriates	22	n.s.
07.10.04	Taba, Ras Sheitan, Nuweiba (EG)	Hotels & camps with predominant Israeli customers	34	105
07.04.05	Cairo (EG)	Suq	3	n.s.
30.05.05	Cairo (EG)	Egyptian museum	0	9
30.05.05	Cairo (EG)	Tourist bus	0	0
07.07.05	London (GB)	Public transport	56	700
16.07.05	Izmir (TR)[d]	Minibus	5	14
23.07.05	Sharm el-Sheikh (EG)	Hotels, minibus-terminal, village center	88	200
09.11.05	Amman (JO)	Three hotels	58	n.s.
24.04.06	Dahab (EG)	Restaurants, supermarket	22	150

[a]FAZ (2005), Spiegel Online (2006a; 2006b), SZ (2005).

[b]Terrorist attacks in Israel/Palestine, Iraq, and Afghanistan have not been included due to the local occupation and (civil) war situation, respectively. The same applies to terrorist attacks in Russia and Chechnya, the kidnapping of 14 Sahara tourists in Algeria, and the recurring kidnapping incidents in Yemen, which are usually not Islamist motivated.

[c]ESP, Spain; ID, Indonesia; JO, Jordan; KE, Kenya; M, Morocco; PK, Pakistan; SA, Saudi Arabia; TN, Tunisia; TR, Turkey; EG, Egypt.

[d]It remains unclear whether this attack has to be attributed to Al-Qa'ida, to the Kurdish PKK, or to a Turkish-nationalist conspiracy group.

Monthly data on tourist arrivals in Egypt, Tunisia, and Dubai clearly (DTCM 2004; MoT div. years; ONTT div. years) show the negative impact of all kinds of violent political unrest associated with the region (Figure 4) and suggest that both "winner" and "loser" destinations were affected. The figures also demonstrate that not only do incidents of violent political unrest repeatedly devastate tourist demand within the region, but also that this influence can be traced back to the neighborhood effects.

However, it is quite surprising that despite the violence following 9/11, SARS, the avian flu, and the economic problems, nearly all Muslim destinations managed to recover and grow again by 2005 (UNWTO 2007). Considering these findings, one has to conclude that 9/11 did not cause a long-term crisis in the tourism industry of the Muslim world. However, the large variations of observations are remarkable and raise the question of how we can explain the varying development paths of different destinations.

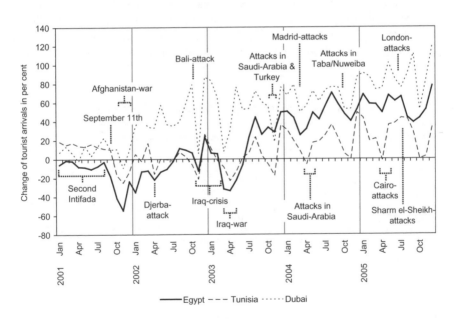

Figure 4. Tourist Arrivals in Egypt, Tunisia, and Dubai (2001–2005). Percentage Change in Comparison to the Year 2000 (DTCM 2004; MoT div. years; ONTT div. years)

Explaining Different Market Performances

The divergent effects of 9/11 result from the country-specific characteristics of Muslim destinations. The various sites have different means of generating tourist markets and offer different key activities (leisure, cultural, pilgrimage/religious, medical, shopping tourism, etc.). Four main aspects of the various tourism structures can be identified (Al-Hamarneh and Steiner 2004). These are Western-oriented leisure and cultural tourism (such as Morocco, Tunisia), intraregional-oriented leisure tourism (Bahrain), multiethnic-oriented mixed-character tourism (Egypt, United Arab Emirates, Indonesia, Malaysia), and multiethnic-oriented cultural and pilgrim tourism (Saudi Arabia, Syria).

After 9/11, the biggest losers were those countries with a narrow orientation toward the Western generating markets (UNWTO 2007a; own calculation). Morocco is a prominent example of such a destination. In this country, 88% of all tourists come from the Western industrialized countries (Table 3). It suffered extraordinarily from travel reluctance in the Western world in general and in Europe in particular. The conflict between Morocco and Spain concerning the sovereignty of the Island of Laila in July 2002 complicated this situation even further. Egypt, one of the main Western European leisure destinations, also suffered from a decrease from its traditional Western European markets.

Table 3. Market Share of Main Generating Markets (2000)

Destination	Generating Market	
	Western Industrialized Countries (%)	Muslim Countries (%)
Turkey	66	8
Malaysia	10	8
Egypt	73	19
Saudi Arabia	3	85
UAE	31	44
Tunisia	68	27
Morocco	88	6
Indonesia	33	9
Bahrain	9	82
Syria	13	81

Source: UNWTO (2007a)

Other destinations, such as Tunisia and Indonesia, faced similar problems but were further hit by local terrorist attacks in Djerba in April 2002 and in Bali in October 2002. The connection of Al-Qa'ida to the attacks in both countries figured prominently in the Western mass media, which damaged each country's destination image and devastated tourism development. According to the Tunisian Tourist Office, the overall number of arrivals in Tunisia immediately declined by 26% after the attack in April and did not fully recover until December 2002 (ONTT, different years). In the case of Bali, the island's most important generating market, Australia, collapsed. Following these attacks, 57% fewer Australian tourists traveled to the island over the next six months (UNWTO 2006a).

Additionally, those destinations that did not depend (solely) on Western markets performed far better. In the United Arab Emirates, Syria, Malaysia, and Bahrain, intraregional tourism boomed. Therefore, a neighborhood effect is statistically not measurable for the group of Muslim tourists (UNWTO 2007a; author's calculation), which is probably because they have better knowledge of the region. Taking these findings into consideration, it is reasonable to assume that the reality construction and risk perception of Muslim tourists seem to differ from those of potential tourists from markets outside the region. Therefore, it is logical to conclude that the occurrence of a neighborhood effect does not refer to physical space, but rather to social distance and proximity.

Dubai, for instance, became increasingly popular for short-term intra-regional holidays with citizens of the Persian Gulf countries, including Iran. The combination of shopping, leisure, entertainment, sports, and cultural attractions in a comparatively liberal environment serves an increasing demand within the region. In comparison, Syria's growth was not only fed by an increasing demand for leisure-oriented holidays in Damascus, but also fed by an increasing number of Shi'ite pilgrims visiting the country's holy sites. Bahrain succeeded in developing itself as one of the most popular weekend and short-term destinations for Saudis. In addition, Turkey and Malaysia benefited from an increase in Muslim travel. Both countries implemented an aggressive marketing strategy to attract more Muslim tourists. While Turkey successfully attracted tourists from Saudi Arabia, Egypt, and Jordan, Malaysia succeeded in convincing 11% more Gulf-Arabs to spend their holidays in the country (Al-Hamarneh and Steiner 2004). This boom of intra-Muslim travel resulted in part from the feeling of many Muslims as being misunderstood and unwelcome in the Western world immediately after 9/11 (Al-Tayar 2002). New visa restrictions and xenophobic outbreaks in the United States, Australia, and Europe forced many Muslims to change their traditional holiday destination plans and travel to destinations in the Muslim world instead (Al-Hamarneh and Steiner 2004).

As a result, 9 of the top 10 Muslim destinations saw an increase in intra-Muslim arrivals between 2000 and 2002. Meanwhile, only four of them also saw an increase in tourists from Western industrialized countries (UNWTO 2007a; own calculation). In addition, only the United Arab Emirates and Bahrain managed to achieve higher growth rates in their Western markets than in their Muslim markets (Figure 5). Because the market share of the Western tourists in both countries is quite limited, compared to North African destinations, this circumstance is not surprising. Furthermore, the development of the Emirates market is largely driven by the rapidly growing Emirates Airlines. In addition, guests who are traveling from Europe to Asia or Bahrain stopover in Dubai. Bahrain also benefited from the Iraqi crisis, which brought large numbers of journalists, media, and civil security personal to Bahrain, where the regional headquarters of the American military were based.

In summary, the neighborhood effect that played a role in the Western industrialized countries did not as strongly affect Muslim markets. Based on

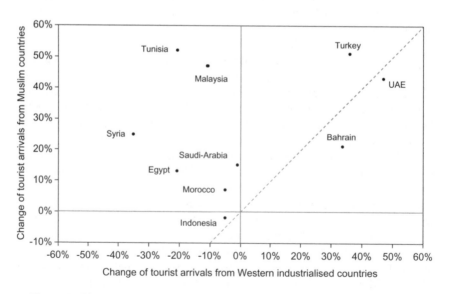

Figure 5. Changes in Tourist Flows in the Top 10 OIC Markets (2000–2002)
Source: UNWTO (2007a)

the above theoretical assumption that actions reflect the reality construction and everyday geographies of people, it is therefore logical to suggest that Arab and Western perceptions of the regional security situation are fundamentally different and that the destination images in both worlds are greatly diverging.

The Rise of Confrontational Geopolitical World Images

Indeed, the polarization between the behavior of tourists from the Muslim and the Western worlds is quite remarkable. The variety of behaviors in the context of the neighborhood effect indicates that the social distance between potential tourists in the Western world and the societies in Muslim host countries has increased. But how can this be explained?

One possible answer is to be found in the changing narratives of the world order after 9/11. McAlister (2005:267) noted that "as a result of September 11 (...), previous constructions of national and transnational identities have been both reaffirmed and revised" and that "the Middle East as a moral geography and a variety of religious beliefs" continued to play a significant role in the identity of societies in the Western industrialized countries in general and in the United States in particular.

Indeed, many geopolitical, generalizing, and confrontational world views that were thought to be obsolete experienced an unexpected renaissance, gained more publicity after 9/11, and became very influential in the way the media and the public interpreted the geopolitical order of the new millennium.

In particular, Huntington's (1993) theory of a "clash of civilizations" was frequently cited by commentators and the media (McAlister 2005), even though it had been intensively debated and rejected by the majority of the academic community in the 1990s. Huntington argues that after the Cold War, conflicts would take place at the borders of allegedly homogeneous cultural spaces and civilizations. This theory is built on an essentialized notion of culture. It operates with quasi-homogeneous and geopolitically motivated abstractions of space (Wolkersdorfer 2006) that can be understood as a "geographical imagination" (Gregory 1998). These abstractions of space replace the analysis of a complex social situation with simple geographical metaphors. Importantly, these geographical imaginations are very influential. As spacialized naturalizations of complex social circumstances, they provide an orientation that unconsciously controls patterns of behavior (Hard 2002; Steiner 2009a). As individuals internalize these socially produced, generalized and confrontational geographical imaginations (Werlen 1993, 2009), they logically refrain from traveling to these places.

However, Huntington's theory is not the only one that became popular after 9/11. Ironically, it is mirrored by the Islamist perspective of Al-Qa'ida (Steinberg 2002). The Al-Qa'ida Islamist and Huntington both need the "other" for the antagonistic reassurance of their own identity. As a result, both perspectives corroborate and reaffirm those long-established essentializations of the respective "other" that are described by the concepts of Orientalism (Said 1978) and Occidentalism (Buruma and Margalit 2004). In this respect, it is highly problematic to operate with terms such as "Muslim world" or "Western industrialized world," because their usage is already incorporating the danger of reaffirming the described differentiation between "the West" and "the Orient." However, because of the purpose of this chapter, it is not possible to avoid such terms. Avoiding them would ironically imply silence—as language is itself the means of thinking (Wittgenstein 1971). Therefore, it is important to emphasize that these terms are simply used here to denote countries belonging to different world regions. They are not meant to refer to some kind of essentialist culturalism.

In addition, an antagonistic, religious interpretation of the conflict became very influential. While supporters of Al-Qa'ida imagined themselves to be fighting against the big "Satan" USA (Bahr 2005), Christian fundamentalists, led by the US President George W. Bush, spoke of a "crusade against terrorism" (Bush 2001a) and a "struggle of good against evil" (Bush 2001b). Although large parts of both the Western industrialized and Muslim societies did not adhere to these interpretations at first, these images have been widely distributed by the mass media. The subsequent reconstruction of notions of "us" and the "other" in both the Orient and the Occident resulted in an increasing social distance. Magazine titles like "Allah's bloody country" (in the reputable German weekly magazine *Der Spiegel*; Spiegel Spezial 2003) were numerous in the Western industrialized countries shortly after 9/11. They corroborated the confrontational distinction between "us" and the "others" and reaffirmed the above-described combination of space and society. This damage to the image of Islam seems to be quite persistent and has been continuously reproduced by the media.

The fact that the 9/11 terrorists were of Muslim origin sparked racist attitudes in the Western societies. In the United States, more than 1,000 incidents of violence against Muslim and Arab Americans were reported by the end of 2001, and at least five persons were killed (McAlister 2005). Anti-Muslim and anti-Arab sentiment became common. Political parties with clear anti-Islamic and xenophobic ideologies gained power in elections in the Netherlands, Denmark, Norway, France, Italy, Belgium, and Portugal. Although many intellectuals (Habermas 2002; Ramadan 2006), politicians, and ordinary citizens in the Western industrialized countries encouraged a more nuanced interpretation of the situation, the Western image of the Muslim world deteriorated. "Islam" was increasingly constructed as a "synecdoche for a particular series of pathologies—an excessive devotion to religion, a tendency toward violence and *jihad*, the oppression of women, a failure of democracy" (McAlister 2005:302), and a synonym of irrationality and hatred of the whole West. As a result, an increasing number of people interpreted 9/11 as part of a clash of civilizations. According to the renowned German Institute für Demoskopie Allensbach (Noelle-Neumann and Petersen 2006), affirmative answers to the question "Do we currently face a clash of civilizations between the Muslim and the Christian World?" increased in Germany from 46% to 58% between August 2004 and May 2006. Inversely, this sentence was rejected by only 22% of Germans in 2006, while it was rejected by 43% of Germans in 2004.

This growing social distance has been reinforced by both recurring terrorist attacks and by the actions and politics of the Western governments, which have been perceived as outrageously unjust by large parts of the Muslim world. The illegal invasion and occupation of Iraq, the general politics of the United States and its allies in the Middle East and in Palestine, the images of the prisoners at Guantanamo Bay, the torture scandal at Abu Ghraib, and the discussions regarding the Mohammed caricatures in Denmark consistently damaged the image of "the West" in the Muslim world (Faath and Mattes 2004). From a theoretical point of view, this increase in confrontational geopolitical world images and the deviating intra- and interregional interpretation schemes of 9/11 must have had an influence on the patterns of travel behavior.

Structural Change of Tourism Flows in the Muslim World

Indeed, the rise of confrontational geopolitical world images simultaneously occurred with structural changes in tourism flows in the Muslim world. Although it is hardly possible to prove a causal relationship between both observations because of methodological reasons, theoretical perspectives give evidence supporting the assumption that the rise of confrontational world images and the increasing social distance between the Western industrialized and the Muslim world significantly impacted the actions of potential tourists.

Table 4. Outbound Tourism from the Middle East (2000–2005)

	Destination	2000	2001	2002	2003	2004	2005
Total (000s)	World	13,762	14,570	17,405	17,497	20,458	22,614
	Middle East	10,139	10,912	13,357	13,538	15,858	17,526
	Europe	1,772	1,631	1,545	1,586	1,844	2,196
	Americas	311	313	183	161	196	218
Market share	Middle East	73.7%	74.9%	76.7%	77.4%	77.5%	77.5%
	Europe	12.9%	11.2%	8.9%	9.1%	9.0%	9.7%
	Americas	2.3%	2.1%	1.1%	0.9%	1.0%	1.0%

Source: UNWTO (various years)

It is undeniable that outbound tourism from Muslim countries changed significantly. The structural transformation is observed in the outbound structures from the Middle East, which is the wealthiest and most attractive generating market in the Muslim world (Table 4). The number of arrivals from the Middle East in Europe did not recover from the 9/11 shock until 2004. Moreover, arrivals in the Americas (predominantly North America) have not yet exceeded their precrisis level. However, although more Arabs from the Middle East are now visiting Europe than ever before, structural changes of tourist flows are obvious. Intraregional destinations gained about 4% of the market share between 2000 and 2005 and accounted for 77.5% of destinations in 2005. In the same period, Europe's market share decreased by a quarter to roughly 10%. The market share of North America decreased by 0.5–1%.

This increase in intraregional tourism was accompanied by a simultaneous decrease in the significance of interregional travel to the Muslim world. While the absolute number of arrivals has more or less recovered in most Muslim countries since 2004, a shift in the structure of the main generating markets is evident.

An analysis of the structural changes in tourist flows to the top 10 destinations of the Muslim world between 2000 and 2005 (UNWTO, various years) reveals an interesting situation (Figure 6). Apart from Tunisia, all others overcame the security-induced crisis at the beginning of the new millennium, and seven of them (the Emirates is not included due to unavailable data) even succeeded in attracting more tourists from the West than ever before (UNWTO 2007a; own calculation).

However, at the same time, growth rates in the Muslim generating markets exceeded the growth in the Western industrialized markets in seven

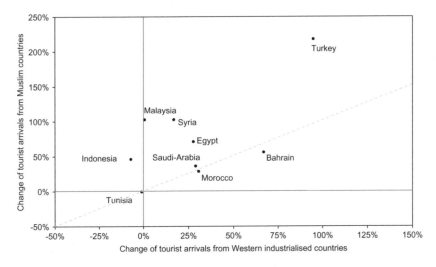

Figure 6. Changes in Tourist Flows in the Top 10 OIC Markets (2000–2005)
Source: UNWTO (2007a)

of the nine countries. Only in Morocco and Bahrain was the growth of tourism from the Western markets slightly larger than the growth from Muslim markets. In the other seven countries, irrespective of differences in market structures and activities, Muslim generating markets were able to increase their market share.

The significance of this change is apparent when one analyzes the structural change of the accumulated market shares of the main generating markets in the top 10 Muslim destinations between 2000 and 2003 (Figure 7).

In 2000, arrivals from the Western industrialized countries accounted for 38% of all tourists in the top 10 Muslim tourism destinations. By 2003, this share decreased to 34%, while the share of intraregional travel in the Muslim world increased from 30 to 33% and is now nearing the levels of the traditional Western tourist markets (UNWTO 2007a; own calculation).

This change in the markets did not occur by chance, but they can be seen as the outcome of strategic decisions within the regional tourism industry. Interviews with leading managers reflect this shift in strategy. Many companies tried to balance losses. A vice president for sales in the Middle East, Africa, and the subcontinent of an American hotel chain described the reactions of his company quite succinctly: "You know, certain markets closed, we opened certain other markets." Furthermore, from the beginning of the crisis, managers intended to minimize their dependence on the volatile

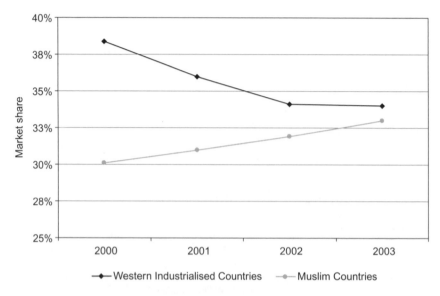

Figure 7. Market Shares for the Top 10 Muslim Tourism Destinations. Time Series Ends in 2003 Because Current Detailed Data for the UAE is Not Yet Available; the Last Year with a Complete Available Set of Data was 2003
Source: UNWTO (2007a)

traditional generating markets. A vice president and area general manager of a British company stated, "What we did is, (…) that was after 9/11, that we changed our market mix. And we really worked with customers that were less sensitive to risk. (…) That's why the second time after the new Iraq War, we actually survived the crises much better."

CONCLUSION

The events following 9/11 caused a recurring neighborhood effect in various Muslim countries, which led to a decline in tourist arrivals. However, while some major destinations in the region severely suffered, others performed extremely well. From a theoretical point of view, this difference in the occurrence of a neighborhood effect is somehow surprising and begged the question of how the varying emergence of neighborhood effects and the varying development paths of different destinations in the Muslim world after 9/11 could be explained.

The analysis presented here demonstrates that the differing performances of destinations in the region can be explained by their varying character-istics. Those destinations that were impacted most seriously were highly dependent on the Western generating markets. Mixed-character destinations and those that concentrated on intraregional markets were more stable, less risk sensitive, and even experienced high growth rates. Indeed, an analysis of the quantitative changes in the structures of inbound and outbound tourist flows shows that the expected neighborhood effect can be observed within the group of tourists from the Western industrialized countries, but is not measurable in the group of intraregional, Muslim tourists. On the contrary, intraregional tourism was booming even after 9/11. This boom mirrored a decrease of travel from the Muslim world in Europe and North America.

These findings point to a weakness in the existing body of theoretical literature on neighborhood effects, which does not sufficiently differentiate between the effects' occurrence, mechanisms, and likeliness of different generating markets. In this respect, the example of the effects of 9/11 on destinations in the Muslim world demonstrated that those with a significant share of intraregional travel do not suffer as much under neighborhood effects as the ones with a strong focus on interregional travel, and more precisely in these cases on the Western industrialized markets.

In summary, the events following 9/11 led to an increase in intraregional tourism and a simultaneous decrease of interregional travel in the Western industrialized and the Muslim world, respectively. From a theoretical point of view, this view can be described as the observation of a novel "two-sided" neighborhood effect, which results in an increasing regionalization of tourist demand. The absolute numbers of arrivals in both regions exceed the precrisis level. Meanwhile, a shift in the structure of the main generating markets persists. Apparently, the 9/11 attacks acted as a catalyst for an increasing and ongoing regionalization of tourist demands in the Muslim world.

Although such a conclusion is methodologically hard to prove, it seems reasonable to assume from a cultural geographical perspective that the differences in travel behavior between the Western and Muslim tourists can be explained by an increasing polarization of different geographical imaginations. From this angle, the mediatized rise and renaissance of confrontational geopolitical world pictures in the Western industrialized and in the Muslim world deteriorated the images of the Occident and the Orient, respectively, and corroborated and reaffirmed the long-established essentializations of the respective "other." This resulted in an increase in social distance between people in the Western and the Muslim worlds.

In this regard, the occurrence of the described two-sided neighborhood effect can be interpreted as an outcome of an increase of social distance of a growing number of people in outbound and inbound tourism markets, which reshapes the individual landscape and geographies of travel risk.

Obviously, the potential of tourism to bridge gaps between people in different cultures and of different religions has suffered in the past few years. The Muslim terrorists, with help from their counterparts in the West, succeeded in this regard. However, the ultimate effects of the described developments are not entirely negative. The resulting growth in intra-Muslim tourism has significantly contributed to the long-term stabilization of the Muslim destinations and to their national economies because of the fact that intraregional travelers seem to perceive risk differently than their interregional counterparts. Furthermore, most destinations have fully recovered from the incidents following the 2001 attacks and exceed the precrisis number of tourist arrivals. Even though 9/11 had a severe impact on the Muslim destinations, it did not cause a long-lasting tourism crisis in the Muslim world, which is partially because tourism agents were proactively dealing with the opportunities presented to them by the markets and adjusted their strategies accordingly. In closing, there is bad news for terrorists targeting the tourism industry. Tourism seems to be more robust in the long run than one would probably have expected in an area that has unfortunately been at the center of global conflict and security concerns for a long time.

Acknowledgments

The author expresses his gratitude to the German Research Foundation (DFG) for financing a three-year research project from which the presented findings are derived.

Chapter 13

IRAN
Tourism, Heritage and Religion

Hamira Zamani-Farahani
Astiaj Tourism Consultancy and Research Centre, Iran

Abridgement: This chapter discusses about tourism in Iran, an old civilization and a theocratic country where Islam is a dominant force. The majority of the people in Iran are Shia Muslims. References are made to conditions in Iran, its tourism industry, and the role of Islam in tourism and society. It is followed by discussion of Shia pilgrimage features. The findings show that while tourism has great potential in Iran, which is renowned for its diversity of attractions, tourism development is, however, constrained by several factors that limit the industry's contribution to economic growth. **Keywords:** Iran; attraction; development; Islam; Shia pilgrimage

INTRODUCTION

This chapter discusses religious and heritage tourism in Iran: a country located in the Middle East with its Persian civilization, with a wealth of historic sites, governed under a strict Islamic state, with an almost all Shia population. According to O'Gorman, McLellan and Baum (2007), Iran's archaeology, cultural heritage, traditions, and natural characteristics are among the main factors that attract inbound tourists. However, lack of information and data render the country less known to the outside world.

In many Muslim countries, Islam is the foundation of society and its principles support tourism policy, development objectives, management, and

Tourism in the Muslim World
Bridging Tourism Theory and Practice, Volume 2, 205–218
Copyright © 2010 by Emerald Group Publishing Limited
All rights of reproduction in any form reserved
ISSN: 2042-1443/doi:10.1108/S2042-1443(2010)0000002016

operation of the industry. Therefore, it is evident that religion (Islam) has an influence on the mode of tourism development and marketing in Muslim countries, but interpretation of Islam in these countries as well as the level of government intervention varies. Moreover, the role played by local culture cannot be ignored. In Iran, ruled by theocratic governments since the Islamic revolution of 1979, the state and religion are virtually indivisible. Thus, this country provides an interesting context to explore these issues, because it is a state where Islam is the dominant influence and demands adherence to strict codes of conduct, a situation that may seem mystifying and alien to non-Muslim tourists.

The literature related to tourism development within Iran is more focused on its heritage and cultural aspects rather than the impact of religion. Weidenfeld and Ron (2008) suggest that the relationship between tourism and religion constitutes a valid and important area of research. Therefore, this study intends to clarify aspects that have received limited attention in the tourism literature to date, namely the strength and impact of Islamic religion on the tourism industry of a country with a civilization older than the religion. The study is aimed at investigating the tourism industry in Iran and the impact of religion on its tourism development. With a focus on Shia pilgrimage, comments are derived from analysis of published materials, supplemented by observations made during fieldwork of other studies, and these are coupled with the author's personal experiences.

IRAN: RELIGION AND TOURISM

Iran is a country that is diverse in both cultural and historical contexts. It represents one of the world's oldest civilizations dating back 10,000 years (O'Gorman et al 2007). Historically, Iran was one of the world's great ancient civilizations "Persian Empire" that made great contributions to science, mathematics, architecture, literature, art, and the spread of religious ideas. It is the fifth largest country in Asia (St. Vincent 1992) and the second largest in the Middle East (Axworthy 2008), The Middle East is recognized as a tourism destination because of its reputation as the birthplace of the three great monotheistic religions (Alavi and Yasin 2000; Rinschede 1992; Uriely Israeli and Reichel 2000). Iran is widely renowned for its diverse attractions such as historic and cultural monuments, landscapes, climate, customs, and the people's lifestyles (O'Gorman et al 2007). The complex climate also means that the country is famed for appearing to have four concurrent yet distinct seasons.

Iran was known as Persia until 1935 and positioned at a crossroads between the East and West, having coastlines on both the Caspian Sea (the world's largest land-locked body of water) and the Persian Gulf. It is bordered by Iraq on the west, Turkey on the northwest, Armenia, Azerbaijan, Turkmenistan, and the Caspian Sea on the north, Afghanistan on the east, Pakistan on the southeast, and the Persian Gulf and the Sea of Oman on the south. With the exception of Armenia, the majority of the populations of all its neighboring countries are Muslim. Article 12 of the Constitution of Iran declares that the official religion of Iran is Islam and the doctrine followed is that of Shi'ism. According to the most recent census, 99.4% of its 73.7 million people are Muslim, with the majority being Shi'as (89%) and the remainder made up of other Muslim sub-groups (Iran National Census 2007), with Sunnis constituting about 10% of the total. Other minor religious communities are Christians and Zoroastrians, as well as Jews. Persian or Farsi is the official language and the Persian script is the only one in use in Iran.

The Islamic Republic of Iran dates from the 1979 revolution when the Shah was deposed and Ayatollah Khomeini installed Islamic rule. The country has a unique political structure whereby the supreme religious leader holds considerable influence, alongside an elected president who has executive powers. The National Assembly is the legislative branch of the government. Its elected candidates must be endorsed by the 12-member Guardian Council, which ensures parliament complies with Islamic principles. The supreme leader has the power to select half of the council members. To streamline its administration, Iran has 30 *ostans* (provinces), each ruled by an *Ostander* (Governor-General).

Iran's economy is mainly based on oil, natural gas, industry (mining and manufacturing), agriculture, and fisheries (caviar). The country holds 10% of the world's petroleum reserves. It also has the world's second largest reserves of natural gas (15% of the world's total). About 85% of its national revenue is derived from oil and natural gas (World Fact Book 2007). Tourism is given low priority, thereby limiting the industry's contribution to the country's economic growth and GNP.

Tourism in Iran

Tourism has great potential in Iran, renowned for its diversity of attractions (Beheshti 2003). It is rich in history and archaeological sites (Zendeh Del 2001). Of the historical sites in Iran, 10 are on the World Heritage List while 59 more are tentatively listed (UNESCO 2009a). Iran has also two World

Intangible Cultural Heritage instances (Nowruz and Radif) (UNESCO 2009b). Nowruz marks the beginning of the Iranian New Year (according to the solar calendar March 21st coincides with the first day of spring and Iranian New Year Day); and Radif is a traditional form of Iranian music. Therefore, according to UNESCO, Iran is ranked as one of the top ten countries in the world in terms of the richness of its ancient and historical sites (Alavi and Yasin 2000). However, having attractions alone is not enough for tourism development. Other factors such as efficient tourism planning, management and marketing, well-trained tourism workforce, and well-developed infrastructure and other facilities are necessary to enable the industry to contribute toward national development.

Iran has a long history of involvement in tourism. There is considerable evidence for hostels that date back to at least 2000 BCE (O'Gorman et al 2007). Iran's tourism was first recognized as an industry worthy to be administered in 1935 (ZamaniZenouzi 1980). Consequently, the country's tourism development was far ahead of its neighbors. Iran has well-established tourism facilities and services in comparison to countries of the surrounding region and its tradition of hospitality exceeds those of many other countries (Zamani-Farahani 2002). Iran offers 729 hotels, 256 hotel-apartments, and 1,481 inns and budget accommodation properties in 2009, as well as many homestay facilities (ICHHTO 2009a). However, many of these properties need to be modernized in light of current international requirements and service levels improved to be at par with standards in other successful destinations. Iran also has 2,156 travel agencies (ICHHTO 2009b) active in inbound, outbound, and domestic tourism. Many provide pilgrimage tours and services as well. There are about 70 tourism teaching/training centers, mostly dependent on the private sector, with 31 of the total located in Tehran province (ICHHTO 2009c).

The development of tourism during the pre- and post-Islamic revolution has not featured as a major economic priority, although it has experienced some progress. The most considerable effort in promoting tourism in Iran before the Islamic revolution was in 1970s, when the government appointed a Swiss consultant (Tourist Consult) to develop a comprehensive plan for expansion of tourism. It was an extensive study of Iran's existing and future tourism markets, policies, resources, priorities, and potentials, along with detailed analysis and suggestions (Zamani-Farahani 2002). However, the study could not be implemented as the country faced several events, including the political developments, pre- and post-1979.

After the declaration of an Islamic Republic and a theocracy led by Ayatollah Khomeini in 1979, tourism activities were hampered by the revolution, political turbulence, conflicts, war with Iraq between 1980 and 1988, and sociocultural barriers (Zamani-Farahani 2009). After the war, a series of five-year development plans was in place in Iran from 1989 until 2009. However, these efforts did not take off because of several problems such as lack of clear policies, insufficient tourism planning, tourism management and marketing, and unavailability of reliable tourism statistical data. The industry faced political and cultural barriers and could not contribute as an effective economic factor in national development.

A 20-year Tourism Plan of Iran was later introduced in 2005, consisting of a 10-year plan and two subsequent 5-year plans. The target was to achieve 20 million tourist arrivals by 2025 with projected investment of over US$32 billion, with $5 billion from the government and the remainder from private enterprise (Faghri 2007). However, the plan experienced setbacks. The goal was optimistic, given the fact that there were only 1.4 million tourists in 2008, mostly from Central and South Asia and the Middle East (Euromonitor 2009). According to the World Travel and Tourism Council (WTTC 2009a), tourism and the wider travel and tourism economy currently contribute 3% and 8% to the GDP, respectively.

The Iran Cultural Heritage, Handicrafts, and Tourism Organization (ICHHTO) has formal responsibility for managing tourism in the country. From 2004, the head of this organization was the country's Vice President. Prior to this, the national tourism administration was under the supervision of the Ministry of Culture and Islamic Guidance. The overall responsibility of this organization is to introduce, protect, and resuscitate the country's historic-cultural legacy, and to also promote the tourism industry. It focused on meeting cultural objectives on attracting tourists who are familiar with and have an interest in the country's rich history and culture and who respect Iranian people as well as Iranian cultural-religious traditions (Paresh 2006, 2007). The reasons for this focus are economic and sociocultural. Iran as an oil- and natural gas-rich nation has little call for extra revenue. As an Islamic country, it wishes to prevent the erosion of religious devoutness and conventions.

The institutional structure and organization of the tourism public sector in Iran displays a number of weaknesses. The selection of top-level managers and key figures in authority appears to be commonly decided by their devotion to Islam and Islamic appearance alongside political allegiance. O'Gorman et al argued, "the leadership of public sector tourism, both in promotional and operational roles, is rarely professional or long term. State and quasi-state tourism organizations do not operate under commercial criteria like profitability and are subject to poor and inconsistent management and high levels of political interference" (2007:307). Males are more prevalent in top-level positions. Proximity to people of religious and political influence is another factor and the skills needed for effective management are secondary (Zamani-Farahani and Henderson 2010). Tourism in Iran also faced interference by influential individuals from both the religious and political arena outside the tourism industry.

Furthermore, local participation in the tourism planning and development process is poor. "Local communities have little awareness of tourism and little control over much potential development or access to tourism markets" (O'Gorman et al 2007:305). They are important players who can influence the success or failure in this industry. In addition to the above shortcomings, over the past decades, the country has experienced several crises, which have restrained its tourism. It also suffered from the intense Western propaganda against the country. This created "an image problem" for Iran in the eyes of tourism markets around the world (Vafadari and Cooper 2007). The image of the Muslim world as portrayed in the Western media often negatively depicts Islamic societies as oppressive, harsh, violent, and intolerant (Armstrong 2002). The political tensions between the West and some Muslim countries have also reinforced mutual suspicions, which may be aggravated by media reporting. The portrayal of Muslims in the media has affected tourism around the world (Timothy and Iverson 2006:201). This also leads to undermining tourism operations in these countries, including Iran.

Political instability or the outbreak of war in one part of the world can dramatically reduce tourist arrival patterns to other parts. During the recent decades, political crises in a neighboring destination also negatively affected the marketability of Iran as a destination. Considering these difficulties, the country may rely on heritage and pilgrimage target audiences; as such tourism products are less vulnerable to crisis situations.

The Impact of Religion

"Religiously motivated tourism is probably as old as religion itself, and is consequently the oldest type of tourism" (Rinschede 1992:53). Tourism, like religion, "provides people with 'non-ordinary or sacred' free time which allows them to reflect, think, and contemplate their lives" (Willson 2007:2). Tourism has also been a way of changing people's attitudes toward other cultures, religions, countries, heritages, and even increasing people's awareness of key world issues (Brown and Morrison 2003; McIntosh and Bonnemann 2006; Schanzel and McIntosh 2000). Iran is the land of the world's first monotheistic religion (Zoroastrianism). It was founded between 1400 and 600 BCE in Persia by Zarathustra. Its teachings influenced mostly monotheistic religions including the world's three main faiths of Judaism, Christianity, and Islam. "By the time the Arabs arrived, bringing what was for them the new idea of worshipping a single God, Persians had been doing it for more than a millennium" (Del Giudice 2008:5). Therefore, in Iranian society, monotheistic religion has a long history and it is associated with Persian history, heritage, and culture. In the 7th century, Islam was accepted as an important religion among the Iranians, but Persian identity remained a strong cultural force in the Muslim world. The next major change came during the Safavid period (1502–1736), when Shi'ism was recognized as the state religion in the country (Faramarzi 1995). Finally, the Islamic revolution in 1979 led to the founding of an Islamic Republic based on a version of politicized Islam and *Shari'a* law (Mackey and Harrop 1998) advocating the return to pure Islam as practiced in the past (Timmer and McClelland 2004).

In fact, Islam is receptive to tourism. There are 16 verses in the *Qur'an*, which directly encourage traveling (Zamani-Farahani and Henderson 2010). Although the doctrine of Islam encourages travel and hospitable behavior, it has little influence on the mode of tourism development in certain Muslim countries. The potential threat of the industry in violating Islamic cultural values and traditions is very much a concern of the locals (Aziz 1995). In some Muslim countries; the state is much more concerned about negative impacts of tourism on their society rather than the public. Therefore, in these countries, tourism development faces a number of challenges. According to Ritter (1975), there are a number of Islamic countries with high tourism potential that are not interested in having non-Islamic tourists. Many Muslims are highly concerned about the immoral influence of tourism, which is why the industry has not been a major development priority in many Islamic nations (Aziz 1995; Baum and Conlin 1997; Mathieson and Wall 1990). In Iranian society, the official fears about the erosion of religious devoutness and conventions meant that there was little demonstration of interest in hosting foreign tourists, especially non-Muslims. It seems religious codes are a factor for tourism restrictions. Islamic religion has influenced the political, cultural, social, and economic environment and the everyday lives of citizens and tourists. That may not seem agreeable and acceptable to the Western and non-Muslim tourists. Studies on local community attitudes toward level of intervention of religion in tourism are limited. However, the results of research on impacts of tourism in Iran conducted in 2006 and 2007 (Zamani-Farahani and Musa

2008) illustrated that the majority of respondents do not question the religious beliefs held by tourists but are more interested in minimizing their discomfort about the Islamic religion.

In Iranian society today, religion is central to public and private life and controls the ways of society. The civil and criminal legal systems, which were in operation before the Islamic revolution, have been replaced by *Shari'a* (Islamic law). Hence, the legal and the whole systems of government reflect the values and the codes of Islam, where the state and religion are virtually indivisible. Religiosity is its most striking feature. Therefore, religious factors have a bearing on policy and development strategy affecting tourism. However, it is evident that national, social, and political conditions play a critical role in enhancing religious commitment in different countries. Hassan (2005) conducted a comparative study of Muslim piety of over 6,000 respondents from Indonesia, Malaysia, Pakistan, Egypt, Turkey, Kazakhstan, and Iran between 1996 and 2003. His findings show that the pattern of response to religious commitments among Muslims from different countries is significantly different. In fact, secular societies such as Kazakhstan and Turkey, as well as Iran with a high attachment to their national/historical identity, were the least likely to express their religiosity in comparison to other countries.

Iran is one of the few Islamic countries that have implemented *Shari'a* law in running the state, as well as the tourism industry. In all the public accommodation, permanent signs are placed in every room where arrows are pointing toward Makkah to indicate the direction of prayer. A copy of the *Qur'an* and other facilities for prayers such as prayer mats are placed in every room. There is also a separate space in hotels for public prayers. Males and females at the public recreational facilities such as beaches, swimming pools, and gyms are segregated. Food and beverages are *halal* (complying with Muslim dietary laws). Tourism industry employees must accord due respect to Islam in terms of dress code and behavior.

Islamic laws also prohibit shaking hands or any physical contact between members of the opposite sex, unmarried couples sharing rooms, gambling, breaking fast in daylight during Ramadan, consumption of pork and other forbidden foods, selling or drinking liquor, public displays of affection, and dressing inappropriately. Both sexes must cover their torso and upper legs at all times, and only women's faces may be exposed (Deng, Jivan and Hassan 1994). Discotheques and bars and other forms of entertainment are deemed unlawful. Tourists (followers of other faiths) are also advised to be respectful to local norms and abide by rules, including the wearing of a head covering by women and modest dress by men in public.

On the other hand, religion brings a certain degree of liberalism for Muslims. They may pray almost anywhere. They as tourists are required to adhere to the customary restrictions where possible and "abstain from profligate consumption and indulgence" (Hashim et al 2007:1085). They may delay Ramadan fasting and curtail regular prayers when they are on the move (Timothy and Iverson 2006). Muslims also observe a tradition of offering hospitality to strangers, which is appreciated by tourists. In Iran the hosts welcome guests with kindness, both as their religious duty, as well as part of Persian culture. While, for example, Jews do not travel on Saturday and other Jewish holidays (Fleischer and Pizam 2002), Friday and holy holidays provide added opportunities for Iranian Muslims to relax, engage in recreational activities, and actually take holiday vacations.

Shia Pilgrimage

Pilgrimage is a popular feature of Islam with a long history. The holy *Ka'ba* in Makkah and the holy Shrine of Prophet Muhammad in Medina in Saudi Arabia are the only pilgrimage destinations formally acknowledged by all Muslims. But there are also a number of other sites deemed holy by the Shia faithful, which are found in Iran, Iraq, Saudi Arabia, and Syria. Non-*Hajj* pilgrimages to these locations are known as *ziarat*. Shia refers to two *Qur'anic* verses (24:36, 42:23) that encourage Muslims to perform this kind of pilgrimage. *Ziarat* are shaped by the culture and traditions of the country where they are made in a manner demonstrated by the circumstances in Iran.

A visit to Makkah for the *Hajj* might be more expensive than pilgrimage to Iran's Shia holy sites. Yet *ziarat* in Iran is valued as a distinct experience rooted in the country's cultural and religious heritage. Therefore, such traveling is strongly encouraged and plays a very important role in Shia religious life in Iran and neighboring Iraq. Unlike the *Hajj*, undertaking *ziarat* does not require extensive preparation and fulfillment of conditions, and it can be repeated as often as desired.

People choose to spend their time in spiritual sites for various reasons such as religious practices, leisure, and work (Ashmos and Duchon 2000; Beck 2003; Schmidt 2005; Tilson 2005; Van Ness 1996; Vukonić 1996; Zinnbauer et al 1997). The religious places are considered by scholars as places that are visited for different reasons, such as their architecture, ambience, and historical importance. Some are visited for holiday and relaxation. They are well known also as tourism attractions (Cohen 1998; Jackson and Hudman 1995; Joseph and Kavoori 2001; Smith 1992). According to the classification made by Bhardwaj (1998), voluntary pilgrimage (including *ziarat*) may be divided based on several motivations: emotive/sentimental reasons, pathogenic (disease/health search), psychosomatic and nonpsychosomatic ailments, fulfillment of a vow (problems of mundane existence) which may be made for reasons related to personal health or health of a loved one or success in life or study, and wish for success, achievement, fulfillment for personal or loves one, or a blessing. In addition to the above categories, Shia pilgrimage in the Iranian community is performed for reasons like supplication, education, discharge of daily stress, recreation and enjoyment, sociocultural communication with other pilgrims, relief from loneliness, eating/offering *nazri* (charitable offering of meals for blessings), and, most importantly, feeling of nearness to God (*Khouda* in Persian).

In Iran, the land of Shia pilgrimage, religious elements are found in its architecture, history, festivals, rituals, and lifestyles. Several magnificent historical monuments with Islamic theme have been constructed. These can be found in Isfahan, Qom, Mashhad, Shiraz, and Tehran. After the revolution, more effort has been given to construction of new places and maintenance, as well as conservation of religious sites. Iran is estimated to have about 9,000 holy places and a large number of these are shrines, 1,200 of which are documented in the official register of National Cultural and Natural Heritage (Kheimehnews 2007). There are around 70,000 mosques (Jahan News 2008) and about 150 notable *imamzadeh* (tombs of the immediate descendants and close descendents of saint imams of the Shia faith) (Iran Touring and Tourism Organization 2009). The most celebrated are those of the Imams and their descendants, but each *imamzadeh* is unique and endowed with a special meaning and status by the local community.

The Shia pilgrimage places in Iran include the Shrine of Shia Imams, mosques, *imamzadeh*, mausoleums of the Muslim saints, martyrs, revered Sufi saints, scholars, and other holy personages, *mazars* (small memorial shrines), cemeteries, *khankahs* (the dervish houses of worship linked to Sufiism, a kind of Islamic mysticism), madrassah (Islamic schools), and *hoseiniyeh* (traditionally served as sites for religious ceremonies and gatherings). Other places may be sacred trees, and wells and footprints identified with particular holy persons who may have visited, or in some other way have been associated with the place. The preeminent sacred site in Iran is the burial ground of Imam Reza, the Shia 8th Imam, in the city of Mashhad, and the shrine of Fatima al-Masuma, the sister of Imam Reza, located in Qom, as the second foremost in the country.

Exhibitions of the *Qur'an* and religion museums are also places of interest to Shi'as. So are bazaars around holy places. New holy places strongly depict the Shia doctrine. After the death of Imam Khomeini (founder of the Islamic Republic regime) in 1989, his golden-domed place of burial, located in the south of Tehran, has became a national-political shrine, which is visited by thousands of local and foreign tourists and by diplomats.

The majority of Shia holy places, especially the Shrine of Imam and *imamzadeh*, are very imposing and well decorated like art galleries. Many types of Persian decorative artwork and embellishments have been used on the Dome. There are *minarets* decorated with gold, tiles, and gild bricks, *Zarih* (the holy burial chamber where the body of the Imam or saint is buried) in gold, silver, or bronze art works, *muqarnas* (honeycomb work), stone and wood fretwork, different colored marble stone, gloriously mirror-worked design, stucco (plaster works, stone works), elaborate *mihrab* (prayer niche), painting on the plaster, golden honeycomb works (stalactite works), and coloring techniques. The mosaic tile works are very delicate and comprise a myriad of colors. In addition, verses of the holy *Qur'an*, traditions, aphorisms, precedents, and Persian poems in "Nashk" script can be observed on the tiles, walls, and ceiling covered with inscriptions in decorative form. The shrine of Imams are furnished with magnificent candelabra and covered by fine Persian carpets or rugs. The aim is to explore the meaning of "Allah, Most Gracious, Most Merciful" via the beauty and grace of the decorations in place. In this sense, the Shia believes that amidst the beauty and the serenity of the location, a adherent is reminded of the delicate elements in his relationship with the Almighty and that God loves beauty and peace.

In addition to holy sites, the Shia faith has many festivals and celebrations. The Shia religious months, days, and holidays have an important role in religious events and ceremonies. The most important months are Muharram and Ramadan. The anniversary of the martyrdom of Imam Hussain and his 72 followers is the most noticeable religious ceremony/event during Muharram. Imam Hussain was the 3rd Shia Imam, the son of Ali and Fatima and the grandson of Prophet Muhammad, and according to Persian legend, the daughter of the last Persian king of the Sasanid dynasty, who was taken captive during the Muslim invasion married Imam Hussain. This ceremony is held every year on *Tasua* (9th day of Muharram), *Ashura* (10th day), and stops on *Arbain* (the 40th day) among Shi'as. The annual Muharram mourning ceremonies where people wear black shirts customary for the mourning season, observed with great pageantry and emotion based on dramatic narration of the life, deeds, suffering, and death of Shia martyrs. The annual drama of *Ashura* reenacts the death of Imam Hussain on the 10th of Muharram called *Ta'ziyeh* (literally means expressions of sympathy, mourning, and consolation). The *Ta'ziyeh* that symbolizes the heroic martyrdom of Imam Hussain is one of the few surviving forms of popular, traditional theater generated by the Islamic (Shia) world from the beginning. The religious ceremonies during Muharram held throughout Iran are observed in subtle variations, according to local subculture. For example at Abiyaneh, a historical village near Isfahan, this event is held with particular pomp. Local people participate with their colorful cultural customs. Another ceremony named *Ghali-shooy-an* (carpet-washing) for the martyred sultan Ali Ibn Mohammad Bagher (the son of the 5th Shia Imam) is performed in the Mashhad-e Ardehal in Isfahan province annually in October. The most significant symbol of this ceremony is the use of carpet. Persian carpets are Iran's most famous cultural export, dating back to the 5th century BCE, and are still an integral part of religious and cultural festivals.

In Iran, pilgrims are primarily Shia Muslim Iranian citizens, although Iranian Christians and Zoroastrians also visit the shrines for the spiritual experience or out of curiosity. Pilgrimage in Iranian culture is spontaneous. Iranians already travel extensively inside or outside of the country for pilgrimage/religious purposes. According to the Iran National Census (2009), during six months (March until September) in 2008, pilgrimage was the most popular purpose of travel after visiting relatives and friends and recreational trips among Iranians. The number of Iranians traveling abroad, especially to Saudi Arabia, Iraq, and Syria for pilgrimage, is also on the rise.

Most foreign pilgrims are from the Middle East or are Iranians living and working abroad. Leading countries of origin include Afghanistan, Iraq, Pakistan, India, Kuwait, Lebanon, Syria, the United Arab Emirates, and Yemen. Saudi Arabia is another source, although most are Sunni who seek recreation in the moderate climate and verdant landscapes of the north of the country. Iraq is an importance source of tourists. Travel to Iran by its nationals has increased since the fall of Saddam Hussein's Sunni regime in 2003 and its eventual replacement by a Shia-led government (Zamani-Farahani 2004). First-time Iraqi pilgrims tend to prefer the better-known sites and then become more adventurous on subsequent visits when they also stay longer. However, the majority of the above-mentioned countries have low average incomes and this limits tourism spending. Muslims from abroad generally have the same access to sites as Iranians and travel individually or with pilgrimage tours, but there is an Office for Non-Iranian Pilgrim Affairs that deals with special arrangements for visits to the holy places of Mashhad and Qom. For non-Muslim tourists, entry to the inner sanctuaries and tombs is disallowed. However, it is usually possible for foreigners who are not Muslims to visit most mosques and *imamzadeh*.

CONCLUSION

This chapter suggests that Iran possesses several strengths as a destination for nationals and foreigners. It has considerable potential for tourism, especially related to heritage, culture, and a diverse assortment of religious attractions, along with reasonably well-established tourism facilities and services. However, the majority of people around the world, including Muslims, are unfamiliar with the country and do not have much idea about what traveling to and in Iran would be like. Lack of appropriate marketing and information about Iran in many countries has led to the misidentification of Iran with its neighboring countries.

The low governmental interest in the economic contribution from tourism and its strict social code impact Iran's image and market potential as a destination for international tourism. The official objective of developing tourism in Iran focuses on cultural aims and is based on attracting tourists who are familiar with and have an interest in the same religion. Consequently, it seems that there is an effort to develop and promote inbound religious tourism, but the match between what happens and what tourism authorities desire to happen is considerable.

Shortcomings exist, particularly with regard to the clear policies, planning, and unity of management. The planning for pilgrimage visits to Iran needs better and more efficient administration. The government needs to make concerted efforts to avoid overlapping duties in management of such programs. Pilgrimage overseas is encouraged by the Iranian government, but better planning, promoting, and organization for inbound pilgrims are required.

Heritage tourism and pilgrimage is attractive as it is less vulnerable to crises. Tourism in Iran under actual sociopolitical conditions requires serious efforts concerning planning, management, marketing, and promotion strategies to increase the number of inbound tourists. Approximately 10–15% of the world's Muslims are Shia (Nasr 2006), which corresponds to about 157–235 million worldwide. Therefore, there is a large pilgrimage market, especially from the countries surrounding the region within which Iran is located, including pilgrims to Iran's Islamic shrines as well as pilgrims transiting through Iran overland to and from Makkah in Saudi Arabia, and Karbala in Iraq. Promoting and marketing inbound pilgrimage from the Persian Gulf (the Shia Muslim communities in regional countries), the Middle East countries, Middle Asia/Caucasia, South Asia and other Organisation of Islamic Conference countries, and Iranians living overseas are suggested. Furthermore, innovative products, which combine pilgrimage and other religious experiences with some of the country's varied cultural and natural heritage resources, could be considered as a means of raising the level of pilgrimage tourism. The interest of non-Muslims from abroad in pilgrimage and other Shia places and practices is one component of a broader itinerary that should be subject of consideration.

PART III

TRAVEL & TOURISM EXPERIENCES

Chapter 14

THE *HAJJ*
Experience of Turkish Female Pilgrims

Ebru Gunlu
Dokuz Eylul University, Turkey
Fevzi Okumus
University of Central Florida, USA

Abridgement: This chapter presents findings from in-depth interviews with female pilgrims traveling from Turkey on their *Hajj*. The three main motives for the respondents were fulfilling one of the Five Pillars of Islam, visiting the center of the Muslim world, and seeing how others practiced Islam. For the majority of female pilgrims, the decision to go was made either jointly with their husbands or by others on their behalf. The long-lasting influences of this pilgrimage may include becoming more spiritual, peaceful, attentive, calm, tolerant, and careful. The experiences reported by respondents are discussed. **Keywords:** Islam; Muslim; experience; female; religious; pilgrimage tourism

INTRODUCTION

Religion has been one of the main purposes of travel since the earliest times (Timothy and Olsen 2006). Today, religious tourism is a significant segment of all tourists, and has major economic and sociocultural impacts on both generating and receiving countries. Over 200 million people per year travel for religious purposes (Jackowski 2000). Previous studies of religious tourism have focused on its definition and types, motives for pilgrimages, impact on destinations, its role in bringing people together from different

Tourism in the Muslim World
Bridging Tourism Theory and Practice, Volume 2, 221–233
Copyright © 2010 by Emerald Group Publishing Limited
All rights of reproduction in any form reserved
ISSN: 2042-1443/doi:10.1108/S2042-1443(2010)0000002017

countries, and the use of sacred sites as attractions (Allcock 1988; Cohen 1998, 2003; Eade 1992; Johnston 2007; Nolan and Nolan 1992; Raj and Morpeth 2007; Rinschede 1992; Rountree 2002; Russell 1999; Singh 2006; Timothy and Olsen 2006; Vukonić 1996; Weidenfeld 2005).

Despite these studies Olsen and Timothy (2006:2) consider that the literature examining religion and tourism "is still fragmented and lacks synthesis and holistic conceptualization." It also appears that there are few studies about religious tourism in and among Muslim countries, or providing empirical evidence on how Muslims engage in their acts of worshipping, and the process of the *Hajj* in Saudi Arabia. In particular, no prior research has empirically investigated Turkish female tourists' experiences on the *Hajj*, the topic of this chapter.

RELIGIOUS TOURISM AND ISLAM

Pilgrimage refers to a relatively demanding physical journey to religious sites to pray, practice rituals, search for truth and enlightenment, and/or for an authentic experience (Digance 2006; Olsen and Timothy 2006; Vukonić 1996), and a pilgrim is a tourist who is motivated by religion (Olsen and Timothy 2006). Digance (2006) claims that since the 15th century, the motives of pilgrims have changed from travel solely for religious purposes and obligations to include curiosity, to desire to see new places, and to have new experiences. Digance (2006) groups religious tourists under two categories: the first travels for religious needs, motives, and obligations, while the second group travels to religious places to gain more knowledge about a religion, religious sites, and practices.

Din (1989) was one of the first scholars who studied the relationship between Islam and tourism. He described the pattern of arrivals in Muslim countries, and analyzed to what extent religion affected tourism policies and development. Taking Malaysia as a case, he concluded that Islamic restrictions on the use of alcohol and gambling prevented tourism development in Muslim countries. Henderson (2003) also used Malaysia as a case in order to examine the problems and the opportunities of Islam and tourism, noting that Malaysia experienced challenges due to conflict between Muslim residents and non-Muslim international tourists. Al-Hamarneh and Steiner (2004) discussed Islamic tourism in relation to the September 11 terrorist attacks, and drew attention to their negative effects for Muslims. As a response they considered that new tourism options were needed, with resorts and hotels targeting

Muslim tourists by providing alcohol-free accommodation, gender segregation, dress code, prayer-rooms on site, Islamic transportation facilities, and entertainment programs respecting Islam.

Din noted that the Islamic concept of tourism focuses on "the sacred goal of submission to the ways of God" (1989:551), and Muslims are encouraged to travel so that they can see and appreciate the greatness of God. According to Din in Islam "travel is meant to be spiritually 'purposeful', to make Muslims aware of the greatness of God, through observing the signs of history and natural and manmade wonders, all of which are gifts of God" (1989:559). Aziz (2001) and Timothy and Iverson (2006) further highlight that Islam encourages Muslims to travel to religious sites and other countries, where they may better realize the greatness of God and may feel closer to God. Aziz (1995) looked at the relationships between tourism and the terrorist attacks in Egypt, and also between Islam, hospitality, and tourism, concluding that Islam does not reject tourism. In another study, Israeli (2000) focused on early Muslim travel and cited *Hadith* to show that Prophet Muhammad urged Muslims to go even to China to seek knowledge and science. Hashim, Murphy, and Muhammad (2009) discussed the importance of tourism in the Middle East, with Saudi Arabia recognized as a special place among Muslims as it is where Islam originated, and it hosts Islam's holiest places. Muslims visit Makkah and Medina for the *Hajj*, one of the Five Pillars of Islam.

The Hajj *and Female Pilgrims*

Numerous studies have provided detailed descriptions and justification of the rituals and prayers required in performing the *Hajj* (Ahmed 1992; Aziz 2001; Bloom and Blair 2000; Din and Hadi 1997; Khan 1986; Long 1979; McDonnell 1990; Peters 1994; Robinson 1999; Rowley 1997; Timothy and Iverson 2006). Simply, the *Hajj* is the most important travel for Muslims, since every Muslim, who is physically fit and has the resources, is required to perform the *Hajj* at least once in their lifetime (Aziz 2001; Robinson 1999; Timothy and Iverson 2006). The *Hajj* begins on the seventh day of the 12th month (Zul-Hijja) of the Islamic lunar calendar, but requires detailed prior planning, preparation, study, and devotion by the *hajji* (Timothy and Iverson 2006). Muslims visit Makkah and Medina in Saudi Arabia in order to visit the *Ka'ba* and undertake religious rituals and prayers (Hashim et al 2009). Over two million people participate in the *Hajj* every year, and Saudi Arabia restricts the number of pilgrims from Muslim countries, since managing and coordinating all activities for such a large number of pilgrims is a complex and challenging process (Aziz 2001; Timothy and Iverson 2006).

Before going on a *Hajj*, pilgrims must put their earthly affairs in order and prepare spiritually, which includes paying all their outstanding debts, resolving any negative feelings and conflicts with family members, relatives, and neighbors before their departure, as well as finding people to take care of family members who stay behind (Khan 1986; Long 1979; Robinson 1999). Pilgrims are also encouraged to find reliable travel companions, since Islamic tradition advocates traveling in groups so that members can help and support each other during their *Hajj* (Timothy and Iverson 2006). In many countries, both state-owned and private agencies organize pilgrims' preparations. For example, in Turkey, private agencies as well as the Presidency of Religious Affairs, a state organization, arrange package tours for the *Hajj*, facilitate applying for visas, and arrange flights and accommodations. They also arrange health checks and any required vaccinations and educate the pilgrims about the procedures and rituals they will undertake.

During the *Hajj* pilgrims devote themselves to God and pledge loyalty and servitude (Khan 1986). During the *Hajj*, pilgrims undertake a series of rites and ceremonies that follow the traditions and experiences of Abraham and Hagar (Timothy and Iverson 2006). There are several steps in performing the *Hajj* (Khan 1986; Long 1979; Timothy and Iverson 2006). The first is the ritual purification or cleansing, called *ihram*. Regular cloths are replaced with simple *ihram* garments, which are loose and simple dresses for women and simple white wrap-around sheets for men. After this, the pilgrims enter the Al-Masjid al-Haram mosque in Makkah through the gate of peace. There they listen to a sermon about the required rituals and prayers that they will be performing during the *Hajj* (Timothy and Iverson 2006). On the eighth day of the month, the pilgrims perform the rituals of *tawaf* and *sai*. *Tawaf* refers to circumambulating the *Ka'ba* seven times, in a counterclockwise direction, followed by prayer at the station of Abraham and drinking water from the Zamzam Well (Timothy and Iverson 2006). *Sai* refers to walking or running between the hills of Safa and Marwa seven times, which takes place after circling the *Ka'ba*.

Following these ceremonies, the pilgrims proceed to Mina, where they pray from the middle of the eighth day to the sunrise of the ninth day. After dawn on the ninth day, they go to the Plain of Arafat to praise God, pray, and ask for forgiveness, which is "considered to be the most important element of the *Hajj*" (Timothy and Iverson 2006:194). From Arafat, the pilgrims walk to Muzdalifa while praying, and upon their arrival, they continue praying at night. The next morning, the pilgrims go to Mina where they throw stones at three *jamaraat* (pillars), an act representing fighting against Shatan. After this, the pilgrims get their hair shaved off or remove a symbolic portion. Those pilgrims who can afford to will sacrifice a sheep, goat, or a camel. The pilgrims then replace the *ihram* with their regular clothes, and they return to Makkah to reperform the *tawaf* and *sai*. On the 11th day, they return to Mina to throw more stones at the *jamaraat* (Timothy and Iverson 2006).

The *Hajj* is one of the world's largest tourist gatherings (Ahmed 1992; Aziz 2001; Timothy and Iverson 2006). Over the last two decades, Saudi Arabia has modernized many aspects of the *Hajj*, including providing air-conditioned and luxury coaches for transport, air-conditioned mosques, and modern airports and hotels (Ahmed 1992; Timothy and Iverson 2006). Air travel and charter flights have made traveling to Saudi Arabia much easier. Bhardwaj (1998) has highlighted several potential *Hajj* problem areas, including transportation, accommodation, health, and hygiene. Transportation problems have been overcome by construction or expansion and upgrading of airports, roads, and routes. New apartments and hotels have been built to reduce accommodation problems. However, health and hygiene remain issues; each year a number of people are injured or killed because of the large crowds and poor health, and sanitation and spread of diseases are major concerns (Ahmed 1992).

Gender differences in religious tourism have been discussed in several studies (Crane 2007; Law 1999; Nobis and Lenz 2005; Omura, Roberts and Talarzyk 1980; Rosenbloom 1978, 2006; Rountree 2002; Taylor and Toohey 2001; Wachs 1987). These studies examined differences concerning transportation mode used, and patterns of domestic and business travel. One of the very few studies concerning Muslim women tourists was conducted by Bhimji (2008), who studied second-generation British Muslim women traveling to South Asia and their parents' places of origin. The author examined to what degree such women related to the simpler lifestyle in South Asian villages, and how their practice of Islam differed from that in their ancestral villages. Thus, although previous studies have focused on religious tourism, Islam, tourism, and the *Hajj*, they have not specifically looked at female pilgrims' experiences when performing the *Hajj*.

The Study Methods and Findings

For this exploratory study, a qualitative approach was chosen to allow collection of firsthand information from female Turkish pilgrims regarding their *Hajj* experiences. The interview schedule included the following open-ended questions:

- Why did you decide to go to the *Hajj*?
- How did you make your *Hajj* decision?
- Tell us about your *Hajj* experience from making the *Hajj* decision to coming back home from Saudi Arabia.
- Tell us about any problems and challenges you faced prior, during, and after the *Hajj*.
- Tell us about how the *Hajj* experience has affected you.
- Do you have anything else to share with us?
- Demographic questions.

Purposive sampling was employed to select the female respondents who had participated in the *Hajj*. Friends, relatives, and colleagues were asked about people meeting the requirements of the study, and based on their recommendations, potential respondents were approached. In total, 18 semistructured interviews were conducted in Izmir, Manisa, Denizli, Aydin, and Bolu provinces of Turkey between June and July 2009, with interviews lasting from 20 minutes to 1 hour. The participants were assured that they would not be identified individually in the research, although the respondents did not express any concerns providing their views, and indeed seemed pleased to talk about their *Hajj* experience. Data saturation was reached after 15 interviews, with three additional interviews undertaken to confirm this. During interviews, the respondents shared a variety of personal stories about their *Hajj* experiences, providing rich and insightful data related to the objectives of the study.

Due to the paucity of prior literature, an inductive data analysis approach was followed with common themes emerging from the analysis (Miles and Huberman 1994). After transcription, commonalities and themes were developed through use of open coding (Creswell 2007), and much of the data analysis consisted of breaking down the interview transcripts into manageable blocks followed by classification into code groups. The original text was cross-referenced so that the source of each code could be traced and the process of abstraction could be examined and replicated. Coding was carried out by both authors.

Table 1 provides descriptive information about the respondents. Respondents' ages were spread between 18 and 86, with the majority in the 31–50 age group. The respondents were mainly homemakers, and a majority had an elementary/middle school education. A majority went on the *Hajj* after 2001 with their husbands.

Table 1. Demographic Profile of the Respondents

Age	Frequency	Hometown	Frequency
18–25	1	İzmir	5
26–30		Aydın	4
31–50	8	Manisa	6
51–60	2	Denizli	1
61–70	4	Bolu	2
71 and over	3		
Total	18	Total	18

Marital Status	Frequency	Year of Travel	Frequency
Married	12	Before 1990	3
Single/Widow	5	1991–2000	3
Divorced	1	2001–2009	12
Total	18	Total	18

Occupation	Frequency	Accompanying Person	Frequency[a]
Housewife	14	Husband	10
Academic	1	Children	1
Student	1	Parents	3
Government official	2	Brothers/Sisters	3
Total	18	Friends	2
		Relatives	1
		Alone	Not applicable

[a]Some respondents were accompanied by more than one type

The research findings that emerged from the data analysis suggest four closely related themes.

Motives for the Hajj. The findings suggest several main motives for participation in the *Hajj*. All of the respondents indicated that they had strong religious motives to undertake the *Hajj*, and felt a strong obligation to perform one of the Five Pillars of Islam. The respondents made statements such as "the *Hajj* is one of Islam's Five Pillars," and "the *Hajj* is a religious obligation for all Muslims"; this was the primary motive for the respondents' decision to go on the *Hajj*. In addition, the respondents stated that Saudi Arabia was an important and sacred country for Muslims, with many religious sites located there. They wanted to see these sacred sites and observe how Muslims from other countries and cultures practiced Islam.

Several respondents also mentioned personal reasons for their *Hajj*. For example, one participant claimed that a dream from 20 years ago was one of her main reasons for going to the *Hajj*:

> Let me tell you why I decided to go to Makkah. I saw my late father-in-law in my dream. He was going to the *Hajj*, but before his departure, he told me to follow him. This was why I intended to go. After twenty years I realized my dream.

None of the respondents made an independent decision to go on the *Hajj*. It was either a joint decision with their husbands or a sole decision by their husbands or other close relatives, such as sons and parents. Several respondents stated that they felt under pressure to go from their family members, with husbands and children a main influence. One participant stated:

> We had just returned to Turkey from the Netherlands with my family members. I was not really ready for such a trip, but my husband insisted heavily. Well, I had to obey.

The Hajj Experience and Challenges. The respondents were asked to describe their overall *Hajj* experience, and whether they faced any challenges during their travel. Respondents described their experience as emotionally rewarding, educational, unique, inspirational, different, and pleasant. The *Hajj* experience helped them to learn more about Islam and their religious obligations, and the reasons behind them. For example, one respondent stated:

> After I came back from the *Hajj*, I started thinking that I had known Islam differently than before I went to the *Hajj*. Before, I was inexperienced and did not have sufficient knowledge about Islam. After the *Hajj*, I started understanding the meanings behind the worship. For example, Muslims throw stones to the devil. Do you know why? The devil is a metaphor. You throw a stone to the bad and wicked feelings hidden in you. The wicked thoughts and feelings are the devil. You try to destroy them and not the devil.

A common theme from the interviews was that the respondents often referred to or explained how they prayed and worshipped for long periods. Unlike other times, during their *Hajj*, they prayed for long hours, asked for forgiveness, and experienced a feeling of belonging, devotion, and self-lessness. Some of the respondents also noted that being able to perform their religious duties and obligations brought more tranquility, satisfaction, and structure to their lives.

Several respondents had gained knowledge about Saudi Arabia and the *Hajj*. For example, one of the respondents stated, "this sacred land was very safe; it was not hard for even women to go out alone after midnight." There were also comments about how the pilgrims from other countries and cultures were supportive and understanding, despite the fact that it was very crowded and they did not speak the same language. Respondents seemed to be moved and emotionally affected by the fact that Muslims from different cultures, countries, races, and ages came together to fulfill their religious obligations.

Many of the respondents initially stated that they did not face any major problems and challenges, perhaps because they were not willing to complain openly about their journey due to its sacred religious nature. Comments included, "There were not any problems," "Everything was fine," "The accommodation, facilities, bathrooms, and food and beverage services were good," "Everything was perfect," and "there were professional people always helping us." However, when probed further, several areas of concern emerged, including warm weather, health issues, application and visa process, hygiene conditions, crowd control, transportation challenges, lack of clear knowledge about religious sites and ceremonies, and language barriers. Certainly, the respondents found Saudi Arabia warmer than Turkey. As most of them were in their middle ages or older, the warm weather and health problems created some challenges. One respondent noted, "Although the accommodation facilities had air conditioning, the temperature outside was high. That is why I couldn't go to some sacred places." Another respondent stated, "It was too hot for us and my health created challenges. But God helps you there, gives you strength to achieve." Another claimed:

> We walked quite long distances. The men and women were separated from each other at nights. We got up at 3:00 AM again for circumambulation. It was very crowded. You could be crushed by this crowd.

The respondents were separated from male relatives on several occasions. For example, they dined separately, slept in different rooms from their husbands, and even prayed separately from their fathers, brothers, and/or husbands. Some respondents spent more time with other female group members than with their husbands or male relatives.

Several referred to visa application procedures for the *Hajj* as one of the major challenges. As noted above, Saudi Arabia allocates an annual quota to each country, and not every applicant from Turkey is able to go to the *Hajj*, depending on the number of applications in that year. When applying for the *Hajj*, each applicant has to provide a health report and receive certain vaccinations. Several respondents also complained about the hygienic conditions of their accommodation, food and beverage outlets, and toilets. Regarding transportation, they noted that some of them could not find a direct route from their hometowns and had to wait long hours at airports for connecting flights.

During their *Hajj*, some of the respondents continued preparing food and drinks and providing clean clothes for their husbands, fathers, or sons. In other words, some of their home duties continued during their travel. One respondent, who was the youngest in her group, helped and served the other group members during their travel, although she did not know most of them. The respondents noted that it was often challenging to move in certain areas due to crowded conditions and the huge mass of people. There were comments from the respondents that before they traveled to the *Hajj*, they were very inexperienced and did not know much about the *Hajj* requirements and procedures. Several wished that they could speak Arabic so that they could communicate with other pilgrims and find directions easier. Two younger respondents noted that before they went to the *Hajj*, they had to find people to look after their children and houses. One other challenge noted was related to the possibility of having their menstruation cycle during the *Hajj*. Several respondents found that their several bags and suitcases were difficult to carry.

Feelings of Female Pilgrims about the Hajj. When respondents were asked about their feelings before, during, and after the *Hajj*, similar and consistent comments were noted. They expressed how they felt before they the trip with the words of "wonder," "excitement," "longing," and "curiosity." During their pilgrimage the feeling were described with the words "excitement," "happiness," "peace," "tranquility," and "enthusiasm." The words used for after the pilgrimage were "calmness," "enthusiasm," "emotional satisfaction," "tranquility," and "happiness."

Four key words were mentioned by almost all the respondents in describing their overall feelings about the *Hajj*: happiness, tranquility, excitement, and peace. All were happy because they had fulfilled one of the Five Pillars of Islam; indeed during the interviews when recalling their experiences, respondents also appeared emotional, happy, and excited. They believed that the *Hajj* was a very different experience, and the sacred land they visited was a kind of heaven for them. For example, statements about the experience included "This can never be explained. You have to experience this," "It is excitement, it is happiness, it is rush," and "indefinable happiness." Several of the respondents noted that during *Hajj*, they felt calm, selflessness, and worthless. All material things that were important before became unimportant, and they did not want to come back to their homes, but wanted to stay there and be close to God. As one respondent noted:

> When you go to the Hajj, you feel yourself free of sins because God forgives you. You feel just like a newborn baby. That is why you feel yourself closer to God.

Influence of the Hajj on Pilgrims' Lives. The respondents were asked whether and how their *Hajj* influenced their lives after returning home. The analysis revealed that the experience positively influenced their lives in many ways. More than half of them stated that after their visit to the *Hajj*, they became more spiritual, peaceful, attentive, and careful in their beliefs and behavior so that they could obey and practice Islam better. It was also apparent that most of the respondents felt satisfied and accomplished because they fulfilled one of the Five Pillars of Islam. They further stated that they learned more about Islam and what and how it requires its followers to behave, pray, and treat others. The respondents expressed that after their *Hajj* experience, they started appreciating what they have and respecting others more. After the experience, they were calmer, more peaceful, and started accepting people as they were. Several stated that since they saw that everyone was equal during the pilgrimage—regardless of their age, wealth, gender, or race—they learned to better appreciate, respect, forgive, and tolerate other human beings. However, there were also comments that after the *Hajj* experience, family members, relatives, and friends changed their expectations of the female pilgrims. The following statement from one of the respondents summarizes these feelings:

> After the travel, there were different expectations from me. For example, the elder parents and relatives become more rigid. They expected that you never participate in social life. This is very hard, indeed.

CONCLUSION

This chapter sought to explore the overall experiences of female pilgrims from Turkey to Makkah for the *Hajj* pilgrimage, an area of limited prior research. The findings offer a number of theoretical and practical implications. First, the main motives of respondents include the religious obligation of performing one of the Five Pillars of Islam, visiting the center of the Muslim world, and seeing how other Muslims practiced Islam. In short, they were inspired by religious motives (Olsen and Timothy 2006), and may be considered as traditional religious pilgrims (Digance 2006) or mandatory religious tourists (Timothy and Iverson 2006). The respondents who participated in this study would not fit the modern secular pilgrim definition of Digance (2006). According to Din, the Islamic concept of travel focuses on "the sacred goal of submission to the ways of God" (1989:551). Muslims are encouraged to travel so that they can see and appreciate the greatness of God. Such appreciation and submission to Allah was often identified in the statements made by the respondents.

Second, it appears that the participants did not make independent decisions to go on the *Hajj*; instead they made a joint decision with their husbands, or the decision was made by their husbands, sons, or other close male family members on their behalf. This finding may be explained by the majority of respondents having a low level of education (elementary or middle school) and being homemakers without financial independence. The *Hajj* from Turkey would cost normally over US$2,000 per person, which is expensive for many in Turkey. Also, men in Turkish society tend to have more power compared to women.

Third, the study suggests that the *Hajj* was an educational, unique, different, and pleasant experience for the participants. Following Pine and Gilmore's (1998) experience economy concept, it is evident that the respondents actively participated in the *Hajj* experience and were fully immersed in their religious duties and obligations. In other words, the *Hajj* was an educational experience (Pine and Gilmore 1998) for them, educating them about Islam and their religious duties. They also learned about Saudi Arabia and the practices of Muslims from other cultures and countries. During the *Hajj* respondents were able to escape from their daily and earthly affairs, and in the process they felt closer to God.

Fourth, the findings reveal that the female pilgrims to the *Hajj* faced certain challenges including warm weather, health problems, application procedures, hygiene conditions, difficulty of moving in crowded areas, transportation challenges, lack of clear knowledge about procedures, and language barriers, in part supporting the findings of a study by Bhardwaj (1998). Given their physical strength, warm weather, and difficulty of moving in crowded areas, the *Hajj* appears to be more challenging for female pilgrims compared to their male counterparts. In addition, the possibility of having their menstruation cycle during certain days of the *Hajj* is also a unique challenge for female pilgrims.

Overall, the respondents had positive feelings regarding their *Hajj* experiences, summarized in four keywords: happiness, tranquility, excitement, and peace. The respondents are considered mandatory/traditional religious tourists. Being able to fulfill one of the Five Pillars of Islam made them feel happy, excited, satisfied, and peaceful. The *Hajj* experience had a positive influence on the lives of these female pilgrims; they became more spiritual, peaceful, attentive, calm, tolerant, and careful in their beliefs and behavior, and as a consequence better practitioners of Islam. This is consistent with findings by Digance (2006) that pilgrims may search for change in their lives through the experience of pilgrimages, and that such experiences may have positive long-lasting impacts on them.

This study has a number of limitations that may be addressed in further research. First, the respondents interviewed included only female pilgrims from Turkey, and future studies may obtain further insights from collecting data from female participants from other countries and cultures. This is because there may be major differences among Islamic countries in terms of customs, traditions, beliefs, and perceptions, which may directly influence female pilgrims' overall *Hajj* experiences. Research into the experiences of female pilgrims who have higher education and more extensive travel experiences may also be of value. Future studies could collect data from both men and women, and hence compare the two genders in terms of their motives, overall experiences, challenges, and feelings, as well as the impact of the *Hajj* on their lives. Finally, the present study collected data through only one data collection method; other studies can collect data through multiple data collection methods such as questionnaires and participant observation.

Chapter 15

TOURISM AND ISLAMOPHOBIA
Muslims in Non-Muslim States

Marcus L. Stephenson
Middlesex University, United Arab Emirates
Nazia Ali
Staffordshire University, UK

Abridgement: This chapter critically focuses on Islamophobic practices that are embedded in travel and tourism environments. Muslims, especially those journeying to other Western nations, are finding that their freedom of movement is restricted within environments perceived to be hostile, particularly in the context of post-September 11. The premise of this chapter is to illustrate the role of travel and tourism in continuing to reinforce Islamophobic attitudes of the West to Muslims worldwide. Importantly, the discussion critically highlights ways in which religious abhorrence, orientalist perspectives, ethnic detestation, and xenophobic intolerance significantly affect tourism experiences. These factors marginalize communities from appreciating the global attributes of tourism, especially elements that express the importance of cosmopolitan forms of citizenship. **Keywords:** Islamophobia; exclusion; discrimination

INTRODUCTION

This chapter critically explores manifestations of Islamophobia in the tourism domain. It seeks to understand the journeys of Muslims in non-Muslim states, emphasizing that the global context of Islamophobia has significant social repercussions for tourists of Muslim origin. The discussions

Tourism in the Muslim World
Bridging Tourism Theory and Practice, Volume 2, 235–251
Copyright © 2010 by Emerald Group Publishing Limited
All rights of reproduction in any form reserved
ISSN: 2042-1443/doi:10.1108/S2042-1443(2010)0000002018

are framed within the context of the global (political) climate following the September 11 terrorist attacks on the World Trade Center. This incident, commonly referred to as 9/11, significantly impacted the journeys of populations affiliated with the religion of Islam. Widespread distrust toward Muslims emerged in the form of anti-Muslim sentiment frequently defined as Islamophobia, which in its purist sense denotes "dread or hatred of Islam, and therefore fear or dislike of all or most Muslims" (Runnymede Trust 1997:1). Islamophobia is represented in the form of direct and indirect types of prejudice, discrimination, religious profiling, xeno-racism, social and political exclusion, and violence. Muslims have been duly caught up in what can be termed the "globalization of fear" (Bianchi 2006).

Given that Muslim tourists are treated with suspicion in a political context where governments and states are waging a war on terror (European Monitoring Centre on Racism and Xenophobia 2006a; European Union Agency for Fundamental Rights 2009; Fekete 2004), the globalized fear of Muslims as terrorists or extremists arguably affects their freedom to travel and liberally participate in tourist activities within the Western states. They have been subjected to extensive random checks from immigration officials and aviation authorities, as well as hostile treatment from other passengers, tourists, and host communities. Members of Muslim communities are genuinely (and politically) concerned about being perceived as a threat to state and public security as a consequence of their religious identities and beliefs. This chapter will thus discuss the limitations and ramifications of the noted failures of the security services to differentiate between "ordinary Muslims and terrorists" at (and within) state borders (Fekete 2004:10). The discussion will highlight the politically ambiguous role of tourism in continuing to reinforce the attitudes and practices in the West toward Muslims worldwide. Here, it is clearly asserted that the demonization of a collective subject described as Muslim has been visible through regulative forms of governance.

The chapter further examines the embodiment of Islamophobic practices and attitudes that shape the tourism movements of Muslim populations. This aspect of the discussion presents a range of personal narratives indicating ways in which religious abhorrence, racist resentment, and xenophobic intolerance have the effect of marginalizing communities from enjoying the benefits and pleasures normatively associated with tourism. As Muslim communities have become extremely vulnerable to religious and racial hatred, there is an urgent need to address ways in which groups experience and encounter xenophobic (and racialized) situations within and across the borders of the Western states. Although there have been some analytical contributions that have deconstructed ways in which the tourism mobilities of ethnic minority citizens (notably the Black Caribbean communities) have been socially and politically restrained by racialized situations (Stephenson 2004, 2006, 2007; Stephenson and Hughes 1995, 2005), tourism studies have not significantly dealt with the tourism mobilities of religious minorities in the Western societies who have also been impacted by social and political circumstance in ways which are uniquely attributed to the condition of Islamophobia.

The work emphasizes that the structural processes at play in monitoring and controlling the mobilities of Muslim tourists fundamentally erodes the freedom associated with travel as a consequence of prejudice or discrimination by other individuals and/or institutions. This contention is dealt with in a final discussion concerning ways in which Islamophobia affects people's opportunity to experience cosmopolitan performances and express a sense of social and religious unity among the global Muslim community, which is, paradoxically, one of the main Islamic principles of travel.

The Association of Chief Police Officers (n.d.) identifies four prominent ways in which Islamophobia has been expressed in British society: attacks, abuse, and violence against Muslims; attacks on Mosques, Islamic Centers, and Muslim cemeteries; discrimination in education, employment, and delivery of goods and services; and lack of provisions and respect for Muslims in public institutions. Anti-Muslim sentiment has been perceived to bear similarities with racial prejudice and discrimination based on color and physical appearance, thus linking Islamophobia with racism. The Commission on British Muslims (2004) emphasizes that Islamophobia can be considered as a form of racism, as anti-Muslim attitudes are reflective of intolerance based upon differences that extend beyond physical appearance and skin color to include religion.

Varying levels of racial intent have been widely reported in a range of member states of the European Union (European Monitoring Centre on Racism and Xenophobia 2006a, 2006b; European Union Agency for Fundamental Rights 2009). Islamophobia can be further linked with racism—and racism with Islamophobia—if the victimization of Muslims is reported to be a direct result of hatred, threats, and/or actual violence (European Monitoring Centre on Racism and Xenophobia 2006a). Islam does not distinguish on the basis of color, nationality, culture, or class, and thus Muslims are not directly categorized on the basis of race and ethnicity. In religious terms, they are formally perceived to belong to one community—the *Ummah*. Nonetheless, the conceptual application of racism toward Muslim communities is still relevant in the context of addressing ways in which they are treated, where racism can be determined by social, political, and ideological determinants rather than biological characteristics. Moreover, it is emphasized that "racism is an enduring, salient aspect of social and global structures" (Lemert 2006:496).

The Council of Europe's European Commission against Racism and Intolerance (ECRI) also acknowledges that racism and Islamophobic practices are in some way interlinked:

> As a result of the fight against terrorism engaged since the events of 11 September 2001, certain groups of persons, notably Arabs, Jews, Muslims, certain asylum seekers, refugees and immigrants, certain visible minorities and persons belonging to such groups, have become particularly vulnerable to racism and/or to racial discrimination across many fields of public life including education, employment, housing, access to goods and services, access to public places and freedom of movement (ECRI 2004 cited in OIC 2008c:18).

The concepts of Islamophobia and racism are further understood by reference to the coexistence of xenophobia and xeno-racism. Xenophobia denotes a fear of foreigners irrespective of their color and phenotypical characteristics. Xeno-racism was initially used to refer to forms of racism directed at such groupings as "political refugees," "alien residents" and "immigrants," and "ethnic" and "racial minorities" living outside of their ancestral homelands (Sivanandan 2001). Given the increased stigmatization and dehumanization of members of Muslim communities post-9/11, especially for those residing in the Western societies and have legal status of residency or citizenship, the conceptual relevance of xeno-racism has now been repositioned in light of the intensification of Islamophobia and xenophobic levels of intolerance toward Muslims in non-Muslim states (Fekete 2004). Muslim Americans in the United States were subjected to post-9/11 hate crimes (such as assaults, vandalism or arson, threats, and intimidation) and verbal abuse (street harassment, name calling, and patronizing statements toward Islam) (Richard 2004). The post-9/11 element of Islamophobia, however, is the process of religious profiling, referring to the criteria by which individuals are singled out often on the basis of their "Islamic religious affiliation" and/or if they originate "from an Islamic state" (Fekete 2004:8). Such discriminative practices can be clearly understood in relation to the propagation of Islamic Orientalism.

ISLAMIC ORIENTALISM, FOLK DEVILS, AND IDENTITY POLITICS

Said's (1978) seminal work, *Orientalism*, is useful in critically understanding the processes responsible for typecasting Muslims as a threat to national and international security. One notable observation concerns the inequitable relationship between Islam and the West, where the Western cultural discourse normatively conceives Muslim populations as a universalized "Other". The media portrayal of Islam in the West, referred to by Said as "Islamic Orientalism" (1978:260), indicated the social construction of the Western fears toward the religion. The projection of stereotypical and standardized images, as well as hegemonic claims to knowledge and power, render the cultural position and social status of Islam inferior to the West. Said's deconstruction of "Islamic Orientalism" is focused on the sociological ramifications of media representations of "Arab others":

> In newsreels or newsphotos, the Arab is always shown in large numbers. No individuality, no personal characteristics or experiences. Most of the pictures represent mass rage and misery, or irrational (hence hopelessly eccentric) gestures. Lurking behind all these images is the menace of *jihad*. Consequence: a fear that the Muslims (or Arabs) will take over the world (1978:287).

Media representations of people and populations affiliated with the theology of Islam, as noted by Said (1978), continue to have an impact upon relations between (and representative of) the Western and non-Western societies. Richard's analysis of Islamophobic manifestations, pre- and post-9/11, highlights orientalist thinking toward Muslims in the West. Although the following claim attempts to overgeneralize, it does indicate underlying stereotypes: "For many Americans, Arabs equal Muslim which equal fanatic, which equals terrorism" (2004:17).

Projections of fear appear to be reflected in the public domain of travel and tourism, where the Muslim is orientalized as a terrorist through a disparaging process of "othering". Such orientalizing is the product of rather populist definitions concerning what constitutes a terrorist in the context of post-9/11. Men sporting beards and females wearing the Islamic head-wrap have been mistaken for terrorists (Glaister 2009; Wazir 2001), which has also intensified in the context of traveling to and from countries listed as state sponsors of terrorism (Iran, Iraq, Syria, Sudan, or Libya) (Goldenberg 2002). The traveler's identity as a Muslim is undermined by being perceived as a potential tourist and an "object of fear" (Aly 2006:22) rather than a subject of religious faith. In view of the experiences of Australian Muslims, Aly states:

> It is this construction of the war on terror as a global battle between 'the West and the rest' that imbues the fear of terrorism with redemptive qualities, enabling and facilitating behavioural responses associated with a reaffirmation of identity and membership of a collective simultaneously denying membership to that collective to those perceived to be "other". This response has found expression in the perception of Muslims as an alien, culturally incompatible and threatening other, creating a state of social tension where the public's anxiety has been and continued to be directed at Australian Muslims who visibly and visually represent the objects of the fear of terrorism (2006:24).

The book by Poynting, Noble, Tabar and Collins (2004), which is sardonically entitled *Bin Laden in the Suburbs: Criminalisation of the Arab Other*, illustrates how 9/11 exacerbated ways in which Muslim and Arab communities are collectively perceived as retrogressive, barbaric, and backward. The level of alienation and the process of alterity can be partly explained by moral panics (Cohen 1972), which relate to ways in which civil societies produce collective hysteria in response to contrived perceptions of others and their patterns of behavior. This concept was further developed by Goode and Ben-Yehuda (1994) to indicate how moral panics explicate levels of hostility toward particular groups, and how they are influenced by a range of functionaries and state representatives (such as politicians, security forces, and journalists). However, Cohen's (1972) original concern of moral panics related to the conceptual significance of folk devils, referring to those who have been socially and politically constructed as the main cause of the public concern or condition. Werbner importantly unearths the ideological ramifications associated with the folk devil phenomenon, emphasizing that the racialized folk devil is

> a displaced figure of collective anxieties and fears and as such, an arbitrary scapegoat embodying racist paranoid convictions

that only cultural, ethnic and racial purity can stem the breakdown of social order and the collapse of society (2005:6).

The labeling of Muslims in the media with words such as "extremists," "terrorists," "fundamentalists," and "fanatics" (Ansari 2002:25) only serves to aggravate anti-Muslim sentiment. Alarmingly, the English politician and television presenter, Robert Kilroy-Silk, writing in the UK newspaper *Sunday Express* (January 4, 2004), branded Arabs as "suicide bombers, limb amputators, women repressors (...) loathsome and threatening terrorists and asylum-seekers" (cited in Dalrymple 2004:18). The BBC suspended Kilroy-Silk's television program following his comments, but this decision was contended by populist discourse on the grounds that freedom of speech was being suppressed by the British media (Dalrymple 2004). These representations cloud the reality that the majority of Muslim populations are not terrorists but actually wish to live in peace with their neighbors (Robinson 1999). Nevertheless, the association of the Islamic world with terrorism has ramifications upon Muslim identities as "terror is transported from the realm of politics into the realm of identity-politics" (Aly 2006:25). According to Said, the politics of identity is

> the feeling that everything you do has to be either legitimated by, or has to pass through the filter of, your national identity, which in most cases is complete fiction (...) I mean, an identity that says all Arabs are homogenously the same and against all Westerners who are all the same (2001:391).

The inferiorization of Arab (and Muslim) others is linked to a historical process of demonization and social exclusion prior to 9/11. This has certainly been observed in situations where Muslims, who are legitimate citizens of the Western states either in terms of rights of residency or rights to domestic nationality, have limited rights to national resources (employment, housing, education, etc.) (Khan 2000; Lewis 1994; Ratcliffe 1999). They also have traditionally experienced social prejudice and discrimination as a consequence of their religious and racialized identities (Werbner 2000).

Impact and Implications on Tourism

The European Monitoring Centre on Racism and Xenophobia (2001) documented evidence concerning increased levels of anti-Islamic hostility taking place in the United Kingdom immediately preceding 9/11. Rayner

(2005) noted that in four years following this incident acts of racism in rural areas in the United Kingdom doubled. Trevor Phillips, Chair of the Commission for Racial Equality, announced that the British countryside sustains a "passive apartheid" where there is a "gradual shift towards a difficult situation in which people from ethnic minorities feel uncomfortable" (The Guardian 2004). Cumbria (northwest England) is now ranked as the most racist region in England and Wales. Other areas deemed dangerous for minority inhabitants and tourists are Cornwall and Devon (southwest England) (Rayner 2005). However, Scotland has also had its share of racial concerns. The Highlands of Scotland Tourist Board, for instance, received racial complaints from a group of Pakistani mountaineers from the West Midlands, who were distressed to find racial graffiti daubed on a cabin at the summit of Ben Nevis with the words: "Keep Pakis off my Mountain" (Eastern Eye 2003:1). It appears that some kind of "purification process" is taking place in those geographic locations which seek to exclude individuals designated at "dangerous outsiders" (Sibley 1997:228).

Nevertheless, common perceptions of others as dangerous beings are significantly expressed at state frontiers and borders. One study conducted in 2008 by the European Union Agency for Fundamental Rights (2009), found that 86% of Muslim respondents of North African origin living in Italy considered themselves to be singled out by immigration customs or border control officials. The physical movement of such groups can arguably be construed as a racialized process and performance, based on Islamophobic and xeno-racist foundations. One specific illustration of this claim relates to the movement of nearly 3 million people of Maghreb origin who travel annually to their ancestral destinations in North Africa for the purpose of visiting friends and relatives, a number that is increasing at an average of 7% every year. Over 6,000 automobiles during the summer months journey from places as far as Germany to Tangiers, via Algeciras—Spain's southern port. In addition to an increased presence of border guards, custom officers, and the local police, a total of 1,200 civil guard officers are commissioned to monitor people's movements across the Gibraltar Straits. Not only have there been cases of intense body and car searches, but lengthy periods of detainment and cases of physical harassment (Gómez 2004).

Two months following 9/11, it was reported that the US authorities required travelers from 26 mainly Muslim states to obtain FBI clearance before their visas could be processed at the US consulates, delaying travels plans and having a direct affect on business tourism and student travel (Goldenberg 2002). A 2006 USA Today/Gallup Poll found 18% of Americans questioned felt nervous if they noticed a Muslim woman aboard the same flight as themselves, while 31% stated they would feel nervous if it was a Muslim man (cited in OIC 2008c).

Perceptions of criminality that obscure the journeys of Muslim minorities infer that aspects of the Lombrosian theory of criminality still have some ontological relevance in explaining why certain individuals and groups are popularly perceived to be involved in activities deemed to be regressive. The late 19th century work of the Italian physician, Cesare Lombroso, is based on the notion that particular physical features of individuals are in some way linked to their potentiality in pursuing criminal acts (Lombroso-Ferrero 1972; Lombroso 2006). Although this perspective has long since been discredited in social sciences, it chillingly illustrates how populist perceptions of others are still influenced by mythical and atavistic notions that certain individuals will commit terrorizing activities on the basis on their genetic features and physical makeup.

Muslims can be excluded from holistic tourism experiences primarily because of the politics of identity. Muslims are arguably typecast more as terrorists than tourists. Identity politics contributes further to the emergence of anti-Muslim sentiments in the guise of Islamophobia and xenophobia/ xeno-racism. Nonetheless, these practices are arguably underpinned by a postcolonial agenda. It has been firmly asserted that:

> For terrorism to be adequate to the project of imperialism, for imperialism to be sustainable publicly and rhetorically, terrorism must be falsely associated with Arabs and Muslims everywhere. For this idea to take hold, ordinary people have to refuse to make distinctions amongst Arabs and Muslims, all of whom are assumed to be actually or potentially guilty of terrorism, just by their ascribed identity (Kateb 2004:3; cited in Aly 2006:26).

The Australian Government introduced a new visa law specifically directed at people and populations of Arab origin applying for entry into Australia. Those submitting visa applications are now asked to disclose their ancestral history by giving the names of their parents and grandfathers. The official rationale for producing this new immigration initiative is based on the view that visa applicants can be more accurately identified in the future. The Islamic Council of Victoria (Australia) condemns such border control measures, viewing the new visa laws aimed at Arab communities as a real indication of the intent of racial and religious profiling (Dunn 2007).

During the boarding of a domestic US flight from Washington DC to Florida nine Muslims, of whom eight were US citizens, were removed from an AirTran flight after their overhead conversations were interpreted as being a threat to security. The Muslim passengers of South Asian decent were planning to travel to a Muslim retreat until their faith, appearance, dress, and form of communication were considered to represent the prototype terrorist. The flight was initially aborted until the remaining passengers were cleared by the FBI. As a safety precaution, the airline refused to carry the Muslim passengers to their given destination, who then had to book a flight with another carrier (Glaister 2009). One of the nine travelers, Kashif Irfan, commented:

> They [*his brother and wife*] were discussing some aspect of airport security ... the only thing he said was "wow, the jets are right next to my window". I think they were remarking about safety (Glaister 2009).

A front page story from the *Sydney Morning Herald* (February 23, 2004) dealt with the circumstances of alleged racism by four young Australians of Sri Lankan origin taken from the plane in the United States and then incarcerated and subsequently questioned as to their purpose of their trip (cited in Kremmer and Banham 2004). Britain's first Muslim minister, Shahid Malik, was stopped, searched, and detained by airport security officials at Washington DC's Dulles Airport after attending a host of meetings to tackle terrorism in October 2007. Ironically, Malik experienced a similar encounter in 2006 at JFK Airport (New York) after attending an event organized by US Department of Homeland Security, where he delivered a keynote speech about combating terrorism. He explained:

> ... two other Muslims were also detained ... I am deeply disappointed ... . The abusive attitude I endured last November [*2006*] I forgot about and I forgave, but I really do believe that British ministers and parliamentarians should be afforded the same respect and dignity at USA airports that we would bestow upon our colleagues in the Senate and Congress (BBC 2007).

The desire or aspiration to visit friends and relatives in such places as America has been problematic for Arab and Asian travelers. In her ethnographic study concerning the travel and tourism perceptions of members of a UK Pakistani community, Ali noted the concerns of one informant, Shazia, who expressed:

> ... I have personally not considered going to America. After September 11, I had a friend whose uncle was in America, there was hostility ... people right or wrong were terrorised in a sense ... I think people think your black or your covering – "OK very dangerous or terrorist" (2008:211).

Disciplinary power and regulative forms of governance have made visible subjects described as "Middle Eastern" or "Muslim". Airports are potent examples of how surveillance techniques operate in a manner that undermine democratic participation and social trust. Lyon (2003:123–124) emphasizes that airports are sites for "security and surveillance practices and process" where travelers are "screened for eligibility to travel and for acceptability on arrival." Augé (1995) describes airports, like refugee camps, service stations, motorways, and train stations, as non-lieux (non-places). Here, mundane locational experiences emerge and organic social interactions cease. Non-places are perceived as places of solitude, anonymity, impermanence, and alienation, as well as being bureaucratic and uniform. Although it cannot be denied that airports manifest officious practices and encompass intrinsically alienating experiences, they are by no means places of anonymity. These sites exhibit stringent practices of top-down security, rigorous information management, and detailed data production, where racialized individuals are systematically identified and documented, often in a surreptitious manner (Stephenson 2006).

Post-9/11 has seen a significant increase in surveillance activities, exemplified through the technological development of screening and data mining processes, operating before individuals depart from the home country and continuing after their arrival at the given destination. Lyon (2003) highlights examples where people's personal data can be gathered from a range of sources: cell phone use, credit card transaction records, traffic control points, ticketing, and Internet data (via computerized reservation systems). Such technologies extend the "capacity to discriminate between different classes of persons, using algorithmic surveillance" (Lyon 2004:310), especially in an effort to establish detailed individual profiles.

The contemporary journeys of Muslims do not systematically constitute legitimate touristic ventures, particularly in situations where one's identity or status as a tourist is not fully sanctioned by state authorities. Therefore, the purpose of travel is potentially perceived to involve criminal or illegal activities as opposed to such touristic activities as educational pursuit, cultural tourism and social recreation. Sorkin informatively presents a reflexive and candid account of how Muslims can quite easily be feared in public spaces in the United States due to the strength of entrenched public opinion, noting:

> Post 9/11, I profiled compulsively. On the subway not long ago I was sitting opposite an elderly Muslim man (bearded and traditionally dressed) who was carrying several large parcels. The well-drilled formula *Muslim plus package equals bomb* fitted through my mind even as I judged it ridiculous (2004:256).

Intense methods of surveillance limit and rigorously control the movements of minority groups within nation-states, where borders and frontiers are localized through the internal monitoring of people's daily mobilities. One such illustration concerns the actions of UK immigration officers (representing HM Customs) operating in such public spaces as the London Underground in a vigorous attempt to refute or validate people's legal status and rights of UK residency. This situation developed as a consequence of the Labour Government's 1999 Asylum and Immigration Act, which provided immigration officers with the power to question and detain individuals beyond ports of entry (Feldman 2004). The methods used to identify illegal entrants are politically uncertain. Feldman raises several important questions:

> How do they select the passengers they pick on? Do they watch out for "foreign-looking" people, or do they wait to hear people speaking to each other in "foreign" languages? (2004:23).

The terrorist attacks on London Underground on July 7, 2005 could be used as formal (and state) justification for future monitoring, detainment and arrest of individuals on the basis of being perceived to be suspicious and/or a direct threat to society and state security. Internal policing of ethnic minority groups is evident in other states. The Vigipirate Anti-Terrorist Initiative in France, for instance, initially unleashed a series of security measures to protect government buildings and tourism sites and was then extended to militarize French housing estates in the Islamic quarters of cities and towns (Fekete 2004:12). The race riots throughout France in November and December 2005 were arguably a reaction to the racial marginalization of North African minorities and the stigmatization of Islam (The Economist 2005).

Destabilization of Religious and Cosmopolitan Forms of Tourism Mobility

Travel for Asian communities has religious, ethnic, and cultural meanings. Although Muslims are encouraged to travel to fulfill the fifth pillar of Islam—*Hajj* (pilgrimage) to Makkah—they are also encouraged to travel to other sites of religious importance such as visit Harem es-Shariff in Jerusalem, Karbala in Iraq, and mosques in Turkey. Several verses from the Qur'an indicate the value of travel associated with the search for knowledge based on the religious importance of Islamic heritage sites:

> And We currently sent into every nation a messenger, (saying), Worship Allah and avoid tāghūt (false objects of worship). And among them were those whom Allah guided, and among them were those upon whom error was (deservedly) decreed. So proceed (*i.e.*, travel) through the earth and observe how was the end of the deniers (the Qur'an, Surah 16:36)... . Say, (O Muhammad), Travel through the land and observe how He began creation. Then Allah will produce the final creation (i.e. development) (the Qur'an, Surah 29:20) ... Say, (O Muhammad), Travel through the land and observe how was the end of those before. Most of them were associators (of others with Allah) (the *Qur'an*, Surah 30:42).

The cultural and religious importance of travel for the Muslim diaspora has been significantly examined in tourism studies (Alhabshi 2001; Ali 2008; Ali and Holden 2006; Din 1989; Timothy and Iverson 2006). The obligatory nature of travel extends to cultural-based aspirations. Ali's (2008) study, for instance, which concerns the tourism practices of a UK Pakistani community, indicates how travels to the ancestral homeland of Pakistan involves visiting of friends and immediate relatives, as well as extended family members located in numerous villages and towns. Individuals and families were sometimes accompanied by relatives of the host society when visiting other kinfolk and attending ceremonial occasions (such as births, deaths, and weddings). Visiting homes of kin to offer condolences for deceased members of the family or community, and visiting their graves and burial grounds, would often involve reciting prayers and verses from the Qur'an. Such forms of travel involving Islamic destinations generally help to secure family networks and uphold kinship membership as well as enable individuals to reaffirm their religious quests and responsibilities.

Din (1989) asserts that Islamic forms of travel can promote cross-cultural communication and understanding, which is essential in endorsing the notion of unity among the *Ummah*. His analysis of tourism and Islam is compelling in that he considers the responsibilities of both the tourist and the host, noting:

> While the spiritual goal is to reinforce one's submission to the ways of God, the social goal which follows is to submission to the ways of God, the social goal which follows is to encourage and strengthen the bond of *sillaturrahim* (Muslim fraternity) among the *Ummah* (Muslim community) … . In sanctioning compassionate treatment for the traveller and in places a high treatment for the traveller and in placing a high premium in travel, Islam enjoins a system of reciprocal (1989:552) hospitality which would promote fraternal affinity among the *Ummah*, and would enable even the poor and less fit to travel … (1989:553).

Some theoretical abstractions of tourism also emphasize that travel can also help to socially bind people together and promote international forms of mutual appreciation, which in many ways complement Islamic principles of travel relating to the importance of achieving congenial relations, auspicious encounters, and spiritual experiences. Therefore, it is thought that tourism can create familiarity and nurture common understanding by acting as a catalyst for dissolving the sociocultural boundaries preexisting between local and foreign cultures. Urry, for instance, maintains that because international tourism encounters have the capacity to produce "familiarization" and "normalization" between host and guest cultures, "countries are no longer seen as particularly dangerous and threatening— just different…" (1995:166–67). This conceptualization suggests the importance of tourism as a vital force for international peace. Such organizations as the UN World Tourism Organization, the World Travel and Tourism Council, and the International Institute for Peace through Tourism firmly maintain that tourists can act as ambassadors for peace. Tourism then can perhaps be viewed as a potential catalyst for nurturing cultural and intercultural learning experiences.

In light of the current climate of "global terrorism," however, Muslim journeys to and within the Western states are politically implicated. Negative portrayals in the media and common perceptions have compromised the safety and security of Muslim tourists in the West. Consequently, anti-Muslim sentiments undermine the cultural duties and religious obligations that influence Muslim populations to travel.

The definitions and understandings of citizenship were advanced by Marshall's (1964) work, which identified the key constituents of modern citizenship as civil, political, and social rights. However, new modes of differentiated types of citizenship emerged in the context of understanding citizenships outside of Marshall's framework, thus perceiving forms of citizenship beyond nation-state boundaries to represent more transnational, global, and cosmopolitan elevations of citizenship (Follesdal 2002; Imber 2002; Kivisto and Faist 2007). However, the 9/11 incident was viewed by Dower and Williams (2002a:xiii) as a defining moment in effacing the "idea" and "ideals" of global citizenship in producing a "sense of common humanity," reflecting Immanuel Kant's (1949) calling for international principles of citizenship that account for "mutual respect" for all of mankind (cited in Dower and Williams 2002b:3).

However, "global terrorism" has led to the need to reconsider matters of citizenship, especially as Muslim identities are implicated in the context of the current sociopolitical climate. As antiterrorist legislation and practices incriminate "Muslims" as "terrorists," this misidentification acts a social impediment by restricting cosmopolitan performances and worldly experiences associated with tourism practices. Such restrictions preclude Muslim tourists, unlike other "ordinary" tourists, from exercising the universalistic human right of freedom of mobility as expressed in Article 13 of the United Nation's Universal Declaration of Human Rights (1948): everyone has the right of freedom to movement and residence within the borders of each state, and everyone has the right to leave any country, including his [sic] own and to return to his [sic] country (The United Nations 1948). However, such declarations are simply conjectural in the sense that rights of mobility associated with tourism can only exists if states are actually proactive in developing and promoting the right to freedom of movement, especially by protecting individuals and groups traveling to, from and within state territory. States may be confronted with the political dilemma associated between the protection of national security and the protection of the personal safety of individuals. Santana notes:

> When tourism is the issue, the meaning of security naturally encompasses 'personal security'. However, national security is not necessarily sufficient to ensure personal security, since it is primarily designed to protect the national territorial integrity and sovereignty of the state from external aggression (2001:223).

Follesdal (2002) crucially writes that one essential principle of (global) citizenship is the social foundation of trust between co-citizens, and also between citizens of different nation-states. Therefore, if trust is over-shadowed with suspicion and fear, then cooperation between humans (and tourists) is indeterminate. Therefore this situation makes it difficult for mutual forms of trust to develop between diverse populations and religions within and beyond the nation-state. Religious abhorrence, xeno-racism, and xenophobic intolerance marginalize Muslim people and populations from enjoying the benefits associated with global forms of citizenship and cosmopolitanism, preventing them from being (or becoming) rooted cosmopolitans and from appreciating the religious benefits associated with being an integral part of the *Ummah*.

CONCLUSION

The terrorist attacks on the World Trade Center on September 11, 2001 have affected the encounter of the Muslim world with the West, and also impacted the identity of its followers globally. A wave of antiterrorism legislation, practices, and procedures emerged to curb terrorist activities in such industry sectors as transport (especially aviation) and tourism. Islamophobia implicates the identities of members of the Muslim diaspora, where they are perceived to pose a serious threat to the safety and security of other tourists and host communities. The structural barriers relating to regulative governance, religious profiling, institutional discrimination, media representation, and populist opinion essentially mystify any attempt to conceive tourism mobility as a marker of cosmopolitan citizenship, or as a symbol of rights associated with the freedom of movement principle.

Muslim tourists are hindered by extensive random checks from immigration officials and aviation personnel, where encounters with tourists and host populations can potentially be met with suspicion and hostility. Consequently, they have restricted access to cosmopolitan privileges because they cannot be trusted, particularly in situations where they are viewed as the "enemy within" (Fekete 2004:3). As Muslim tourists are considered a threat to humanity, cultural harmony, and the global order, they could perhaps be viewed as anti-cosmopolitan subjects, despite genuine intentions to travel for meaningful quests and experiences.

Although the conceptualization of cosmopolitanism is multifaceted (Hill 2000; Keith 2005; Roudometof 2005; Szerszynski and Urry 2002), the intersection of global citizenship and cosmopolitanism with Islamic religion and tourism, particularly in the context of post-9/11, needs to be further explored in the field of tourism studies and within different destination contexts. As the 10th anniversary of 9/11 approaches, research ought to reconsider through empirically focused study ways in which Islamophobic encounters in the realm of tourism hinder the formation of bilateral affinities between individuals and groups.

Research that is embedded in critical discourses of citizenship could enable inquires to think politically about the difficulties of achieving transnational and cosmopolitan forms of citizenship through the lens of tourism mobilities. This approach could contribute further to conceptualizations of civil, political, and social rights of Muslims (and other disenfranchised communities) in host countries, whether as tourists or hosts. It is important to bear in mind that Muslim tourists are also victims of terrorist attacks in both Muslim (such as Indonesia, Egypt, Turkey) and non-Muslim destinations (the United States, the United Kingdom, Spain), and thus future inquiries should attempt to readdress such issues in order to provide a more balanced inquiry as well as consider the wider impacts of terrorism on the Muslim community.

Chapter 16

TOURISM SHOPPING IN JEDDAH
Female Domestic Tourists' Experiences

Samirah Al-Saleh
King Abdul Aziz University, Saudi Arabia
Kevin Hannam
University of Sunderland, UK

Abridgement: This chapter examines the consumption experiences of Saudi Arabian female domestic tourists visiting the shopping malls of Jeddah and contextualizes this in terms of Islamic consumption more generally. First, the wider academic literature on the relations between shopping and tourism is discussed, and then aspects of Islamic consumption in terms of both shopping and tourism. Next, a review of the context of tourism development in Saudi Arabia and specifically Jeddah is provided. After a brief note on the methodology used for this study, the results from the focus groups conducted with female domestic tourists about their shopping experiences in Jeddah are discussed.
Keywords: shopping; Islamic consumption; Jeddah; Saudi Arabia

INTRODUCTION

Contemporary tourism has brought both risks and opportunities for culture and development in the Muslim world, depending on how it is managed. Indeed, as Sadi and Henderson note: "For many Middle Eastern societies, Western style tourism is considered to be fundamentally incompatible with the Islamic religion and way of life" (2005:95). Nevertheless, tourism developments have proceeded, and for many there are increasing

Tourism in the Muslim World
Bridging Tourism Theory and Practice, Volume 2, 253–264
Copyright © 2010 by Emerald Group Publishing Limited
All rights of reproduction in any form reserved
ISSN: 2042-1443/doi:10.1108/S2042-1443(2010)0000002019

opportunities for free time; thus, a high percentage of disposable income is being spent on various forms of tourism and leisure. However, for many others the opportunities afforded by tourism are restricted to relatively low-paid employment and relative immobility (Singh, Timothy and Dowling 2003; Hannam, Sheller and Urry 2006). Other barriers to tourism development have been regional political instability and visa restrictions (Hazbun 2008).

For the hypermobile elite, however, the relations between tourism and shopping have been showcased by research into the developments in the United Arab Emirates and Jordan (Al-Hamarneh and Steiner 2004). Like Las Vegas, Dubai was literally created out of nothing as an instant city in the deserts. Indeed, Dubai has quickly become a commercial capital comparable to Las Vegas in terms of shopping and tourism. According to Bagaeen, "combining the involvement of local businesses and innovative strategies of urban marketing with headline catching projects, Dubai has set out to transform its urban landscape and its image" (2007:173). With luxury residences, hotels, offices, and shopping malls, as well as a spectacular airport, the rulers of Dubai have consciously sought to enter the world stage of consumption by extravagantly spending their income from oil. It is the world's biggest building site, but its success is also built on the labor of the poorly paid workers from the Indian subcontinent (Stephenson and Ali-Knight 2009). As Steiner observes, Dubai has become "a completely commoditized hyperreal Orient, designed for the purpose of consumption and the stabilisation of the existing authoritarian regimes" (2009b:10). Outside the United Arab Emirates, many other Islamic cities have also sought to emulate the grand shopping malls of Dubai by constructing their own. This chapter examines the consumption experiences of Saudi Arabian female domestic tourists visiting the shopping malls of Jeddah and is contextualized in terms of Islamic consumption more generally.

SHOPPING AND TOURISM

Shopping has proved to be a major motivation for tourists (Cohen 1995; Di Matteo and Di Matteo 1996; Turner and Reisinger 2001). Indeed, it can be argued that tourism experience is not complete without some form of shopping (Timothy and Butler 1995). This also has considerable economic significance to local merchants and has become the highest ranking tourist expenditure in certain areas of the world (Kent, Schock and Snow 1983; Turner and Reisinger 2001). Timothy and Butler (1995) further explain that shopping can be a great attraction for tourists from developed countries visiting less developed ones who look for bargains in destinations where the prices of merchandise may be relatively lower.

Shopping specifically for souvenirs and gifts for friends and family as a way of sharing of their experience far from home is also a significant factor in tourism (Littrell, Anderson and Brown 1993; MacCannell 2002; Snepenger, Murphy, O'Connell and Gregg 2003). Particular places can be developed into tourist shopping grounds such as in Asia, where craftwork or souvenirs typical of the local culture in night markets can be purchased (Littrell et al 1993; Hsieh and Chang 2006). Away from traditional markets, shopping as an activity has grown in large retail stores, shopping arcades, and shopping malls (Turner and Reisinger 2001). Shopping opportunities have also become an important factor in destination marketing and a key component of package tours (Timothy and Butler 1995). Moreover, the planning strategy for tourist shopping villages (Getz 1993), use of a shopping space by both tourists and residents (Snepenger et al 2003), and cross-border shopping behaviors (Timothy and Butler 1995) have all been examined recently.

However, tourists sometimes treat their visits to shops as a form of entertainment or recreation, perhaps without even purchasing a product (Jones 1999). In that case, their primary motivation is not utilitarian, but hedonistic. Tourists can lose themselves in shopping to escape from daily routine or to experience another culture (Babin, Chebat and Michon 2004). The possibility of shopping developing into a tourist resource depends on the degree of quality, attractiveness, and safety of the environment. Perceived and/or real risks associated with shopping while on holiday may lead to real confusion, affecting tourists' shopping behavior. Incidents like muggings while shopping or the fear of being conned may inhibit tourists' shopping activities at destinations and change their future plans as a result of incidents. Perceived risk affects present and future decisions, in spite of perceived hospitality in other resort domains (Yuksel and Yuksel 2007). However, local shopping customs may amuse and induce tourists to change their normal shopping patterns. In most less developed countries, bargaining is a widespread practice in specific types of small retail business, whereas it is not common in most of the West. The practice may be interesting to tourists, but it can also be seen as frustrating (Lee 2000).

Overall, it is clear that the retail sector gives important support to the tourism industry and even constitutes a key form of tourist activity. Moreover, contemporary shopping may also present many positives for various groups, particularly in non-Western societies. The greatest beneficiaries of shopping malls, for example, may be females (Featherstone 1998) who are often excluded from many locations, especially in the evenings by various traditions (Abaza 2001), a topic which is treated later.

Islamic Consumption

In an important recent paper, Essoo and Dibb (2004) discuss the significance of religious influences on shopping behavior. They argue that although the sociology of religion has long been a topic for research, few have linked it to the study of consumption. However, the latter is central to all religions in various ways. Bailey and Sood summarize the effects of religious beliefs on consumption habits: "Prominent examples are the importance of fasting and feasting to patterns of food purchases, belief in taboos on clothing styles and activities of women, practices of personal hygiene related to purchases of toiletries and cosmetics, and influences on housing and entertainment patterns" (1993:328).

In terms of Islam, this is evident through definitions of what is *halal* or permitted and what is *haram* or prohibited by Allah. This is most commonly related to items of food and drink (such as pork or alcohol), but has now filtered into all aspects of Islamic life such as the wearing of jewelry, using cosmetics, purchasing works of art, keeping pets, and other areas. In particular, though, the *Qur'an* specifically highlights a dislike of excess. Moreover, the entry of Western franchised food outlets has changed the eating landscape in many Muslim countries, while simultaneously subjecting the Western food companies to new standards of *halal* certification, a process termed *halalisation* (Fischer 2008).

Central to this process has been the construction of large shopping malls in many Muslim countries for the growing middle classes to consume a wide range of Western designer brands. Fischer writes of how "shopping in malls is a constructive example of how proper Islamic consumption can be ritualized.... These rituals are attempts at transforming what could be seen as excessive consumption into meaningful and acceptable practices" (2008:162). But these are also contested public spaces where "the behavior of teenagers has become a site for the negotiation of anxieties about possible ills of modernity, the embodiment of parental and societal failures to produce the right kind of Asian family values and Islamic modernity" (Stivens 1998:70). There is thus certainly a contemporary tension between "on the one hand, the invocation of Islam as a worldview and a performance of acts of piety; on the other hand a range of consumer practices and lifestyle choices made by, and within, families" (Fischer 2008:8).

This tension is also manifest in the consumption of contemporary tourism in many Muslim countries. A number of studies have examined the implications of Islam on tourist practices (Alavi and Yasin 2000; Alhemoud and Armstrong 1996; Aziz 2001; Baum and Conlin 1997; Bhardwaj 1998; Burns and Cooper 1997; Daher 2007b; Hazbun 2008; Henderson 2003; Poirier 1995; Zamani-Farahani and Henderson 2010). As Timothy and Iverson note, "Muslim leadership and citizenry recognize the negative social impacts that tourism typically brings with it—drugs, alcohol consumption, lewd behavior, gambling, immodest dress, open affection between males and females, sexual promiscuity and prostitution ... which are all forbidden by Islamic law" (2006:189). Although some Muslim countries are more tolerant of the behavior of Western tourists, tensions still arise when they misbehave. Moreover, negative images of the Islamic world, particularly post September 11, have prevented the growth of international tourism to many countries. Some have responded by developing segregated tourism areas and others, as in the following case of Saudi Arabia, by emphasizing domestic tourism and the encouragement of international tourists from other Muslim countries (Rimmawi and Ibrahim 1992). Islam, though, has historically emphasized travel as an important attribute particularly for learning (Timothy and Iverson 2006; Zamani-Farahani and Henderson 2010). Furthermore, it is also noted:

> Islamic tradition advocates traveling in groups on trips to faraway places. As a result, most Muslims, especially from the Arabian Peninsula, prefer to travel in groups of family members of friends ... Likewise, religion has a bearing on the types of accommodations the travelers will select and where they will eat. For devout Muslims, hotels that offer gender segregated swimming and recreational facilities ... prayer rooms or that are near mosques are more desirable ... (Timothy and Iverson 2006:199).

Overall, Islamic tourism is widely seen as a potential powerful commercial force with excellent prospects (Zamani-Farahani and Henderson 2010).

Tourism Development in Saudi Arabia

In the past Saudi Arabia devoted little attention to tourism development for a variety of religious, social, economic, and political reasons. Tourism in the Kingdom has gained increasing importance more recently as the government identified it as a key strategy to diversify its economy away from reliance upon oil. To this effect, in 2000 the Supreme Commission for Tourism and Antiquities was established by the government with the purpose to develop, promote, and enhance the tourism sector in the Kingdom and to facilitate the growth of a sector that is deemed to be an important resource for the national economy (SCTA 2010). Specifically, and in contrast to most other governments around the world, the Saudi tourism development plan emphasizes domestic tourism growth for the nationals rather than international tourists. However, concerns have been raised over the sustainability of recent mass tourism developments in the Kingdom, as these are taking place without proper environmental impact assessments (Seddon and Khoja 2003). Nevertheless, it is estimated that tourism will provide an additional 1.5 million new jobs for Saudis by 2020 (Sadi and Henderson 2005).

For an increasing number of Saudi nationals, traveling to destinations, internationally or domestically, and spending the annual holiday away from home is now the norm. Domestic tourism, including short-break trips to the coast, the desert, or to urban destinations for shopping dominate with 14.5 million participants (Bogari 2002; Bogari et al 2004; Sadi and Henderson 2005; Seddon and Khoja 2003). While Saudi Arabia has over five million international tourists annually, these are predominantly Muslims making a *Hajj* or *Umrah* pilgrimage to the holy Islamic cities of Makkah and Medina (Seddon and Khoja 2003; Timothy and Iverson 2006). The importance of these pilgrimages cannot be underestimated both spiritually and economically, as it accounts for nearly half of all tourism expenditure (Sadi and Henderson 2005). In addition to these pilgrimages, many Muslims undertake other religiously motivated trips. These may be for sentimental, emotive, and spiritual reasons, to participate in religious festivals, to visit other famous religious places, or to celebrate special days related to births and marriages (Timothy and Iverson 2006). Other trips may be more to do with the problems of everyday life such as the health of a relative or more recently to engage in the practices of consumption described above. International Western tourists, though, are relatively infrequent as it is not possible to obtain an individual tourist visa only to visit for business purposes or as part of a heavily controlled special group tour (Hazbun 2008).

For the purposes of this study, Jeddah was selected as it has historically been one of the most important areas for tourism. More recently, the Jeddah Governorate has been able to develop a substantial tourism infrastructure, thus attracting increasing numbers of tourists over the last decade. The city of Jeddah has a rich architectural heritage, and at the same time is considered as the commercial center of Saudi Arabia. Situated on the coast,

Jeddah is used as a sea-based attraction, as well as the gateway for those making pilgrimages to the nearby holy cities of Medina and Makkah. Geographically, Jeddah is centered on Al-Balad, the strip of buildings along its coast road, and the old city directly behind these.

Tourism development in Jeddah as in the rest of Saudi Arabia, however, still faces financial and social obstacles. In this context, the study by Abu-Dawood (2002) discussed the development of tourist resources and activities in the Governorate of Jeddah and tried to identify the role of the government and private sectors in furthering sustainable tourism development. Moreover, Bogari has also noted:

> Since 1997 private companies and government bodies have taken part in the two-month summer programs, which is aimed at promoting domestic tourism and attracting visitors and holidaymakers from outside the Jeddah area sectors and the Gulf State to visit Jeddah during the summer holiday period. For this purpose, the Summer festival was organized and included many activities like circus, fireworks, dolphin shows and water-skiing. According to the Jeddah Chamber of Commerce and Industry the summer festival in 1999 raised U.S.$ 212 million (SR 795 million) and recorded over one million visitors (2002:38).

Further, Bogari also studied the motivations for domestic tourism in Saudi Arabia, concluding that the most important push and pull factors as perceived by Saudi tourists are cultural and religious values. Jeddah has some significant museums and some of the most renowned souks (markets) in the Kingdom. It has the highest number of hotels in the country, and has also witnessed the construction of a large number of large shopping malls—a trend recognized back in the late 1980s (Abdulaal and Al-Rahman 1991). As a result, a strong relation between shopping and tourism has developed in Jeddah.

Empirical Findings

The methods of study reported here were qualitative in nature. Focus groups comprising female tourists visiting Jeddah were structured into six groups, with each of approximately six women according to age groups (18–30, 31–49, 50 and above). A discussion was held with each group twice, once when they arrived in Jeddah and once before they left, to obtain data about their tourism experiences in general and their shopping experiences in particular. All focus group information was recorded, transcribed, and then coded and analyzed. The focus group discussions inquired about respondents' favorite places to shop, the nature of purchases, whether shopping was alone or with husband or another person and their experience, in particular, of the shopping malls and the souks in Jeddah. This chapter reports solely their experiences of shopping malls.

Among participants, there was consensus that the most visited places and the main attractions in Jeddah were the shopping malls and restaurants, and the favorite time for shopping was in the morning because it is quieter and less crowded in the peak of the summer season. Shopping in malls in Saudi Arabia is governed by strict Islamic codes of behavior, which mean that men and women are segregated and there are none of the entertainments available in similar shopping malls elsewhere in the world such as cinemas. All the sales people in Kingdom's shopping malls' mixed floors are male foreign workers, but many malls have women-only floors. Jeddah has seen an exponential growth in the construction of large new shopping malls in recent years. Respondents in the study contrasted their experiences of traveling internationally and domestically, with the latter being described relatively unfavorably. Shopping in small groups in malls is now widely prevalent and that conspicuous consumption is significant, particularly for younger generations. The respondents also recognized the problems of adhering to the tenets of Islam and shopping in the malls.

Participants in some focus groups contrasted their different tourist experiences internationally and domestically, as well as their dissatisfaction with their domestic experience; for example:

> The difference between here [Jeddah] and travelling abroad is that there ... there are a lot of opportunities besides shopping, I mean here all you can do is shopping or go to a restaurant, there are not many places you can go to, but abroad it is very nice, the weather is good for walking. Here, if you go out for a stroll, it's like some kind of punishment and you just have to get back home (Focus group aged 31-49 years, February 2009).

As the preceding discussion of the importance of souvenir shopping in tourism has indicated, all participants were interested in discussing the souvenirs that they brought back from their international travels. They argued that they always tried to find as much as they could to keep for themselves or to give as gifts, like t-shirts, cards, pictures, and mugs, carrying images of landmarks, or other features. All participants agreed that the tourism industry in Jeddah and Saudi Arabia is relatively under-developed compared to other Muslim countries such as the United Arab Emirates, as the following comment demonstrates:

> I would like to add that we can have fantastic things that we find abroad but unfortunately not here in the Kingdom, or at least only restricted access, like, for example, sports clubs ... archery, rallies, marathons like in Dubai ... they have created an artificial ski slope ... I wish we could have all these things here ... of course a circus throughout the year, a cinema ... at least cartoons for the children as recreation for them (Focus group aged 31–49, February 2009).

This provides evidence that for the hypermobile elite in Saudi Arabia, traveling abroad has led to a Westernization of tastes and the search for more forms of entertainment than are currently on offer in Saudi Arabia.

All participants preferred to shop in malls, rather than in individual stores (boutiques), as they could find many different stores in one place: supermarkets, clothes shops, toy shops, jewelry stores, makeup, perfume, bookstores and shoe shops, in particular. They preferred indoor shopping, with outdoor shopping being preferred by those who felt oppressed by the enclosed atmosphere. Most of the participants focused on two kinds of purchases: clothes and jewelry, while shoes, watches, bags, and electronic goods were secondary purchases. Moreover, they were conscious of price differences from store to store and from mall to mall. Importantly, one of the participants insisted on the importance of window shopping as a form of leisure:

> I do not like shopping too much, but I love walking, window shopping ... maybe I go inside a store and have a look ... if I admire something inside the store, I hold it in my hands and walk all around the store before deciding whether to buy it or not (Focus group aged 31–49, February 2009).

Significantly, when participants were asked about their preferences about going shopping alone or accompanied by their husband, children, or friends, it was found that they consistently preferred going in small groups with their sisters, daughter(s), perhaps with friends, mother or sons, but shopping with their husbands usually came in last place. It was also noted that, with age, the desire to go shopping alone increased, perhaps mainly because it is easier to take decisions and not be pressured into changing a decision. Younger women wanted the company of sisters and friends to confer with on purchase decisions, but this also confirms the importance of adhering to the Islamic customs relating to shopping in public discussed above. Hence, the pleasure was not in shopping itself, but the sociable experience of going out in a group with daughters, talking together, and maybe drinking tea. Moreover, some participants used shopping as a kind of reward, first as a self-reward after making progress with studies, and, second, to lift a depressed mood. For example:

> I love rewarding myself, particularly when I am studying. When I visit my supervisor and he makes me happy by giving me good news about my work ... that is excellent, and I go straight home and dump my books in exchange for shopping bags (Focus group aged above 50, February 2009).

> Sometimes I feel a strange state of mind, if I am absolutely depressed, maybe I go to reward myself with a gift (Focus group aged above 50, February 2009).

In contrast, in terms of their purchase behavior, it was found that some of the over 50-year-old participants worked with limited budgets. One of the participants explained the differences in her purchasing behavior just in terms of age as follows:

> In the past, I loved shopping, but lately, maybe in the last five years, shopping does not mean anything to me. Age, believe me, plays a big role. When I went shopping before, if I liked a blouse, I would buy it in all available colors ... if I liked some shoes, I would also buy them in all the colors available, but now this kind of thing does not mean anything (Focus group aged above 50, February 2009).

Indeed, many of the participants considered that age was a major factor in changing purchasing behavior. They become more rational and look at prices before purchasing, whereas previously they would buy straight off without caring about the price. Another participant from a different group described her purchasing behavior and considered her shopping as a hobby:

> In the past I was fond of shopping, it was one of my hobbies ... I mean I felt comfortable when I went into the shops and I would buy buy buy. I would come out with many things (laughing) that were a highlight for me. But recently, I don't know ... maybe its age ... I have become more reasonable ... I feel that it was wrong what I was doing. I started a few months ago to think about my previous behavior and I started to realize what I need exactly, not like before. I used to buy things that I liked and also things that I did not like. Sometimes if I liked something but could not find my size or if it was not entirely suitable for me, I would buy it anyway for my friend or anyone, just buy it and that's that (Focus group aged 18–30, February 2009).

From a Muslim perspective, many participants suggested lengthening shopping hours; they also suggested that stores did not need to close during the Isha prayer, which continues until midnight. Otherwise they have to wait in front of the store, which causes confusion with some men and women mingling together. Such a situation is in contradiction with Islamic tenets:

> They follow the Holy *Qur'an*, which says no selling or buying at certain times. We do not mind them closing, but we do not like them putting us outside, because men and women are not supposed to mix in a crowd in front of the store (Focus group aged 31–49, February 2009).

Previously, they had allowed for people to stay inside the supermarket during prayer time, but because of a high percentage of theft, they have made everyone go outside.

CONCLUSION

The main aim of this chapter was to focus on the relations between tourism and shopping in a Muslim context. In doing so it has focused primarily upon domestic female tourists' experiences of Jeddah, Saudi Arabia. Jeddah is the primary destination in the Kingdom for domestic tourism and shopping because of its lifestyle, atmosphere, and perceived freedom and safety.

The attraction of Jeddah for Saudi women was confirmed to be its shopping malls. However, it can be concluded that many of the focus group participants were significantly unhappy about their tourism-shopping experiences in Jeddah, as well as Saudi Arabia generally, due to the restrictions that are sometimes placed upon them. More positively, many respondents noted the affordances that had been given to them in terms of lifestyle shopping (Shields 1992). Nevertheless, further comparative research needs to be done on both international and domestic, male and female, tourists and hosts in order to examine the nuances of the relations between tourism and shopping in the Muslim world.

PART IV

PROMOTION AND MARKETING

Chapter 17

ISLAMICIZATION OF PROMOTION

Deepak Chhabra
Arizona State University, USA

Abridgement: For sustainable progress of heritage tourism in Muslim regions, exaggerated and distorted notions of Islam have to be dispelled. To accomplish such an arduous task, the first step is to examine media content employed by key tourism organizations/agencies in Muslim countries. This chapter examines the heritage environments and contemporary macro environment factors in Muslim countries that are either secular or Islamic in nature. Using cultural indicators, it further analyzes the content of website marketing employed by the leading tourism authorities in the selected regions to understand if considerations and efforts are made to market Muslim heritage. The findings indicate mixed results. **Keywords:** sustainability; Islam; cultural indicators; website marketing

INTRODUCTION

Heritage tourism has become a widespread currency at the global level. Although this form of tourism is omnipresent across the world, it has recently emerged in the Muslim countries. Because the significance of religion in the Muslim world is more prominent (Din 1989), Islamic principles have distinct imprints on policies shaping tourism in developing countries (Ritter 1975). After Christianity, Islam is the next major religion with around 25% of the world population as its followers.

According to CIA (2009c), approximately 40 countries in the world have a Muslim majority, with the lead ones situated in South and Southeast Asia and the Middle East, such as Indonesia, Bangladesh, Pakistan, Turkey, Iran,

Tourism in the Muslim World
Bridging Tourism Theory and Practice, Volume 2, 267–285
Copyright © 2010 by Emerald Group Publishing Limited
All rights of reproduction in any form reserved
ISSN: 2042-1443/doi:10.1108/S2042-1443(2010)0000002020

and Maldives, Russia, the Balkan Peninsula, and China. Traveling in Islam is viewed "as a trying task which subjects individuals to the test of patience and perseverance. There is no real division between the physical and spiritual aspects of travel" (Din 1989:555). According to Graburn (1977), contrary to the commercial goals of modern mass tourism, the Islamic concept of tourism stresses on the sacred goal of submission to the ways of God. Prodigal consumption and extreme indulgences is forbidden. The same inclination is expected of tourists to Muslim regions (Henderson 2003). That is, serious travel rather than mass travel is preferred by Muslim communities.

Despite the claims made by most documented literature that Islam is not a marketable commodity (Kesler 1992; Said 1981), a parallel growing body of literature in the last decade suggests otherwise. It is being suggested that Muslim-friendly marketing be employed and tour companies design Islamic tour packages dedicated to Muslim heritage (Sayed 2001). With regard to Muslim attractions, Henderson argues that, "there is scope for consultation with religious figures, as well as local communities, regarding the formulation of codes of conduct and presentation of sites such as mosques and shrines as tourist attractions" (2003:454). This is by no means an easy task. Major ideological barriers have to be overcome so that sustainable heritage tourism aligned with the needs and goodwill of the Muslim communities can be envisioned.

Often stereotype images and distorted media messages pertaining to Islam are portrayed to the Western audience and this has damaged perceptions of the Muslim countries (Din 1989). For sustainable prosperity of heritage tourism, untrue notions and promotional exhibits depicting Muslim countries as conservative and anti-Western need to be discontinued. To accomplish such an arduous task, one crucial step can be to examine media content employed by key tourism organizations/agencies in Muslim countries. It has been pointed out that websites provide extensive multimedia information, thereby generating images of a destination and these online image-forming agents shape tourist perceptions and selection of destinations (Beerli and Martin 2004; Hashim et al 2007).

Govers and Go (2004), Hashim et al (2007), and Henderson (2003) are among the few scholars who have examined the online imagery of Muslim countries. Govers and Go (2004) content analyzed 20 websites focusing on Dubai tourism. The authors focused on projections of Dubai's image using pictures and narrative text and showed that the websites failed to promote its cultural identity and sustainability. The focus extensively rested on the commercial facets of the city such as shopping and dining experiences. Henderson (2003) examined the Tourism Malaysia website and reported only a meager mention of Islam within the context of Islamic museums. The pronounced focus on the website was focused on narrations and photographs related to the country's culture, traditions, and crafts. Malaysia thus succeeded in providing information on local culture and traditions while at the same time made an attempt to promote the local crafts. Hashim et al (2007) extended Henderson's discourse on online religious imagery by examining websites of destination marketing organizations at the state level. In congruence with the findings of Henderson (2003), the authors found inadequate projection of Islam. Only prayer schedules were included. However, the authors noted that close to the time of religious events, more evidence related to religion and its narration and the Muslim dress code appeared on the websites. Thus, predominant themes focused on contemporary tourism offerings. It was noted that regardless of contemporary focus, all websites offered pronounced coverage to nature, history, and culture of Malaysia.

From the preceding text it is clear that in light of concerns associated with moral debauchery, an accommodationist attitude of tourists is desired. That is, their adherence to Islamic dress code and demeanor can help soothe the discord (Henderson 2003). It is then crucial that imprints of Islamic principles are made visible in promotion strategies. Given the limited contemporary academic attention on this subject, this chapter examines the extent to which cultural and religious sensitivities are portrayed in the promotional material employed by Muslim countries. Cultural sustainability indicators to gauge responsible tourism promotion to Muslim countries are identified and matched with the pronounced themes portrayed in the promotional materials.

Website marketing content of Muslim countries, both at the national and regional level, in the selected regions (secular or Islamic in nature) is content analyzed to comprehend if considerations and efforts are being made to market Muslim heritage in a sustainable manner. That is, is tourism marketing sensitive to the Islamic principles? If so, does such an attempt strive to effectively balance the demands of a unique religion central to everyday life and the demands triggered by postmodern tourism? The appraisal is of websites only, using content analysis techniques.

For the purpose of this study, a qualitative version of the content analysis is employed. As pointed out by Krippendorf (2004), this method has received increasing attention in the assessment of media evaluations. A qualitative approach in content analysis focuses on communication content such as images, written text, speech by creating categorizations. Two coders were used in this study and intercoder reliability was determined, which refers to the level of agreement between two or more coders (Neuendorf 2002). Predominant themes in the promotional material on the webpages were identified and these were matched with the predetermined cultural sustainability indicators to determine the extent of Islamicization embraced by the marketing strategies. Four steps defined the content analysis process: data reduction, data display, conclusion drawing, and verification. Contingent on the findings, a culturally sustainable heritage tourism marketing model is suggested for the Muslim countries. In other words, the Islamicization of tourism promotion in Muslim countries is proposed.

SUSTAINABLE CULTURAL AND HERITAGE INDICATORS

The purpose of cultural sustainability is to conserve, maintain, and protect local rituals, customs, and norms; and to minimize the possible friction that might arise between the tourists and the host communities (Carbone 2005). Culture is discursive, so the process of cultural adaptation may be unavoidable. Therefore, cultural sustainability seeks to curtail and reduce harmful effects, and educate tourists to behave in a responsible manner in order to prevent local culture alterations (Mowforth and Munt 2003). Cultural sustainability ensures that tourism development preserves community identity (Mill and Morrison 2006); at the same time, it informs tourists about the host community culture and its sensitivities, and promotes a mutually beneficial relationship between the guests and the hosts.

Several indicators to detect cultural sustainability in tourism promotions are suggested by literature. For instance, Harris and Nelson's (1993) list of social indicators includes the degree to which tourism is planned in a culturally appropriate manner and builds on the cultural heritage of a community; it does not conflict with the community "vision" or plan; local community opinions are sought; and measures are taken so that the privacy, spiritual values, and cultural integrity are not threatened. Another list of indicators was presented by Choi and Sirakaya (2006), which include taking the host community and stakeholders' attitudes and satisfaction, responsible use of community resources, cultural (site) management, retention efforts of local customs and language, and efforts to diminish loss of authenticity by promoting cultural integrity. Drawn from a literature review, Aguilar (2009) used the following indicators in her examination of signature websites of destination marketing organizations: information on local customs such as festivals; education about the sensitivities associated with the cultural aspects of the local community; and how to behave responsibly.

Moreover, Chhabra (2009) suggests several indicators for sustainable marketing of cultural and heritage tourism. They are local community involvement and collaboration among stakeholders in terms of marketing together or managing the tourism flow and impact and local community benefit, conservation emphasis and promoting objective authenticity of tangible and intangible heritage, strategic planning in marketing with a long-term focus including ongoing SWOT analysis of the macro and micro environments, creating mindful tourists, careful interpretation content and communication of other educational tools, and ongoing research on how best to sell a sustainable heritage product and promote responsible behavior.

Seven Themes of Indicators

To detect the extent of Islamicization content in promotion by Muslim countries, a list of cultural sustainability indicators, as they relate to the Muslim environment, are drawn from a review of literature focusing on both Islamic and non-Islamic tourism (Figure 1). It is purported that the Islamicization framework can enhance the sustainability of host cultures in an attempt to make them status rather than commodity areas. Gilbert (1996) introduced a strategic framework by positioning destinations on a scale between status and commodity areas. Status areas reach desired demand as a consequence of distinct product attributes while in commodity areas destinations can be substituted and are price sensitive. Consumers have little awareness of any exclusive benefits or features. In this study, it is suggested that a destination can become a status area in terms of cultural sustainability

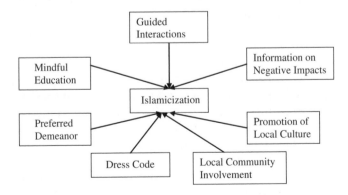

Figure 1. The Islamicization Framework

if a Muslim country incorporates the following seven themes of indicators in its marketing content.

Education on How to be Mindful of Local Culture.   Muslims fear that tourism will have an immoral impact on their culture. This can be minimized by educating tourists of the desired behavior and local community norms. For instance, alcohol, prostitution, and mixing of men and women is not welcomed (Henderson 2003; Scott 2003). Furthermore, it has been extensively reported that the West holds a stereotype notion of Muslims because of terror attacks (Din 1989; Timothy and Olsen 2006) and touted perspectives of a handful of fundamentalists. According to Din (1989), Muslims are stereotyped by the Western media as representing terror, danger, intolerance toward other religions, and violence. Most terror-related incidents are blown out of proportion, thereby creating a negative image of the Muslims throughout the world.

Contrary to this perception, Islam requires Muslims to be friendly, compassionate, and hospitable toward their guests (Din 1989). Tourists are qualified as recipients of several religious endowments and can seek permission to sleep in mosques. According to Din, "Muslims are bound by religious duty to extend a personal welcome to the travelers and offer good food for at least three days. In short, charity to the travelers is obligatory to the host community" (1989:552). This view is in stark contrast to the stereotype conservative and unfriendly images of Muslims often portrayed by the Western media. Hence, an actual picture of the friendly disposition of Muslim communities and their religion needs to be communicated through tourism promotion. A Muslim-friendly image can help determine if such a cultural sustainability measure is pursued by tourism organizations. This indicator will help determine if an accurate picture of the Muslim communities is portrayed.

Information on How to Behave.   According to Olsen and Timothy (2006), Muslim citizenry can get offended if tourists ignore local customs and take their pictures. Sindiga reported that the local Muslims do not approve of "kissing or fondling by tourists in front of a mosque when prayers are going on" (1996:429). Information on appropriate behavior at the mosque needs to be communicated to tourists as irreverent conduct in and around sacred places is not tolerated (Timothy and Olsen 2006). For instance, shoes should be removed before going inside the mosque. As warned by Poirier, many times "tourists knowingly or unknowingly violate rules of propriety in and around mosques and Islamic religious activities, and provide fuel to Islamic fundamentalists who criticize the excessive Westernization" of Muslim societies (1995:167). Further, the Sahib mentality of some tourists needs to be dispelled.

Dress Code. Dressing scantily in public and sacred places is not favored by Muslims (Din 1989). With the proliferation of tourism in their region, Muslims have to cope with intrusion into their cultural and religious environments (Burns and Cooper 1997). Dress codes for women have to be diligently followed in countries like Saudi Arabia. These require women to cover their hands and face and avoid scant clothing (Din 1989). Men are also discouraged to wear shorts that reach above the knee.

Local Community Involvement in Promotional Efforts. Evidence of local community involvement in the overall planning and marketing needs to be reflected in the overall promotional efforts of tourism organizations, both at the national and local levels. Islam guides Muslims to be compassionate toward their guests. Hence, it is important for destination marketing organizations, both national and international, to take into account their views on promotional messages and images so that friendly disposition of the community is maintained and its concerns are addressed in an ongoing manner. Information on host community involvement in different tourism projects on the website can suggest an image that the organization is coordinating the industry in conjunction with the host community. An overall coordinated image can go far in presenting a host friendly environment. As suggested by Henderson, "there is scope for consultation with religious figures, as well as the local communities, regarding formulation of codes of conduct and presentation of sites such as mosques and shrines as tourist attractions" (2003:454).

Promotion of Local Handicrafts. Extant literature acknowledges that local handicrafts receive a boost if there is tourism demand for them. While several developing countries depend on Islamic handicrafts as a source of supplemental income, promotional images have not extensively focused or utilized this viable cultural identity and economic tool (Faroqhi and Deguilhem 2005). It is argued that an increasing coverage on a variety of Islamic handicrafts can provide economic benefits to the local community while at the same time instill a sense of pride. In this study, efforts were made by coders to identify themes focused on the promotion of local handicrafts.

Information on Possible Negative Impacts on the Host Community Culture. It has been extensively reported that tourism has been a cause of adverse cultural impact and facilitated moral decadence in Muslim countries (Hashim et al 2007; Poirier 1995). For example, commercial aspects of *Hajj* pilgrimage in Saudi Arabia have annoyed fundamentalist Muslims. The immoral impacts of irresponsible behavior should be communicated to tourists. Negative effects include demonstration effects and excessive use of extravagance through display of personal items such as expensive jewelry and dress. Exploitative acts that result in profiteering from tourists is not encouraged, because it compromises local standards and results in malpractices (Din 1989). Externalities generated by irresponsible tourism need to be highlighted so that tourists and the suppliers of tourism are informed and can be more mindful.

Availability of Guided Opportunities for Guest–Host Interactions. As stated by Din, "host-guest relations can be congenial when both are sensitive to one another's feelings and needs" (1989:553). For instance, Malaysia allows non-Muslim tourists to explore Islam in a friendly and less threatening environment. Hashim et al (2007) maintain that Malaysia's religious tolerance has earned it the title of a liberal and multicultural Muslim country. Friendly host–guest environments can help counter negative images. Friendliness of the hosts is crucial to the long-term viability of tourism success. Promotion of local events is one example where local heritage can be promoted, providing a platform for friendly host–guest interactions. It remains to be seen in this analysis if friendly host–guest environments are communicated to tourists in the promotional messages.

Evidence of Indicators

Using the aforementioned indicators as a guide, this chapter examines efforts of cultural sustainability of a geographically dispersed selection of Islamic countries: Saudi Arabia, Indonesia, Maldives, and Algeria. Each subsection examines the extent to which tourism promotion by the government follows the theory of Islamicization in these countries. Information on its characteristics is obtained from one or more of such sources as CIA World Factbook, US Department of State, official tourism websites, official country websites, and Economic Intelligence Unit.

Saudi Arabia. Saudi Arabia has a population of more than 28.5 million, of which 90% are Sunni Muslims. The official religion is Islam. For the most part, the Sunni Muslims follow the interpretation of Islam as enforced by the Government. In fact, the legal system is guided by the government's official version of *Shari'a* (Islamic law). According to the International Religious Freedom Report, people, both Muslims and non-Muslims who do not adhere to the government-sanctioned interpretation face discrimination and restrictions. The official title of the King of Saudi Arabia is "Custodian of the Two Holy Mosques." Evidently then, of utmost importance in the country is the support and advocacy of Islam. Public practice of a non-Muslim religion is not permitted in Saudi Arabia. Moreover, it has been noted that although the government accords to every citizen the right to private worship, incidents show that personal religious material of non-Muslim residents is often confiscated. Nevertheless, several improvements regarding freedom of religion issues have been reported recently by the US Department of State. Improvements are noted with regard to better protection of the right to possess and use personal religious materials. Efforts have also been made to curtail and investigate misuse and harassment by the *Mutawwa'in* (volunteer officers of the Commission to Promote Virtue and Prevent Vice).

Saudi Arabia has government monopoly in major economic areas. It has strongly relied on oil for its economic growth. Roughly 6.4 million foreign workers play an important role in the Saudi economy, particularly in the oil and service sectors. High oil prices have facilitated growth and government revenues. Saudi ownership of foreign assets has increased and thus the country has been able to address its domestic debt. Of late, the government has shifted its economic focus and is promoting private sector investment to boost local economy. The aim is to diminish the country's dependence on oil exports and enhance employment opportunities for the growing population. Approximately 40% of the population is below the age of 15 years. The government is planning to set up six economic cities in its spatially dispersed regions to encourage development and diversification. Although high oil prices have provided adequate financial capital to curtail the negative effects of the global economic recession, it is predicted that tight international credit, falling oil prices, and the global economic slowdown will slow the country's economic growth in the future. This has led the government to explore other areas to boost economic growth such as cultural tourism. Moreover, increasing interactions with the West has fostered religious toleration and several committees are set to protect the rights of non-Muslims.

Tourism in Saudi Arabia, till recently, mainly centered on religious travel. It is mandatory of every Muslim to participate in the *Hajj* pilgrimage to the holy city of Makkah at least once in their lifetime. Pilgrims also visit Medina to pay their respects at the Mosque, which houses the tomb of Prophet Mohammed. This pilgrimage attracts more than 2 million pilgrims (both international and domestic) to Makkah and Medina each year. To manage this massive demand for the *Hajj*, the Saudi government has invested extensively in building appropriate infrastructure to manage the pilgrims. Special visas are issued for the pilgrims based on quote system. Non-Muslims are prohibited to enter Makkah as it is considered the holy city of Islam. Thus, the aforesaid religious places have placed Saudi Arabia firmly on the world tourism map because pilgrimage tourism is considered an important component of heritage tourism (Timothy and Boyd 2003). As pointed out by Lew, Hall, and Timothy, "their location in Saudi Arabia gives the Saudi government and the Saudi royal family an enormous role and responsibility with respect to Islamic affairs" (2008:161). Coupled with oil wealth, this has given Saudi Arabia an edge over other Middle Eastern countries and made its rulers powerful and their opinions are eagerly sought on political matters.

Earlier, Saudi Arabia followed a heavily restrictive policy with regard to the promotion of international tourism. Tourist visas were not issued prior to 2004. Tourists used to come to the country either under guest worker programs or to participate in the *Hajj* pilgrimage. Political environments since then have forged a better relationship with different countries across the globe to facilitate travel to Saudi Arabia. The main incentive in tourism promotion lies in diversifying the country's economy that has been traditionally dependent on oil. Another aim is to provide social benefits to local population by developing countryside and desert regions. The objective is to discourage populations from rural areas to migrating to already crowded cities. For the past several years, the government has become actively involved in developing infrastructure plans to promote tourism. Examples include setting up schools for tourism and hotel management and building resorts and cable cars. Further, in 2003 the Secretary General of the Tourism Higher Authority inaugurated a workshop to facilitate planning of natural heritage sites for tourism. Massive restoration projects were set in place to restore old buildings, palaces, museums, and antiquities. The main goal is to set up cultural centers that can regularly host lectures, exhibitions, symposiums, and folklore performances. This is done to enhance social ties by connecting the Saudis with each other and provide a sense of belonging among domestic tourists.

Two main attractions in Saudi Arabia are religion and heritage. As stated earlier, religious tourism is an ancient phenomenon in the country. Heritage tourism is new and in its infancy. The country is promoting visits to its ancient sites, most of which are organized by group tours. Tourists, in packaged tours, are in fact beginning to show up now on the Saudi soil. Although they are expected to respect the local culture and traditions, the main tourism websites in Saudi Arabia do not provide adequate information on Islam and its customs. A brief overview of the themes promoted on the signature websites is given below.

The Saudi Commission for Tourism and Antiquities (SCTA) plans and manages tourism in Saudi Arabia in conjunction with the Ministry of Education. It is focused on the sustainable promotion of Saudi Arabia and facilitates effective partnerships and local employment. As Table 1 illustrates, it advocates Islamic principles (Supreme Commission on Tourism and Antiquities 2010). Examples of programs supported by the Commission for Tourism and Antiquities include the "Smile," "Tourism Enriches," and "Leave No Trace" programs. The first one is a society-based program. It aims to facilitate local involvement and participation, and create a compatible social environment for tourism that "enhances the role of the society (individuals, establishments and institutions), encourage their participation in developing and nationalizing the sustainable tourism and performing the maximum social utilities for them" (Supreme Commission on Tourism and Antiquities 2010). The "Tourism Enriches" is a project devoted toward creating awareness through different local community groups and facilitating their involvement in the development of the national tourism

Table 1. Commission for Tourism and Antiquities Vision and Mission

Saudi Tourism Vision
Saudi Arabia is the cradle of Islam. [The vision is] to develop tourism, characteristic of its social, cultural, environmental, and economic values, on the basis of Islamic principles and the authenticity of its ancient heritage and traditional hospitality.

SCTA Mission
SCTA is working toward facilitating the development of sustainable and successful tourism industry in the Kingdom through the provision of clear direction for the industry, working in close partnership with industry leaders and partners to find and create a climate in this emerging industry and to achieve a high degree of self-sufficiency. With respect to SCTA's mission toward antiquities and museums, it will strengthen its capacity to protect, register, conduct exploration studies related to antiquities, develop museums and architectural heritage, increase knowledge of the elements of the cultural heritage of the Kingdom, effectively manage museums and antiquities, and create cultural resources to be developed and presented to the members of the society.

sector. It aims to inform and educate leaders and local community members about the social, economic, and cultural prospects of the tourism industry.

The Saudi Arabia travel guide website provides basic information on the beliefs and customs of Muslim people and how these are upheld in day-to-day living. The guide informs tourists of clothing guidelines. Because of the strict policies, all women are required to wear *abaya* (a long black dress that is able to cover women from ankle to knees). Saudi Arabia is very strict with clothing policies. Mini-skirts and shorts are not allowed. Violators run the risk of being arrested by the *Muttawas* (religious police). Other information listed on the website pertains to hot weather, local transportation, and popular shopping venues. Additional information on lack of nightlife and alcoholic regulations are provided. Several cultural sustainability indicators were remiss on the website.

An examination of a couple of other travel related nongovernment websites showed less pronounced themes related to cultural sustainability, although information was offered on religion and preferred demeanor. The majority of the focus was on attractions and sites, transportation, and accommodations. One interesting point of note across most websites was that the tourism industry has started promoting its local brands such as hotel chains.

Indonesia.   This archipelago country of approximately 18,000 islands, 6,000 of which are inhabited, has a population that includes more than 300 distinct ethnic groups and speaks over 250 languages (Lew et al 2008). The main religion is Islam. Approximately 88% of the people are Sunni Muslims. Tropical agriculture makes the main source of income for Indonesians. The country was under the Dutch colonial rule and professed its independence from this rule in 1945, although the Dutch handed over their authority another four years later.

The Indonesian constitution supports freedom of religion and grants all people the right to worship as per their religious beliefs. The basic principle of the country's nationalist ideology is called "Pancasila," which supports belief in one supreme God. Despite religious tolerance policies, the Ministry of Religious Affairs accords official recognition to only six religious groups: Islam, Catholicism, Protestantism, Buddhism, Hinduism, and Confucianism. Unrecognized groups are registered with the Ministry of Tourism and Culture and regarded as social organizations. Short programs related to educational travel are promoted through which Indonesians are invited to visit countries in the West such as the United States, so that a dialogue with

US counterparts can happen in areas associated with religious diversity, interfaith discussions, and multiculturalism in a democratic society.

Indonesia has made significant economic advances, but it has been affected by the global financial crisis and downward trend in the world economy. Its debt-to-GDP ratio in recent years has declined steadily because of increasingly robust GDP growth and sound fiscal stewardship. Recently significant reforms were introduced by the government in the financial sector to boost the relationship with both domestic and foreign investors. These were in the areas of tax and customs, the use of Treasury bills, and capital market supervision. Contemporary challenges in Indonesia are focused on poverty and unemployment, poor infrastructure, corruption, complicated regulatory environment, and unfair resource allocation among regions. From an economic perspective, tourism is considered an important industry in Indonesia.

The country is a popular nature-based, cultural, and heritage destination. More than 5 million foreign tourists visit Indonesia each year and incur an average spending of US$100 per day. The top five markets are reported to be Singapore, Malaysia, Australia, Japan, and South Korea. Western tourists mostly belong to the United Kingdom, France, Germany, and the Netherlands. Dutch tourists seek their colonial ties, while those from other countries are attracted because Indonesia offers a wide range of nature-based activities such as trekking, bird and animal watching, and diving. Cultural tourism and the opportunity to meet ethnic communities are also important attractions. The island of Bali is the main destination. Among cultural tourism attractions, Toraja, Prambanam, and Borobudur temples draw huge crowds of tourists. All three enjoy the world heritage status. Hindu festivals, Yogyakarta, and Minangkabau are also popular cultural attractions. During the early years of the 21st century, domestic tourism was heavily promoted in Indonesia. Several recent events have adversely affected the country, such as the Tsunami, the 2002 and 2005 terrorist bombings in popular venues in Bali, the outbreak of SARS, and the Bird Flu. Foreign governments remain vigilant of the safety and health climate in the country.

"My Indonesia" is the official tourism website of Indonesia. It provides information on various tour packages, offers image galleries with spectacular pictures of key attractions. Additionally, information is offered on important events happening in the country, such as the "Sumatera International Travel Fair." There are six icons on the left side of the website titled: What's new, Events, Traveler's Tools, Activities, Indonesia by Province, and Promotional Media. Under the first one traces of Indonesia's awareness toward environmental sustainability are visible. For example, there is information on efforts made to participate in World Oceans Forums and discuss climate change issues. However, no evidence exists of the inclusion of cultural sustainability criteria.

The country was running a special promotion campaign titled "Visit Indonesia 2009." There is a "contact us" icon at the bottom of the "My Indonesia" website that leads to the "Visit Indonesia" website. It also offers several subheadings such as Visiting Indonesia, Indonesia at a Glance, Events, and Activities. Indonesia at a Glance offers a brief introduction of the country, its climate, history, language, flora and fauna, geography, and important cities. Visiting Indonesia offers information on entry points, foreign representatives, time zones, electricity, office hours, banking hours, currency, Indonesian phrases, and Dos and Don'ts. Indonesian phrases educates tourists about basic words needed to converse in the local language. Dos and Don'ts provide several guidelines on how to behave when interacting with the local community. As Table 2 illustrates, this information satisfies several cultural sustainability indicators (Visit Indonesia 2009).

Tourists are informed of the sensitivities of the Muslim culture and how to behave, dress, and the possible negative impacts on some aspects of local culture. However, these promotional efforts do not reflect a focus on local heritage. Local community involvement is not evident, nor is an effort to promote local handicrafts or guided opportunities for guest–host interactions.

Table 2. Dos and Don'ts in Indonesia

When visiting Indonesia, visitors should observe local traditions and attitudes. Number of traditions and attitudes is:

- Though shaking hands is generally accepted in social intercourse between man and woman, but a number of Muslim women introduce themselves to men by nodding their head and smiling.
- Greeting traditionally is shaking hands by two hands, but without holding in grasp.
- Making a phone call before a visit is polite.
- Shoes must be taken off before entering house or house of worship.
- In general, drink is offered to a guest when visiting, receiving the drink is polite.
- Right hand is always used when eating, receiving something, or giving something.
- Right index finger should not be used to appoint a place, goods, or person. Use the right hand thumb with four other fingers folded back.
- Taking photographs at house of worships is allowed, but permission to do so should be obtained first.
- Toasting is not generally accepted.
- Most of Indonesian Muslims do not consume alcoholic drinks.

It appears that Indonesia, at the national level, is moving away from being a pure commodity area to embracing attributes of cultural sensitivity. Few sustainability themes were found in other tourism agency websites. Traces included the involvement of conservation organizations in monitoring nature-based products, and also information on local culture and local handicrafts.

Algeria. This North African country has a population of 35 million (CIA 2009c), of which 99% are Sunni Muslims. Its constitution declares Islam as the state religion and prohibits any behavior that is not aligned with the Islamic moral values, but it respects the freedom of other religious beliefs. Nevertheless, several sources suggest that freedom of religion status has received a setback over the recent years. The law requires all non-Muslim religious organizations to register with the government before they are allowed to operate or perform any religious activity. The only non-Islamic group that has successfully registered with the government is the Catholic Church.

The main source of Algeria's economic wealth is the hydrocarbons sector. Algeria is also known for its large natural gas reserves and as the fourth largest gas exporter in the world. High oil prices in recent years have boosted its financial situation. The government, however, is making consistent efforts to diversify its economy and encourage both foreign and domestic investment. An effort is being made to provide employment opportunities to the rising youth population and thus reduce poverty. However, corruption and bureaucratic resistance continues to challenge the efforts to reform the economy, such as development of the banking sector and infrastructure.

The Algerian government is keen on developing its tourism industry. Of interest is the promotion of Saharan and cultural tourism. Algerian legislation eased regulations for foreign and local investments in 2005. Initially, the country's tourism services were poor, such as hotel accommodation and terrorism threats. The government has worked hard to improve the facilities and break free of its past stigmatized image. Today, foreign companies are allowed to operate several state-owned hotels and the national tourism organization is decentralized. The country also hopes to increase hotel capacity in the nearby future.

A plan titled "Horizon 2005" was adopted, which focused on improving infrastructure. The government hoped to attract a large number of foreign tourists to strengthen its economy and international ties. Key attractions in the country include the Sahara Desert, Cirta (the capital city of the Numidia Kingdom), Al Qal'a of Beni Hammad (the original capital of the Hammadid Empire), Belzma National Park, and Algiers (the country's capital). A key event happening in July 2009 was the Pan-African Cultural Festival. The government hoped that this event would draw a huge crowd of tourists to celebrate the artistic renaissance of Africa. The event was of historical significance for Algeria, as it was considered the cultural capital of the African continent in 1969. The event was spearheaded by the Ministry of Tourism and musicians, artists, writers, and poets, among other, from different parts of the world were invited to celebrate the history, culture, and civilization of the African continent.

The Tourism in Algeria website does not reflect any of the cultural sustainability indicators. It only offers information on geography, topography, popular attractions, and tourist activities in the country. Several needs for investment are mentioned, in addition to the proposed expansion in tourism infrastructure by 2015. Information is also given on historical cities such as Timgad and Tipaza, which are known for their archaeological value and historic and scientific symbolism. Local festivals are promoted as symbols of Algerian's cultural identity. Examples include Tafsit of Tamanrasset and S'biba of Djanet. Hosted by the Embassy of Algeria in the United States, this link promotes tourism to Algeria among US residents. It appears that the government is more or less driven by the commodity area perspective. Other tourism websites also follow the commodity perspective. For instance, the pronounced focus is on a variety of activities and attractions in the country. Information on Arabic language and local music and history appeared in all of them, but in a brief manner. Other cultural sustainability themes were absent.

Maldives. The total population of Maldives is 270,000. It is one of the smallest nations in Asia. It comprises of approximately 1,191 islands, of which only 200 are inhabited. The greatest concentration of population is on Malé, the capital island of Maldives. Women enjoy special privilege and play a significant role in the family and the community. The average age is almost 26 years. Archaeological evidence indicates the presence of Hinduism and Buddhism in the region before it predominantly embraced Islam in 1153 CE. Since time immemorial, the Maldives has been a melting pot for African, Arab, and Southeast Asian mariners. Nevertheless, the Muslim calendar is followed to set up main events and festivals. Islam is compulsory in the school curriculum. From infancy, children are taught religious education at school and home.

The Maldivian economy was earlier reliant on fishing, but in the recent few decades, the emphasis has shifted to tourism. In fact, the emergence of tourism in 1972 transformed the economy of the Maldives. It has become the sole source of revenue and livelihood. The majority of its development has been driven by the tourism sectors such as transport, distribution, real estate, construction, and government. Taxes derived from the industry have helped develop infrastructure and improve technology in the agricultural sector. According to the Ministry of Tourism, it is also Maldives' major foreign currency earner and the single biggest contributor to the GDP with an average above 7.5% in 2005. The country suffered a severe setback because of the Tsunami in 2004. However, tourism revival, post-tsunami reconstruction, and development of a new resort facilitated its economic recovery. The year of 2008 witnessed slow economic growth because of high oil prices and imports of construction material. Additionally a large deficit occurred due to government spending on social needs, subsidies, and civil servant income. As a result, high inflation hit the country and reached 13% in the latter half of 2008. The government today is interested in diversifying its economy beyond tourism and fishing. Public finance reformation and unemployment are other main challenges. Long-term challenges include erosion and harmful effects of global warming on the low-lying country (CIA 2009c).

"Visit Maldives" is the official site of Maldives. It is operated and managed by the Maldives Tourism Promotion Board that came into existence in 1998. Its core purpose is to promote its tourism industry across the globe. The website offers three main icons: Accommodations, Airport Information, and Travel Agents. The left side offers help as to "Getting there, Where to stay, and Things to do." The host community is described briefly under the "Things to do" option. The website also offers an icon on Environment Friendly Tourism, Photo Gallery, Media Center, FAQ, and Live Video. FAQ (frequently asked questions) are associated with information on visa, medicine, vaccinations, credit card, safe drinking water, and electrical equipment facilities.

No information on the local community, its culture, or tourist mindfulness guidelines is offered. Examination of other tourism websites revealed somewhat different traces of cultural sustainability. Predominant sustainability themes were related to local culture, people, and language. Under local culture, most focus was given to traditional music and dance. Information about people was related to demographics. The majority of the homepage themes centered on attractions, weather, resorts, and activities. The Maldives has enjoyed the high-end (upscale) market due to its location and ocean ambience. Upscale prices have served to sustain the carrying capacity of the destination. Hence, it has positioned itself in the status area. However, from a cultural sustainability perspective, it follows the commodity status.

CONCLUSION

It is apparent that there is scope for misunderstanding between Muslim residents and the non-Muslim tourists, because they follow polarized faiths (Henderson 2003). Previous studies have acknowledged that the travel media has compounded the drift by projecting stereotyped images of the Muslims and their faith, thereby generating feelings of mutual distrust. However, with more Muslims countries showing interest in promoting tourism, it has become pertinent to dispel the Western notions of Islamic heritage and provide a balancing ground of religious adherence and tourist needs (Timothy and Olsen 2006). This chapter examines websites of tourism organizations and other tourism agencies in a selected group of Muslim countries with different degrees of liberalization to gauge the extent to which cultural sustainability is promoted in the tourism promotion material. Themes identified from the electronic material are likened to the cultural sustainability indicators and mixed results are noted. The degree of liberalization has determined the portrayed levels of Islamicization.

Indonesia and Maldives are more devoted to their nature-based attractions because of their proximity to the ocean, and are in comparison more moderate and more tolerant of tourists. Most of their promotional content is focused on attractions. Compared to Indonesia, Maldives gives less attention to the promotion of cultural sustainability in its tourism marketing strategies. In line with the results reported by Hashim et al "minimal albeit varying portrayals of Muslim values on the website" (2007:13) is illustrated. The national tourism organization of Saudi Arabia presents a postmodern model of tourism development by engaging the interests of the Muslim community. Their contemporary theme is "Sauditization" of tourism, although the efforts are still in its infancy. At the national level, results remain unclear. Sustainable emphasis calls for more attention on "Islamicization" in the overall Sauditization strategy. Algeria, on the other hand, is dabbling in secular tourism. In fact, in the case of Algeria and Saudi Arabia, recent impetus is driven by the need to diversify the local economy. Both Indonesia and Maldives are established destinations although they have suffered a severe setback due to the Tsunami. In the case of Indonesia, other factors such as terrorism and SARS have damaged the destination. Thus, several dilemmas confront Muslim nations as they step forward to promote mass tourism.

In addition to the national tourism organizations, websites of several other tourism agencies were examined. They partially passed the cultural sustainability test. The government and private agencies were found to differ in their portrayal of Islam and its sensitivities on their websites. Several critical aspects of cultural sustainability were missing in the promotional content of these other sites such as information on possible negative impacts of tourism (Timothy and Olsen 2006), comprehension of religious sensitivities (Henderson 2003), and an insight into the friendly nature of Islamic religion (Din 1989). Such deficiencies can trigger an uneasy environment and a troubled relationship between Islam and tourism if not resolved in the near future. National tourism policies need to trickle down all tourism agencies and serve as a guide to advocate cultural sustainability so that tourist demeanor is not disruptive and immoral.

Several scholars report that post-9/11, many Westerners perceive Islam as an unfriendly religion (Armstrong 2001 see Chapters 12 and 15 this volume). This stereotyped image of the Muslims needs to be dispelled. Hospitality in fact is a core characteristic of Islam. Islamic countries need to educate the West by using a variety of distribution and promotion tools such as television, radio, intermediaries, and the Internet. For cultural and heritage tourism to flourish in Muslim countries, tourist friendly messages and effective interpretation techniques are required. This calls for a comprehensive long-term marketing strategy that can leverage the uniqueness of Muslim culture while at the same time safeguarding the interests of the Muslims. The proposed Islamicization framework stresses the involvement of the local community in tourism development decisions, making known the rules of appropriate behavior at the mosques, creating tourist mindfulness techniques, facilitating guided interactions between the guests and the hosts, and making the Muslim destinations economically viable. The aim is not only to plan tourism based on cultural sustainability measures in Muslim destinations in the short term, but also to ensure long-term success.

Websites offer a unique way to promote religious heritage through destination images. Advocacy of Islamic principles by official destination marketing organization websites can help market ethical behavior among tourists. Adequate portrayal of Islamic imagery associated with lifestyle and hospitality is required to dispel stereotyped myths on Muslim inhospitality. As suggested by Hashim et al, "the Internet can convey Islamic messages to non-Muslims and Muslims" (2007:1095). It can help create appealing and sincere messages for tourists who have a genuine desire to visit a Muslim country and learn about it. In this way, Islam can become more influential with sincere, realistic, and positive images.

Chapter 18

ARABIAN SIGHTS
Muslim States' Shared Photos

Sharifah Fatimah Syed-Ahmad
University of Malaya, Malaysia
Dayangku Ida Nurul-Fitri Pengiran-Kahar
Institute of Technology, Brunei
Ali Medabesh
Jazan University, Saudi Arabia
Jamie Murphy
University of Western Australia, Australia

Abridgement: This chapter examines a popular online trend—photo-sharing—in an understudied region, the League of Arab States. In contrast to online information from official bodies, anyone with Internet access can view and create destination photos. This study first searched for destination photos on Flickr.com, a popular photo-sharing website, from 22 Arab countries, and then content analyzed 589 Muslim and travel photos. The key results included Egypt with the most destination photos and Saudi Arabia with the most Muslim images. Common Muslim images were mosques and women with headscarves. This chapter shows that Flickr photos represent Arab images and are possible destination recommendations. **Keywords:** user-generated content; photo; Arab; word-of-mouth

Tourism in the Muslim World
Bridging Tourism Theory and Practice, Volume 2, 287–302
Copyright © 2010 by Emerald Group Publishing Limited
All rights of reproduction in any form reserved
ISSN: 2042-1443/doi:10.1108/S2042-1443(2010)0000002021

INTRODUCTION

The Internet changes distribution, pricing, and customer interactions in the tourism industry (O'Connor and Murphy 2004). In addition to traditional sources, tourists today rely on information from the Web (Lee, Soutar and Daly 2007; Tjostheim, Tussyadiah and Hoem 2007). Top sources for destination information include tourism websites and tourists (Lee et al 2007), with the Web becoming the main source for potential tourists (Morosan and Jeong 2008). Furthermore, word-of-mouth, offline interaction among individuals regarding a product such as destinations, is thriving online (Litvin, Goldsmith and Pan 2008; Puczko, Ratz and Smith 2007).

Tourism Internet studies often focus on the roles and impact of email and websites for promotion and information (Choi, Lehto and Morrison 2007; Gretzel and Yoo 2008; Litvin et al 2008). Some online and offline studies converge by focusing on how tourism organizations project destination images through brochures and websites (Hashim et al 2007; Hunter 2008). Until late last century, the media and destinations managed travel images. However, new technology applications such as user-generated content (UGC) wrest some control of destination image away from traditional media.

With UGC, individuals create and share destination photos, text, video, and audio (Choi et al 2007; Daugherty, Eastin and Bright 2008). As Alexa rankings indicate, tourism UGC websites such as TripAdvisor (rank 389), Virtual Tourist (2,737), and TravelPod (3,890) thrive (Alexa 2009). Non-tourism UGC websites are even more popular, with eight ranked in Alexa's (2009) top 40 of all websites—Facebook (2), YouTube (4), Wikipedia (6), Blogger.com (7), MySpace (11), Twitter (14), Flickr (33), and LinkedIn (38).

The most viewed UGC is photos (Daugherty et al 2008). The top photo website, Flickr.com, enables users to view and share destination photos, as well as artistic, family, and friend photos (Alexa 2009; Cox, Clough and Marlow 2008). As part of their gaze on destinations, tourists take and share photographs (Urry 1990)—offline and online—to inform, show, and possibly recommend selected destinations such as the Arab world. For instance, Flickr photos can show cultural and religious norms such as praying in public and women wearing headscarves. What locals, as well as regional and worldwide tourists, portray via Flickr photos could shape viewers' destination gaze and promote that destination to both Muslims and non-Muslims.

As the West dominates mainstream tourism studies, including technology research (Hashim et al 2007), this study helps close gaps regarding tourism and technology in Muslim countries. Furthermore, the study extends the word-of-mouth concept to include UGC photos. A quantitative content analysis focuses on a new trend in sharing tourism photography in an understudied market—the League of Arab States—and addresses three research questions: how Arab countries vary in their presence of travel and Muslim photos posted on Flickr, how Flickr users depict Muslim images in Arab countries, and how Arab countries vary in Muslim images posted on Flickr. The results could assist tourism organizations, particularly in Arab and other Muslim countries, understand the destination photo-sharing trend, and incorporate shared photos in destination image promotions.

USER-GENERATED PHOTOS

Tourism organizations and photographers shape destination images through photos (Hunter 2008; Stalker 1988). The photo portrayals include destinations' customs and tourism activities (Hunter 2008). They can create lasting impressions as adults remember destination photos well (Smith and MacKay 2001). Tourism photography studies examine destination-marketing organizations' brochures and websites, focusing on the official portrayal of a city, region, or country. These producer-generated photos highlight the best of destinations such as nature (Hashim et al 2007) and heritage (Choi et al 2007; Hunter 2008), or project images such as wealth, power, and patriotism (Huang and Lee 2009).

Yet there can be contradictory messages. In Dubai, the government promotes heritage and culture, while hospitality operators focus on amenities in their promotions (Govers and Go 2004). Furthermore, as destination image interpretations differ between marketers and individuals (Choi et al 2007; MacKay and Fesenmaier 1997), viewers face inconsistent images. If so, individuals might refer to tourists to understand destinations.

Tourists photograph unique landscapes, locals, family members, and mundane images (Haldrup and Larsen 2003; Urry 1990). While studies focus on tourists' photos, few, if any, examine sharing photos—offline and online. Sites such as Flickr, Facebook, and TripAdvisor facilitate the sharing with personal contacts and the public (Cox et al 2008; Syed-Ahmad, Hashim, Horrigan and Murphy 2009).

User-generated photos represent a broad range of destination perspectives, similar to asking individuals to capture destinations, as in visitor-employed photographs (VEP) (Cherem and Driver 1983; Garrod 2009;

MacKay and Couldwell 2004). While these researchers provide cameras and instruct participants to take photos, a new version of VEP emerges as users willingly take and share photos on UGC websites. Aside from Flickr, photo channels emerge via ranked sites—Photobucket (47), ImageShack.us (69), Panoramio (908), and Photo.net (2,132)—with increasing importance as consumers prefer to gather information from others rather than from official sources (Alexa 2009; Cheong and Morrison 2008).

Photos as Destination Recommendations

UGC can resemble word-of-mouth for destinations and tourism services. Word-of-mouth is interaction among individuals without any financial incentives regarding a product or organization (Litvin et al 2008). These recommendations play an important role in tourists' destination choices (Puczko et al 2007). When the Internet mediates this informal interaction, such as TripAdvisor text reviews, word-of-mouth reaches beyond family and friends (Litvin et al 2008). For example, reviews help tourists discover new hotels (Vermeulen and Seegers 2009), and positive hotel reviews lead to increased bookings (Ye, Law and Gu 2009).

The impact of this online word-of-mouth is a popular UGC research stream, yet few studies examine it from non-tourism and photo-based UGC websites (Cantoni, Tardini, Inversini and Marchiori 2009; Gretzel and Yoo 2008; Vermeulen and Seegers 2009; Ye et al 2009). Shared online photographs help create destination interest, excitement, and plans (Syed-Ahmad et al 2009), and might relay more information than official channels. For example, users share more photos of historic buildings, scenic views, and local cuisine than tourism organizations do (Choi et al 2007). Furthermore, photos have more media richness—and thus more possible persuasiveness—than simple text (Daft and Lengel 1984). User-generated photographs, such as those on Flickr, could represent destinations and persuade tourists.

Established in 2004, Flickr features photo-sharing with the ability to network and socialize (Boyd and Ellison 2007). Flickr users post self-expressive photos as well as people in activities such as tourism (Cox et al 2008). Users set privacy levels for sharing photos with four groups—family, friends, contacts, and the public (Cox et al 2008). Flickr generates possible recommendations with millions of destination photos in December 2009: United States (7 million), United Kingdom (5 million), and Australia (5 million). Muslim countries also have Flickr presence, such as Turkey (1.8 million), Malaysia (1.4 million), and Egypt (1.3 million).

Muslims and Muslim Images

Tourism is a growing industry in Muslim countries (Al-Hamarneh and Steiner 2004). In 1985, Malaysia, Turkey, and Morocco were the top three Muslim destinations (Din 1989). A couple decades later, Turkey and Malaysia still lead Muslim tourism with over 17 million tourists each (World Tourism Organization 2008). Five other popular Muslim destinations, with over six million tourists in 2005–2006, are from the Arab League: Egypt, Saudi Arabia, United Arab Emirates, Morocco, and Tunisia (World Tourism Organization 2008). Established in 1945, the 22 League of Arab States member countries, mostly in the Middle East and North Africa, share a common language, identity, and culture (Otterman 2009). They are Algeria, Bahrain, Comoros, Djibouti, Egypt, Iraq, Jordan, Kuwait, Lebanon, Libya, Mauritania, Morocco, Oman, Palestine, Qatar, Saudi Arabia, Somalia, Sudan, Syria, Tunisia, United Arab Emirates (UAE), and Yemen.

The World Travel and Tourism Council forecasts annual tourism growth until the year 2019 of 4.3% and 5.1%, respectively, for the Middle East and North Africa, higher than the global average of 4.0% (2009a, 2009b). The top three Arab destinations (Egypt, Saudi Arabia, and UAE) account for two-thirds of tourists in the region. Local and international tourists view Egypt as a leisure destination (World Tourism Organization 2007). Aside from tourists who make their *Hajj*, Saudi Arabia expands its religious tourism by attracting off-season and long-term tourists (Hazbun 2006). UAE, a federation of seven emirates, benefits from Dubai's standing as a popular destination (Govers and Go 2004). UAE's capital, Abu Dhabi, receives business tourists (Sharpley 2002; Wells 2007).

Arab countries have high Muslim populations, ranging from 60% for Lebanon to 100% for four countries (CIA 2009a). The encounters between tourists and Muslim locals have three dimensions: both groups' personalities, the interaction, and how both parties deal with the encounter (Din 1989). In most Arab countries, locals are uncomfortable with displays of overly affectionate relationships and scantily-clad female tourists. They see these behaviors as disrespectful to the Islamic religion and local culture (Dluzewska 2008).

Muslim culture comes from the holy book *Qur'an*, the revelations from God to Muhammad, and *Hadith*, a compilation of his actions and sayings (Nigosian 1987). Muslims' basic tenet embraces five obligatory actions: *Shahadah*, prayer, almsgiving, fasting, and pilgrimage (Nigosian 1987). Muslims believe and voice the *Shahadah*, a sentence declaring that Allah is the only God and Muhammad is God's messenger (Mawdudi 1985). Second,

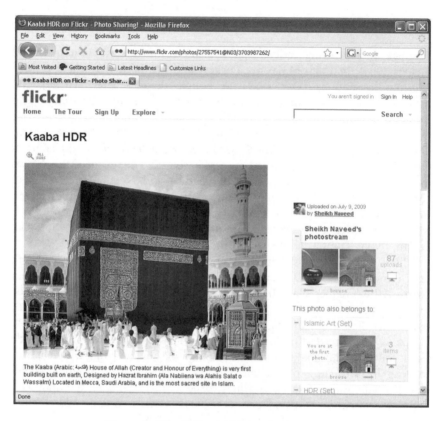

Figure 1. The *Ka'ba* on Flickr (22 July, 2009)

Muslims pray five times a day to worship God, privately or in public settings such as mosques (Nigosian 1987). As Figure 1 shows, they pray toward but do not worship the *Ka'ba*, a black holy shrine in Makkah (Tabbarah 1993). Third, Muslims give alms according to their wealth. Fourth, from sunrise to sunset in the month of Ramadan, they abstain from activities that would nullify their fast (Mawdudi 1985). Last, able Muslims perform the *Hajj* pilgrimage centering around the *Ka'ba* (Nigosian 1987).

Only some of these Islamic practices, such as praying as opposed to fasting, are observable and photographable. Studies of images in Dubai and Malaysia identified three observable Muslim images: mosques, women in headscarves, and the *Qur'an* (Govers and Go 2004; Hashim et al 2007). Table 1 lists eight observable Muslim images based around Muslim

Table 1. Eight Observable Muslim Images and 11 Coding Variables

Muslim Images	Description	Operationalization
Muslim Association (six coding variables)		
1. *Qur'an*	A holy book in Arabic calligraphy of God's revelations to Muhammad (Nigosian 1987)	A book with Arabic calligraphy. Read in mosques or in private
2. Allah or Muhammad	Allah means God; Muhammad is God's Messenger	The word Allah or Muhammad in Arabic or Latin writing
3. *Ka'ba* image	A holy shrine in Makkah, Saudi Arabia that Muslims pray toward (Nigosian 1987)	The black holy shrine in Makkah, Saudi Arabia
4. Prayer Hall (mosque)	Muslims congregate for prayers here	Clear prayer row markings parallel to the *mihrab* wall
5. *Mihrab* (mosque)	A decorated niche in Prayer Hall's front wall, showing the direction of *Ka'ba* (Insoll 1999)	A decorated niche in prayer hall's front wall
6. *Minaret* (mosque)	A tower for prayer calls (Polk 2004)	A tower attached to a mosque
7. Muslim conduct (one coding variable)		
Praying	Muslims pray five times a day by praising God, performing a set of movements, and reciting verses from the *Qur'an*. Prayers can be alone or with a leader	The subject stands, sits, bends halfway down or to the ground during prayer
Wudu	Before praying, Muslims cleanse their faces, hands, and feet by performing *wudu*	The subject is washing the face, hand, or feet
Du'a	An appeal for special needs or solace (Nigosian 1987)	The subject has palms facing upward and at shoulder level
Dhikir	Praising God through repeating God's name usually with rosary beads (Nigosian 1987)	The subject is in sitting position with fingers handling a set of rosary beads to count the repetitions
Reading the *Qur'an*	Muslims can read or recite the *Qur'an* placed on a "*rihal*" (wooden *Qur'an* holder) in front of them	The subject's eyes are cast down toward the opened *Qur'an* in front

Table 1 (*Continued*)

Muslim Images	Description	Operationalization
Listening to sermon	Muslims need to seek and increase Islamic knowledge, an act of piety to God. Listening to sermons traditionally occurred in mosques; however in recent times, Muslims listen to sermons through cassettes (Hirschkind 2001), CDs, and the Internet	Physical presence for sermons with preacher at the front and facing subjects
8. Female headscarf (four coding variables)	Muslim women cover themselves, except faces and hands during prayers and in public (Tabbarah 1993)	A female using any of four headscarf variations

association and conduct, mosques, and the female headscarf, also known as the *hijab* or *abaya*. As Flickr photos range from the mundane to destinations (Cox et al 2008), its users post tourism shots as well as Islamic images. The number of country and tourism photos are considered here as a measure of each nation's general and tourism presence on Flickr, and Islamic images reflect the country's Islamic culture.

As Flickr photos range from the mundane to destinations (Cox et al 2008), its users post travel photos as well as Muslim images. The number of photos with travel and Muslim keywords suggests a country's tourism and Muslim presence. Furthermore, exploring photos for Muslim images could reflect a destination's Islamic culture. To examine these photos and images, this study focused on the League of Arab States due to their high Muslim population and tourism growth.

The Study and its Findings

This study compares how Flickr destination photos and Muslim images vary for the 22 League of Arab States. It employed content analysis, which is prevalent in tourism and photography research (Choi et al 2007; Hashim et al 2007; Huang and Lee 2009; Hunter 2008) and UGC studies

(Jones, Millermaier, Goya-Martinez and Schuler 2008; Meyer, Rosenbaum and Hara 2005). Critical steps in content analysis include sampling, operationalizing the variables, and reliability test of the coding (Neuendorf 2002).

Prior to sampling, researchers tested Flickr keyword results. Viewers search Flickr photos using keywords, with the returned results listed on one of three listing criteria: relevance, recency, and interesting. They observe the returned photos (Figure 2) and can click for a close-up (Figure 1). In addition, viewers can access accompanying information such as the photograph title, poster's name, taken and posted dates, and location. Figure 2 illustrates a Flickr results page for all three keywords "Yemen, Muslim, travel."

Figure 2. Results Page for "Yemen Muslim Travel" (July 22, 2009)

To choose suitable keywords, Flickr searches in June 2009 returned nearly 192,000 photos for the keyword "Muslim" and over 154,000 photos for "Islam," making Muslim a better keyword for Muslim image searches. A search for "travel" returned over nine million photos, the highest among other tourism words such as vacation, holiday, tour, tourist, and tourism. Thus, the keywords in this study, using the Boolean "AND," were the "Arab country, Muslim *and* travel." The searches according to the relevance criteria ensured that the results related to the chosen keywords.

Table 2 shows the number of Flickr photos by various keyword searches on June 18, 2009, as well as percentages from each destination's photos. For the United Arab Emirates, the sampling was for all seven emirates (Abu Dhabi, Ajman, Dubai, Fujairah, Sharjah, Ras al-Khaimah, and Umm al-Quwain), as they are autonomous and diverse (UAE Government 2006). Table 2 lists the Arab countries in descending order according to the results for the three keywords. The last column indicates quota sampling to analyze up to the first 30 returned photos, or 589 photos, across 21 countries and seven emirates.

Flickr users displayed over four million photos for the League of Arab States; Egypt led with over one million. Those found with travel as the keyword made up 4.8% of the overall, and those with Muslim as the keyword had 1.7% presence. Egypt had the highest number of travel photos and over half the Arab countries, 15 states, portrayed over 2,000 travel photos. Yemen, however, led the travel photo presence at 10.9%, with three Arab countries having less than 1% travel photos. Palestine led Muslim photos at 12.3%, while 15 states had less than 1%. There were more photos in each country for the keyword travel than Muslim, except Palestine, Lebanon, Syria, Iraq, and Mauritania. For photos with both keywords Muslim and travel (Muslim-travel), 23 states had 4 to over 2,000 photos and 5 states had no photos. The percentage of Muslim-travel photos was less than 1% for all countries except Yemen.

Non-Arab Muslim countries aided the operationalization of variables to investigate photo content in addition to photo keywords. Examining Flickr results for Malaysia and Turkey helped define 11 coding variables in Table 1. These were coded separately as a photo could contain several Muslim images, such as Figure 1, which includes the *Ka'ba*, *minaret*, and women's headscarf. The unit of analysis was the photo from the results page, noting the presence of variables without interpreting meanings (Ball and Smith 1992).

Two Muslim postgraduate students (authors of this chapter) refined and managed the coding process from April to June 2009. Pretests with Iran,

Table 2. Arab Countries' Flickr Photos (June 18, 2009)[a]

Flickr Keywords	Country	Country + Travel	% Travel Photos	Country + Muslim	% Muslim Photos	Country + Muslim + Travel	% Muslim Travel Photos	Country + Muslim + Travel [studied]
Egypt	**1,143,702**	**77,441**	6.8	8,271	0.7	**2,280**	0.20	30
Morocco	649,199	47,939	7.4	5,716	0.9	1,615	0.25	30
Jordan	676,124	20,973	3.1	1,688	0.2	920	0.14	30
Yemen	49,783	5,411	**10.9**	1,753	3.5	874	**1.76**	30
Syria	145,696	10,337	7.1	13,854	9.5	792	0.54	30
Palestine	148,159	3,657	2.5	**18,181**	**12.3**	600	0.40	30
Tunisia	181,764	12,479	6.9	1,030	0.6	348	0.19	30
Lebanon	214,952	5,410	2.5	14,430	6.7	187	0.09	30
Dubai (UAE)	428,332	12,966	3.0	1,307	0.3	171	0.04	30
Bahrain	75,751	2,017	2.7	420	0.6	133	0.18	30
Saudi Arabia	50,455	2,871	5.7	1,355	2.7	104	0.21	30
Sharjah (UAE)	13,454	321	2.4	164	1.2	92	0.68	30
Iraq	276,940	2,127	0.8	2,660	1.0	85	0.03	30
Oman	102,958	2,344	2.3	1,358	1.3	39	0.04	30
Abu Dhabi (UAE)	40,505	1,306	3.2	439	1.1	38	0.09	30
Somalia	10,046	438	4.4	188	1.9	30	0.30	30
Kuwait	114,565	1,593	1.4	652	0.6	26	0.02	26
Mauritania	15,295	646	4.2	1,049	6.9	21	0.14	21
Algeria	36,063	1,483	4.1	489	1.4	18	0.05	17
Sudan	55,190	2,359	4.3	580	1.1	15	0.03	15
Qatar	95,278	2,179	2.3	382	0.4	14	0.01	14
Libya	50,075	1,715	3.4	276	0.6	10	0.02	12
Djibouti	7,846	244	3.1	25	0.3	4	0.05	4
Comoros	1,483	20	1.3	5	0.3	0	0	0
Fujairah (UAE)	4,472	41	0.9	14	0.3	0	0	0
Ajman (UAE)	1,759	39	2.2	4	0.2	0	0	0
Ras al-Khaimah(UAE)	1,729	58	3.4	3	0.2	0	0	0
Umm al-Quwain (UAE)	221	0	0	0	0	0	0	0
Total	4,591,796	218,414	4.8	76,293	1.7	8,416	0.18	589

[a]Numbers in **bold** represent column leader.

Pakistan, and Turkey familiarized coders with the variables, helped revise them, and tested coding reliability. The pretest on Turkey had a Scott's pi intercoder reliability coefficient of 0.86 for the most disagreed variable and 100% agreement on 4 of the 11 variables (Neuendorf 2002). Coders disagreed on 7, or 4%, of the total 165 (15 photos × 11 variables) coding entries for Turkey.

From May 15 to June 2, 2009, the coders studied the 589 Flickr photos tagged with one of the League of Arab States' countries/emirates, "Muslim," and "travel" (Table 2), and posted before May 12, 2009 for a standard timeframe. The coders used Explorer 7.0 Web browsers through the same Internet connection. Reliability increased during the study. Independent coding for Egypt showed Scott's pi of 0.88–1.0, with 100% agreement on five variables. Both coders agreed on 321 coding entries, or 97% of the 330 Egyptian entries (30 photos × 11 variables).

Table 3 shows that of the 589 photos studied, 235 Muslim images appeared in 215 photos (36.5%). Across all Muslim images, the female headscarf had the highest visibility with 118 photos (20%), followed by *minarets* (13%). Three Muslim images that made up the mosque (prayer hall, *mihrab*, and *minaret*) appeared in 16% of the photos. Other Muslim images had low visibility with no more than 2% of all photos. Female headscarves and *minarets* were evident, respectively, in 20 and 21 countries/ emirates, with other images present in up to seven of the studied Arab countries and emirates. Saudi Arabia had the highest number of Muslim images (83%) of total photos, while 15 countries/emirates had less than 50% of Muslim images.

Arab states with the most Muslim images were Somalia (headscarf), Saudi Arabia (*minaret* and *Ka'ba*), Abu Dhabi (*mihrab*), Yemen (prayer hall), Dubai (Allah or Muhammad), and Qatar (Muslim conduct). Across the eight Muslim images, Saudi Arabia and Yemen photos depicted six and five images, respectively. Five Arab countries and emirates had half the images present, and 16 other countries/emirates had three or less.

The top five Arab countries, Egypt, Morocco, Jordan, UAE, and Tunisia, with over 10,000 travel photos listed in Table 2, were among the top destinations in the region (World Tourism Organization 2008). In addition, Flickr's top three Arab states for destination and travel photos—Egypt, Jordan, and Morocco—were among the region's most affordable destinations (Gursoy, Baloglu and Chi 2009).

While tourists cluster the Arab world together (Winckler 2007), Flickr photos did not portray the Arab world as a single entity. Flickr users' postings differentiated Egypt, Saudi Arabia, and the UAE. Consistent with

Table 3. Arab Countries' Muslim Images[a]

Muslim Images	Muslim Association						Muslim Conduct	Female Headscarf	Total Muslim Images	Total Photos Studied	% Muslim Images
	Qur'an	Allah or Muhammad Image	Ka'ba Image	Prayer Hall	Mihrab	Minaret					
Saudi Arabia	0	0	**7**	2	1	**10**	1	4	**25**	30	**83**
Algeria	0	0	0	0	0	6	0	5	11	17	65
Qatar	0	0	0	0	0	4	**2**	3	9	14	64
Somalia	0	0	0	0	0	3	0	**16**	19	30	63
Yemen	0	0	2	**3**	1	7	0	6	19	30	63
Egypt	0	0	0	0	0	8	0	10	18	30	60
Libya	0	0	0	0	0	2	1	4	7	12	58
Oman	0	0	0	1	0	4	1	10	16	30	53
Bahrain	0	0	0	2	0	4	1	5	12	30	40
Lebanon	0	0	0	0	0	5	0	7	12	30	40
Syria	0	0	0	1	0	4	0	7	12	30	40
Morocco	0	0	0	0	0	1	0	10	11	30	37
Dubai (UAE)	0	**2**	0	0	0	4	1	3	10	30	33
Iraq	1	0	0	0	1	3	0	5	10	30	33
Tunisia	0	1	0	0	0	3	0	5	10	30	33
Jordan	0	0	0	0	0	1	0	7	8	30	26
Djibouti	0	0	0	0	0	1	0	0	1	4	25
Mauritania	0	0	0	0	0	0	1	4	5	21	24
Abu Dhabi (UAE)	0	0	0	0	**3**	2	0	1	6	30	20
Kuwait	1	0	0	0	0	2	0	2	5	26	19
Palestine	0	0	0	1	0	0	0	4	5	30	17
Sudan	0	0	0	0	0	2	0	0	2	15	13
Sharjah (UAE)	0	0	0	1	0	1	0	0	2	30	7
Total	2	3	9	11	7	77	8	118	235	589	
% of all photos	0.3	0.5	1.5	1.9	1.2	13.1	1.4	20	39.9	100	

[a]Numbers in **bold** represent column leader.

its position as the top Arab destination, Egypt dominated Flickr for the keyword results in Table 2. In addition, the data on Muslim images given in Table 3 reflect Saudi Arabia's role as a focus of Islamic tourism. Among the states of the UAE, Dubai had nearly 13,000 travel photos, surpassing countries such as Tunisia, Syria, and Saudi Arabia. The emirates received differing Flickr coverage, possibly reflecting emirate-level activities (Sharpley 2002), with three of seven emirates (Dubai, Abu Dhabi, and Sharjah) having the most travel and Muslim presence.

The Flickr photo results reflect the low tourism activities in some Arab states, such as Iraq with 0.8% travel photos. In addition, possibly due to unstable situations in Palestine and Iraq (Gregory 2004; Sirriyeh 2007), four neighboring countries—Palestine, Lebanon, Syria, and Iraq—had more Muslim than travel photos, suggesting lower tourism than Muslim associations. Palestine had the highest Muslim photo percentage (12.3%), possibly as users associate Palestine with Muslims in the country.

The female headscarf had the highest Muslim image percentage for Arab countries. Aside from informing the Muslim identity, the veil can correspond to social class, political symbol, maturity, and privacy, as well as facilitate women's movements in public (El Guindi 1999; Insoll 1999). Perhaps Flickr users associate female headscarves as the prominent Muslim norm or encountered more Muslim women with headscarves than other Muslim images. Another possibility is taking headscarf shots makes photographers feel they understand the destination's culture (Urry 1990).

After headscarves, mosques had prominence with *minarets* as the most common image. This outdoor mosque feature is more accessible for photos compared to the indoor prayer hall and *mihrab*. Some mosque interiors are only accessible to Muslims, who would usually focus on worshipping God rather than taking photos inside mosques. The same reasons could contribute to the low presence of Muslim conducts that typically appear inside mosques, such as praying and listening to sermons. Possible reasons for the exceptional number of mosque photos in the study are the number of mosques in a country, posters' fascination with mosque architecture, and Islamic norms' understanding.

Depicted Muslim images could inform and possibly attract tourists. Muslim tourists' impressions could pertain to assurances of their abilities to practice and conduct their religious responsibilities while traveling. In addition, certain images such as the holy *Ka'ba* could remind and motivate Muslims to visit Saudi Arabia or conduct their obligatory *Hajj*. Non-Muslims could perceive the Muslim images as unique due to low exposure to Islam (Urry 1990), possibly creating interest. In addition, countries with larger number of Muslim images may assist others' understanding of Islam as a religion.

This study supports Flickr as an avenue for destination recommendations. Compared to text, pictures are better at getting tourism information across, especially among inexperienced Internet users (Frias, Rodriguez and Castaneda 2008). As benefits, customization, and security ensure website satisfaction and repeat visits (Morosan and Jeong 2008), Flickr flourishes as it fulfills all three criteria. First, users benefit through the search function and may ask posters about a destination or join discussion groups. Second, users can customize photo searches and collect photos on their Flickr profile by labeling their favorites, thus creating readily available images for future reference. Last, after visiting a destination, Flickr users might want to share photos with just friends or family. Privacy features can limit photo viewing.

CONCLUSION

Egypt dominated destination, travel, and Muslim-travel photos, while Palestine had the highest percentage of Muslim photos. All League of Arab States and emirates, except five, had more travel than Muslim photos. Within Arab Muslim-travel photos, Flickr users depicted 36.5% Muslim images, mostly female headscarves followed by mosques. Other Muslim images were less prominent than the headscarf and mosque, with only up to 2% visibility and each image in less than seven countries. The countries vary in Muslim images depicted. Saudi Arabia had the highest percentage of images, while most Arab countries and emirates had fewer than 50% such images.

Tourism organizations could use these images for education and promotion. Future tourists to Arab countries unfamiliar with Muslim norms might turn to official websites for information. To educate viewers of the countries' Muslim norms, tourism representatives could link to specific Flickr images. Organizations could also employ these shared photos in brochures, minimizing time and possibly cost to produce photographs. Furthermore, photos on Flickr and other UGC websites resemble word-of-mouth rather than official recommendations.

Each destination's photos revealed various Muslim images. With Saudi Arabia, for example, aside from the photos of *Ka'ba* and *Hajj*, users shared mosque images such as the Floating Mosque in Jeddah and Al-Najedi in the Farasan Islands. These photos could interest and lead tourists to include these attractions in their Saudi Arabian itinerary. In Oman, two studied photos featured Prophet Ayoub's mausoleum, which could interest Muslim tourists. Destination officials could use these photos to understand what attractions posters share, or ignore, to assist promotion of these attractions. Additionally, historical and religious tourism could develop through users having visual access to shared places. The previous example could draw tourists to prophet's lands and tombs.

The study reported in this chapter contributes to the limited body of knowledge of how tourists photograph destinations, and how they are viewed (Cherem and Driver 1983; Garrod 2009). While this Flickr case is a small part of the emerging UGC trend, its role in the Internet, photo, and tourism studies could grow together with global users, which increased by 350% in the last decade (Internet World Stats 2009). The findings indicate that UGC such as Flickr could be another destination gaze (Urry 1990), in addition to various online and offline destination visuals. They illustrate that users share destination photographs with religious images. The study sets a benchmark of Muslim images and opens future research avenues for studying photos as destination recommendations.

Limitations of the study illustrate abundant future research opportunities. First, this chapter only examined a keyword combination: "Arab country, Muslim and travel." Future studies could explore keywords that capture specific tourist activities, attractions, or festivals. Second, the results might not reflect all keywords specified such as Muslim. For example, some photos did not have obvious Islamic elements in them, such as a tourism district in Sharjah and a flower petal in Kuwait. Third, this study focused on Flickr photos. Researchers could consider other popular UGC sites such as Facebook and YouTube for Muslim destination recommendations via texts, photos, or videos. Last, the focus was Arab countries; future studies could seek other emerging tourism destinations such as ASEAN countries.

Acknowledgments

The authors thank Krystyna Haq for feedback on the manuscript and the three Flickr posters for permission to use their photographs.

Chapter 19

ISLAMIC HERITAGE IN SINGAPORE
The Kampong Glam Historic District

David Tantow
National University of Singapore, Singapore

Abridgement: This chapter discusses the impact of tourism on the Kampong Glam Islamic heritage site in Singapore. For tourism development purposes, the main artery of the district was converted into a pedestrian mall. Planners tried to connect contemporary marketing initiatives for Islamic heritage with the historic role of Kampong Glam as a pilgrim destination, and attempted to legitimize the intense interventions. Despite these efforts, the rapidly induced changes have caused alienation of parts of the local Muslim community from the district. The chapter portrays the challenge to showcase Kampong Glam as a center of Singapore's Islamic heritage for interested tourists, while retaining the district's role as a homestead for the local Muslim minority.
Keywords: Singapore; Muslim minority; Islamic heritage; marginalization; cultural tourism

INTRODUCTION

The city-state of Singapore in Southeast Asia categorizes its citizens in three main ethnic groups: Chinese, Malays, and Indians, who make up 75%, 14%, and 9% of the population, respectively (Wong 2007). According to this multiracial ideology, each is free and even encouraged to keep up a distinct identity as long as the cohesion of the nation-state is not compromised. A similar idea applies to religion. Its practice is encouraged as a moral basis

Tourism in the Muslim World
Bridging Tourism Theory and Practice, Volume 2, 303–319
Copyright © 2010 by Emerald Group Publishing Limited
All rights of reproduction in any form reserved
ISSN: 2042-1443/doi:10.1108/S2042-1443(2010)0000002022

for good citizenry, but must be kept separate from national politics (Nasir and Pereira 2008).

In the case of Singapore's Malays, the link between ethnicity and religion is a peculiar one. As the indigenous Malay community is almost entirely Islamic, the terms "Malay" and "Muslim" are sometimes used as synonyms. The problem with using the term "Malays" as an umbrella term for all Muslims in Singapore is that there are also Arab, Indian, and even Chinese Muslims. All of them would be excluded by such a terminology. For this research work, Kampong Glam is discussed as the heritage district for Singapore's Muslim community—as it is a central venue for many Islamic religious and cultural institutions. Other heritage districts, Little India and, to a lesser degree, Chinatown are also a draw for local Muslim tourists, but Kampong Glam is the only central area where commercial life and cultural venues have been predominantly catering to Muslims. However, Kampong Glam's Islamic space is heavily influenced by non-Islamic culture, as it is home to some traditional Chinese clan associations and a hub for many Indian textile outlets (only some of them are owned by Indian Muslims, many belong to local Hindu or Sikh families). Despite these influences, Kampong Glam has always remained decidedly Islamic in character and is as such a unique urban quarter in Singapore's central city area.

Singapore's urban planning agency, Urban Renewal Agency (URA) tried to bridge the gap between the rigid labeling of heritage districts according to ethnic affiliation ("Malayness") and the multitude of hitherto unrecognized other Islamic influences in Singapore's Kampong Glam with a hyphenated or composite terminology. The Kampong Glam conservation zone has been relabeled as the Malay *and* Muslim heritage district to integrate Islamic culture of nonlocal origin into the official discourse (URA 1995). In contrast to this quite recent inclusion of Islamic space into heritage planning, the spatial manifestation of religious differences (in ethno-religious districts like Kampong Glam) was a taboo in the immediate aftermath of Singapore's independence. Urban redevelopment, among its other intentions such as economic uplifting, aimed to balance out the ratios of ethnicity and religious affiliation in all districts of the city-state to avoid racial and religious ghettoization. During this phase of urban renewal, existing ethnic or religious enclaves thus often underwent wholesale demolition (Gamer 1972).

In the new towns to which former inner-city residents were resettled, an ethno-religious quota of a maximum of 20% Malay/Muslim dwellers meant to preclude the evolution of new enclaves, at the same time manifesting the Singapore government's uneasiness with the nation's Malay and Muslim minority (Chih 2003). While commonly regarded as a success in economic terms, Singapore's urban renewal policies soon faced criticism for erasing religious and cultural heritage, hence leaving a vacuum for local identities. The interchangeable new towns and increasingly the inner-city area were devoid of meaningful places for the citizens; furthering the clearance strategy meant to risk the loss of their sense of belonging to Singapore (Kong 2000).

Postcolonial nation building, however, required the preservation of local heritage, especially if the citizens of independent Singapore were to develop a sense of belonging to their young nation-state. The government hence identified the need to maintain ethnic heritage in the urban environment to conserve a cultural homestead for every ethnicity (Tay 1988). Beyond their local relevance, these ethnic districts could fulfill a dual function, similarly serving as tourism attractions. But, in the course of conservation, the role of ethnic districts as an attraction at times dwarfed their intended function as a center for local ethnic culture (Kong 2000). However, whether directed at national or foreign tourists, the spatial adjustments in Kampong Glam are state-engineered representations of Islamic heritage. They manifest the racial and religious ideologies that developed over the past decades of postcolonial nation building.

The government ultimately acknowledged the increasing modernization of the downtown area as a threat to Singapore's Asian identity in the 1980s. As a consequence, it proclaimed ethnic heritage districts for the three ethnic groups. This proclamation of heritage districts aimed to spare certain areas from the pressures of modernization. The conservation zones should help the citizens to stay in touch with the city's multiethnic and multireligious history (Yeoh and Huang 1996). The government intended the districts to showcase local ethnic and religious identities to both tourists and young Singaporeans, for which it feared that they had lost touch with their "Asian roots" (Chang and Yeoh 1999). The government's URA hence drafted conservation manuals with the intention not only to preserve, but possibly to enhance the heritage of the particular areas (URA 1991).

While heritage preservation in Singapore started out as a top-down approach, communities can usually shape heritage spaces with their acceptance, contestation of, or even total resistance to policy-induced spatial adjustments in turn (Merrifield 2000). Based on a case study on Singapore's Muslim community in the Kampong Glam heritage district, this chapter analyzes the impact of tourism policies on ethnic heritage districts in postcolonial nations, and discusses how the representation of Islamic heritage for nation-building and tourism purposes has been received by local Muslims. The spatial redevelopment of Bussorah Street, as Kampong Glam's main artery leading to the Mosque's doorstep, exemplifies the potential for conflict between tourism development and Islamic community interests. Anchored to the Kampong Glam case study, the chapter discusses local sensitivities with tourism development in Islamic heritage areas. It emphasizes that Muslim communities' concerns have to be negotiated with tourism policymakers and urban planners, also in Islamic diasporas, such as in the Chinese-dominated global city of Singapore.

CULTURAL POLICIES, TOURISM, AND ISLAMIC SPACES

The case study is based on a combination of qualitative methods and quantitative forms of inquiry. The latter consisting of two separate "street surveys" of tourists and locals to Kampong Glam and a business survey distributed to shop owners. During fieldwork, approximately 40 semi-structured interviews were conducted to gain qualitative insights about life in the heritage district. Quantitative data was collected at three points in time, for three subpopulations, with a total of 500 questionnaires each time (200 from tourists, 200 from locals, 100 from shop and restaurant owners). In addition to the interviews and surveys, participant observation was carried out onsite, with an emphasis on the photographic documentation of local activities and a mapping exercise on the social history of the district's subzones.

As for the historic background for the representation of heritage in Kampong Glam today, Singapore merged with Malaysia in 1963 for gaining full independence from the United Kingdom. In the new nation-state, Islam was the prevailing religion and the Muslim Malays the majority population group. After only two years of merger, however, Malaysia and Singapore went separate ways in 1965. Since then the Muslims are a minority in the city-state and remain marginalized in economic and political life (Rahim 1998). After its independence from Britain and Malaysia, Kampong Glam's strong Islamic character was anathema to the Singapore government when it was to shape a coherent society out of the many ethnicities and religions of the newly independent city-state. The government arranged for pilot projects of urban renewal in the Kampong Glam area. This resulted in the demolition of some traditional Muslim neighborhoods for the Crawford public housing estate (Gamer 1972). Today, Kampong Glam's remaining historic rows of shop houses and the golden roof of the Sultan Mosque are surrounded by a high-rise jungle of urban renewal (Figure 1).

Ethnic and religious spaces (or their repression) thus played a key role in the struggle for a Singaporean identity during nation building, since the government initially considered the existence of such spaces as

Figure 1. Kampong Glam Heritage District, Sultan Mosque as a Landmark

counterproductive to its nation-building goal (Betts 1975). Ethnic and religious enclaves were a taboo in postcolonial Singapore, whereby the government perceived Muslim-Malay heritage with its communalist tendencies as representing half-hearted loyalty to the nation and thus as particularly problematic (Rahim 1998).

For tourism promotion, multiculturalism and multireligious heritage were officially endorsed, while their actual spatial manifestation in particular ethnic or religious heritage districts was initially kept to a minimum. Chang and Yeoh state that virtually all new cultural attractions "were housed in modern buildings rather than at historic staged sites" (1999:104) in the 1970s. Examples include the Asia Cultural Show featuring dances of various local cultures and religions, inaugurated in 1970, the Singapore Handicraft Center that showcased Asian artifacts and artisans of 1976, and the Rasa Singapura Food Centre that boasted the best of national cuisines of 1978. Most of these 1970s' ethno-cultural attractions were conveniently located along Orchard Road, Singapore's main shopping strip. All these central locations were racially and religiously neutral, since they represent selected cultural practices of various ethnicities and religions comprehensively in indoor exhibition spaces. Therefore, most of the newly erected ethno-religious attractions displayed heritage categorized into activities or aspects of life. They did not present all main components of a particular ethnic or religious heritage, a practice that left a lot of room for selective representations of religion and ethnicity. A possible cause for this instant approach could have been the uneasiness about components of the real ethno-religious spaces as opposed to confidence in merely staged performances held in neutral, purposefully built locations.

The uneasiness toward ethno-religious spaces would especially apply to the Malay and Muslim heritage of Singapore, since it has at times been associated with separatism and fundamentalism (Rahim 1998). Kampong Glam was a hot spot for a number of religiously motivated riots in the 1950s and early 1960s, such as the Maria Hertogh riots, prompted by the police-enforced handover of a Muslim educated girl from her Islamic adoptive parents to her Christian relatives (Khoo, Abdullah and Wan 2006). After Singapore's independence in 1965, Kampong Glam's association with Islamic activism became a problematic fact for the young nation, as it was seeking to mitigate its racial and religious discrepancies (Hussin 2005). In the 1960s and early 1970s, many Muslim Malays considered themselves as eligible for certain privileges as they were the indigenous ethnicity and religion of Singapore, yet socially marginalized. In contrast, these privileges were legalized in neighboring Malaysia. Kampong Glam's two principal landmarks—the *Istana* or palace of Kampong Glam, which is a symbol for Malay royalty and leadership, and Sultan Mosque as the island's oldest place of Islamic worship—were mobilized by activists to illuminate the aspired special status of the Islamic Malays in Singapore society. These declarations, however, stood in strong contrast to a multiracial and multireligious society as envisioned by the government (Betts 1975).

Due to this gap between official ideas about national identity and Muslim-Malay activism, Kampong Glam's Islamic heritage was initially sidelined by cultural policies. The district even shrank due to the allocation of urban renewal pilot projects next to the area. However, as the 1970s had passed without religious unrest, an attitude change toward Kampong Glam occurred.

Ethno-Religious Spaces Reconstructed for Tourism

In the 1980s, Singapore society had reached an unprecedented level of wealth and stability; hence ethno-religious incoherence seemed less threatening. The government became more confident to showcase the nation's diverse heritage, which was now deemed fitting to the island's aspired global-city status (Olds and Yeung 2004). As part of its cosmopolitan aspirations, the government then wished to develop the country as a cultural hub, world city, and "tourism capital." One aspect of becoming such a cultural hub was the urban enhancement of city spaces, for which the Singapore Tourism Board (STB) identified experiential themes such as "Ethnic Singapore" (STB 1996:29). "Ethnic Singapore" should emphasize the importance of ethnic spaces, multireligious diversity, and heritage. Kampong Glam's Arab Street was listed as an extension of the inner city's shopping district (STB 1996). The "Ethnic Singapore" program represented a fine-tuning of the prior conservation efforts of heritage spaces for the various religions and ethnicities of Singapore. It aimed both at repackaging the heritage experience according to coherent themes for respective target groups, locals and tourists alike, and at diversifying the heritage spaces at display. This tourism draft laid the basis for the more prominent representation of Kampong Glam as an Islamic heritage district.

Hence, the government recently rediscovered Islamic influences as quaint and complementary to the Chinese mainstream heritage and the Little India ethnic enclave. Numerous influences of the policy change can be noticed. Recent migrants from Muslim countries have opened new businesses in the gastronomic sector. In addition, government publications reemphasized transnational Muslim heritage, the historic pilgrim route connections to the Arabian Peninsula (URA 2005). Numerous newspaper articles proudly present the Middle Eastern influences in Kampong Glam. The district has become hip and draws a reasonably huge crowd of mostly youth especially on weekends. Most popular are the Arabian-inspired Shishah cafés offering smokes of the water pipe with aromatized tobaccos (Yong 2007). Almost 20 years after being demarcated as a heritage district, Kampong Glam's Muslim heritage is finally prominently on display.

The Islamic Pilgrim Tourism Legacy

Before 1819, Singapore was under Johor Sultanate and hence under a Muslim leadership. The Johor Sultanate originated from Malacca (present-day Malaysia) and Islam has been in Malacca since the 15th century (Sandhu and Wheatley 1983). Kampong Glam started off as a maritime settlement east of the Singapore river mouth (Imran 2005). *Kampong* is the Malay term for village or compound, *Glam* is believed to be derived from the endemic *Gelam* tree. Kampong Glam is older than modern Singapore. It existed prior to the colonial foundation of the city (URA 1995). However, the settlement only started to grow rapidly after the ceding of Singapore Island to the British in 1819 by a local chieftain. After its foundation in 1819 by British colonizer Sir Raffles, the open port settlement attracted Muslim traders from various regional backgrounds. They settled in Kampong Glam, as it was the area designated to them by the Raffles' town plan of 1823. The Islamic district gained popularity for tourism activities, as it became a center for *Hajj* pilgrimage. This era can generally be described as the time when the Malay and Muslim character of the district came into being. Within the next two decades, the economy flourished and the area's two principal landmarks were erected. The Sultan Mosque at the end of Bussorah Street dates back to 1828 and the *Istana Kampong Glam*—the Malay term for "the palace of Kampong Glam"—was completed around 1840 (Lou 1985).

Subsequently, Kampong Glam became renowned as the homestead of the Arab merchant elite of Singapore and as a center for pilgrim tourism, where Southeast Asian Makkah pilgrims stopped over to embark on ocean liners to the Arabian Peninsula. While the colonial administration did assign special districts to Singapore's various ethnicities and religious groups, it stopped short of strictly enforcing racial or religious boundaries. Hence, by the end of the colonial era, Kampong Glam was a predominately Malay and Muslim inner city quarter, albeit one with a fair share of Chinese population and regularly frequented by all ethnicities (Perkins 1984).

Another inheritance of the colonial era is the relocation of the harbor to the mouth of the Singapore River. The British directed the relocation in order to exercise tighter controls over traded goods as early as the 1820s. However, the port of Kampong Glam remained in operation, but subsequently had to focus on trades in which the British were apparently not interested. Kampong Glam as a coastal settlement specialized in trades catering to the city's Islamic community, while Chinese businesses also showed a presence (Lou 1985). Its seafront became a hub for Islamic traders and pilgrim brokers, whose activities started shaping the spaces in the area. A Bugis–Hadramauti shipping alliance managed the sea transport of the pilgrims. The Bugis as a regional Islamic ethnicity shipped them to Singapore, while the Hadramauti, originating from the Arabian Peninsula itself, would provide transport to the holy sites. The pilgrim brokers of Kampong Glam arranged the travel for the *Hajj* pilgrims, who intended to visit the holy sites of Makkah and Medina, via Singapore. These pilgrims from all over Southeast Asia would come to Singapore's Kampong Glam to await the second leg of their journeys.

At the seaside, the Hadramauti ships from Jemen would be anchored for further transportation to the final destinations on the Arabian Peninsula. In the meantime between ship passages, the brokers would provide the pilgrims with lodging and *halal* food. The brokers also assigned them to selected ships and equipped them with such attire as sandals and head ware. As the scope of activities suggests, pilgrim tourism, even though merely a stopover, supported many businesses in Kampong Glam and grew into a major sector of the local economy.

Imran (2005) provides detailed information about the whereabouts of the pilgrim trades during the 19th century in Singapore. Bussorah Street, as the main artery leading from the shore to Sultan Mosque, became known as *Kampung Kaji* (meaning *Hajji* Compound in Javanese). Other pilgrim centers existed, but they were demolished during urban renewal in the 1960s and 1970s. However, Bussorah Street as a former hub for pilgrims remained intact and offers potentially interesting insights into pilgrim tourism legacy. The street featured a considerable infrastructure for long-haul pilgrims, such as lodging, food stalls, and sellers of travel utensils.

However, when Kampong Glam was declared a heritage district in 1989, the pilgrim trade had already declined. Ismail (2006) argues that *Hajj*-related business continues to make an impact in the area and declares it an Islamic place, but admits that a strong manifestation of Muslim character in street life is now seasonally limited to the holy month of Ramadan. While she is certainly correct that the overall Islamic character of Kampong Glam has been persistent over the decades, the remaining *Hajj* businesses today cannot be equated with the major role Islamic pilgrim brokers played up to the mid-20th century.

At a closer look, two fundamental changes occurred in the nonrecent past, which preclude all notions of continuity. First, pilgrims do not stay in Kampong Glam any more for stopovers, since air travel has replaced sea travel to Makkah since the 1960s. Bussorah Street has not been a center for the accommodations of Muslim pilgrims or related businesses for decades. Second, the pilgrim brokers and their travel agencies are now forced to concentrate on local Muslims who intend to undertake *Hajj*, which has caused some entrepreneurs to cease their operations. Most of the remaining travel agencies have migrated out of Kampong Glam's conservation zone to the neighboring Golden Landmark shopping complex at around 1980. Therefore, pilgrim trades have not shaped the streetscapes of Kampong Glam's Bussorah Street for almost a quarter of a century. The STB's recent attempts to promote Islamic heritage try to link current tourism development with the bygone pilgrim legacy. However, the connectivity of earlier

Hajj and recent heritage tourism is weak and has furthermore been interrupted by the heavy-handed refurbishment procedures of the 1990s, which overlooked concerns of the local Islamic community.

Reengineered Survivor of the Pilgrim Era

Initiatives to revitalize Islamic heritage in Singapore focused on Kampong Glam due to the concentration of tangible heritage in the area (Imran 2005). After it was declared a heritage district for Malays and Muslims in 1989, Singapore's urban redevelopment authority started several conservation projects (initiated by a complete revamp of Bussorah Street) within the district in order to enhance the historic atmosphere. The two main intentions of STB and URA—as the state agencies in charge—were to commercially revitalize Kampong Glam, for both the tourists and locals, and sharpen its Islamic identity by means of a redesign of streetscapes and the beautification of shop houses. Since earlier attempts of state intervention within heritage districts had received sharp criticism for downplaying the importance of lived culture (Yeoh and Kong 1994), URA and STB were warned about the pitfalls of the state-engineered re-creation of ethno-religious heritage spaces that it could be interpreted as other-directed development targeted at tourists. The long history of pilgrim tourism in Kampong Glam came in handy for both agencies in this context. Their common basic assumption was that the historically important role of tourism since the district's foundation would lend some legitimacy for tourism-induced changes, even if fundamental adjustments had to be undertaken.

When the re-creation of ethno-religious spaces in Kampong Glam, according to popular tourism demand, began in 1994, the said pilgrim trades and connections were used as a vehicle to evoke a feeling of historicity by means of a reloaded Arab architectural theme initiated by URA and STB. Traditionally being a residential street (Ahmad 1987), Bussorah Street was turned into a pedestrian mall as a first step of the joint project by the two agencies. URA acquired all houses from the owners, refurbished them at the state's expense, removed the tenants, zoned the strip as commercial, and sold the now empty units to the highest bidder for the return of prior investment. This draconian approach left all facades intact but fundamentally changed the character of the street at the National Mosque's doorstep (Imran 2005). After the removal of former tenants, STB took care of visual details and infused the street with an Arabian flavor, such as orient-inspired mosaics on the plaster, supposedly reviving the ancient Middle Eastern connections (Figure 2). URA and STB deemed this creation of a redesigned tourism

Figure 2. Arab Elements after Bussorah's Redecoration

flagship commercial strip necessary to attract new tourists and thus make the district commercially viable.

While admitting that the Middle East is an increasingly important tourism-generating market, STB is careful to emphasize that the Arab design theme does not signify that non-Islamic tourists are not welcome to Kampong Glam. "The STB does not cater to any tourist group specifically, but Middle Eastern tourists are very welcome to visit a piece of Arab heritage in Kampong Glam," as Kelvin Leong, STB's spokesperson for historic districts, puts it (personal communication 2008). There is no comprehensive plan to market the Kampong Glam district specifically to Islamic tourists. The tourism infrastructure has been laid out to accommodate a wide range of possible touristic demands (Ismail 2006). Hence, the ancient pilgrim trade and its transcontinental connections serve the board as a justification for the reinfusion of exotic Arab elements into the locally built environment for general marketing purposes and not for specifically enhancing the share of Islamic tourists in Singapore. This nonexclusive tourism development strategy is common practice in destination branding, but because the needs and expectations of Western tourists tend to stand in contrast with local sensitivities, this very open approach gives rise to conflicts. It is especially problematic since the local Malay-Muslim community cannot identify with the Arab-Muslim theme which has been selectively enhanced for marketing.

Islamic pilgrim tourism has historically played an important role in Kampong Glam. However, forcibly tying it to an Arab theme does injustice to the district's history. The same can be said for attempts to construct a continuous legacy of inbound Islamic tourism. Urban renewal has caused a lot of ruptures both in and around Kampong Glam which preclude these notions of continuity. The Islamic heritage of Kampong Glam has *not* always been appreciated, as already discussed. Recent attempts to reinfuse Malay and Muslim spirit into the conservation zone might help to reconnect future generations of locals with their past, but to base those attempts on incorrect assumptions of continuity would mean to distort historical facts.

Reactions of Local Muslims

The flagship development of Bussorah Street into a pedestrianized mall has received mixed reviews. From the point of conservation, it is important to state that the architectural heritage has survived and has been refurbished for improved presentation. However, the enforced change of use of shop houses from residential to commercial has caused social disruption of Islamic community life in Kampong Glam, a point which is meanwhile acknowledged from official side, at least to some extent. For instance, Kelvin Ang, head of URA's conservation department, firmly insists that refurbishment works of the 1990s had not compromised on the architectural authenticity of the street, but concedes that other problems with the adaptive reuse exist (personal communication 2008).

This acknowledgment hints at the downside of the tourism flagship approach, highlighting adaptation problems as implications of the policy-induced rapid change of use. The strictly enforced sudden changes preclude continuity and complicate the organic social and economic redevelopment of the district. Subsequently, three interrelated issues have evolved: the rapid disappearance of traditional shops catering to local customers; the start-up of new, at times inappropriate, businesses in empty premises; and the arguably culturally insensitive promotion of Kampong Glam.

The Decline of Traditional Businesses. Many local residents and commercial residents think that the tourism flagship approach has backfired in terms of the conservation of Malay and Muslim culture. They believe that this rapid top-down development approach with its total clearance strategy has prevented most remaining Malay-Muslim shops to reoccupy their previous units (Ismail 2006). For redevelopment, URA lifted rent control for Kampong Glam to encourage investment and similar to the policy for the Chinese and Indian heritage districts put state properties on the market (Chang 1996). As URA offered tenders strictly to the highest bidder, the newly available shop units, after renovation, went to affluent investors rather than locally rooted tenants. Since Bussorah Street is the main artery to the Mosque and the central street of the conservation zone, the few remaining traditional Malay shops had only a slim chance to adjust to the sudden tourism-induced change in rental price levels. Representatives of traditional businesses face a difficult situation: "due to the high rentals in this area, most shops dealing in traditional trades like *songkok* and *kapals* have to move out. So, no more traditional Malay headwares and footwares" (personal communication 2008). The new commercial heart of the district did not develop organically, but was designed from scratch according to URA's plans. This ensured high architectural and physical conservation standards but no continued occupancy of Islamic residents or shopkeepers.

The Start-Up of New Businesses in Empty Premises. The 1997 Asian financial crises slowed down tourism development and prolonged the vacancy period of state property awaiting private occupation, such that the time gap till reoccupation of the empty units had a worse impact than expected. URA as the owner of all upper Bussorah Street units initially insisted on full return of investments and refused to lower the rental fees or purchase price for units. There were no restrictions on the commercial use as long as the new occupancy was a nonpolluting business (URA 1991). Nearly all lines of businesses were welcome as long as they could purchase the formally state-owned units. Today, vacancies as such are not a major problem along Bussorah Street but the occupancy with the highest bidder continues to spark resentments among business owners. "There are many unsuitable businesses and activities such as places where liquors are sold. There is an undesirable social crowd. All those facts do not project a good Malay and Muslim character" (Malay-Muslim shop owner in 2008).

The presence of the 7-Eleven convenience store along Bussorah Street has, in particular, sparked controversy. Located in front of the Mosque and amidst the conservation zone's dry area where an alcohol-serving ban applies, it uses a loophole in the law and sells beer to customers, because the alcohol is not served but sold. The widespread negative comments about such practices and unsuitable uses have meanwhile caused unease over the commercial developments in Bussorah Mall. Initial responses from URA to criticism were quite defensive, claiming that the pedestrianization of Bussorah as a festival street potentially gave room for Islamic festivities to be held, thus incorporating a cultural component into the commercial development (URA 1995:79). Not all local cultural researchers were convinced by such arguments. Rahil Ismail from the Center for Muslim States and Societies retorts that:

> [those statements are] ignoring the fact that Bussorah Street was already an authentic 'festival street' before conservation, it is this cookie-cutter pedestrianised shopping mall that had caused most consternation as gentrification of the street had erased both life and authenticity to a historic street (2006:248).

Finally, even spokespersons of URA, representatives of the responsible agency itself, expressed concern. Kelvin Ang, head of the conservation department, explains that "once units have been sold the new owner freely chooses the tenants," making it impossible for the state agency to ensure culturally appropriate uses (personal communication 2008). He elaborates that URA is currently in a dilemma. Previously critiqued for too heavy-handed approaches such as wholesale demolition, its conservation department now wants to step away from the image of a merely restricting and limiting agency. Conservation of heritage districts should be experienced as providing a pleasant spatial environment rather than acting as a constrictive force. However, Ang understands when concerned local Muslims complain to URA about unsuitable uses brought about by the agency's very own highest-bidder principle but refuses to revert back to state-centered approaches. He urges the new owners to be considerate and to carefully select tenants.

This appeal is respectable, but will likely remain without impact, since it is lacking a legally binding preclusion of inappropriate building uses. In recent years, Chinese-owned Karaoke lounges have sprung up in direct proximity to the Mosque, not on Bussorah Street but on adjacent North Bridge Road.

Karaoke lounges not only serve alcohol, some of them also function as brothels, which is arguably the case along North Bridge Road (Aziz 1998). Aziz (1998) and other exponents of Islamic cultural revitalization blame the destabilization of the traditional Malay-Muslim commercial community of Kampong Glam by the tourism-directed development plans for the relatively recent surge of un-Islamic businesses activities. The tough competition from solvent tourism business on Bussorah Street would have caused the decline of Islamic commerce in neighboring streets, and initiated the buyout of locally rooted Muslim shops by Chinese entrepreneurs. This argument is plausible but hard to prove. The problem of rapidly spreading inappropriate businesses does not only concern culturally inclined observers, but has meanwhile also alarmed the local commercial community, initially not a friend of the limitation of permitted business activities. The head of the Kampong Glam Business Association clearly states that his organization opposes the selling of alcohol in the district, since it is often combined with highly offensive activities, such as soliciting of young females in front of said karaoke bars (personal communication 2008).

As a further concession to concerned local Muslims, URA initiated an amendment to conservation guidelines, which extended the alcohol-serving ban from Bussorah Street into neighboring streets, albeit without closing the legal loophole of permitted alcohol purchase when not served. Meanwhile, a backpacker hostel has also opened up on Bussorah Street, whose guests enjoy alcoholic drinks in the open (a couple of meters from the Sultan Mosque's main entrance). Despite this coincidence, Kampong Glam remains a relatively quiet area, and rowdy behavior of tourist has so far not been reported (personal communication 2008). Furthermore, official representatives emphasize that the introduction of an alcohol ban, despite loopholes, is already a drastic measure to accommodate the local Muslim population with concessions regarding free-market activities, and as such without precedence in Singapore (personal communication 2008).

Culturally Insensitive Promotion of Kampong Glam. The third point of local critique is the arguably one-sided marketing of Kampong Glam as a hip shopping area with exotic nightlife. In addition to reports in popular magazines, STB directly promotes the area as a hot spot for designer shopping, where "glittery and lavish fashion items [are] abound" (STB 2008c). The good news about this somewhat unexpected amount of publicity is clearly that Kampong Glam's Islamic heritage is finally prominently on display and increasingly appreciated by young Singaporean. The downside is that those who are expected to enter a freshly evolving party zone are difficult to sensitize to appropriate and respectful behavior around a religious landmark.

A resident proposed bilingual street signs as a simple means to underline the Islamic character of Kampong Glam, asking people for due respect around the Sultan Mosque as an important spiritual center for Singapore Muslims (personal communication 2008). With the street name announced in both Latin script and in Arab writing, tourists would be reminded of the Islamic character of Kampong Glam in a subtle yet potentially effective manner. In addition to this possible adjustment of *in situ* signposting, more in-depth information about Islamic minority culture in Singapore in written form was deemed necessary. Granted not all reports about Kampong Glam can be centrally stirred into the direction of a cultural awareness campaign, but STB could enhance its efforts to bring background facts about the customs of Muslim minority across, via the inclusion of related information in its promotion material about Kampong Glam.

CONCLUSION

Bussorah Street is a "survivor" of urban renewal mostly in terms of architectural features. In contrast, the enhancement of Muslim-Malay characteristics of Kampong Glam in the post-urban renewal conservation zone largely failed because the top-down approach to conservation planning did not adequately account for the need of local residents and commercial operators. Their discontent with the nonconsultative planning approach is not primarily rooted in their religious affiliation to Islam, but the initial disregard for Muslim sensitivities has further antagonized the local population. Recent initiatives to pursue a more sensitive tourism development approach (the installation of a dry core zone around the Mosque where alcohol consumption is prohibited, etc.) are still in their infant stage. The URA–STB redevelopment alliance profoundly changed the character of the historic district with the conversion of Bussorah Street into a tourism flagship project. Despite being commercially successful, many locals describe its new representation of Islamic space as inappropriate. URA's role as the facilitator of Bussorah Mall is now limited. It contents itself with the role of mediator, conciliating conflicts between profit-maximizing owners and stakeholders emphasizing the local Muslim character. The tradition as an Islamic tourism hub had been steadily declining since the 1960s, but the radical 1990s revamp irrevocably interrupted continuity. If Bussorah Street is to develop into a more authentic Islamic heritage space again, URA must tread carefully as mediator.

In the future, it might in some instances be forced to stand ground against commercially viable uses that violate alcohol bans or engage in other locally contested activities in order to keep up the Islamic legacy of Bussorah Street.

At the same time, STB should rethink its all-encompassing promotion strategy of Kampong Glam, which to date is praising a wide range of shops and bars, inviting tourists across the board, from pleasure-seeking youngsters to aficionados of Islamic culture. While the business-friendly perspective of the agency is self-evident, a somewhat more targeted marketing of Islamic heritage might well pay off as a more sustainable form of tourism development, as it would enable a long-term growth perspective by means of the avoidance of clashes between the local population and tourists.

Singapore likes to portray itself as a global city and cultural hub. In the past 20 years, the city-state has made considerable efforts to conserve the multicultural and multireligious heritage of its citizens. These efforts have incorporated the Kampong Glam district as the traditional Islamic area, despite initial hesitations to showcase its arguably problematic and divisive heritage. The unfortunate start of heritage enhancement, with a tourism flagship project on Bussorah Street and implicating the displacement of former tenants, has quickly resulted in reservation of the local Islamic community about heritage initiatives. Since then, the understanding of authorities for the sensitivities of Kampong Glam's Muslim community has somewhat improved. Yet, URA and STB, as the agencies involved in heritage refurbishment and promotion, are in the difficult position to gradually gain back the trust of the community, since they squandered away confidence in tourism planning with initially rigid and nonconsultative project implementations in the 1990s. For a sustainable development of Islamic heritage in Singapore, the participation of the Islamic community in planning processes is a must in order to avoid further alienation of local Muslims from their designated heritage district.

Chapter 20

THE *HAJJ*
An Illustration of 360-Degree Authenticity

Nathalie Collins
Jamie Murphy
University of Western Australia, Australia

Abridgement: The chapter explores authenticity by proposing a 360-degree perspective based on tourism and philosophy literature. The Islamic religious pilgrimage or *Hajj* serves as an exemplary case for a proposed model. It merges theories of authenticity into a 360-degree multidimensional analysis. The dimensions are objective, constructive, existential, and commercial. Embracing authenticity as a multidimensional concept creates room for varying and valid authenticity perceptions, as well as validating the partnership of participants and producers as cocreators of value within the tourism experience. **Keywords:** authenticity; *Hajj*; pilgrimage; communitas; value cocreation

INTRODUCTION

Authenticity in the tourism experience has been a source of debate, starting with the meaning itself. Several definitions of authenticity exist, with much of the discussion about which definition to use or how to integrate them. This chapter explores the concept of authenticity by proposing a 360-degree perspective based on tourism and philosophy literature and using, as an exemplary case, the Islamic religious pilgrimage or *Hajj*. In this discussion the *Hajj* is acknowledged as a spiritual and holy experience and that it

Tourism in the Muslim World
Bridging Tourism Theory and Practice, Volume 2, 321–330
Copyright © 2010 by Emerald Group Publishing Limited
All rights of reproduction in any form reserved
ISSN: 2042-1443/doi:10.1108/S2042-1443(2010)0000002023

cannot be compared to commercial products. However, by contemplating it we may be inspired to better understand qualities of ordinary categories of goods, as discussed below.

Tourism has always dealt with the "theater" of the constructed experience (Vukonić 1996). Although there is consensus that authenticity is important to tourists, how to deliver it or if it is required for a satisfactory experience remains unclear. Yet the literature indicates tourists know authenticity when they see it, and they want to experience more of it (Wang 1999). The paradox of authenticity is that it is often mistaken for an objective truth or scientific fact. A common definition of "authentic" is something that can be objectively confirmed (Burchfield 1987). An object is an original or it is not. The conjecture is in the process of confirmation more than the definition of authenticity.

With experiences, authenticity takes on another quality. Wang (1999) calls this "existential authenticity," as it arises from a phenomenological perspective first posited by modern philosopher Soren Kierkegaard, who approached it not as an objective position, but as a quality of life, a pattern of behavior, and a personal connection. This approach was a departure from those who came before him in the Western philosophical tradition. It also opened the door to valuing the subjective experience, with all of its complexities and contradictions (Golomb 1995). Kierkegaard departs from the Western notion of separating spiritual and rational thinking. He posits that authenticity is ongoing, an internal struggle not to compartmentalize oneself and to live a whole and complete existence (Golomb 1995). And yet tourism tends to offer an opportunity to get away from the stresses and constraints of everyday life.

Does a tourism perspective take a holistic view of experience, or leave one place to exist authentically in another? Greek philosophers set the stage for the categorization and separation that seems to ring true in a Western context, which is why Kierkegaard's holistic approach to authenticity seems so radical (Golomb 1995). The *Hajj* balances these perspectives by being both an experience away from daily life and an experience integrated into the daily life of aspiring pilgrims and those who returned from the journey. The *Hajj* presents an ideal case in which to examine these experiential issues for several reasons. Islam is unique, with both a rich tradition of travel as well as an imperative to make specific journeys. The religion recognizes the potential for growth with any journey, and travel as both an external and internal transformative experience (Vukonić 1996). The largest single pilgrimage event in the world, the *Hajj*, is an Islamic one.

The *Hajj* is also an exclusive experience. Non-Muslims cannot participate in *it* and are forbidden from visiting the sacred sites in Saudi Arabia. Furthermore, to examine the *Hajj* experience without addressing the significant spiritual component is problematic from a methodological perspective and carries the risk of approaching the subject matter without the due respect. It is acknowledged here that the profound seriousness of the *Hajj* is the primary reason for its selection in this text. In the context of 360-degree authenticity, it is hard to find an exemplar as effective as this mandatory pilgrimage. The chapter intends to demonstrate that the seriousness of the journey by all participants is precisely why the example of the *Hajj* is so effective, and such effective examples are so rare.

Treating the *Hajj* experience as an exemplary case raises several points. Approaching the concept of tourism from a holistic context, as an interior and exterior transformation, helps reveal a way to understand the essential nature of authentic experiences richly and thoroughly. Examining the experience and its importance in a world context acknowledges the unique and profound nature of the event. Although non-Muslims cannot take part in the journey, they are well placed to learn from it, and in so doing increase their understanding of Islam. It is important to place the *Hajj* in its cultural and religious context. It is not a leisure activity. It is a mandatory journey for every Muslim able to complete it. The effects of the pilgrimage resonate throughout the life of the individuals who have made the journey, as well as their community (Vukonić 1996).

PILGRIMAGE TOURISM

As far back as the ancient Greeks, the literature has romanticized religious quests. A pilgrimage was a journey of sacrifice fraught with risk for the pilgrims, but showering spiritual rewards on the brave ones. The word has a looser meaning today, applying to all journeys of significance, whether they apply to conventional religion or not (Turner 1974; Vukonić 1996). An essentialist criticism of the word "pilgrimage" in modern usage is that it can apply to profane settings such as sports tourism and other types of "brand community" tourism (Gamin 2004).

The inner and outer journeys sit at the heart of the pilgrimage experience. Victor Turner's (1974) view of ritual pilgrimage has three steps: separation from ordinary life and the social/economic structures therein, entrance into the "liminal world" of "communitas," and then re-entry into the ordinary world with perspectives from the liminal world.

Turner's liminal world is analogous to a third place (Belk, Ger and Askegaard 2003), where the rules governing society no longer exist. *Communitas* suspends the traditional hierarchy and division between individuals and imposes a social order based on the essential nature of the activity. Ordinary social structures tend to emphasize differences. Communitas emphasizes sameness or unity (Turner 1974). Signifiers of communitas are the lack of emphasis on material wealth or social standing from secular power constructs, joy, and spiritual connection with a common source or focus (Belk, Wallendorf and Sherry 1989).

The liminal world and communitas are key components of tourism marketing (Vukonić 1996). The implication is that communitas and a liminal state are available through the tourism experience, no matter the nature of the activity or the sacredness of it. Similarly, churches advertise the lure of the liminal world. Promising a liminal experience is problematic due to its subjective nature. However, the potential for such an experience is attractive to tourists and a selling point for many tour operators.

This juxtaposition of religious and leisure imagery, and of authenticity and escape, seems to cloud the issue. What is authentic? Can it be measured objectively? Is a subjective perspective of it required to experience its efficacy? The traditional view of authenticity is something that can be independently verified as an objective fact about a place or an object.

Types of Authenticity

When Lionel Trilling (1974) started discussions on authenticity over 40 years ago, he used "To thine own self be true," a quote from Shakespeare's *Hamlet*, to summarize his philosophical view of it. Yet Trilling's seminal work indicates that a standard definition of authenticity is illusive.

Traditionally, authenticity relates to the physical state of an object. Object-related authenticity also has two distinctions. Objective authenticity relates to the "genuineness" of an object due to its originality. Constructive authenticity relates to the symbolic or constructed value of an object (Wang 1999). In this latter distinction, perception creeps in to an objective concept. This constructive authenticity can exist regardless of the genuineness of the object or place in question.

Recently, scholars added "existential" to concepts of authenticity. This addition is a nod to Kierkegaard, which Wang (1999) uses to draw a distinction between object-related authenticity and activity-related authenticity. Although Wang does not explicitly make this distinction, a close reading of his text in conjunction with Turner (1974) suggests an individual state of existential authenticity and a communal state that Turner (1974) and others (Belk et al 1989; Carse 2008; Vukonić 1996) call communitas.

Departing from the philosophical perspectives above, another type of authenticity can be in a commercial context. As marketing researchers examine the rising experience economy (Pine and Gilmore 1999), service-dominant logic (Vargo and Lusch 2004), and consumer cocreation of value (Prahalad and Ramaswamy 2000; Vargo and Lusch 2004), authenticity takes center stage. In a matrix categorizing levels of authenticity, the pinnacle is the product that is what it says it is and is true to itself (Gilmore and Pine 2007; Pine 2004). At this pinnacle, products that are what they purport to be and are true to themselves are "real real" (as opposed to a "real fake" or a "fake real"). Although simplistic, the model introduces "fake" and "real" into the discussion—a reference to authenticity and inauthenticity.

In popular culture, the "realness" of an activity makes it powerful. Reality television gets its punch from the claim that people in the shows behave authentically in extreme situations (Gilmore and Pine 2007). Phrases such as "keeping it real" and "being real" are slang terms introduced into common language through music and other cultural products. These terms refer positively to people who represent themselves authentically, ironically claiming to be unswayed by popular culture or fashion (Urban Dictionary: Keeping It Real 2009).

These phrases have made it into mainstream marketing slogans as well, such as Coca Cola's "The Real Thing." Tourism advertisements use "real" to discuss both a place and a state of being (Gilmore and Pine 2007). Trilling (1974) discusses "being true to oneself," but Pine (2004) discusses the importance of *being what you say you are* (emphasis added). With cultural authenticity it is insufficient to be who you say you are. One must also behave in an authentic manner. In this way, popular culture integrates Kierkegaard's holistic view of authenticity.

Gilmore and Pine (2007) build a matrix regarding natural authenticity (artificial/natural), original authenticity (imitation/original), exceptional authenticity (disingenuous/genuine), referential authenticity (fake/real), and influential authenticity (insincere/sincere). For this chapter, Pine's matrix as commercial authenticity refers to commercial products in a cultural context. For clarity, Table 1 reiterates different kinds of authenticity.

Rather than letting these definitions of authenticity be at odds with each other, it is useful to see them as discrete parts of a holistic authentic experience. A model adapted from the discipline of human resources is a shorthand way of analyzing the complex issue of authenticity: 360-degree

Table 1. Types of Authenticity

Authenticity Types	Description	Created by	Source
Objective	An object is genuine, an original	Producer	Wang (1999)
Constructive	Something that has constructed, symbolic value	Producer and consumer	Wang (1999)
Existential (self)	The liminal state of an individual	Consumer and producer	Wang (1999)
Existential (others)	The liminal state of a group; communitas	Consumers among themselves	Turner (1974); Wang (1999)
Commercial	A product is what it says it is and is true to itself	The culture at large, consumers, and producers	Gilmore and Pine (2007)

evaluation. Measuring work performance with a 360-degree evaluation helps one understand an employee's knowledge, leadership, and management skills by surveying individuals throughout their network on their performance. A 360-degree evaluation usually includes supervisors, clients, colleagues, and subordinates. Ideally, this evaluation provides a complete picture of the person and how others regard them (Nowack 1993). Similarly, a 360-degree authenticity model would look at a product or experience from all angles: objective, constructive, existential, and commercial. The model also looks at a product or experience from the point of view of both producers and consumers. Ideally, this multidimensional view creates an accurate analysis of the authenticity in a product experience.

The Hajj *as a Prototype of a 360-Degree Authenticity*

The *Hajj* is an annual pilgrimage ritual, mandatory for all Muslims at least once in their lifetime if they are able. The pilgrimage is both intensely personal and intensely public. It is an inner and outer journey, culminating in ancient rites performed in the holiest place in the world. The sheer numbers of pilgrims, almost two million per year, means pilgrims rarely have a moment alone, and all aspects of the journey are performed publicly as part of a community (Saudi Embassy 2009).

The famous *Hajji* (a returned *Hajj* pilgrim) Malcolm X described the experience this way:

> I have never before seen sincere and *true* brotherhood practiced by all colors together, irrespective of their color.... . During the past eleven days here in the Muslim world, I have eaten from the same plate, drunk from the same glass, and slept on the same rug—while praying to the same God—with fellow Muslims, whose eyes were the bluest of blue, whose hair was the blondest of blond, and whose skin was the whitest of white. And in the words and in the deeds of the white Muslims, I felt the same *sincerity* that I felt among the black African Muslims of Nigeria, Sudan and Ghana (Haley 1965:346; emphasis added).

X is describing existential authenticity, which is explored later in the chapter. If one reads his entire account of the experience, he is clear that it is all aspects of the authentic experience (objective, constructive, existential, and commercial) that impact his internal and external transformation. X's account is interesting because at the time he was one of the few Americans to make the journey. He also demonstrated a marked change in his rhetoric after the journey, making his transformation public, as he was such an outspoken public figure. As a civil rights activist who spent much of his life seeing European Americans as his enemy and oppressors, X returned from Makkah transformed in many ways. His view toward people of other races was just one aspect of his transformation.

To examine the *Hajj* pilgrimage without acknowledging its central spiritual nature is to discount the key point of the experience. This spiritual significance and its radiance shine brightly in the Muslim world. This genuineness is the very authenticity that this chapter examines, and in the process of examination, the potential of 360-degree authenticity will reveal itself as illusive by discounting the *Hajj's* significant religiosity. To shed light on this subject, it is necessary to explore the various types of authenticity and how they relate to the *Hajj* experience.

Object and Constructed Authenticity

Saudi Arabia is the caretaker of Islam's holiest sites, Makkah and Medina. The government dictates access to each site and licenses tourism operators to bring pilgrims into the country. They restrict the site to Muslims, and ensure that the

Hajj logistics are as safe as possible for the pilgrims and the place. The government's Ministry of the *Hajj* coordinates the massive effort (Saudi Embassy 2009). That the *Hajj* takes place on the original site is significant. It gives the journey an objective authenticity. Pilgrims perform all the symbolic actions in the original places where Muhammed performed them. The actions follow a sequence, and each ritual in the sequence has a specific meaning understood by all who participate (Public Broadcasting System 2009; Saudi Embassy 2009). These actions have significant constructed authenticity in Islamic culture.

After the journey, the pilgrim earns the title of *Hajji*. No specific individual or organization confers the title, but all in the community familiar with the culture of Islam (including non-Muslims) recognize the *Hajji* title (Public Broadcasting System 2009). Therefore, a Muslim contemplating the *Hajj* plans for the trip well in advance, as the trip requires preparation on many levels. The religious requirement to embark on the journey is clear: one must have the means, the freedom to travel, the ability to ensure that their dependants are cared for in their absence, and unencumbered and safe passage to what is now known as Saudi Arabia. According to Saudi Embassy (2009), it is unadvisable to make the journey without all of these conditions in place.

It is a religious requirement that the journey be on a secure path, avoiding treacherous passages and ensuring, as far as possible, the safety of pilgrims. Most of them enjoy safe travel, but some do not return from the *Hajj*. The Ministry of *Hajj* publishes tips, particularly for dealing with possible medical risks due to the close proximity of large groups of people, carefully controlled and limited resources, and other conditions. Occasionally, people are trampled a stampede while performing the rites (Saudi Embassy 2009).

The *Hajj* Ministry requires pilgrims to have a *Hajj* travel visa, which may require a mosque verifying that the pilgrim is a Muslim. Non-Muslims may not participate or visit the sites during the *Hajj* or at any other times. The Saudi government also licenses external touring companies, familiar with the risks and challenges of *Hajj* travel, as guides. These travel agents are audited and are the only ones who can facilitate *Hajj* visas and travel to Makkah and Medina during the key times. The agents are largely responsible for the pilgrims in their care. To that end, mosques, in partnership with the agents, educate and train pilgrims on their forthcoming experience before they depart (Saudi Embassy 2009). These predeparture activities become part of the ritual. Procuring all the necessary documents and training to participate in the trip is part of what Turner (1974) refers to as the ritual of separation from the ordinary world and entry into the liminal world.

These activities also familiarize the pilgrim with the significance of objective authentic experience in the constructed cultural context. Therefore, pilgrims are familiar with the meaning of what they are about to do. By excluding non-Muslims from the experience, the Saudi government ensures that the pilgrims on the *Hajj* are the ones who will experience the full spiritual impact of the journey. No spaces can be spared for bystanders or spectators—everyone participates in the cultural construct of the place and activities.

Existential Authenticity

When the pilgrims board the plane with their fellow Muslims, they enter the in-between place of the liminal experience and the start of the communitas. The final entry into the liminal world is when the pilgrims consciously leave behind their identity and acknowledge that, upon entrance to Makkah, they leave behind their race, nationality, social class, and other vestiges of the ordinary world and become a person dedicated to God, like the others on the journey (Public Broadcasting System 2009). This falling away of the last vestige of the old identity and the acknowledgment of the new identity is another ritual that underscores the concept of the *Hajj* as a liminal world for the self and in between all the selves on the journey.

The rites during the trip have profound spiritual meaning to the pilgrims, but the group experience of everyone's reverence for the rites and each other, along with the performance of the rites in concert, exponentially increases their symbolic impact. Although some on the journey are more devout than others, the feeling of community beyond national and social class lines is one of the most powerful aspects of the liminal space. Malcolm X's feelings of sincerity, brotherhood, equality, and spirituality, as well as his changed worldview, appear in other literature from returned *Hajjis* and reinforce the existential authenticity for both the pilgrims and the community (Public Broadcasting System 2009).

Once the pilgrims return from the experience and re-enter their ordinary life, they will reflect on the journey. This reflection can come in private moments, in communication with other pilgrims, and with the larger community. Reliving the experience in thoughts and discussions, one recreates and reconsumes the experience. The attributes in the imagination— authenticity, meaning, and sincerity—gain momentum upon reflection, and recollecting the experience enhances the transformative experience of the journey (Featherstone 1991).

Commercial Authenticity

The postmodern view of consumer culture suggests that individuals construct their identity through consumption (Featherstone 1991; Lewis and Bridger 2000; Schouten and McAlexander 1995). However, in this case, the pilgrims, as well as those who did not participate in the journey, validate the authenticity and importance of the *Hajj* through their reverence for it. The experience resonates long after it is over for the pilgrim and those who know him or her.

A key point with commercial authenticity is reverence. A commercially successful enterprise that is also respectful and spiritually appropriate is possible in Islam because of how Islamic culture blends the commercial, cultural, and spiritual aspects. The commercial enterprises involved with the *Hajj* must adhere to strict guidelines and are monitored to ensure their compliance. However, these commercial industries participate beyond compliance. Their reverence is, commercially speaking, authentic.

CONCLUSION

This chapter introduced the concept of 360-degree multidimensional authenticity, which comprises its main definitions in the literature. This approach allows for the objective and subjective, as well as the commercial and existential, authenticity. By taking into account the multiple discussions in the literature and binding them into one analysis, a sharp picture emerges of what authenticity can mean overall, and perhaps forms a new measure of it in experiences. The model also allows for the incorporation of more accounts of authenticity should they develop in future.

The chapter draws on themes that resonate when discussing tourism and religion. Anthropological, sociological, philosophical, and religious studies literature all play a role in discovering what makes particular experiences resonate with some individuals. Perhaps, looking back at Kierkegaard, one can posit that the persons most likely to find an experience authentic are those steeped in authenticity themselves. Surely, a pilgrim is an easier fit into that category than a different type of tourist. The most significant and popular pilgrimage in the world, the *Hajj*, helps initiate the exploration of how genuine meaning can be experienced: individually, as a group, and as a culture.

Chapter 21

CONCLUSION
Exploring the Muslim World

Noel Scott
The University of Queensland, Australia
Jafar Jafari
University of Wisconsin-Stout, USA
University of Algarve, Portugal

After 20 chapters exploring the intersection of the Muslim world and tourism, what conclusions can be drawn, and where might further explorers of tourism and the Muslim world look? These last pages provide the editors' reflections concerning common themes found in the chapters of this book, and also areas where there may be opportunities for further research.

In reflecting on the title chosen for this book, perhaps it should have been *Tourism in the Muslim Worlds*, as the chapter authors have provided insights into a diverse set of Muslim worlds, based on different viewpoints, such as those of the *Hajjis* and that of the Islamophobics. On the other hand, Islam provides the basis for unification, allowing a synthesis of this diversity.

From an academic perspective, this volume provides a view of tourism in the Muslim world that is vibrant and developing rapidly. Its 21 chapters by international authors indicate that tourism in the Muslim world is a topic of academic and practical interest, and one where there is a "critical mass" of authors and papers. While the volume contains contributions from established authors, it also includes a number of papers involving contributions from doctoral candidates or early career researchers. The interest demonstrated by contributors is heartening for the editors, and suggests that there is an opportunity for further joint scholarly activity. This could take the form of academic conferences, review papers, additional

Tourism in the Muslim World
Bridging Tourism Theory and Practice, Volume 2, 331–335
Copyright © 2010 by Emerald Group Publishing Limited
All rights of reproduction in any form reserved
ISSN: 2042-1443/doi:10.1108/S2042-1443(2010)0000002024

edited books, and building relationships among universities. Certainly these occur already, but perhaps there is an opportunity for increased activity.

This book has also provided readers with insight into the nature of Islam. Its first five chapters provide insights into the history, legal structure, labor force issues, and dietary requirements of the Muslim world, as well as the potential for mutual misunderstandings, whether related to tourism or to wider society. Of particular importance is the nature of *Shari'a* law, which indicates what is *halal* and what is *haram*. The significance of Chapter 2 is that it provides an argument that tourism is lawful. From a non-Muslim perspective, this may seem trivial and unnecessary, but within the Muslim world it is of paramount importance. Such an understanding is critical to tourism professionals who seek to host Muslim tourists.

The academic interest in this topic, as evident in this volume, is also in part due to the growth of tourism as an economic activity in many Muslim societies, including those in countries examined in this book: China, Brunei, Indonesia, Iran, Jordan, Malaysia, Maldives, Singapore, Saudi Arabia, Thailand, Turkey, and Turkmenistan. These countries are all grappling with policies and plans to manage this growth, balancing economic benefits and the social impacts of tourism development (Fredline 2002; King, Pizam and Milman 1993; Lindberg and Johnson 1997; Tovar and Lockwood 2008). There is significant variation across countries in the influence of the values and beliefs of Islam, and in their implementation in tourism policies and planning, indicating the practical value of the study of the topic, and also indicating a fruitful area for comparative research.

THEMES AND AREAS FOR FURTHER RESEARCH

One important reason for study of the Muslim world is that the trajectory of tourism development may not follow a pattern identical to that found in other countries. Many of the case studies of destination development found in the literature indicate a lack of control by those within the destination, even after negative effects have become apparent, leading to the development path described by Butler's lifecycle model (Butler 1980, 2005a, 2005b). In a number of countries, and particularly in Saudi Arabia, planning for tourism has taken a different and proactive strategy that encourages tourism by Muslims from neighboring countries. The same approach has also been observed in some regions of Western China, whereby people from Korea and Japan are preferred as tourists due to their similar cultural background. This strategy may be interpreted as a means of managing the development of tourism in a manner that minimizes its sociocultural impacts, an outcome consistent with principles of sustainability. The encouragement of tourists likely to meet the requirements of *Shari'a* law is termed Muslim tourism.

The development of tourism in the Muslim world is subject to actions derived from a set of beliefs and principles that are different from those found in many other destinations, and hence provides a contrast to that of mainstream tourism. A number of authors have highlighted the need for responsible tourism, where the tourist engages with the local community and is respectful of the values of the host in their behavior (Harrison and Husbands 1996; Spenceley 2008). In essence, this is what Muslim tourism seeks to encourage. However, its implementation in practice raises questions about the use of alcohol during leisure activities, wearing a bikini at the beach, and how these impact the decisionmaking process for a holiday. If tourists from countries used to freedom of action in their holidays are not likely to travel to a destination that practices Muslim tourism, then why should they be respectful in other destinations? Is it that tourists will practice responsible tourism only if they share the same beliefs as the local community?

Consideration of such issues as the impact of Islam on tourism development also encourages reflection on the existing patterns and activities taken for granted in many traditional tourism destinations. One of the fundamental issues in a globalizing world is how different religious and cultural values are accommodated. Tourism is often discussed as encouraging peace and understanding, and thus one might imagine that the tensions inherent in different beliefs may be more likely to be addressed within destinations, and that they may serve as important contexts within which to examine "accommodation" of different values. Unfortunately, the volume also provides some evidence that such accommodations may be difficult, such as in Chapters 12 and 16 where examples of Islamophobia are discussed.

Thus, examination of tourism in the Muslim world provides a useful perspective with which to view the discourses of "conventional tourism." A number of researchers have noted the need to examine the discourses of tourism (Azcairate 2006; Bramwell 2006; Bryce 2007; Burns 2008; Hollinshead and Jamal 2001; Markwick 2000; McGehee and Santos 2005; Papanicolaou 2009). In the context of ecotourism, Fletcher writes:

> In a wide variety of respects, therefore, we can observe that the promotion and practice of ecotourism tends to be framed within a constellation of beliefs, values and assumptions

largely peculiar to the white, upper-middle-class members of post-industrial societies who comprise the majority of ecotourism providers and clients globally. In promoting ecotourism as a strategy for sustainable development in poor rural areas of less-developed societies, therefore, providers and planners advocate viewing and engaging with the world from this perspective on the part of the local people with whom they work as well. While ecotourism planners may claim that they are merely offering locals an economic activity, we can observe in their practice an attempt to promote a variety of cultural or ideological changes among local people as well that planners shorthand as "education" (2009:280–281).

Similarly, by examining the intersection between tourism and the Muslim world, one may also find a sharper focus on the relationship of traditional values and tourism discourses.

A more practical theme found in a number of chapters relates to the planning, promotion, and marketing of tourism in the Islamic world. The theme of contrast between Islamic principles and those underpinning development in other destinations extends through many chapters, and a number of authors seek to better understand the interface of Islamic principles and planning and marketing. In particular, the studies of tourism photographs in this book (Chapters 18) illustrate that:

Photographs are a powerful and plentiful medium for tourism destination promotion. They cast the natural and cultural resources of a destination in the best light and even prescribe the proper host–tourist interactions through their depictions. It could be said that their representational power functionally transforms a place into a destination—a commodity (Hunter 2008:354).

In these and other respects, the book as a whole indicates a number of areas for further research within the intersection of Islam and tourism. One issue that has been discussed is religious tolerance (or intolerance). This has been studied in the hospitality industry in terms of the impact of religious tolerance on hotel employees (Huntley and Barnes-Reid 2003), and in Chapter 5 of this volume, religion is found to be a significant factor influencing women's employment in the tourism industry of the Maldives, particularly in terms of a woman working at an enclave resort. Related topics that merit attention include the effect of the perceived tolerance of the host community on Muslim tourist satisfaction.

Another area for further research that appears promising, given the differences in tourist motivations and behavior noted for the Muslim tourist, may be broadly described as product development. Opportunities have been identified in some countries (Iran, China, Jordan, and Saudi Arabia) for research regarding non-*Hajj*-related tourism. One area of potential is in development of shrine tourism (Bhardwaj 1998), while various mosques and historical sites are also being redeveloped (Chapter 10). It would appear there are also opportunities for innovative products that combine traditional pilgrimage and additional religious experiences with other activities, such as those related to culture and natural heritage resources. Similarly, it may be that there are other ways of structuring tours from developing countries that better take into account the beliefs of the Islamic host community.

Further, it is important to compare Islamic touristic policy in various countries to evaluate their effect on tourism development and local community. Studies may examine characteristics of demand and supply of *halal* food for Muslims, or the availability of alcohol for non-Muslims on destination choice. A number of chapters in this volume have called for studies on the difference between genders in terms of challenges, feelings, and impacts from experiences as diverse as pilgrimage and shopping in the Muslim world. There would also appear to be an opportunity for the study of the development of tourism training and education in Muslim countries.

In conclusion, this collection provides an illumination of Islam and its relation to and effects on tourism as an individual belief and as a source of economic development. But it is important to keep in mind that "Islam is not just a religion and certainly not just a fundamentalist political movement. It is a civilization and a way of life that varies from one Muslim country to another but is animated by a common spirit" (Mazrui 1997:118). Studies similar to what appears in this collection contribute to a better understanding of both the Muslim and non-Muslim worlds, for often by looking at another, people are better able to understand each other.

References

Ababsa, M.
2001 Les mausolées invisibles: Raqqa, ville de pèlerinage chiite ou pôle étatique en Jazîra syrienne. Annales de Géographie 622:647–664.

Abaza, M.
2001 Shopping Malls, Consumer Culture and the Reshaping of Public Space in Egypt. Theory, Culture and Society 18:97–122.

Abdulaal, W., and H. Al-Rahman
1991 Development of Shopping Centres in Jeddah. Journal of Environmental Planning and Management 34:10–19.

Abdulaziz, B.
2007 General Strategy for the Development of National Tourism. Riyadh, Saudi Arabia: Supreme Commission for Tourism.

'Âbed al-Qa'îd, M.
2002 Al-Siyâha al-diniyya fi al-Urdun (The Religious Tourism in Jordan). Amman, Jordan: Dar al-Hâmid.

Abel, A.
1960 Bahîrâ. In Encyclopédie de l'islam (new edition), Tome I, A-B, XX-VIII, pp. 950–951. Paris: E.J Brill Leiden and Maisonneuve et Larose.

Abrahamian, E.
2008 A History of Modern Iran. Cambridge, UK: Cambridge University Press.

Abu-Dawood, A.
2002 Development of Tourism in the Governorate of Jeddah: A Study in the Geography of Tourism. Riyadh, Saudi Arabia: The Saudi Geographical Society.

Adams, T.
2003 The Power of Perceptions: Measuring Wellness in a Globally Acceptable, Philosophically Consistent Way, Wellness Management. Sourced <www.hedir.org>.

Adelkhah, F.
2007 Economie morale du pèlerinage et société civile en Iran: les voyages religieux, commerciaux et touristiques à Damas. Politix 77:39–54.

Aguilar, M.
2009 Examining Destination Marketing from the Lens of Sustainability, unpublished master's thesis, Arizona State University, Phoenix.

Ahmad, N.
1987 Kampong Glam-the Genre de Vie of Urban Malays, unpublished bachelor's honours thesis, National University of Singapore, Singapore.

Ahmed, Z.
  1992 Islamic Pilgrimage (*Hajj*) to Ka'aba in Makkah (Saudi Arabia): An Important International Tourism Activity. Journal of Tourism Studies 3:35–43.
Ahmed, Z., and F. Krohn
  1992 Understanding the Unique Consumer Behavior of Japanese Tourists. Journal of Travel and Tourism Marketing 1(3):73–86.
Akbarzadeh, S.
  1999 National Identity and Political Legitimacy in Turkmenistan. Nationalities Papers 27:271–290.
Alavi, J., and M. Yasin
  2000 Iran's Tourism Potential and Market Realities: An Empirical Approach to Closing the Gap. Journal of Travel & Tourism Marketing 9(3):1–22.
Alexa
  2009 Top Sites. Sourced <http://www.alexa.com/topsites/global> (15 December 2009).
Al-Gendy, M.
  2005 The Right of Tourist in Safety and Security of the View of Islam Conference, Helwan University (in Arabic).
Alhabshi, S.
  2001 Catering to the Needs of Muslim Travellers. Paper presented at the Second Conference of Ministers from Muslim Countries: Tourism: Challenges and Opportunities, Palace of the Golden Horses Hotel, Kuala Lumpur, Malaysia, 10–13 October 2001. Sourced <http://www.bernama.com/oic_tourism/speeches1.htm>.
Al-Hamarneh, A., and C. Steiner
  2004 Islamic Tourism: Rethinking the Strategies of Tourism Development in the Arab World after September 11, 2001. Comparative Studies of South Asia, Africa and the Middle East 24:175–186.
Alhemoud, A., and E. Armstrong
  1996 Image of Tourism Attractions in Kuwait. Journal of Travel Research 34(4):76–80.
Ali, N.
  2008 The Significance of Ethnic Identity upon Tourism Participation within the Pakistani Community. PhD dissertation in Tourism Studies. University of Bedfordshire, UK.
Ali, N., and A. Holden
  2006 Post-Colonial Pakistani Mobilities: The Embodiment of the 'Myth of Return' in Tourism. Mobilities 1:217–242.
Ali Khan, G.
  2009 Tourism Industry Urged to Employ Saudi Women. Arab News (12 February).
Alipour, H., and R. Heydari
  2005 Tourism Revival and Planning in Islamic Republic of Iran: Challenges and Prospects. Anatolia 16:39–61.

Allcock, J.B.
  1988 Tourism as a Sacred Journey. Society and Leisure 11:33–38.
Al-Tayar, N.
  2002 A Prototype Experiment of Islamic Tourism (in Arabic). Al-Mousafir
    92:5.
Al-Shatibi, E.
  1960 Al-Mufwafqut Part 1. Mohamed A. Sobeh Press.
Aly, A.
  2006 The AtmosFEAR of Terror: Australian Muslims as Objects of Fear and
    Othering. Paper presented at the International Conference on Racisms in
    the New World Order: Realities of Culture, Colour and Identity Conference,
    Hyatt Regency Coolum, Queensland, Australia, 8–9 December 2005. Sourced
    <http://www.usc.edu.au/NR/rdonlyres/FF483353-FE64-49C9-84EF627B6961
    70CB/0/RacismsConf1revised.pdf#page=22>.
AME Info
  2002 Tourism and Saudi Arabia, Business Features. Sourced <www.ameinfo.
    com> (27 October 2003).
  2006 Eid Travel Packages Set to Attract Middle East Travellers to Singapore.
    Sourced <http://www.ameinfo.com/98315.html>.
  2008a Singapore Adds Visa Agencies in UAE. Sourced <http://www.ameinfo.
    com/143779.html>.
  2008b Singapore Honours Ramadan with Hari Raya Celebrations. Sourced
    <http://www.ameinfo.com/167773.html>.
Amin, S., and I. Alam
  2008 Women's Employment Decisions in Malaysia: Does Religion Matter? The
    Journal of Socio-Economics 37:2368–2379.
Anderson, B.
  2002 L'imaginaire National. Paris, France: La Découverte.
Anderson, B.A.
  2006 Crisis Management in the Australian Tourism Industry: Preparedness,
    Personnel and Postscript. Tourism Management 27:1290–1297.
Anderson, J.
  1959 Islamic Law in the Modern World. London, UK: Stevens and Sons.
Andreu, L., E. Bigne, and C. Cooper
  2000 Projected and Perceived Images of Spain as a Tourist Destination for British
    Travelers. Journal of Travel and Tourism Marketing 9(4):47–67.
Andreu, L., M. Kozak, N. Avci, and N. Cifter
  2005 Market Segmentation by Motivations to Travel: British Tourists Visiting
    Turkey. Journal of Travel & Tourism Marketing 19(1):1–13.
Anonymous
  2009 The Intangible Cultural Heritage in China. Sourced <http://www.china.
    com.cn/culture/zhuanti/whycml/node_7021179.htm> (10 April 2010).
Ansari, H.
  2002 Muslims in Britain. London, UK: Minority Rights Group International.

Armstrong, K.
  2001 Islam: A Short History. Toronto, Canada: Random House Inc.
  2002 Islam. New York: Random House.
ASEAN
  2008 International Visitor Arrivals to ASEAN 2005. Association of South East
    Asia Nations. Sourced <http://www.aseansec.org/tour_stat>.
  2009a ASEAN Statistics. Association of South East Asia Nations. Sourced
    <http://www.aseansec.org>.
  2009b ASEAN Statistical Yearbook. Jakarta, Indonesia: ASEAN Secretariat.
Ashley, C., D. Roe, and H. Goodwin
  2001 Pro-Poor Tourism Strategies: Making Tourism Work for the Poor: A
    Review of Experience. Nottingham, UK: Overseas Development Institute.
Ashmos, D., and D. Duchon
  2000 Spirituality at Work. A Conceptualization and Measure. Journal of
    Management Inquiry 9(2):134–145.
AsiaTravelTips.com
  2006 Singapore Tourism Board Launches Muslim Visitor's Guide. Sourced
    <http://www.asiatraveltips.com>.
Association of Chief Police Officers, The
  n.d. Stop Islamophobia. London: The Association of Chief Police Officers and the
    Muslim Safety Forum.
Au, N., and R. Law
  2002 Categorical Classification of Tourism Dinning. Annals of Tourism Research
    29:819–833.
Aubin-Boltanski, E.
  2004 Prophètes héros et ancêtres. Les pèlerinages musulmans de Nabî Mûsâ et
    Nabî Salîh dans la construction nationale palestinienne. PhD dissertation in
    Ethnologies. EHESS, France.
Augé, M.
  1995 Non-Places: Introduction to the Anthropology of Supermodernity. London,
    UK: Verson.
Axworthy, M.
  2008 A History of Iran. New York: Basic Books.
Ayata, S.
  1996 Patronage, Party, and State: The Politicization of Islam in Turkey. Middle
    East Journal 50:40–56.
Azcairate, M.
  2006 Between Local and Global, Discourses and Practices: Rethinking
    Ecotourism Development in Celestan (Yucatan, Mexico). Journal of Ecotour-
    ism 5:97–111.
Aziz, A.
  1998 On Royal Ground: Heritage Site Management in Kampong Glam. B.A.
    thesis in Southeast Asian Studies. National University of Singapore, Singapore.

Aziz, H.

1995 Understanding Attacks on Tourists in Egypt. Tourism Management 16(2): 91–95.

2001 The Journey: An Overview of Tourism and Travel in the Arab Islamic Context. *In* Tourism and the Less Developed Word: Issues and Case Studies, D. Harrison ed., pp. 151–159. Wallington: CABI.

Babin, B., J. Chebat, and R. Michon

2004 Perceived Appropriateness and its Effect on Quality, Affect and Behavior. Journal of Retailing and Consumer Services 11:287–298.

Badawi, S.

2006 The Effects of GATTS in Egypt's G.D.P (in Arabic).

Bagaeen, S.

2007 Dubai: The Instant City; or, the Instantly Recognizable City. International Planning Studies 12:173–197.

Bahr, H.

2005 Kreuzzug gegen Terror: Politik mit der Apokalypse. Blätter für Deutsche und Internationale Politik 9:1111–1118.

Bai, K.

2009 External Recognition of Urban Ethnic Communities: Islamic Traditional Community in the Hui Nationality Residential Area in Xi'an. China Population Resources and Environment 3:169–174.

Bai, S.

2000 History of Hui Religion in China (3rd ed.). Yinchuan, China: Ningxia People's Publication.

Bailey, J., and J. Sood

1993 The Effects of Religious Affiliation on Consumer Behavior: A Preliminary Investigation. Journal of Managerial Issues 5:328–352.

Ball, M.S., and G.W.H. Smith

1992 Analyzing Visual Data. Newbury Park, CA: Sage Publications.

Bandyopadhyay, R., D. Morais, and G. Chick

2008 Religion and identity in India's heritage tourism. Annals of Tourism Research 35:790–808.

Bar-On, R.

1996 Measuring the Effects on Tourism of Violence and of Promotion Following Violent Acts. *In* Tourism, Crime and International Security Issues, A. Pizam and Y. Mansfeld, eds., pp. 164–182. Chichester, UK: Wiley.

Baum, T.

2007 Human Resources in Tourism: Still Waiting for Change. Tourism Management 28:1383–1399.

Baum, T., and M. Conlin

1997 Brunei Darussalam: Sustainable Tourism Development within an Islamic Cultural Ethos. *In* Tourism and Economic Development in Asia and Australasia, F. Go and C. Carson, eds., pp. 91–102. London, UK: Cassell.

BBC
    2004 Iran Police in Fashion Crackdown. Sourced <http://news.bbc.co.uk/1/hi/
    world/middle_east/3887311.stm>.
    2007 Minister Detained at US Airport, BBC News Channel. Sourced <http://
    news.bbc.co.uk/1/hi/england/west_yorkshire/7066944.stm> (29 October).
Beck, J.
    2003 Self and Soul: Exploring the Boundary between Psychotherapy and Spiritual
    Formation. Journal of Psychology and Theology 31:24–36.
Beerli, A., and J. Martin
    2004 Factors Influencing Destination Image. Annals of Tourism Research 31(3):
    657–681.
Beheshti, O.
    2003 Travel Guide to Esfahan, Kashan and More. Tehran, Iran: Rowzaneh
    Publication.
Belhassen, Y., K. Caton, and W. Stewart
    2008 The Search for Authenticity in the Pilgrim Experience. Annals of Tourism
    Research 35:668–689.
Belk, R., G. Ger, and S. Askegaard
    2003 The Fire of Desire: A Multisited Inquiry into Consumer Passion. Journal of
    Consumer Research 30:326–351.
Belk, R., M. Wallendorf, and J. Sherry
    1989 The Sacred and the Profane in Consumer Behaviour: Theodicy on the
    Odyssey. The Journal of Consumer Research 16:1–38.
Bennigsen, A., and S. Wimbush
    1985 Muslims of the Soviet Empire. London, UK: Hurst.
Benny, R., and S. Nasr
    1975 Persia Bridge of Turquoise. Boston, MA: New York Graphic Society.
Berger, P., and T. Luckmann
    1966 The Social Construction of Reality. New York: Doubleday.
Bernama
    2009 Islamic Theme Park Not a Waste Says Azalina. Bernama News Agency
    (16 January).
Betts, R.
    1975 Multiracialism, Meritocracy and the Malays of Singapore. Dissertation
    thesis. Massachusetts Institute of Technology, Boston.
Bhardwaj, S.
    1998 Non-Hajj Pilgrimage in Islam: A Neglected Dimension of Religious
    Circulation. Journal of Cultural Geography 17(2):69–87.
Bhimji, F.
    2008 Cosmopolitan Belonging and Diaspora: Second-Generation British Muslim
    Women Travelling to South Asia. Citizenship Studies 12:413–427.
Bianchi, R.
    2006 Tourism and the Globalisation of Fear: Analysing the Politics of Risk and
    (In)security in Global Travel. Tourism and Hospitality Research 7:64–74.

Bin Muhammad, G.
1999 The Holy Sites of Jordan. Amman, Jordan: Turab.
Bin Salman, B.
2009 Kingdom Eyes SR101bn Revenue from Tourism. Arab News (3 May 2009).
Bitner, M.
1995 Building Service Relationships: It's All about Promises. Journal of the Academy of Marketing Science 23:246–251.
Bloom, J., and S. Blair
2000 Islam: A Thousand Years of Faith and Power. New York: TV Books.
Bogari, N.
2002 Motivation for Domestic Tourism: A Case Study of the Kingdom of Saudi Arabia. PhD thesis. The University of Huddersfield, Huddersfield, UK.
Bogari, N., G. Crowther, and N. Marr
2004 Motivation for Domestic Tourism: A Case Study of the Kingdom of Saudi Arabia. *In* Consumer Psychology of Tourism, Hospitality and Leisure, G. Crouch, R. Perdue, H. Timmermans, and M. Uysal, eds., Vol. 3, pp. 51–63. Oxford, UK: CABI.
Bonavia, J.
2004 The Silk Road. Hong Kong: Airphoto International.
Bonne, K., and W. Verbeke
2008 Muslim Consumer Trust in Halal Meat Status and Control in Belgium. Meat Science 79:113–123.
Bonne, K., I. Vermeir, F. Bergeaud-Blackler, and W. Verbeke
2007a Determinants of Halal Meat Consumption in France. British Food Journal 109:367–386.
2007b Religious Values Informing Halal Meat Production and the Control and Delivery of Halal Credence Quality. Agriculture and Human Values 25:35–47.
Boucek, C.
2007a Energy Security Implications in Post-Niyazov Turkmenistan. Central Asia-Caucasus Institute (CACI) Analyst. Sourced <http://www.cacianalyst.org/newsite/?q=node/4378>.
2007b Berdymukhammedov Burnishes Muslim Credentials on Visit to Saudi Arabia. Central Asia-Caucasus Institute (CACI) Analyst. Sourced <http://www.cacianalyst.org/?q=node/4594>.
Boyd, D., and N. Ellison
2007 Social Network Sites: Definition, History, Scholarship. Journal of Computer-Mediated Communication. Sourced <13:jcmc.indiana.edu/vol13/issue1/boyd.ellison.html13:jcmc.indiana.edu/vol13/issue1/boyd.ellison.html>.
Bramwell, B.
2006 Actors, Power, and Discourses of Growth Limits. Annals of Tourism Research 33:957–978.
Briant, P.
2002 From Cyrus to Alexander: A History of the Persian Empire. Winona Lake, IN: Eisenbrauns.

Brown, S., and A. Morrison
  2003 Expanding Volunteer Vacation Participation—An Exploratory Study on the Mini-Mission Concept. Tourism Recreation Research 28(3):73–82.
Brummell, P.
  2005 Turkmenistan. St Peters, UK: Bradt Travel Guides.
Brunei Times
  2008 Sultanate can be promoted as Hub for *Halal* Tourism. Sourced <http://www.halalfocus.com> (18 August 2008).
Brunei Tourism
  2008 Concept Statement. Brunei Tourism. Sourced <http://www.tourismbrunei.com/contact/concept.html>.
Brunt, P., and K. Cousins
  2000 The Extent of the Impact of Terrorism on International Travel and Tourism at Specific Tourist Destinations. Crime Prevention and Community Safety: An International Journal 4(3):7–21.
Bryce, D.
  2007 Repackaging Orientalism: Discourses on Egypt and Turkey in British Outbound Tourism. Tourist Studies 7:165–191.
Buhalis, D.
  2000 Marketing the Competitive Destination of the Future. Tourism Management 21:97–116.
Burchfield, R. ed.
  1987 The Compact Oxford English Dictionary. (2nd ed.). Oxford, UK: Oxford University Press.
Burns, P.
  2007 From Hajj to Hedonism? Paradoxes of Developing Tourism in Saudi Arabia. *In* Tourism in the Middle East, Continuity, Change and Transformation, R. Daher, ed., pp. 215–236. Clevedon, UK: Channel View Publications.
  2008 Tourism, Political Discourse, and Post-Colonialism. Tourism and Hospitality Planning & Development 5:61–71.
Burns, P., and C. Cooper
  1997 Yemen: Tourism and a Tribal Marxist Dichotomy. Tourism Management 18:555–563.
Burton, R.
  1995 Patterns of Tourism in the World's Regions: Africa and the Middle East. *In* Travel Geography, R. Burton, ed., pp. 348–370. London, UK: Pitman Publishing Limited.
Buruma, I., and A. Margalit
  2004 Occidentalism. The West in the Eyes of its Enemies. New York: Atlantic Books.
Bush, G. W.
  2001a Remarks by the President upon Arrival, September 16, 2001. Sourced <http://www.whitehouse.gov/news/releases/2001/09/20010916-2.html>.

2001b Address to a joint Session of Congress and the American People, September 20, 2001. Sourced <http://www.whitehouse.gov/news/releases/2001/09/20010920-8.html>.

Butler, R.
1980 The Concept of a Tourist Area Cycle of Evolution: Implications for Management of Resources. Canadian Geographer 24:7–14.
2005a The Tourism Area Life Cycle, Vol. 1, Applications and Modifications. London, UK: Channel View Publications.
2005b The Tourism Area Life Cycle, Vol. 2, Conceptual and Theoretical Issues. London, UK: Channel View Publications.

Cantoni, L., S. Tardini, A. Inversini, and E. Marchiori
2009 From Paradigmatic to Syntagmatic Communities: A Socio-Semiotic Approach to the Evolution Pattern of Online Travel Communities. *In* Information and Communication Technologies in Tourism (ENTER) 2009, W. Hopken, U. Gretzel, and R. Law, eds., pp. 13–24. Amsterdam, The Netherlands: Springer-Verlag/Wien.

Cao, H.
2002 The Research on Current Development and Management of China Religion Tourism. Social Scientist 4:48–51.

Carbone, M.
2005 Sustainable Tourism in Developing Countries: Poverty Alleviation, Participatory Planning, and Ethical Issues. The European Journal of Development Research 17:559–565.

Carlile, L.
1996 Economic Development and the Evolution of Japanese Overseas Tourism 1964–1994. Tourism Recreation Research 2:11–18.

Carmouche, R., and N. Kelly
1995 Behavioral Studies in Hospitality Management. London, UK: Chapman & Hall.

Carpenter, W. and D. Wienek, eds.
2004 Asian Security Handbook: Terrorism and the New Security Environment. Armonk, NY: M.E. Sharpe.

Carse, J.
2008 The Religious Case against Belief. New York: Penguin Press.

Caswell, M.
2008 King of the Desert. Business Traveller December:64–67.

Cavlek, N.
2002 Tour Operators and Destination Safety. Annals of Tourism Research 29: 478–496.

Central Intelligence Agency (CIA)
2009a The World Factbook. Sourced <http://www.cia.gov/library/publications/the-world-factbook/index.html> (29 April 2009).
2009b Turkmenistan. *In* The World Fact Book. Washington DC: Central Intelligence Agency. Sourced <https://www.cia.gov/library/publications/the-world-factbook/geos/tx.html>.

2009c Various Sourced. <https://www.cia.gov/library/publications/the-world-factbook/>.

Centre for Asian Studies Michigan State University
n.d. Turkmenistan-Religion. Sourced <http://www.asia.msu.edu/central_asia/turkmenistan/religion.php>.

Cha, S., K. McCleary, and M. Usal
1995 Travel Motivations of Japanese Overseas Travelers: A Factor Cluster Segmentation Approach. Journal of Travel Research 34:33–39.

Chang, T. C.
1996 Local Uniqueness in the Global Village: Heritage Tourism in Singapore, unpublished doctoral dissertation, Department of Geography, McGill University.

Chang, T., and B. Yeoh
1999 New Asia-Singapore: Communicating Local Cultures through Global Tourism. Geoforum 30(2):101–115.

Chhabra, D.
2009 Sustainable Marketing of Cultural and Heritage Tourism. London, UK: Taylor and Francis.

Channel News Asia
2008 S'pore and Gulf States Sign FTA, Recognise MUIS Halal Certification. Sourced <http://channelnewsasia.com>.

Chatelard, G.
2005a Un système en reconfiguration: l'émigration des Irakiens de la guerre du Golfe à la guerre d'Irak (1990–2003). *In* Monde en mouvement au Moyen-Orient au tournant du XXe siècle, H. Jaber and F. Métral, eds., pp. 113–155. Beyrouth, Lebanon: IFPO.
2005b Tourism and Representation: Of Social Change and Power Relation in Wadi Ramm. *In* Représentation et construction de la réalité sociale en Jordanie et Palestine, S. Latte-Abdallah, ed., pp. 53–82. Beyrouth, Lebanon: IFPO.

Cheong, H., and M. Morrison
2008 Consumers' Reliance on Product Information and Recommendations Found in UGC. Journal of Interactive Advertising. Sourced <8://jiad.org/article103>.

Cherem, G., and B. Driver
1983 Visitor Employed Photography: A Technique to Measure Common Perceptions of Natural Environments. Journal of Leisure Research 15:65–83.

Chevalier, J.
2008 Iran Sets a High Standard for Dialogue and Understanding. eTN Global Travel Industry News. Sourced <http://www.eturbonews.com>.

Chih, H.S.
2003 The Politics of Ethnic Integration in Singapore: Malay—Re-grouping as an Ideological Construct. International Journal of Urban and Regional Research 27(3):527–544.

China National Knowledge Infrastructure (CNKI) Database
2009 Tsinghua University, Beijing, China.

Choi, S., X. Lehto, and A. Morrison
2007 Destination Image Representation on the Web: Content Analysis of Macau Travel Related Websites. Tourism Management 28:118–129.

Choi, H., and E. Sirakaya
2006 Sustainability Indicators for Managing Community Tourism. Tourism Management 27:1274–1289.

Chon, K., T. Inagaki, and T. Ohashi
2000 Japanese Tourists: Socio-Economic, Marketing and Psychological Analysis. New York: Haworth.

Clique Associate Trainers and Consultants (CATC)
2007 Human Resource Needs Study 2007: Tourism Sector. Malé, Maldives: Clique Associate Trainers and Consultants Pvt. Ltd.

Cohen, E.
1995 Touristic Craft Ribbon Development in Thailand. Tourism Management 16:225–235.
1998 Tourism and Religion: A Comparative Perspective. Pacific Tourism Review 2:1–10.
2003 Tourism and Religion: A Case Study—Visiting Students in Israeli Universities. Journal of Travel Research 42:36–47.

Cohen, S.
1972 Folk Devils and Moral Panics: The Creation of Mods and Rockers. London, UK: MacGibbon and Kee.

Cohen-Hattab, K., and Y. Katz
2001 The Attraction of Palestine: Tourism in the Years 1850–1948. Journal of Historical Geography 27:166–177.

Coles, T., C.M. Hall, and D. Duval
2006 Tourism and Post-Disciplinary Enquiry. Current Issues in Tourism 9:293–319.

Collins-Kreiner, N.
2010 The Geography of Pilgrimage and Tourism: Transformations and Implications for Applied Geography. Applied Geography 30:153–164.

Collins-Kreiner, N., and J. Gatrell
2006 Tourism, Heritage and Pilgrimage: The Case of Haifa's Bahá'í Gardens. Journal of Heritage Tourism 1:32–50.

Commission on British Muslims and Islamophobia
2004 Islamophobia: Issues, Challenges and Actions. Stoke-on-Trent, UK: Trentham Books Ltd.

Constance, H.
2005 Working Women in English Society, 1300–1620. Canadian Journal of History 40:506–508.

Constitution of the Republic of Maldives
2008 Constitution of the Republic of Maldives. Malé, Maldives: Presidents Office.

Cooper, M.
2008 Tourism in the Middle East. Tourism Culture and Communication 8:55–56.
Cooper, M., B. Abubakar, and P. Erfurt
2001 Eco-Tourism Development into the New Millennium on Fraser Island: Tour Operators Perspectives. Tourism 49:359–367.
Cooper, M., M. Ogata, and J. Eades
2008 Heritage Tourism in Japan—A Synthesis and Comment. *In* Culture and Heritage Tourism in the Asia Pacific, B. Prideaux, D. Timothy, and K. Chon, eds., pp. 107–117. London, UK: Routledge.
Cowan, J. ed.
1976 Arabic-English Dictionary: The Hans Wehr Dictionary of Modern Written Arabic. London, UK: Harrap.
Cox, A., P. Clough, and J. Marlow
2008 Flickr: A First Look at User Behaviour in the Context of Photography as Serious Leisure. Information Research. Sourced < 13:http://informationr.net/ir/13-11/paper336.html >.
Crane, R.
2007 Is There a Quiet Revolution in Womens' Travel? Revisiting the Gender Gap in Commuting. Journal of the American Planning Association 73: 298–316.
Creswell, J.
2007 Qualitative Inquiry and Research Design: Choosing Among Five Approaches (2nd ed.). Thousand Oaks, CA: Sage Publications.
Crompton, J.
1979 Motivations for Pleasure Vacation. Annals of Tourism Research 6:408–424.
Crouch, D., and N. Lubbren
2003 Visual Culture and Tourism. London, UK: Berg.
Crouch, H.
2001 Managing Ethnic Tensions through Affirmative Action. *In* Social Cohesion and Conflict Prevention in Asia, N.J. Colletta, T.G. Lim, and A. Kelles-Viitanen, eds., pp. 225–262. Washington, DC: The World Bank.
Curtis, G. ed.
1996 Turkmenistan: A Country Study. Washington, DC: GPO for the Library of Congress, Sourced < http://countrystudies.us/turkmenistan/14.htm >.
Daft, R., and R. Lengel
1984 Information Richness: A New Approach to Managerial Behavior and Organization Design. *In* Research in Organizational Behavior, B. Staw and L. Cummings, eds., pp. 191–233. Greenwich, CT: JAI Press, Inc.
Daher, R.
2007a Tourism, Heritage and Urban Transformation in Jordan and Lebanon: Emerging Actors and Global-Local Juxtaposition. *In* Tourism in the Middle East, Continuity, Change and Transformation, R. Daher, ed., pp. 263–307. Clevedon, UK: Channel View Publications.

Daher, R. ed.
2007b Tourism in the Middle East. Clevedon, UK: Channel View.

Dalrymple, W.
2004 Islamophobia. New Statesman (19 January) pp. 18–20.

Daugherty, T., M. Eastin, and L. Bright
2008 Exploring Consumer Motivations for Creating User-Generated Content. Journal of Interactive Advertising. Sourced <//jiad.org/vol8/no2/daugherty/index.htm>.

Dayal, R., and S. Didi
2001 Women in the Republic of Maldives: Country Briefing Paper. Manila, Philippines: Asian Development Bank.

Delaney, C.
1990 The "Hajj": Sacred and Secular. American Ethnologist 17:513–530.

Del Giudice, M.
2008 Persia: Ancient Soul of Iran: A Glorious Past Inspires a Conflicted Nation: They Can't Control What's Inside us. National Geographic Magazine. Sourced <http://www.davidproject.org/resources/TeachersGuides/TeachersGuides_NationalGeographicMagazine.pdf> (August).

Deng, S., S. Jivan, and M.L. Hassan
1994 Advertising in Malaysia: A Cultural Perspective. International Journal of Advertising 13:153–166.

Department for International Development (DFID)
1999 Tourism and Poverty Elimination: Untapped Potential London. Sourced <http://www.propoortourism.org.uk/dfid_summary.PDF>.

Department of National Planning (DNP)
2009a Statistical Year Book of Maldives 2008, Department of National Planning. Sourced <http://planning.gov.mv/en/content/view/206/34/>.
2009b Statistical Year Book of Maldives 2009, Department of National Planning. Sourced <http://planning.gov.mv/yearbook2009/>.

Department of Tourism and Commerce Marketing (DTCM), Government of Dubai
2004 Hotel Statistics 1994–2003. Dubai.

Dewey, J.
2001 Die Suche nach Gewißheit. Eine Untersuchung des Verhältnisses von Erkenntnis und Handeln. Frankfurt/Main: Suhrkamp.
2002 Logik: die Theorie der Forschung. Frankfurt/Main: Suhrkamp.

Digance, J.
2003 Pilgrimage at Contested Sites. Annals of Tourism Research 30:143–159.
2006 Religious and Secular Pilgrimage: Journeys Redolent with Meaning. *In* Tourism, Religion and Spiritual Journeys, D.J. Timothy and D.H. Olsen, eds., pp. 36–48. Abington, MA: Routledge.

Di Matteo, L., and R. Di Matteo
1996 An Analysis of Canadian Cross-Border Travel. Annals of Tourism Research 23:103–122.

Din, A., and A. Hadi
   1997 Muslim Pilgrimage from Malaysia. *In* Sacred Places, Sacred Spaces: The Geography of Pilgrimages, R. Stoddard and A. Morinis, eds. Baton Rouge, LA: Louisiana State University.
Din, K.
   1982 Tourism in Malaysia competing needs in a plural society. Annals of Tourism Research 9:453–480.
   1989 Islam and Tourism: Patterns, Issues, and Options. Annals of Tourism Research 16:542–563.
Dluzewska, A.
   2008 The Influence of Religion on Global and Local Conflict in Tourism: Case Studies in Muslim Countries. *In* Tourism Development: Growth, Myths and Inequalities, P.M. Burns and M. Novelli, eds., pp. 52–67. Oxfordshire: CAB International.
Donner, F.
   2004 Expansion. *In* Encyclopedia of Islam and the Muslim World, R.C. Martin, ed., pp. 239–245. New York: Macmillan Reference USA.
Doron, A.
   2005 Encountering the 'Other': Pilgrims, Tourists and Boatmen in the City of Varanasi. The Australian Journal of Anthropology 16:157–178.
Dou, J.
   2006 The Study of Kashgar Folklore-Culture Traveling's Development. Urumchi, China: Xinjiang University.
Dower, N., and J. Williams
   2002a Preface. *In* Global Citizenship: A Critical Reader, N. Dower and J. Williams, eds., pp. xiii–xv. Edinburgh, UK: Edinburgh University Press.
   2002b Introduction. *In* Global Citizenship: A Critical Reader, N. Dower and J. Williams, eds., pp. 1–8. Edinburgh, UK: Edinburgh University Press.
Dunn, M.
   2007 Visa Laws 'Unfair' to Muslims, Herald Sun, 18 July. Sourced <http://www.news.com.au/heraldsun/story/0,21985,22092556-662,00.html>.
Du Rand, G., E. Heath, and N. Alberts
   2003 The Role of Local and Regional Food in Destination Marketing: A South African Situation Analysis. Journal of Travel & Tourism Marketing 14:97–112.
Eade, J.
   1992 Pilgrimage and Tourism at Lourdes, France. Annals of Tourism Research 19:18–32.
Eastern Eye
   2003 Racism Scales New Heights (M. Mann), 3 October, pp. 1–2.
ECOTimes
   2009 "Avaza" National Tourist Zone. ECOTimes (6):24–30. Sourced <http://www.ecieco.org/Portals/ee7fd74a-9a9b-4cb5-bf1b-9f8c85228be0/Publications%20E-Books/ECO%20Times%20,%20June%202009%20Web%20Edition.pdf>.

Edgar, A.
2004 Tribal Nation: The Making of Soviet Turkmenistan. Princeton, NJ: Princeton University Press.

Editorial Committee of Encyclopedia of China Islam
1995 Encyclopedia of China Islam. Chengdu, China: Sichuan Dictionary Press.

Edmonds, C., and J. Mak
2006 Terrorism and Tourism in the Asia Pacific Region: Is Travel and Tourism in a New World After 9/11? Department of Economics, University of Hawaii at Manoa.

EIU
2008a Country Profile 2008 Brunei. London, UK: Economist Intelligence Unit.
2008b Country Profile 2008 Malaysia. London, UK: Economist Intelligence Unit.
2008c Country Profile 2008 Indonesia. London, UK: Economist Intelligence Unit.
2008d Country Profile 2008 Singapore. London, UK: Economist Intelligence Unit.

El Guindi, F.
1999 Veil: Modesty, Privacy and Resistance. Oxford: Berg.

Elliot, J.
1997 Tourism Politics and Public Sector Management. New York: Routledge.

Enders, W., and T. Sandler
1991 Causality between Transnational Terrorism and Tourism: The Case of Spain. Terrorism 14:49–58.

Enders, W., T. Sandler, and G. Parise
1992 An Econometric Analysis of the Impact of Terrorism on Tourism. KYKLOS 45:531–554.

Esposito, J., and F. Donner
1999 The Oxford History of Islam. Oxford, UK: Oxford University Press.

Essoo, N., and S. Dibb
2004 Religious Influences on Shopping Behavior: An Exploratory Study. Journal of Marketing Management 20:683–712.

Euromonitor
2007 Executive Summary: Travel and Tourism in Iran. Sourced <http://www.euromonitor.com/Travel_And_Tourism_in_Iran>.
2009 Travel and Tourism: Iran. London, UK: Euromonitor Intelligence.

European Monitoring Centre on Racism and Xenophobia
2001 Anti-Islamic Reactions in the EU after the Terrorist Acts against USA: A Collection of Country Reports from RAXEN, National Focal Points (NFP)—United Kingdom, 12 September to 31 December. Vienna, Austria: European Monitoring Centre on Racism and Xenophobia.
2006a Muslims in the European Union: Discrimination and Islamophobia. Vienna, Austria: European Monitoring Centre on Racism and Xenophobia.
2006b Perceptions of Discrimination and Islamophobia: Voices from Members of Muslims Communities in the European Union. Vienna, Austria: European Monitoring Centre on Racism and Xenophobia.

European Union Agency for Fundamental Rights
2009 Data in Focus Report: Muslims. Austria: European Union Agency for Fundamental Rights.

Faath, S., and H. Mattes
2004 Misstrauen, Feindseligkeit und Gegnerschaft gegenüber "dem Westen"-ein künftig dominierende Einstellung in Nordafrika, Nah- und Mittelost? Hamburg. Sourced <http://www.giga-hamburg.de/dlcounter/download.php? d = /content/imes/menastabilisierung/pdf/mena_tp3_aspekte_3.pdf>.

Faghri, R.
2007 Tourism Planning and Policy Making of the Islamic Republic of Iran: Analysis of the Four Five-Year Development Plans. MA thesis. Lulea University of Technology, Sweden.

Fall, L., and J. Massey
2005 The Significance of Crisis Communication in the Aftermath of 9/11: A National Investigation of How Tourism Managers Have Re-Tooled their Promotional Campaigns. Journal of Travel & Tourism Marketing 19(2/3):77–90.

Faramarzi, M.
1995 A Travel Guide to Iran. Tehran, Iran: Published by Author.

Faroqhi, S., and R. Deguilhem
2005 Crafts and Craftsmen of the Middle East: Fashioning the Individual in the Muslim Mediterranean. London, UK: I.B. Tauris.

Fayazmanesh, S.
2003 The Politics of U.S. Economic Sanctions against Iran. Review of Radical Political Economics 35(3):221–240.

Featherstone, M.
1991 Consumer Culture and Postmodernism. London, UK: Sage Publications.
1998 The Flaneur, the City and Virtual Public Life. Urban Studies 35:909–925.

Fekete, L.
2004 Anti-Muslim Racism and the European Security State. Race and Class 46:3–29.

Feldman, R.
2004 Asylum Watch. Red Pepper 155:34.

Feldmann, H.
2007 Protestantism, Labor Force Participation, and Employment Across Countries. The American Journal of Economics and Sociology 66:795–816.

Fischer, J.
2008 Proper Islamic Consumption: Shopping Among the Malays in Modern Malaysia. Copenhagen, Denmark: NIAS.

Fisher, J., R. Nawaz, R. Fauzi, F. Nawaz, S. Eran Sadek, L. Zulkiflee Abd, and M. Blackett
2008 Balancing Water, Religion and Tourism on Redang Island, Malaysia. Environmental Research Letters 3:1–6.

Fleischer, A.
2000 The Tourist behind the Pilgrim in the Holy Land. International Journal of Hospitality Management 19:311–326.

Fleischer, A., and A. Pizam
2002 Tourism Constraints among Israeli Seniors. Annals of Tourism Research 29:106–123.

Fletcher, R.
2009 Ecotourism Discourse: Challenging the Stakeholders Theory. Journal of Ecotourism 8:269–285.

Flounders, S.
2006 Why the US is Targeting Iran, Stop War on Iran Organization. Sourced <http://www.axisoflogic.com/artman/publish/article_24499.shtml>.

Foroutan, Y.
2008 Women's Employment, Religion and Multiculturalism: Socio-Demongraphic Emphasis. Journal of Population Research 25:63–90.

Follesdal, A.
2002 Citizenship: European and Global. In Global Citizenship: A Critical Reader, N. Dower and J. Williams, eds., pp. 71–83. Edinburgh, UK: Edinburgh University Press.

Francis, L., E. Williams, J. Annis, and M. Robbins
2008 Understanding Cathedral Visitors: Psychological Type and Individual Differences in Experience and Appreciation. Tourism Analysis 13: 71–80.

Frangialli, F.
2002 Final Statement at the Third Meeting of the Tourism Recovery Commitee, London, 12.11.2002. Retrieved February 13, 2003, from World Tourism Organization Website <www.world-tourism.org>.

Frankfurter Allgemeine Zeitung (FAZ)
2005 Schwere Terroranschläge seit dem 11.September 2001-Attentate die islamistischen Terroristen zugeschrieben werden. Published July 25, 2005:3.

Fredline, E.
2002 Social Impacts of Tourism on the Gold Coast. Gold Coast, Australia: Cooperative Research Centre for Sustainable Tourism.

Frias, D., M. Rodriguez, and K. Castaneda
2008 Internet vs. Travel Agencies on Pre-Visit Destination Image Formation: An Information Processing View. Tourism Management 29:163–179.

Gamer, R.
1972 The Politics of Urban Development in Singapore. Ithaca, NY: Cornell University Press.

Gamin, S.
2004 Secular Pilgrimage and Sport Tourism. In Sport Tourism: Interrelationships, Impacts and Issues, B. Ritchie and D. Adair, eds., pp. 30–45. Clevedon, UK: Channel View Publications.

Ganguly, R.
2003 Ethnic Conflict and Secessionism in South and Southeast Asia: Causes, Dynamics, Solutions. New York: Sage Publications.
Gardet, L.
2005 Islām. *In* Encyclopaedia of Islam online, P. Bearman, T. Bianquis, C.E. Bosworth, E. van Donzel, and W.P. Heinrichs, eds. Leiden, The Netherlands: Brill.
Garrod, B.
2009 Understanding the Relationship between Tourism Destination Imagery and Tourist Photography. Journal of Travel Research 47:346–358.
Gee, C.
1997 The Role of Government in Tourism Policy and Administration. *In* International Tourism: A Global Perspective, C. Gee and E. Fayos-Sola, eds., pp. 281–300. Madrid, Spain: UN World Tourism Organization.
George, R.
2004 Marketing South African Tourism. Cape Town, South Africa: Oxford Southern Africa.
Getz, D.
1993 Tourist Shopping Villages: Development and Planning Strategies. Tourism Management 14:15–26.
Ghawânmeh, Y.
1995 "Maqâmat al-Sahâba fî al-Urdun" (The Shrines of the Companions of the Prophet in Jordan). Amman, Jordan: Ministry of the Youth.
Gilbert, D.
1996 Relationship Marketing and Airline Loyalty Schemes. Tourism Management 17:575–582.
Gilmore, J., and B. Pine, II
2007 Authenticity: Contending with the New Customer Sensibility. Boston, MA: Harvard Business School Publishing.
Gladney, D.
2003 Islam in China: Accommodation or Separatism? The China Quarterly 174:451–467.
Glaister, D.
2009 Muslim Family Thrown Off US Jet for Remarks. The Guardian. Sourced <http://www.guardian.co.uk/world/2009/jan/03/airtran-flight-muslim-passengers> (3 January).
Goeldner, C., and J.R. Ritchie
2006 Tourism Principles, Practices, Philosophies (11th ed.). Hoboken, NJ: Wiley.
Golomb, J.
1995 In Search of Authenticity: From Kierkegaard to Camus. London, UK: Routledge.
Government of the UAE
2004 UAE interact—Dubai GDP gets tourism boost. Sourced <http://uaeinteract.com/docs/Dubai_GDP_gets_tourism_boost/12003.htm>.

Goldenberg, S.
2002 Arabs and Muslims to be Fingerprinted at US Airports. The Guardian. Sourced <http://www.guardian.co.uk/international/story/0,3604,802729,00html> (2 October).

Gómez, L.
2004 Vvelta a casa. El Pais Semanal 1454:44–51.

Goode, E., and N. Ben-Yehuda
1994 Moral Panics: The Social Construction of Deviance. Oxford: Blackwell.

Government of Singapore
2006 The Singapore Constitution. Sourced <http://statutes.agc.gov.sg>.

Govers, R., and F. Go
2004 Projected Destination Image Online: Website Content Analysis of Pictures and Text. Journal of Information Technology & Tourism 7: 73–89.

Graburn, N.
1977 Tourism: The Sacred Journey. *In* Hosts and Guests: The Anthropology of Tourism, V. Smith, ed., pp. 17–31. Philadelphia, PA: University of Pennsylvania Press.

Gray, M.
2002 Development Strategies and the Political Economy of Tourism in Contemporary Jordan. *In* Jordan in Transition, 1990–2001, G. Joffé, ed., pp. 308–329. London, UK: Hurst and Co.

Gregory, D.
1998 Geographical Imaginations. Malden, MA: Blackwell Publishers.
2004 Palestine and the "War on Terror". Comparative Studies of South Asia, Africa and the Middle East 24:183–195.

Gretzel, U., and K. Yoo
2008 Use and Impact of Online Travel Reviews. *In* Information and Communication Technologies in Tourism, P. O'Connor, W. Hopken, and U. Gretzel, eds., pp. 35–46. Innsbruck, Austria: Springer-Verlag Wien.

Gunn, C., and T. Var
2002 Tourism Planning: Basics, Concepts, Cases (4th ed.). New York: Routledge.

Gursoy, D., S. Baloglu, and C. Chi
2009 Destination Competitiveness of Middle Eastern Countries: An Examination of Relative Positioning. Anatolia: An International Journal of Tourism and Hospitality Research 20:151–163.

Habermas, J.
2002 Fundamentalismus und Terror. Antworten auf Fragen zum 11. September 2001. Blätter für Deutsche und Internationale Politik 2:165–178.

Halal Focus
2009 Halal on the Rise. Sourced < http://halalfocus.net/2009/08/07/halal-on-the-rise/>.

Haldrup, M., and J. Larsen
2003 The Family Gaze. Tourist Studies 3:23–45.
Haley, A.
1965 The Autobiography of Malcolm X. New York: Grove Press.
Hall, C.M.
1994 Tourism and Politics: Policy, Power and Place. New York: Wiley.
2002 Travel Safety, Terrorism and the Media: The Significance of the Issue-Attention Cycle. Current Issues in Tourism 5:458–467.
2008 Tourism Planning: Policies, Processes and Relationships (2nd ed.). Essex, UK: Pearson-Prentice Hall.
Hall, C.M., and R. Mitchell
2005 Gastronomic Tourism: Comparing Food and Wine Tourism Experiences. In Niche Tourism: Contemporary Issues, Trends and Cases, M. Novelli, ed., pp. 73–87. Burlington, MA: Elsevier.
Hall, C.M., and V. O'Sullivan
1996 Tourism, Political Stability and Violence. In Tourism, Crime and International Security Issues, A. Pizam and Y. Mansfeld, eds., pp. 105–121. Chichester, UK: Wiley.
Hamdhoon, A.
2010 Banguralah Hulhuvifaivaa Enmme Dhorehves Huregen Nuvaane, Haveeru Daily Online. Sourced < http://haveeru.com.mv/?page = details&id = 93585& cat = search >.
Hannam, K., M. Sheller, and J. Urry
2006 Mobilities, Immobilities and Moorings. Mobilities 1:1–18.
Haq, F., and J. Jackson
2009 Spiritual Journey to Hajj: Australian and Pakistani Experience and Expectations. Journal of Management, Spirituality & Religion 6:141–156.
Hard, G.
2002 Über Räume reden. Zum Gebrauch des Wortes "Raum" in sozialwissenschaftlichem Zusammenhang. In Landschaft und Raum. Aufsätze zur Theorie der Geographie Band 1, G. Hard, ed., pp. 235–252. Osnabrück, Germany: Universitätsverlag Rasch.
Harris, J., and J. Nelson
1993 Monitoring Tourism from a Whole Economy Perspective: A Case from Indonesia. In Tourism and Sustainable Development: Monitoring, Planning and Managing, J. Nelson, R. Butler, and G. Wall, eds., pp. 179–200. Waterloo, Canada: Heritage Resources Centre, University of Waterloo.
Harrison, D.
2007 Towards Developing a Framework for Analyzing Tourism Phenomena: A Discussion. Current Issues in Tourism 30:61–86.
Harrison, L.C., and W. Husbands
1996 Practicing Responsible Tourism: International Case Studies in Tourism Planning, Policy, and Development. Brisbane, Australia: Wiley.

Hashim, N., J. Murphy, and N. Hashim
2007 Islam and Online Imagery on Malaysian Tourist Destination Websites. Journal of Computer-Mediated Communication 12:1082–1102.

Hashim, N., J. Murphy, and N. Muhammad
2003 Tourism and Islam: Understanding and Embracing the Opportunity. Ehlite Magazine 14:11–13.
2009 Tourism and Islam: Understanding and Embracing the Opportunity. Inside-Out Sourced <http://web.biz.uwa.edu.au/staff/jmurphy/Touirsm_and_Islam.pdf>.

Hassan, R.
2005 On Being Religious: Of Religious Commitment in Muslim Societies. Singapore: Institute of Defense and Strategic Studies. Sourced <www.ntu.edu.sg/rsis/publications/WorkingPapers/WP80.pdf>.

Hazbun, W.
2002 Mapping the Landscape of the New Middle East. The Politics of Tourism Development and the Peace Process in Jordan. *In* Jordan in Transition, 1990–2001, G. Joffé, ed., pp. 330–345. London, UK: Hurst & Company.
2006 Explaining the Arab Middle East Tourism Paradox. The Arab World Geographer 9:206–218.
2008 Beaches, Ruins, Resorts: The Politics of Tourism in the Arab World. London, UK: University of Minnesota Press.

Hejazeen, E.
2007 Tourism and Local Communities in Jordan. Munich, Vienna: Profil.

Henderson, J.
2003 Managing Tourism and Islam in Peninsular Malaysia. Tourism Management 24:447-456.2003 Terrorism and Tourism: Managing the Consequences of the Bali Bombings. Journal of Travel & Tourism Marketing 15(1):41–58.
2008a Tourism Destination Development: The Case of Malaysia. Tourism Recreation Research 33:49–58.
2008b Representations of Islam in Official Tourism Promotion. Tourism, Culture and Communication 8:135–146.
2008c The Politics of Tourism: A Perspective from the Maldives. Tourismos 3:99–115.
2009 Food Tourism Reviewed. British Food Journal 111:317–326.

Heyerdahl, T.
1986 The Maldive Mystery. London, UK: Allen and Unwin.

Hijawî, A.
2005 3,000 Pilgrims Visit Muta and Mazar. Sourced <www.jordan.jo> (19 September 2005).

Hill, J.
2000 Becoming a Cosmopolitan. Lanham, MD: Rowman and Littlefield Publishers, Inc.

Hillenbrand, R.
1999 Islamic Art and Architecture. London, UK: Thames and Hudson.

Hirschkind, C.
   2001 The Ethics of Listening: Cassette-Sermon Audition in Contemporary Egypt. American Ethnologist 28:623–649.
Hitchcock, M., and I. Putra
   2007 Tourism, Development and Terrorism in Bali. Aldershot, UK: Ashgate Publishing Ltd.
Hjalanger, A., and M. Corigliano
   2000 Food for Tourists: Determinants of an Image. International Journal of Tourism Research 2:28–293.
Hollier, R.
   1991 Conflict in the Gulf: Response of the Tourism Industry. Tourism Management 12:2–4.
Hollinshead, K., and T. Jamal
   2001 Delving into Discourse: Excavating the Inbuilt Power-Logic (S) of Tourism. Tourism Analysis 6:61–73.
Horak, S.
   2005 The Ideology of the Turkmenbashy Regime. Perspectives on European Politics and Society 6:305–319.
Horak, S., and J. Sir
   2009 Dismantling Totalitarianism: Turkmenistan under Berbiduhamedov. CACI—Silk Road Studies Programme.
Hsieh, A., and J. Chang
   2006 Shopping and Tourist Night Markets in Taiwan. Tourism Management 27:138–145.
Huang, W., and B. Lee
   2009 Capital City Tourism: Online Destination Image of Washington, DC. *In* Information and Communication Technologies in Tourism (ENTER), W. Hopken, U. Gretzel, and R. Law, eds., pp. 355–367. Amsterdam, The Netherlands: Springer-Verlag/Wien.
Hudman, L., and R. Jackson
   2002 Geography of Travel and Tourism (4th ed.). London, United Kingdom: Thompson.
Human Rights Watch
   2004 Turkmenistan: Human Rights Update Human Rights Watch submission to EBRD. Sourced <http://www.hrw.org/en/reports/2004/05/14/turkmenistan-human-rights-update>.
Hunter, W.
   2008 A Typology of Photographic Representations for Tourism: Depictions of Groomed Spaces. Tourism Management 29:354–365.
Huntington, S.
   1993 The Clash of Civilizations. Foreign Affairs (3):22–49.

Huntley, E., and C. Barnes-Reid
 2003 The Feasibility of Sabbath-Keeping in the Caribbean Hospitality Industry. International Journal of Contemporary Hospitality Management 15:172–175.
Hussain, J.
 1999 Islamic Law and Society: An Introduction. Sydney, Australia: The Federation Press.
Hussin, N.
 2005 Malay Press and Malay Politics: The Hertogh Riots in Singapore. Asia Europe Journal 4:561–571.
Ibn Al-Qaiem,
 1940 Aalam Al-Mwaqaien, Part 1. Demashk Press.
ICHHTO
 2009a Public Accommodation in Iran. Tehran, Iran: ICHHTO Statistics and Information Bureau.
 2009b Travel Agencies in Iran. Tehran, Iran: ICHHTO Statistics and Information Bureau.
 2009c Tourism Teaching and Training Centers in Iran. Tehran, Iran: ICHHTO Statistics and Information Bureau.
Imber, M.
 2002 The UN and Global Citizenship. *In* Global Citizenship: A Critical Reader, N. Dower and J. Williams, eds., pp. 114–124. Edinburgh, UK: Edinburgh University Press.
Imran, T.
 2005 Reading the Traditional City of Maritime Southeast Asia: Reconstructing the last Century Port Town at Gelam-Rochor-Kallang, Singapore. Journal of Southeast Asian Architecture 8:1–25.
Insoll, T.
 1999 The Archaeology of Islam. Oxford: Blackwell Publishers Ltd.
International Air Transport Association
 2007 Unpublished data of monthly passenger kilometres and passenger capacities. Received on September 11, 2007 by email.
International Crisis Group (ICG)
 2009 Women and Radicalization in Kyrgyzstan: Asia Report No. 176. International Crisis Group Asia. Sourced <http://www.crisisgroup.org/en/regions/asia/central-asia/kyrgyzstan/176-women-and-radicalisation-in-kyrgyzstan.aspx>.
International Labour Organization (ILO)
 2007 Global Employment Trends: Brief, January 2007. Geneva, Switzerland: International Labour Organization.
Internet World Stats
 2009 World Internet Users and Population Statistics. Sourced <http://www.internetworldstats.com/stats.htm> (11 December 2009).

Iqbal, A.
  2003 Sahrhe hale Abdollah bin Moqaffa Farsi (Biography of Ibn Moqaffa Farsi). Tehran, Iran: Asatir.
Iran National Census
  2007 Iran's National Census Statistical Pocketbook, (Selected Outcomes of 2006). Tehran, Iran: Statistical Center of Iran.
  2009 Statistical Data of Domestic Tourist in Iran. (In Persian). Sourced <www.sci.org.ir> and <www.amar.org.ir>.
Iran News Agency
  2007 Iran Exports Wheat from This Year. Sourced <http://www.iribnews.ir/Default.aspx?Page=MainContentandnews_num=106112>.
Iranian Qur'an News Agency (IQNA)
  2007 Grand Ayatollah Makarem Shirazi Threatens to Boycotts Minor Hajj. Sourced <http://www.iqna.ir/en/news_detail.php?ProdID=137970>.
Iran Touring and Tourism Organization (ITTO)
  2001 Tourism Development and Management Plan for the Islamic Republic of Iran. Tehran, Iran: ITTO.
  2009 List of all Shrines. Iran Tourism and Touring Organization. Sourced <http://www.itto.org/tourismattractions/index.asp?srch2=23&pg=8>.
IslamiCity
  2010 Sunnah, IslamiCity. Sourced <http://www.islamicity.com/mosque/sunnah/#Hadith>.
Islamic Republic of Iran Broadcasting (IRIB)
  2006 Saudi Tourism Officials Met Iran. Sourced <http://www.iribnews.ir>.
Ismail, R.
  2006 Ramadan and Bussorah Street: The Spirit of Place. GeoJournal 66(3):243–256.
Israeli, R.
  2000 Medieval Muslim Travelers to China. Journal of Muslim Minority Affairs 20:313–321.
Issa, I., and L. Altinay
  2006 Impacts of Political Instability on Tourism Planning and Development: The Case of Lebanon. Tourism Economics 12:361–381.
ITM
  2008a 50% Rise in Egyptian Tourists Visiting Malaysia, 5 November. Islamic Tourism Media. Sourced <http://www.islamictourism.com/news>.
  2008b Malaysia Seeks to Promote Islamic Tourism, 23 July. Islamic Tourism Media. Sourced <http://www.islamictourism.com/news>.
Jackowski, A.
  2000 Religious Tourism: Problems with Terminology. *In* Peregrinus Cracoviensis, A. Jackowski, ed. Krakow, Poland: Institute of Geography, Jagiellonian University.
Jackson, R., and L. Hudman
  1995 Pilgrimage Tourism and English Cathedrals: The Role of Religion in Travel. Tourism Review 50(4):40–48.

Jahan News
  2008 Holy Shrines. (In Persian). Sourced <http://www.jahannews.com/vdcevx8e. jh8epi9bbj.html>.
Jamieson, W.
  2003 Poverty Alleviation Through Sustainable Tourism Development. New York: United Nations.
Jenkins, C.
  2008 Tourism in Developing Countries. Annals of Tourism Research 35: 604–605.
Jenkins, C., and B. Henry
  1982 Government Involvement in Tourism in Developing Countries. Annals of Tourism Research 9:499–521.
Jesudason, J.
  2001 State Legitimacy, Minority Political Participation and Ethnic Conflict in Indonesia and Malaysia. *In* Social Cohesion and Conflict Prevention in Asia, N.J. Colletta, T.G. Lim, and A. Kelles-Viitanen, eds., pp. 65–98. Washington, DC: The World Bank.
Jing, X.
  1999 Advantages and Strategy on Islam Cultural Tourism Development in Quanzhou. Minjiang Vocational University Journal 2:39–40.
Johnston, A.
  2007 Is the Sacred for Sale? Tourism and Indigenous People. London, UK: Earthscan.
Jones, M.
  1999 Entertaining Shopping Experiences: An Exploratory Investigation. Journal of Retailing and Consumer Services 6:129–139.
Jones, S., S. Millermaier, M. Goya-Martinez, and J. Schuler
  2008 Whose Space is MySpace? A Content Analysis of MySpace Profiles. First Monday. Sourced <www.uic.edu/htbin/cgiwrap/bin/ojs/index.php/fm/article/view/2202/2024>.
Jordan Tourism Board
  2002 Tracing Islam in Jordan. Amman, Jordan: Jordan Tourism Board.
Joseph, C., and A. Kavoori
  2001 Mediated Resistance: Tourism and the Host Community. Annals of Tourism Research 28:998–1009.
JTMC
  2009 Japanese Overseas Travelers by Destination. Tokyo, Japan: JTMC.
Jukić, J.
  1977 Pluralistički pristup religiji (The Pluralistic Approach to the Religion). Crkva u svijetu 1:25.
Kadyrov, S.
  1996 Turkmenistan v XX veke: probely i problemy (Turkmenistan in the 20th Century: Deficiencies and Problems). Bergen, Norway.

Kagelmann, H., and S. Rösch
2002 Der 11. September und die Folgen für die US-amerikanischen Freizeitparks. Tourismus Journal 6:451–469.
Kant, I.
1949 Fundamental Principles of the Metaphysics of Morals (translated by Thomas Abbott Kingsmill). New York: Liberal Arts Press.
Katz, K.
2003 Legitimizing Jordan as the Holy Land: Papal Pilgrimages, 1964–2000. Comparative Studies of South Asia, Africa and the Middle East 23:181–189.
Keith, M.
2005 After the Cosmopolitan? Multicultural Cities and the Future of Racism. Abingdon, Oxon: Routledge.
Kelly, M.
1998 Jordan's Potential for Tourism Development. Annals of Tourism Research 25:304–918.
Kent, W., P. Schock, and R. Snow
1983 Shopping Tourism's Unsung Hero(ine). Journal of Travel Research 21(4):2–4.
Keown, C.
1989 A Model of Tourist Propensity to Buy: The Case of Japanese Visitor to Hawaii. Journal of Travel Research 18(3):31–34.
Kesler, C.
1992 Pilgrim's Progress: The Travelers of Islam. Annals of Tourism Research 19:147–153.
Khan, W.
1986 Hajj and Islamic Da'wah. *In* Hajj in Focus, Z. Khan and Y. Zaki, eds. London, UK: Open Press.
Khan, Z.
2000 Muslim Presence in Europe: The British Dimension—Identity, Integration and Community Activism. Current Sociology 48(4):29–43.
Kheimehnews
2007 The Necessity of Expanding Religion tourism in Iran. In Persian. Sourced <http://www.kheimehnews.com/vdcf.vdmiw6decgiaw>.
Khodadadian, A.
1999 History of Ancient Persia: Achaemenids. Tehran, Iran: Nashr-e Behdid.
Khoo, K., E. Abdullah, and M.H. Wan, eds.
2006 Malay/Muslims in Singapore: Selected Readings in History 1819–1965. Subang Jaya, Malaysia: Pelanduk Publications.
Kiepenheuer-Drechsler, B.
2006 Trapped in Permanent Neutrality: Looking behind the Symbolic Production of the Turkmen Nation. Central Asian Survey 25:129–141.
King, B., A. Pizam, and A. Milman
1993 The Social Impacts of Tourism on Nadi Fiji as Perceived by its Residents. Annals of Tourism Research 20:650–665.

Kingdom of Saudi Arabia Central Department of Statistics and Information
2009 Hajj Statistics. Sourced <http://www.cdsi.gov.sa/showsection.aspx?lid=
26&id=308>.
Kingdom of Saudi Arabia Ministry of Hajj
2009 Hajj. Sourced <http://www.hajinformation.com/>.
Kivisto, P., and T. Faist
2007 Citizenship: Discourse, Theory and Transnational Prospects. Oxford: Blackwell.
Kong, L.
2000 Value Conflicts, Identity Construction and Urban Change. *In* A
Companion to the City, G. Bridge and S. Watson, eds., pp. 354–365. Oxford:
Blackwell.
Kotler, P., J. Bowen, and J. Makens
1999 Marketing for Hospitality and Tourism. Upper Saddle River, NJ: Prentice
Hall.
Kozak, M.
2002 Comparative Analysis of Tourist Motivations by Nationality and Destina-
tions. Tourism Management 23:221–232.
Kramer, G. and R. Allen, eds.
2009 The Encyclopaedia of Islam Three. Lieden, The Netherlands: Koninklijke Brill.
Kremmer, C., and C. Banham
2004 US Targeted us on Racial Grounds: Australians. The Sydney Morning
Herald. Sourced <http://www.smh.com.au/articles/2004/02/22/1077384639114.
html>(23 February).
Krippendorf, K.
2004 Content Analysis: An Introduction to its Methods. Thousand Oaks, CA:
Sage Publications.
Kuru, A.
2002 Between the State and Cultural Zones: Nation Building in Turkmenistan.
Central Asian Survey 21:71–90.
Law, R.
1999 Beyond "Women and Transport": Towards New Geographies of Gender
and Daily Mobility. Progress in Human Geography 23:567–588.
Lawrence, B.
1999 The Eastward Journey of Muslim Kingship: Islam in South and Southeast
Asia. *In* The Oxford History of Islam, J. Esposito, ed., pp. 395–432. New York:
Oxford University Press.
Laws, E.
2006 Considerations in Improving Services. *In* Managing Tourism and Hospitality
Services, B. Prideaux, G. Moscardo, and E. Laws, eds., pp. 225–236.
Wallingford, CT: CABI.
Lee, J., G. Soutar, and T. Daly
2007 Tourists' Search for Different Types of Information: A Cross-National
Study. Journal of Information Technology & Tourism 9:165–176.

Lee, Y.
2000 Retail Bargaining Behavior of American and Chinese Customers. European Journal of Marketing 34:190–206.
Lemert, C.
2006 Racism. *In* The Cambridge Dictionary of Sociology, B. Turner, ed., p. 496. New York: Cambridge University Press.
Levin, G.
2006 Pomegranate Roads. Forestville, CA: Floreant Press.
Lew, A., C.M. Hall, and D. Timothy
2008 World Geography of Travel and Tourism: A Regional Approach. Oxford: Butterworth-Heinemann.
Lewis, D., and D. Bridger
2000 The Soul of the New Consumer: Authenticity—What We Buy and Why in the New Economy. London, UK: Nicholas Brealey Publishing.
Lewis, H.
2007 The 'Magnificent Seven' Food Trends to 2013—Management Briefing: Megatrend 5: Halal Food. Just-Food (May): 19.
Lewis, P.
1994 Islamic Britain: Religion, Politics and Identity among British Muslims. London, UK: I.B. Tauris.
Li, H.
2002 Research on the Population of Muslim in China. Researches on the Hui 4:111–115.
Li, N.
2008 Between the Rural and the Urban—A Uygur Rural Society in the Tourism Development. Journal of Xinjiang University (Philosophy,Humanities and Social Sciences) 5:77–81.
Li, N., and P. Jia
2009 The Development of Students at Ethnic Universities and Colleges. Sourced <http://zt.jyb.cn/china/gnxw/200907/t20090721_293378.html> (10 April 2010).
Lindberg, K., and R. Johnson
1997 The Economic Values of Tourism's Social Impacts. Annals of Tourism Research 24:90–116.
Linhart, S. and S. Frühstuck, eds.
1998 The Culture of Japan as Seen Through its Leisure. New York: SUNY.
Littrell, M., L. Anderson, and P. Brown
1993 What makes a Craft Souvenir Authentic? Annals of Tourism Research 20:197–215.
Litvin, S., R. Goldsmith, and B. Pan
2008 Electronic Word-of-Mouth in Hospitality and Tourism Management. Tourism Management 29:458–468.
Liu, A., and G. Wall
2006 Differentiating Education and Training Needs. Asia Pacific Journal of Tourism Research 11:17–28.

Liuzhou Tourism Bureau
2008 Guilin Begin to Develop International Muslim Tourism Market. Sourced
   <http://www.lztour.gov.cn/html/lydt/2008-08/3090.html> (10 April 2010).
Lombroso, C.
2006 Criminal Man. Durham, NC: Duke University Press.
Lombroso-Ferrero, G.
1972 Criminal Man: According to the Classification of Cesare Lombroso.
   Montclair, NJ: Patterson Smith.
Long, D.
1979 The Hajj Today: A Survey of the Contemporary Makkah Pilgrimage.
   Albany, NY: State University of New York Press.
Lou, E.
1985 Conserving the Ethnic Enclave: The Case of Kampong Glam in Singapore.
   Master thesis in Architecture. Massachusetts Institute of Technology,
   Singapore.
Lyon, D.
2003 Surveillance After September 11. London, UK: Polity.
2004 Technology vs. 'Terrorism': Circuits of City Surveillance since September 11,
   2001. *In* Cities, War, and Terrorism: Towards an Urban Geopolitics, S.
   Graham, ed., pp. 297–311. Oxford: Blackwell.
Ma, J.
1997 Religious Tourist Resources and their Further Exploitation in China.
   Journal of Shaanxi Normal University (Natural Science Edition) 25:107–112.
Ma, L.
2009 Research on Tourism Development of Uygur Catering Culture in Xinjiang.
   Urumchi, China: Xinjiang University.
MacCannell, D.
2002 Reflections and Reviews: The Ego Factor in Tourism. Journal of Consumer
   Research 29:146–151.
MacKay, K.J., and C.M. Couldwell
2004 Using Visitor-Employed Photography to Investigate Destination Image.
   Journal of Travel Research 42:390–396.
MacKay, K.J., and D.R. Fesenmaier
1997 Pictorial Element of Destination in Image Formation. Annals of Tourism
   Research 24:537–565.
Mackey, S., and S. Harrop
1998 The Iranians: Persia, Islam, and the Soul of a Nation. New York: Penguin.
Maffi, I.
2004 Pratique du patrimoine et politique de la mémoire en Jordanie. Entre histoire
   dynastique et récits communautaires. Lausanne, Switzerland: Payot.
Mahdavi, M.
2004 Islamic Forces of the Iranian Revolution: A Critique of Cultural
   Essentialism. Iran Analysis Quarterly 2(2) <http://web.mit.edu/ISG/iaqfall04-
   mahdavi.htm> (February 2007).

Markwick, M.
   2000 Golf Tourism Development, Stakeholders, Differing Discourses and Alternative Agendas: The Case of Malta. Tourism Management 21: 515–524.
Marshall, T.
   1964 Class, Citizenship and Social Development. Garden City, NY: Doubleday.
Mashai, R.
   2005 Islamic Nations Prioritized in Tourism Investment. Tehran: Iran Daily, December 28. Sourced <http://iran-daily.com/1384/2462/html/economy. htm>.
Mathieson, A., and G. Wall
   1990 Tourism, Economic, Physical and Social Impacts. Harlow, UK: Longman.
Matson, S., and V. Vermignon
   2006 Gastronomy Tourism: A Comparative Study of Two French Regions: Brittany and La Martinique. Sustainable Tourism with Special Reference to Islands and Small States Conference 25–27th May, Malta.
Mawdudi, S.
   1985 Let us be Muslims. Leicester, UK: The Islamic Foundation.
Mawlawy, F.
   1987 The Islamic Principles for the Relation between Muslim and Non-Muslim, pp. 5–111. Beirut, Lebanon (in Arabic).
Mazari, S.
   1983 'Islamisation' and the Status of Women in Pakistan: A Note. South Asia Bulletin 3:79–82.
Mazrui, A.
   1997 Islamic and Western Values. Foreign Affairs 76:118–132.
McAlister, M.
   2005 Epic Encounters: Culture, Media & U.S. Interests in the Middle East since 1945. Berkeley, CA: University of California Press.
McDonnell, M.
   1990 Patterns of Muslim Pilgrimage from Malaysia, 1885–1985. *In* Muslim Travellers: Pilgrimage, Migration, and the Religious Imagination, J.P. Piscatori and D.F. Eickelman, eds., pp. 111–130. Berkley, CA: University of California Press.
McGehee, N., and C. Santos
   2005 Social Change, Discourse and Volunteer Tourism. Annals of Tourism Research 32:760–779.
McIntosh, A., and S. Bonnemann
   2006 Willing Workers on Organic Farms (WWOOF): The Alternative Farm Stay Experience? Journal of Sustainable Tourism 14:82–99.
MCT Ministry of Culture and Tourism, Republic of Indonesia
   2005 Monthly Distribution of Visitor Arrivals to Indonesia 1994–2004. Sourced <http://www.my-indonesia.info/filedata/180_334-STAT2004.pdf>.

Mehmet, O.
  1991 Islamic Identity and Development: Study of the Islamic Periphery. London, United Kingdom: Routledge.
Merrifield, A.
  2000 Henri Lefebvre: A Socialist in Space. *In* Thinking Space, N. Thrift and M. Crang, eds., pp. 167–182. New York: Routledge.
Mervin, S.
  1996 Sayyida Zaynab, banlieue de Damas ou nouvelle ville sainte chiite. Cermoti 22:149–162.
Metcalf, B.
  1990 The Pilgrimage Remembered: South Asian Accounts of the Hajj. *In* Muslim travellers: Pilgrimage, Migration, and the Religious Imagination, J.P. Piscatori and D.F. Eickelman, eds., pp. 85–110. Berkley, CA: University of California Press.
Meyer, G.
  1996 Tourism Development in Egypt Overshadowed by Middle East Politics. Applied Geography and Development 48:69–84.
Meyer, E., H. Rosenbaum, and N. Hara
  2005 How Photobloggers Are Framing a New Computerization Movement. *In* Association of Internet Researchers Annual Meeting. Sourced <http://ssrn.com/abstract=1353879. Chicago, Illinois, USA>.
Mi, S., and J. You
  2004 Islam in China. Beijing, China: China Intercontinental Press.
Middleton, N.
  2005 Extremes along the Silk Road. London, UK: John Murray.
Mideast Mirror
  1998 IRAN: The Case for a U.S.-Iran Thaw. Teheran: Mideast Mirror (12 January).
Miles, M., and A. Huberman
  1994 Qualitative Data Analysis. London, UK: Sage Publications.
Mill, R., and A. Morrison
  2006 The Tourism System: An Introductory Textbook. Dubuque, IA: Kendall Hunt Publishing.
Ministry of Awqâf
  2000 Hashemite Constructions of Mosques and Shrines of Prophets and their Companions, and the Most Important Islamic and Historical Sites. Ministry of.
  2004 *Ma'lim al-siyâha al-dînyya fi al-mamlaka al-Urduniyya al-Hashimiyya* (The Sites of the Religious Tourism in the Hashemite Kingdom of Jordan). Ministry of.
Ministry of Human Resources Youth and Sports (MHRYS)
  2009 Statistics, Ministry of Human Resources Youth and Sports. Sourced <http://www.employment.gov.mv/Resources/MonthlyData.asp>.
Ministry of Tourism (MOT)
  1996 Maldives Tourism Master Plan 1996–2005: Main Report. Malé, Maldives: Ministry of Tourism.
  1998 Dhivehiraajeygai Tourism. Malé, Maldives: Ministry of Tourism.

Minkus McKenna, D.
2007 The Pursuit of Halal. Progressive Grocer 86(17):42.
Ministry of Tourism and Antiquities
2000 Statistics about the Entry of Tourists by Nationality (2000). Sourced <http://www.mota.gov.jo>.
2001 Statistics about the Entry of Tourists by Nationality (2001). Sourced <http://www.mota.gov.jo>.
2002 Statistics about the Entry of Tourists by Nationality (2002). Sourced <http://www.mota.gov.jo>.
2003 Statistics about the Entry of Tourists by Nationality (2003). Sourced <http://www.mota.gov.jo>.
2004a National Tourism Strategy, 2004–2010. Sourced <http://www.mota.gov.jo>.
2004b Statistics about the Entry of Tourists by Nationality (2004). Sourced <http://www.mota.gov.jo>.
2005 Statistics about the Entry of Tourists by Nationality (2005). Sourced <http://www.mota.gov.jo>.
2006 Statistics about the Entry of Tourists by Nationality (2006). Sourced <http://www.mota.gov.jo>.
2007 Statistics about the Entry of Tourists by Nationality (2007). Sourced <http://www.mota.gov.jo>.
2008 Statistics about the Entry of Tourists by Nationality (2008). Sourced <http://www.mota.gov.jo>.
2009 Statistics about the Entry of Tourists by Nationality (2009). Sourced <http://www.mota.gov.jo>.
Ministry of Tourism Arts and Culture (MTAC)
2009 Tourism Year Book 2009. Malé, Maldives: Ministry of Tourism Arts and Culture.
Ministry of Tourism and Civil Aviation (MTCA)
2007 Maldives Third Tourism Master Plan 2007–2011. Malé, Maldives: Ministry of Tourism and Civil Aviation.
2008 Fathuruverikamuge Tharageege 35 Aharu. Malé, Maldives: Ministry of Tourism and Civil Aviation.
Mintel
2002 Country Reports—The Middle East. Travel & Tourism Intelligence, pp. 1–29.
Mitchell, R., and C.M. Hall
2003 Consuming Tourists: Food Tourism Consumer Behavior. *In* Food Tourism around the World, C.M. Hall and L. Sharples, eds., pp. 60–61. Oxford: Butterworth-Heinemann.
Mok, C., and T. Lam
2000 Travel Related Behavior of Japanese Leisure Tourists: A Review and Discussion. Journal of Travel & Tourism Marketing 9(1/2):171–184.

Morgunov, S.
2003 Autocratic Turkmen leader hailed as prophet on birthday. Sourced <www.afp.com>.

Morosan, C., and M. Jeong
2008 The Role of the Internet in the Process of Travel Information Search. Information Technology in Tourism 5:13–23.

Moscardo, G., A. Morrison, P. Pearce, C. Lang, and J. O'Leary
1996 Understanding Vacation Destination Choice through Travel Motivation and Activities. Journal of Vacation Marketing 2(2):109–121.

MoT Ministry of Tourism, Arab Republic of Egypt div. years
Tourism in Figures (1993–2006). Cairo.

Mowforth, M., and I. Munt
2003 Tourism and Sustainability. New Tourism in the Third World. London, UK: Routledge.

MSNBC
2007 Iran Arrests 300 Insufficiently Veiled Women. Sourced <http://www.msnbc.msn.com/id/18277927/#storyContinued>.

Muñoz-Bullón, F.
2009 The Gap Between Male and Female Pay in the Spanish Tourism Industry. Tourism Management 30:638–649.

Murphy, A.
1995 Female Labour Force Participation and Unemployment in Northern Ireland: Religion and Family Effects. The Economic and Social Review 27:67–84.

Naghi, S.
2000 Tourism Development and Management Plan for the Islamic Republic of Iran, Activity 1.1.3. Tehran, Iran: Unpublished Report for ITTO.

Nasir, K., and A. Pereira
2008 Defensive Dining: Notes on the Public Dining Experiences in Singapore. Contemporary Islam 2:61–73.

Nasr, V.
2006 The Revival of Shia Islam. Sourced <http://pewforum.org/events/index.php?EventID=R120>.

Neuendorf, K.
2002 The Content Analysis Guidebook. Thousand Oaks, CA: Sage Publications.

News Central Asia
2009 Sourced <http://www.newscentralasia.net/Regional-News/131.html>.

Nigosian, S.
1987 Islam: The Way of Submission. Great Britain, UK: Crucible.

Nitta, H.
2006 Capitalizing on the Retirement of Japan's First Baby-Boomers, Japan Economic Report, JETRO. Sourced <www.jetro.go.jp/en/market/trend/special/pdf/jem0605-1e.pdf>.

Niyaz, A.
  2002 Tourism in Maldives: A Brief History of Development. Malé, Maldives: Novelty Printers and Publishers.
Nobis, C., and B. Lenz
  2005 Gender Differences in Travel Patterns: The Role of Employment Status and Household Structure. *In* Research on Women's Issues in Transportation 2: Technical Papers, Transportation Research Board Conference Proceedings 35, pp. 114–123. Washington, DC: National Research Council.
Noelle-Neumann, E., and T. Petersen
  2006 Eine fremde, bedrohliche Welt. Die Einstellungen der Deutschen zum Islam. Frankfurter Allgemeine Zeitung 114:115.
Nolan, M., and S. Nolan
  1992 Religious Sites as Tourism Attractions in Europe. Annals of Tourism Research 19:68–78.
Noor, F.
  2008 Islamic Theme Park Fails to Impress. Malaysia Votes. Sourced <http:// malaysiavotes.com>.
Nora, P.
  1984 Entre mémoire et histoire. La problématique des lieux. *In* Les lieux de mémoire, P. Nora, Tome 1, pp. 15–42. Paris: Gallimard.
Nordic World Heritage Organization (NWHO)
  1999 Sustainable Tourism and Cultural Heritage: A Review of Development Assistance and its Potential to Promote Sustainability, Nordic World Heritage Office. Sourced <http://www.nwhf.no/files/File/culture_fulltext. pdf>.
Nowack, K.
  1993 360-Degree Feedback: The Whole Story. Training and Development 47: 69–72.
O'Gorman, K., L. McLellan, and T. Baum
  2007 Tourism in Iran: Central Control and Indigeneity. *In* Tourism and Indigenous Peoples: Issues and Implications, R.W. Butler and T. Hinch, eds., pp. 301–317. Oxford: Elsevier.
O'Connor, P., and J. Murphy
  2004 A Review of Research on Information Technology in the Hospitality Industry. International Journal of Hospitality Management 23:473–484.
OIC Journal
  2008 Damascus Declaration, July–September, 60–61.
Olds, K., and H. Yeung
  2004 Pathways to Global City Formation: A View from the Developmental City-State of Singapore. Review of International Political Economy 11(3):489–521.
Organization of the Islamic Conference (OIC)
  2008a International Tourism in the OIC Countries—Prospects and Challanges. Ankara, Turkey: OIC.

2008b Framework for Development and Cooperation in the Domain of Tourism between OIC Member States 2008–2018. Organisation of the Islamic Conference. Sourced <http://www.oic-oci.org/oicnew/page>.

2008c 1st OIC Observatory Report on Islamophobia—May 2007–March 2008. Istanbul, Turkey: The Union of NGOs of the Islamic World.

Olsen, D., and D. Timothy

2006 Tourism and Religious Journeys. *In* Tourism, Religion and Spiritual Journeys, D. Timothy and D. Olsen, eds., pp. 1–21. Abingdon, Oxon: Rutledge.

Omura, G., M. Roberts, and W. Talarzyk

1980 An Exploratory Survey of Women's Travel Attitudes and Behavior: Directions for Research. Advances in Consumer Research 7:705–708.

ONTT Office National du Tourisme Tunesien

div. years Le Tourisme Tunisien en Chiffres. Tunis.

O'Pachler, W.

2008 King of the Desert. Business Traveller (December):64–67.

Otterman, S.

2009 Arab League. Sourced <http://topics.nytimes.com/topics/reference/timestopics/organizations/a/arab_league/> (22 June 2009).

OTTI Office of Travel and Tourism Industries U.S. Department of Commerce

2007 Monthly Tourism Statistics. Sourced <http://tinet.ita.doc.gov/research/monthly/arrivals/index.html>.

Pambudi, D., N. McCaughey, and R. Smyth

2009 Computable General Equilibrium Estimates of the Impact of the Bali Bombing on the Indonesian Economy. Tourism Management 30:232–239.

Papanicolaou, A.

2009 Representing Mexicans: Tourism, Immigration and the Myth of the Nation. Journal of Policy Research in Tourism, Leisure and Events 1:105–114.

Paresh

2006 ICHTO's Monthly Newspaper in English, 3 (December): 5–8.

2007 ICHTO's Weekly Newspaper in Persian, 114 (November): 5.

Pearce, P., and P. Benckendorff

2006 Benchmarking, Usable Knowledge and Tourist Attractions. Journal of Quality Assurance in Hospitality and Tourism 7:29–52.

Perkins, J.

1984 Kampong Glam: Spirit of a Community. Singapore: Times Publishing.

Peters, F.

1994 The Hajj: The Muslim Pilgrimage to Mecca and the Holy Places. Princeton, NJ: Princeton University Press.

Pew Research Centre

2009 Mapping the Global Muslim Population: A Report on the Size and Distribution of the World's Muslim Population. Washington, DC: Pew Forum on Religion & Public Life.

Pine II, J.
   2004 What do Consumers Really Want? On TEDTalks: http://www.ted.com/
   talks/joseph_pine_on_what_consumers_want.html
Pine II, J., and J. Gilmore
   1998 Welcome to the Experience Economy. Harvard Business Review 76:
   97–105.
   1999 The Experience Economy. Boston, MA: Harvard Business School Press.
Pinto, P.
   2007 Pilgrimage, Commodities, and Religious Objectification: The Making of
   Transnational Shiism between Iran and Syria. Comparative Studies of South
   Asia, Africa and the Middle East 27:109–125.
Pizam, A., and A. Fleischer
   2002 Security versus Frequency of Acts of Terrorism: Which has the larger Impact
   on Tourist Demand? Journal of Travel Research 40:337–339.
Pizam, A. and Y. Mansfeld, eds.
   1996 Tourism, Crime and International Security. Chichester, UK: Wiley.
Poirier, R.
   1995 Tourism and Development in Tunisia. Annals of Tourism Research 22:
   157–171.
   1997 Political Risk Analysis and Tourism. Annals of Tourism Research 24:675–686.
Polk, W.
   2004 Gropius and Fathy Remembered. Architectural Design: Islam and
   Architecture 74:38–45.
Poria, Y., R. Butler, and D. Airey
   2003 Tourism, Religion and Religiosity: A Holy Mess. Current Issues in Tourism
   6:340–363.
Poynting, S., G. Noble, P. Tabar, and J. Collins
   2004 Bin Laden in the Suburbs: Criminalisation of the Arab Other. Sydney,
   Australia: Sydney Institute of Criminology Series.
Prahalad, C., and V. Ramaswamy
   2000 Co-Opting Customer Competence. Harvard Business Review 78:79–87.
Prevost, V.
   2009 Les mosquées Ibadites au Maghreb. *Les mosquées. Espace, institutions et
   pratiques.* Adelkah F. et Moussaoui A., ed, REMMM 125:217–232.
Public Broadcasting System (PBS)
   2009 Legacy of a Prophet. Sourced <http://www.pbs.org/muhammad/index.
   shtml>.
Puczko, L., T. Ratz, and M. Smith
   2007 Old City, New Image: Perception, Positioning and Promotion of Budapest.
   Journal of Travel and Tourism Marketing 22:21–34.
Putra, I., and M. Hitchcock
   2006 The Bali Bombs and the Tourism Development Cycle. Progress in
   Development Studies 6:157–166.

Quan, S., and N. Wang
  2004 Towards a Structural Model of the Tourist Experience: An Illustration from Food Experiences in Tourism. Tourism Management 25:297–305.
Rahim, L.Z.
  1998 The Singapore Dilemma: The Political and Educational Marginality of the Malay Community. Kuala Lumpur: Oxford University Press.
Raj, R. and N. Morpeth, eds.
  2007 Religious Tourism and Pilgrimage Management. Wallingford, CT: CAB International.
Ramadan, T.
  2006 Kein Kampf der Kulturen. Published February 06, 2006. Retrieved September 14, 2007, from Welt Online Website <http://www.welt.de/print-welt/article196024/Kein_Kampf_der_Kulturen.html>.
Ran, H., and Y. Lu
  2005 Islam Cultural Tourism of Xinjiang. Journal of Xingjiang Normal University (Natural Sciences Edition) 3:317–341.
Rasooldeen, M.
  2009 SCTA Body to Promote Hospitality Sector. Arab News (15 March).
Ratcliffe, P.
  1999 Housing Inequality and "Race": Some Critical Reflections on the Concept of "Social Exclusion". Ethnic and Racial Studies 22:1–21.
Rayner, J.
  2005 Racist Attacks on the Rise in Rural Britain. Observer, 27 March, pp. 1–16.
Read, J.
  2004 Family, Religion, and Work Among Arab American Women. Journal of Marriage and Family 66:1042–1050.
Read, J., and S. Oselin
  2008 Gender and the Education-Employment Paradox in Ethnic and Religious Contexts: The Case of Arab Americans. American Sociological Review 73: 296–313.
Rice, G., and M. Al-Mossawi
  2002 The implications of Islam for advertising messages: The Middle Eastern context. Journal of Euromarketing 11:71–96.
Richard, S.
  2004 Post 9/11 Islamophobia in the United States. Senior thesis in Justice and Peace Studies. Georgetown University, Washington, DC.
Richards, G., and J. Wilson
  2007 Tourism, Creativity and Development. London, UK: Routledge.
Richter, L.
  1994 The Political Dimension of Tourism. *In* Travel, Tourism and Hospitality Research: A Handbook for Managers and Researchers, B.W. Ritchie, C. Goeldner, and N. Ritchie, eds., pp. 219–232. New York: Wiley.

1999 After Political Turmoil: The Lessons of Rebuilding Tourism in Three Asian Countries. Journal of Travel Research 38:41–45.

Richter, L., and W. Waugh
1986 Terrorism and Tourism as Logical Companions. Tourism Management 7:230–238.

Rimmawi, H., and A. Ibrahim
1992 Culture and Tourism in Saudi Arabia. Journal of Cultural Geography 12(2):93–98.

Rinschede, G.
1992 Forms of Religious Tourism. Annals of Tourism Research 19:51–67.

Ritter, W.
1975 Recreation and Tourism in the Islamic Countries. Ekistics 40(236): 149–152.

Robinson, N.
1999 Islam: A Concise Introduction. Washington, DC: Georgetown University Press.

Rogan, E.
1986 Physical Islamisation in Amman. The Muslim World 76(1):24–42.

Rojek, C.
2000 Indexing, Dragging and the Social Construction of Tourist Sights. *In* Touring Cultures, Transformations of Travel and Theory, C. Rojek and J. Urry, eds., pp. 52–74. London, UK: Routledge.

Rojek, C., and J. Urry
2000 Transformations of Travel and Theory. *In* Touring Cultures, Transformations of Travel and Theory, C. Rojek and J. Urry, eds., pp. 1–19. London, UK: Routledge.

Rosenbloom, S.
1978 The Need for Study of Women's Travel Issues: Editorial. Transportation. 7:347–350.
2006 Understanding Women and Men's Travel Patterns: The Research Challenge. *In* Research on Women's Issues in Transportation, I: Conference Overview and Plenary Papers, Transportation Research Board Conference Proceedings 35, pp. 7–28. Washington, DC: National Research Council.

Rotar, I.
2005 Turkmenistan: More Pressure Against Islamic Religious Practice Forum 18. Sourced <http://www.forum18.org/Archive.php?article_id=675>.

Roudometof, V.
2005 Transnationalism, Cosmopolitanism and Glocalization. Current Sociology 53(11):113–135.

Rountree, K.
2002 Goddess Pilgrims as Tourists: Inscribing the Body through Sacred Travel. Sociology of Religion 63:475–496.

Rowley, G.
1997 The Pilgrimage to Mecca and the Centrality of Islam. *In* Sacred Places, Sacred Spaces: The Geography of Pilgrimages, R.H. Stoddard and A. Morinis, eds. Baton Rouge, LA: Louisiana State University.

Royal Committee for the Construction of Mosques and Shrines of Prophets, Companions and Martyrs
1996 Hashemite Construction of the Grand Islamic Complex Where Mu'ta Commanders are Buried.

Runnymede Trust, The.
1997 Islamophobia: A Challenge for us All. London, UK: The Runnymede Trust.

Russell, P.
1999 Religious Travel in the New Millennium. Travel & Tourism Analyst 5:39–68.

Sadi, M., and J. Henderson
2005 Tourism in Saudi Arabia and its Future Development. Cornell Hospitality Quarterly 46:247–257.

Saeidi, A.
2002 Dislocation of the State and the Emergence of Factional Politics in Post-Revolutionary Iran. Political Geography 21:525–546.

Said, E.
1978 Orientalism. London, UK: Routledge and Kegan Paul.
1981 Covering Islam: How the Media and Experts Determine How We See the Rest of the World. New York: Pantheon.
2001 Europe and its Others: An Arab Perspective. *In* Power, Politics, and Culture: Interviews with Edward W. Said, G. Viswanathan, ed., pp. 385–393. New York: Pantheon Books.

Sanad, H.
2008 Tourism Legislation. Egypt: Minia University.

Sandhu, K., and P. Wheatley
1983 Melaka: The Transformation of a Malay Capital C. 1400–1980. Kuala Lumpur: Oxford University Press.

Santana, G.
2001 Globalisation, Safety and National Security. *In* Tourism in the Age of Globalisation, S. Wahab and C. Cooper, eds., pp. 213–241. London, UK: Routledge.

Saudi Embassy
2009 A record Number of Pilgrims Arrive for the Hajj (2008). Sourced <http://www.saudiembassy.net/affairs/recent-news/news12060801.aspx> (26 October 2009).

Savory, R.
2008 Rise of a Shi'a State in Iran and a New Orientation in Islamic Thought and Culture. *In* UNESCO: History of Humanity, P. Burke and H. Inalcik, eds., Vol. 5, p. 263. London, UK: Routledge.

Sayed, M.
  2001 Cooperative Marketing among OIC countries. Paper presented at the Second Conference of Ministers from Muslim Countries, Tourism: Challenges and Opportunities, 10–13 October, Kuala Lumpur.
Schacht, J.
  1959 Islamic Law in Contemporary States. The American Journal of Comparative Law 8(2):133–147.
Schanzel, H., and A. McIntosh
  2000 An Insight into the Personal and Emotive Context of Wildlife Viewing at the Penguin Place, Otago Peninsula, New Zealand. Journal of Sustainable Tourism 8:36–52.
Scheuch, E.
  1976 Ferien und Tourismus als Neuen Formen des Freizeit, *In* H. Prahl, ed., p. 305. Sociologie der Freizeit.
Scheyvens, R., and J. Momsen
  2008 Tourism and Poverty Reduction: Issues for Small Island States. Tourism Geographies 10:22–41.
Schmidt, C.
  2005 Being, Becoming and Belonging: The Phenomenological Essence of Spiritual Leisure Experiences. PhD dissertation in Tourism. Griffith University, Australia.
Schneider, I., and S. Sönmez
  1999 Exploring the Touristic Image of Jordan. Tourism Management 20:539–542.
Schouten, J., and J. McAlexander
  1995 Subcultures of Consumption: An Ethnography of the New Bikers. The Journal of Consumer Research 22:43–61.
Schumann, F.
  2006 Changing trends in Japanese Overseas Travel: Implications for Guam as a Resort Destination. Ritsumeikan Journal of Asia Pacific Studies 21: 125–149.
Scott, R.
  2003 An 'Official' Islamic Response to the Egyptian *al-Jihad* Movement. The Journal of Political Ideologies 8(1):39–61.
Scott, N., and J. Jafari
  2010 Islam and Tourism: Asia and the Pacific in Focus. *In* UNWTO Study on Religious Tourism in Asia and the Pacific. Madrid, Spain: World Tourism Organization.
Seddon, P., and A. Khoja
  2003 Saudi Arabian Tourism Patterns and Attitudes. Annals of Tourism Research 30:957–959.
Sha, H.
  2009 Research on Interest Groups in Kazak Tourism Development. Beijing, China: The Central University for Nationalities.

Sha, Z.
2004 Islam of China and the Silk Road. Journal of Shihezi University (Philosophy and Social Science) 4(3):1–6.

Shakeela, A., N. Breakey, and L. Ruhanen
2010 Dilemma of a Paradise Destination: Tourism Education and Local Employment as Contributors to Sustainable Development. A paper presented to the Council of Australian University Hospitality and Tourism Education (CAUTHE) Conference, Hobart, Australia, 8–11 February.

Shakeela, A., and C. Cooper
2009 Human Resource Issues in a Small Island Setting: The Case of the Maldivian Tourism Industry. Tourism Recreation Research 34:67–78.

Shani, A., M. Rivera, and D. Severt
2007 "To bring God's Word to all People": The Case of a Religious Theme-Site. Tourism Review 55:39–50.

Sharpley, R.
2002 The Challenges of Economic Diversification through Tourism: The Case of Abu Dhabi. International Journal of Tourism Research 4:120–130.
2008 Planning for Tourism: The Case of Dubai. Tourism and Hospitality Planning and Development 5:13–30.

Shehata, R.
2005 The Safety and the Security of the Tourist in Islam. A conference held at Helwan University, Egypt, pp. 230–280 (in Arabic).

Shields, R.
1992 Lifestyle Shopping: The Subject of Consumption. London, UK: Routledge.

Shono, S., D. Fisher, and A. McIntosh
2005 The Changing Gaze of Japanese Tourists. Tourism Review International 9:224–237.

Shunnaq, M., W. Schwab, and M. Reid
2008 Community Development Using a Sustainable Tourism Strategy: A Case Study of the Jordan River Valley Touristway. International Journal of Tourism Research 10:1–14.

Sibley, D.
1997 Endangering the Sacred: Nomad, Youth Cultures and the English Countryside. In Contested Countryside Cultures: Otherness, Marginalization and Rurality, P. Cloke and J. Little, eds., pp. 218–231. London, UK: Routledge.

Silayi, A.
2008 A Ethnological Study of International Bazaar in Urumqi. Lanzhou, China: Northwest University for Nationalities.

Sinclair, M.T. ed.
1997 Gender, Work, and Tourism. London, UK: Routledge.

Sindiga, K.
1996 International Tourism in Kenya and the Marginalization of the Swahili. Tourism Management 17:425–432.

Singapore Tourism Board
  1996 Tourism 21. Vision of a Tourism Capital. Singapore: STB Media Division.
  2007 A Unique Transformation Gains Momentum. Annual Report 2006/2007.
    Singapore: Singapore Tourism Board.
  2008a Uniquely Singapore. Singapore Tourism Board. Sourced <http://
    www.visitsingapore.com>.
  2008b Muslim Visitor's Guide. Singapore: Singapore Tourism Board.
  2008c One City three Festivals. Hari Raya Aidilfitri Celebrations at Kampong
    Glam. Singapore: STB Media Division.
  2009a Visitor Arrivals Statistics. Singapore Tourism Board. Sourced <http://
    app.stb.gov.sg/asp/tou/tou02.asp>.
  2009b South Asia, Middle East and Africa. Singapore Tourism Board. Sourced
    <http://app.stb.gov.sg/asp>.
Singh, S.
  2006 Tourism in the Sacred Indian Himalayas: An Incipient Theology of
    Tourism? Asia Pacific Journal of Tourism Research 11:375–389.
Singh, S., D. Timothy, and R. Dowling, eds.
  2003 Tourism in Destination Communities. Oxford: CABI.
Sirriyeh, H.
  2007 Iraq and the Region since the War of 2003. Civil Wars 9:106–125.
Sivanandan, A.
  2001 Poverty is the New Black. Race and Class 43(2):1–5.
Smith, M., and K. MacKay
  2001 The Organization of Information in Memory for Pictures of Tourist Destina
    tions: Are There Age-Related Differences? Journal of Travel Research 39:261–266.
Smith, V.
  1992 Introduction: The Quest in Guest. Annals of Tourism Research 19:1–17.
Snepenger, D., L. Murphy, R. O'Connell, and E. Gregg
  2003 Tourists and Residents Use of a Shopping Space. Annals of Tourism
    Research 30:567–580.
Sonmez, S.
  1998 Tourism, Terrorism, and Political Instability. Annals of Tourism Research
    25:416–456.
  2001 Tourism Behind the Veil of Tourism: Women and Development in the
    Middle East. *In* Women as Producers and Consumers of Tourism in
    Developing Regions, Y. Apostolopoulos, S. Sonmez, and D. Timothy, eds.,
    pp. 113–142. Westport, CT: Praeger.
Sönmez, S., Y. Apostopoulos, and P. Tarlow
  1999 Tourism in Crisis: Managing the Effects of Terrorism. Journal of Travel
    Research 38:13–18.
Sönmez, S.F., and A.R. Graefe
  1998 Influence of Terrorism Risk on Foreign Tourism Decisions. Annals of
    Tourism Research 25:112–144.

Sorkin, M.
2004 Urban Warfare: A Tour of the Battlefield. *In* Cities, War, and Terrorism: Towards an Urban Geopolitics, S. Graham, ed., pp. 251–262. Oxford: Blackwell Publishing.

Spenceley, A.
2008 Responsible Tourism: Critical Issues for Conservation and Development. London, United Kingdom: Earthscan/James & James.

Spiegel Online
2006a Chronik: Anschläge auf Ausländer in Ägypten. Published April 24, 2006. Retrieved April 24, 2006, from Spiegel Online Website <http://www.spiegel.de/politik/ausland/0,1518,412871,00.html>.
2006b Islamistischer Terror: Die schlimmsten Anschläge seit 9/11. Published July 11, 2006. Retrieved September 11, 2007, from Spiegel Online Website <http://www.spiegel.de/panorama/justiz/0,1518,426226,00.html>.

Spiegel Spezial
2003 Allahs blutiges Land—der Islam und der Nahe Osten. Hamburg.

Somers Heidhues, M.
2001 Southeast Asia: A Concise History. London, UK: Thames and Hudson.

St. Vincent, D.
1992 Iran: A Travel Survival Kit. Singapore: Lonely Planet Publication.

Stake, R.
1995 The Art of Case Study Research. Thousand Oaks, CA: Sage Publications.

Stalker, P.
1988 Can I Take Your Picture? The Strange World of Photography. Sourced <http://www.newint.org/issue185/keynote.htm> (14 December 2009).

State Administration for Religious Affairs, P. R. C.
2009 Freedom of Religious Belief in China. Sourced <http://www.sara.gov.cn/GB/zgzj/default.htm> (10 Feburary, 2009).

State News Agency of Turkmenistan
2007 Sourced <http://turkmenistan.gov.tm/_eng/2007/10/06/today_the_people_of_turkmenistanmourn_for_those_perished_in_the_1948_ashgabat_earthquake.html>.

Steinberg, G.
2002 Islamismus und islamistischer Terrorismus im Nahen und Mittleren Osten. Ursachen der Anschläge vom 11 September 2001. Sankt Augustin: Konrad-Adenauer-Stiftung.

Steiner, C.
2007 Political Instability, Transnational Tourist Companies and Destination Recovery in the Middle East after 9/11. Tourism and Hospitality Planning and Development 4:167–188.
2009a Tourismuskrisen und organisationales Lernen. Akteursstrategien in der Hotelwirtschaft der Arabischen Welt. Eine Pragmatische Geographie. Bielefeld, Germany: Transcript.

2009b From Heritage to Hyperreality? Prospects for Tourism Development in the Middle East between Petra and the Palm. Paper presented at the Traditions and Transformations: Tourism, Heritage and Cultural Change in the Middle East and North Africa Region Conference, 4–7 April, Amman, Jordan.

2010 An Overestimated Relationship? Violent Political Unrest and Tourism Foreign Direct Investment in the Middle East. International Journal of Tourism Research 12 (in press). Available online at http://onlinelibrary.wiley.com/doi/10.1002/jtr.788/abstract

Stephenson, M.

2004 Tourism, Racism and the UK Afro-Caribbean Diaspora. *In* Tourism, Diasporas and Space, T. Coles and D.J. Timothy, eds., pp. 62–77. London, UK: Routledge.

2006 Travel and the 'Freedom of Movement': Racialised Encounters and Experiences amongst Ethnic Minority Tourists in the EU. Mobilities 1(2): 285–306.

2007 The Socio-Political Implications of Rural Racism and Tourism Experiences. *In* Developments in Tourism Research: New Directions, Challenges and Applications, J. Tribe and D. Airey, eds., pp. 171–184. Oxford: Elsevier.

Stephenson, M., and J. Ali-Knight

2009 Societal and Social Implications of Dubai's Tourism Industry—A Sociological Assessment. Paper presented at the Traditions and Transformations: Tourism, Heritage and Cultural Change in the Middle East and North Africa Region Conference, 4–7 April, Amman, Jordan.

Stephenson, M., and H.L. Hughes

1995 Holidays and the UK Afro-Caribbean Community. Tourism Management 16:429–435.

2005 Racialised Boundaries in Tourism and Travel: A Case Study of the UK Black Caribbean Community. Leisure Studies 24(3):137–160.

Stivens, M.

1998 Modernizing the Malay Mother. *In* Materialities and Modernities: Colonial and Postcolonial Experiences in Asia and the Pacific, K. Ram and M. Jolly, eds. Cambridge, UK: Cambridge University Press.

Süddeutsche Zeitung (SZ)

2005 Selbstmordanschlag: Terror in türkischem Urlaubsparadies. Published July 16, 2005. Retrieved September 11, 2007, from Süddeutsche Zeitung Online Website <http://www.sueddeutsche.de/ausland/artikel/870/56814/>.

Sungkar, I.

2009 The Global Halal Food Industry Revisited. The Halal Journal May/June.

Supreme Commission for Tourism (SCT)

2006 National Tourism Plan of the Kingdom of Saudi Arabia. Riyadh, Saudi Arabia: Supreme Commission for Tourism.

Supreme Commission on Tourism and Antiquities (SCTA)

2010 Supreme Commission on Tourism and Antiquities. Sourced <http://www.
scta.gov.sa/sites/english/General_Strategy/TourismDevelopmentProjectPlan/
Pages/default.aspx>.

Syed-Ahmad, S., N. Hashim, D. Horrigan, and J. Murphy

2009 Travel Research and Sharing through User-Generated Content. *In* 7th Asia
Pacific CHRIE Conference Singapore, 28–31 May. Pusan, Korea: Asia Pacific
Tourism Association.

Szerszynski, B., and J. Urry

2002 Cultures of Cosmopolitanism. Sociological Review 50:461–481.

Tabbarah, A.

1993 The Spirit of Islam: Doctrine and Teachings. Beirut, Lebanon: Dar El-Ilm
Lilmalayin.

Taman Tamadun Islam

2009 Taman Tamadun Islam. Sourced <http://www.tti.com.my/>.

Tapper, N.

1990 Ziyaret: Gender, Movement and Exchange in a Turkish Community. *In*
Muslim Travellers: Pilgrimage, Migration, and the Religious Imagination,
D. Eickelman and J. Piscatori, eds. Los Angeles, CA: University of California
Press.

Tay, K.

1988 The Committee on Heritage Report. Singapore: Advisory Council on
Culture and the Arts.

Taylor, P.

2006 Getting them to Forgive and Forget: Cognitive Based Marketing Responses
to Terrorist Acts. International Journal of Tourism Research 8:171–183.

Taylor, T., and K. Toohey

2001 Behind the Veil: Exploring the recreation needs of Muslim Women. Leisure/
Loisir 26:85–105.

The Economist

2005 Special Report- France's Riots: An Underclass Rebellion, 377(8452):31–33.

2007 Malaysia at 50: Tall Buildings, Narrow Minds? The Economist,
384(8544):12.

2009 Halal food: Cut-throat Competition. Sourced <http://www.economist.com/
businessfinance/displayStory.cfm?story_id=14460095>.

The Guardian

2004 Villagers Bristle at Accusation of Rural Prejudice (L. Smith) (9 August).

The Government Administration Council of PRC

1956 The Notification of the Name of Islam.

The Halal Journal

2009a Halal tourism for Gulf Citizens on Rise. Sourced <http://www.Halaljournal.
com/article/1800/-'Halal-tourism'-for-gulf-citizens-on-rise#>.

2009b Ministry Targets 400,000 Tourists from Middle East This Year. Sourced <http://www.halaljournal.com/article/1734/-ministry-targets-400,000-tourists-from-middle-east-this-year>.

The New Straits Times
2008a Panel Discussion Defines Islamic Tourism (18 August).
2008b Islamic Theme Park Attracted 1.9 Million Visitors (17 December).

The New Sunday Times
2004 The Arabs have Arrived (15 August).

The State Council of the Peoples Republic of China
2006 The State Council's Notification of the Name of Islam.

The Straits Times
2005 Rolling out the Red Carpet for the Arabs (4 May).
2009a Timely Push to Woo Tourists (6 February).
2009b More Mid-East Tourists Coming Here (24 July).

The United Nations
1948 Universal Declaration of Human Rights. Sourced <http://www.un.org/en/documents/udhr/>.

The World Bank
2004 The World Bank in Maldives, The World Bank. Sourced <http://siteresources.worldbank.org/INTMALDIVES/Resources/MV05.pdf>.

Thubron, C.
1994 The Lost Heart of Asia. New York: HarperCollins.

Tilson, D.
2005 Religious-Spiritual Tourism and Promotional Campaiging: A Church-State Partnership for St. James and Spain. Journal of Hospitality and Leisure Marketing 12:9–40.

Timmer, P., and D. McClelland
2004 Economic Growth in the Muslim World, How Can USAID Help? Washington, DC: Bureau for Policy and Program Coordination, U.S. Agency for International Development (3).

Timothy, D., and S. Boyd
2003 Heritage Tourism. New York: Prentice Hall.

Timothy, D., and R. Butler
1995 Cross-Border Shopping: A North American Perspective. Annals of Tourism Research 22:16–34.

Timothy, D., and T. Iverson
2006 Tourism and Islam Considerations of Culture and Duty. In Tourism, Religion and Spiritual Journeys, D. Timothy and D. Olsen, eds., pp. 186–205. London, UK: Routledge.

Timothy, D. and D. Olsen, eds.
2006 Tourism, Religion and Spiritual Journeys. London, UK: Routledge.

Tjostheim, I., I. Tussyadiah, and S. Hoem
2007 Combination of Information Sources in Travel Planning: A Cross-National Study. *In* Information and Communication Technologies in Tourism, M. Sigala, L. Mich, and J. Murphy, eds., pp. 153–162. New York: Springer.

Todays' zaman
2009 Turkey Gears up Secure Share in Huge *Halal* Food Market. Sourced < http://www.todayszaman.com/tz-web/news-173625-turkey-gears-up-secure-share-in-huge-halal-food-market.html >.

Tong, D.
2005 A Comparison between Chinese and Western View of Religion. Journal of The Central University for Nationalities (Philosophy and Social Sciences Edition) 1:39–48.

Tovar, C., and M. Lockwood
2008 Social Impacts of Tourism: An Australian Regional Case Study. International Journal of Tourism Research 10:365–378.

Trilling, L.
1974 Sincerity and Authenticity. Oxford: Oxford University Press.

TTG
2009a Kuala Lumpur to Welcome First 'Dry' Hotel from UAE. TTG TravelHub.Net. Sourced < ttgasia2email12.museondemand.com >.
2009b Malaysia Eyes Iranian Market. TTG TravelHub.Net. Sourced < ttgasia2email12.museondemand.com >.

TTI
2009 About Taman Tamadun Islam. Sourced < http://www.tti.com.my/aboutus.htm >.

Tugores, M.
2008 Reconciling Work and Family from a Gender Perspective: An Application to the Balearic Hotel Industry. Tourism Economics 14:223–239.

Turner, L., and Y. Reisinger
2001 Shopping Satisfaction for Domestic Tourists. Journal of Retailing and Consumer Services 8:15–27.

Turner, V.
1973 The Center out There: Pilgrim's Goal. History of Religions 12:191–230.
1974 Drama, Fields and Metaphors: Symbolic, Action in Human Society. Ithaca, NY: Cornell University Press.

Tyson, D.
1997 Shrine Pilgrimage in Turkmenistan as a means to understand Islam among the Turkmen Central Asia Monitor: On line Supplement 1. Sourced < http://www.uga.edu/islam/turkmen.html >.

UAE Government
2006 About UAE. Sourced < http://www.government.ae/gov/en/general/uae/country.jsp > (26 June 2009).

Ulmann, U.
   2002 Die Auswirkungen des 11. September 2001 auf die Destination New York
   City. Tourismus Journal 6:471–474.
Um, S., and J. Crompton
   1992 The Roles of Perceived Inhibitors and Facilitators in Pleasure Travel
   Destination Decisions. Journal of Travel Research 30(3):18–25.
UNDP
   2008 Human Development Report 2007/2008. Sourced <http://hdrstats.undp.
   org/countries/country_fact_sheets/cty_fs_BRN.html>.
UNESCO
   1999 Merv. Sourced <http://whc.unesco.org/en/list/886>.
   2005 Kunya Urgench. Sourced <http://whc.unesco.org/en/list/1199>.
   2006 Population of Turkmenistan. Sourced <http://stats.uis.unesco.org/unesco/
   TableViewer/document.aspx?ReportId=121&IF_Language=eng&BR_Country
   =7940>.
   2007 Parthian Fortress of Nisa. Sourced <http://whc.unesco.org/en/list/1242>.
   2009a World Heritage. Sourced <http://whc.unesco.org/en/statesparties/ir>.
   2009b The Intangible Heritage List. Sourced <http://www.unesco.org/culture/
   ich/index.php?RL=00282>.
United Nations World Tourism Organization (UNWTO)
   1997 Tourism 2000 Building a Suitable Future for Asia-Pacific, Final Report.
   Madrid, Spain: UN World Tourism Organization.
   2000 Maldives Study Points the Way for Small Islands UN World Tourism
   Organization. Sourced <http://www.world-tourism.org/newsroom/Bulletin/
   archives/son2000/B0007015.html>.
   2001a Study on Visa Facilitation in the Silk Road Countries. Madrid, Spain:
   WTO.
   2001b Tourism after 11 September 2001: Analysis, Remedial Actions and
   Prospects. Madrid, Spain: WTO.
   2002a The Impact of the September 11th Attacks on Tourism: The Light at the
   End of the Tunnel. Madrid, Spain: WTO.
   2002b. News from the World Tourism Organization: World Tourism Stalls in
   2001. Sourced <http://www.attto.org.nz/worldtourismstalls.pdf>.
   2006a Australia-Asia and the Pacific Intra-regional Outbound Series. Sourced
   <http://pub.unwto.org/WebRoot/Store/Shops/Infoshop/453C/C9AF/46B1/
   A458/3DB6/C0A8/0164/C6E7/061205_australia_extract.pdf>.
   2006b Tourism Highlights 2006 Edition. Sourced <http://www.unwto.org/facts/
   eng/pdf/highlights/highlights_06_eng_hr.pdf>.
   2006c Tourism Market Trends 2006 Edition. Sourced <http://www.unwto.org/
   facts/eng/ITA&TR.htm> (16 April 2007).
   2007a Compendium of World Tourism Statistics 1995–2005 by Country
   (CD-Rom). Madrid, Spain: WTO.

Various years Tourism Market Trends Middle East 2003–2007 edition. Madrid, Spain: WTO.

2007b Tourism Market Trends: Middle East. Madrid, Spain: World Tourism Organization.

2008 Tourism Market Trends: Middle East. Madrid, Spain: World Tourism Organization.

2003 Tourism Market Trends, 2003 Edition-Middle East. Madrid, Spain: UN World Tourism Organization.

2008 World Tourism Barometer 2008. Madrid, Spain: UNWTO.

2009 UNTWO World Tourism Barometer Interim Update. Sourced <http://www.unwto.org/facts/eng/pdf/barometer/UNWTO_Barom09_update_sept_en.pdf>.

University of Southern California

2010 Sunnah and Hadith, University of Southern California. Sourced <http://www.usc.edu/schools/college/crcc/engagement/resources/texts/muslim/hadith/>.

UN News Center

2007 UN Awards Four Population Laureates, PressTV, 9 June 2007. Sourced <http://www.presstv.ir/detail.aspx?id=12511andsectionid=3510203>.

URA

1991 Conservation Guidelines for Kampong Glam Conservation Area. Singapore: Urban Redevelopment Authority.

1995 The Kampong Glam Historic District. Our Heritage is in our Hands. Singapore: URA Conservation Department.

2005 Celebrating the City-Kampong Glam. Singapore: Conservation Department.

Urban Dictionary

2009 Keeping it Real. Sourced <http://www.urbandictionary.com/define.php?term=keeping+it+real>.

Uriely, N., A. Israeli, and A. Reichel

2000 Residents Attitudes towards Tourism Events: The Case of Nazareth. *In* Proceedings of the Second International Seminar on Tourism Management in Heritage Cities, A. P. Russo, ed., pp. 99–116, Nazareth, 3–5 February.

2003 Religious Identity and Residents' Attitudes towards Heritage Tourism Development: The Case of Nazareth. Journal of Hospitality & Tourism Research 27:69–84.

Urry, J.

1990 The Tourist Gaze: Leisure and Travel in Contemporary Societies. London, UK: Sage Publications.

1995 Consuming Places. London, UK: Routledge.

US Mission to OSCE

2008 Sourced <http://osce.usmission.gov/media/pdfs/2008-statements/st_1218008_turkmenistan.pdf>.

Vafadari, K., and M. Cooper
  2007 Japan-Iran Tourism Relations: Opportunities and limitations in promoting Iran's Cultural and Heritage Tourism in the Japanese Market. Ritsumeikan Journal of Asia Pacific Studies 23:75–88.
  2008 Non-Institutionalized Working Tourists in Japan: The Case Study of Iranians in Tokyo as a Social Phenomenon of the Early 1990s. International Journal of Tourism and Travel 1:7–12.
Van Ness, P. ed.
  1996 Spirituality and the Secular Quest. New York: The Crossroad Publishing Company.
Vargo, S., and R. Lusch
  2004 Evolving to a New Dominant Logic for Marketing. Journal of Marketing 68:1–17.
Vermeulen, I., and D. Seegers
  2009 Tried and Tested: The Impact of Online Hotel Reviews on Consumer Consideration. Tourism Management 30:123–127.
Visit Indonesia
  2009 Dos and Don'ts in Indonesia. Sourced < http://www.indonesia.travel/ >.
Vukonić, B.
  1996 Tourism and Religion. London, UK: Pergamon Press.
Wachs, M.
  1987 Men, Women, and Wheels: The Historical Basis of Sex Differences in Travel Patterns. Transportation Research Record 1135:10–16.
Wahab, S.
  1996 Tourism and Terrorism: Synthesis of the Problem with Emphasis on Egypt. *In* Tourism, Crime and International Security Issues, A. Pizam and Y. Mansfeld, eds., pp. 175–186. Chichester, UK: Wiley.
Wahîb, M.
  2004 *Al-Siyâha al-diniyya fi 'Ammân* (The Religious Tourism in Amman). al-Zarqa, Jordan.
Wajdhee, M.
  2010 Rah Rashugai Banguraa Vikkun Hudhakurun: Sarukaarun Gengulhenee Laadheenee Siyaasatheh. Haveeru Daily Online. Sourced < http://haveeru. com.mv/?page = details&id = 93524&cat = search >.
Walker, E.
  2003 Islam, Islamism and Political order in Central Asia. Journal of International Affairs 56(2):21–41.
Wan Hassan, W.
  2007 Globalizing Halal Standards: Issues and Challenges. The Halal Journal (July/August):38–40.
Wan Hassan, W., and C.M. Hall
  2003 The Demand for Halal Food among Muslim Travelers in New Zealand. *In* Food Tourism around the World, C.M. Hall, L. Sharples, R. Mitchell, B. Cambourne, and N. Macionis, eds., pp. 81–101. Oxford: Butterworth-Heinemann.

Wang, N.
1999 Rethinking Authenticity in Tourism Experience. Annals of Tourism Research 26:349–370.

Wang, W.
2007 Tourism Development Research on Unique Ethnic Minority Region in Gansu Province. Research on the Development of Chaidamu Basin 4:39–41.

Wang, X., T. Xu, and B. Liu
2009 Xinjiang Tourism: confidence is important than profits. China Youth. WITCX.

Wazir, B.
2001 British Muslims Fly into a Hostile Climate. The Observer (21 October), p. 4.

Weidenfeld, A.
2005 Religious Needs in the Hospitality Industry. Tourism and Hospitality Research 6:143–159.

Weidenfeld, A., and A. Ron
2008 Religious Needs in the Tourism Industry. Anatolia: An International Journal of Tourism and Hospitality Research 19:357–361.

Weimann, G., and C. Winn
1994 The Theatre of Terror: Mass Media and International Terrorism. New York: Longman.

Wells, R.
2007 The Arabian Dream Becomes Reality. The Middle East 42–47.

Werbner, P.
2005 Islamophobia: Incitement to Religious Hatred—Legislating for a New Fear? Anthropology Today 21:5–9.
2000 Divided Loyalties, Empowered Citizenship? Muslims in Britain. Citizenship Studies 4:307–324.

Werlen, B.
1993 Society, Action and Space: An Alternative Human Geography. London, UK: Routledge.
2009 Everyday Regionalisations. *In* The International Encyclopaedia of Human Geography, R. Kitchin and N. Thrift, eds., pp. 286–292. Oxford: Elsevier.

Wikimedia Commons
2010 File:Map of the Achaemenid Empire.jpg <http://en.wikipedia.org/wiki/File:Map_of_the_Achaemenid_Empire.jp>.

Willson, G.
2007 Conceptualizing Spirituality in the Context of Tourism. Sourced <ictlconference.googlepages.com/53.Gregory.Willson.RP.pdf>.

Wilson, R.
2006 Islam and Business. Thunderbird International Business Review 48:109–123.

Winckler, O.
2007 The Birth of Oman's Tourism Industry. Tourism 55:221–234.

WITCX
2008 World Islamic Tourism Conference & Expo 2008, press release, 24 June 2008.

Wittgenstein, L.
1971 Philosophische Untersuchungen. Frankfurt/Main: Suhrkamp.
Wolkersdorfer, G.
2006 Das Konzept der Kulturerdteile und der "Kampf der Kulturen". *In* "Orient" versus "Okzident"? Zum Verhältnis von Kultur und Raum in einer globalisierten Welt, G. Glasze and J. Thielmann, eds., pp. 9–17. Mainz, Germany: Geographisches Institut der Johannes Gutenberg Universität Mainz.
Wong, W. K.
2007 Monthly Digest of Statistic Singapore, August 2007. Singapore: Ministry for Trade and Industry.
Woodward, S.
2004 Faith and Tourism: Planning Tourism in Relation to Places of Worship. Tourism and Hospitality Planning & Development 1:173–186.
World Factbook
2007 Country List: Iran, New York, Library of Congress. Sourced < https://www.cia.gov/library/publications/the-world-factbook/index.html >.
Wupur, K.
2006 A Research on the Development of Minority Event and Rural Tourism in Xinjiang A Case Study of the Nuoluzi Festival. Market Modernization 20:194–196.
World Travel and Tourism Council (WTTC)
2009a Travel and Tourism Economic Impact 2009: Iran. London, UK: World Travel and Tourism Council.
2009b Travel and Tourism Economic Impact 2009: Middle East. London, UK: World Travel and Tourism Council.
2009c Travel and Tourism Economic Impact 2009: North Africa. London, UK: World Travel and Tourism Council.
Wupur, K.
2006 A Research on the Development of Minority Event and Rural Tourism in Xinjiang: A Case Study of the Nuoluzi Festival. Market Modernization 20:194–196.
Xie, L.
2005 Research on the Development of the Border Tourism in West China. Tropical Geography 2:181–184.
Xu, F.
1993 A Trial of Developing Special Tourism Products for the Muslims. Tourism Tribune 5:13–15.
Xu, L., and X. Yu
2009 The Problem and Coping of Non-Traditional Safety in the Ethnic Frontier Regions: An Example of Xinjiang. Ethno-Nations Studies 5: 34–43,108.

Yaapar, S.
2005 Negotiating Identity in Malaysia: Multi-Cultural Society, Islam, Theatre and Tourism. Asian Journal of Social Science 33:473–485.

Yang, W.
1997 Islamic Culture and Theme Tourism in Quanzhou. Development Research 4:42–43.

Yang, X.
2008a A Case Study about the Different Attitude towards the Tourism Development among the Community Resident in Hui Ethnic People-Take Najiahu Village and Huoshizhai Village for Examples. Economic Geography 6:1068–1072.
2008b Tourism Development of the Folk Culture of Hui Ethnic Based on the Resident's Perception of Tourism Impacts—Taking the Village of Najiahu in Yongning County of Ningxia Hui Autonomous Region as Example. Journal of Ningxia University (Natural Science Edition) 1:86–90.

Yang, Z., T. Xie, and X. Li
2001 Development and Protection of Minority Culture Tourism Spots in Kashi Area. Arid Land Geography 4:332–337.

Ye, Q., R. Law, and B. Gu
2009 The Impact of Online User Reviews on Hotel Room Sales. International Journal of Hospitality Management 28:180–182.

Yeoh, B., and L. Kong
1994 Reading Landscape meanings: State Constructions and Lived Experiences in Singapore's Chinatown. Habitat International 18(4):17–35.

Yeoh, B., and S. Huang
1996 The Conservation-Redevelopment Dilemma in Singapore: The Case of the Kampong Glam Historic District. Cities 13:411–422.

Yimamu, R.
2008 The Study of Folk-Custom Tourism Depth Explotation in High Platform Folk Houses. Urumqi, China: Xinjing University.

Yong, L.
2007 Chill-Out Street: Kampong Glam has Come Alive with New Shops and Cafes to Rival Holland Village in the Hip Quotient. Singapore: The Sunday Times, pp. L6–L7.

Yu, L.
1999 The International Hospitality Business: Management and Operations. New York: Haworth Press.

Yuksel, A., and F. Yuksel
2007 Shopping Risk Perceptions: Effects on Tourists' Emotions, Satisfaction and Expressed Loyalty Intentions. Tourism Management 28:703–713.

Yunanto, S. ed.
2003 Militant Islamic Movements in Indonesia and South-East Asia. Jakarta, Indonesia: Ridep Institute.

Zadeh, V.

   2001 Women's Employment Situation in Iran, Hamshahri. Daily Newspaper (22 April).

Zamani-Farahani, H.

   2002 Iran, Tourism, and Travel Services. (In Persian). Tehran, Iran: Zohed Publications.

   2004 Religion Tourism in Iran: Stop in Starting Point? (In Persian). Shargh Newspaper, pp. 175.

   2009 The Impacts of Crises on Tourism Development: Case of Iran. A paper presented to the International Conference: Positioning Planning in the Global Crises, 12–13 November, Bandung: Indonesia.

Zamani-Farahani, H., and J. Henderson

   2010 Islamic Tourism and Managing Tourism Development in Islamic Societies: The Cases of Iran and Saudi Arabia. International Journal of Tourism Research 12:79–89.

Zamani-Farahani, H., and G. Musa

   2008 Residents' Attitudes and Perception towards Tourism Development: A Case Study of Masooleh, Iran. Tourism Management 29:1233–1236.

ZamaniZenouzi, E.

   1980 A Summarized Report on the Role of Tourism in Iran. Tehran, Iran: Planning and Budget Organization (Department of Guidance, Culture, and Arts).

Zeithaml, V., and M. Bitner

   1996 Services Marketing. New York: McGraw-Hill.

Zendeh Del, H.

   2001 Iran at a Glance. Tehran, Iran: Irangardan.

Zhang, H., and C. Wang

   2007 On the Pervasion of Ethnic Cultures in the Tourist Development. Journal of Urumqi Adult Education Institute 1:61–64.

Zhang, T., C. Song, and Z. Ma

   1991 Muslim Population in China. Yinchuan, China: Ningxia People's Publishing House.

Zhang, Y.

   2008 Research on Preferential Policies for Tourism in Minority Areas. Guizhou Ethnic Studies 28:113–117.

Zhang, Y., and B. Hanaiti

   2008 The Development of Traditional Food Culture Tourism Attractions of the Hazak in Yili. Journal of Urumqi Vocational University (Humanities and Social Sciences) 1:14–16.

   2009 Tangible Traditional Culture of Hazak and the Development of Tourism Industry in Yili. Northern Economy 7:59–60.

Zhou, J.
2000 Discussion on the Identity Definition of Chinese Muslim. Journal of Hui Muslim Minority Study 1:25–27.
Zinnbauer, B., K. Pargament, H. Cole, M. Rye, E. Buffer, and T. Belavich
1997 Religion and Spirituality: Unfuzzying the Fuzzy. Journal for the Scientific Study of Religion 36:549–564.
Zirinsky, M.P.
1992 Imperial Power and dictatorship: Britain and the Rise of Reza Shah 1921–1926. International Journal of Middle Eastern Studies 24(4):639–663.
Zubaida, S.
2003 Law and Power in the Islamic World. London, UK: IB Tauris.

About the Authors

Samirah Al-Saleh <sameeraalsaleh@hotmail.com> is a lecturer in geography and tourism at King Abdul Aziz University, Jeddah, Saudi Arabia. She is also a doctoral candidate in the Faculty of Business and Law at the University of Sunderland, United Kingdom. She has participated in numerous tourism conferences in Saudi Arabia and abroad. She has contributed to the journal, *Al Aqiq*, in a recent special edition on the topic of domestic tourism in Saudi Arabia.

Nazia Ali <nazia.ali@staffs.ac.uk> was awarded her Ph.D. in tourism studies from the University of Bedfordshire (United Kingdom) in 2008. Theoretically, her work largely takes on board postcolonial perspectives to interpret the relationship between tourism and ethnicity. Nazia's research agenda is largely ethnographic, operating within an interpretive framework to investigate tourism's relationship with such characteristics of identity as religion, culture, race, and diaspora. She is currently positioned within the Business School at Staffordshire University, United Kingdom.

Maedeh Bon <maedeh_bon@ut.ac.ir> is a part time lecturer in the ATU Open Courses Center of the Allameh Tabataba'i University, Tehran, Iran. She holds a master's degree in Tourism Planning and Development from University of Tehran and bachelor's degree in Tourism Management from Allameh Tabataba'i University. Her main tourism research interests include culture and heritage, food tourism and tourism impacts on cultural destinations. She has edited a bibliography of Persian leisure and tourism literature. Her master's thesis examined tourism development impacts in Tehran's Grand Bazaar as an important urban-historical tourism destination.

Noreen Breakey <noreen.breakey@uq.edu.au> is the UQ tourism undergraduate coordinator with research interests in sustainable visitor usage of tourism destinations. Dr Breakey has more than a decade of industry experience, having worked in hotels and resorts throughout Australia and in the travel industry in the United Kingdom. Immediately prior to joining the School, she was a project officer with Tourism Queensland, working on Destination Management Plans for each region of Queensland. Her research interests are in sustainable visitor usage of the world's existing, developing, and potential tourism destinations and she recently completed her Ph.D. in tourism destination development.

Deepak Chhabra <deepak.chhabra@asu.edu> teaches at Arizona State University, USA. Her research interests focus on evaluating and designing sustainable marketing strategies for the travel and tourism industry; application of different theories of authenticity to advance sustainability of heritage; and determination of visitor expenditures and assessment of viable economic benefits of different forms of hospitality and tourism industries for the local community and local and state governments. She has worked on a variety of grants, and is a resource editor for the *Annals of Tourism Research,* also serves on the editorial board of the *Journal of Travel Research.*

Nathalie Collins <nathaliescollins@gmail.com> divides her time between Western Australia and the United States. She works for Edith Cowan University as their Regional Marketing Manager. Nathalie's areas of research interest include religious studies, service-dominant logic, and subcultures of consumption. Nathalie enjoys looking at Marketing and Consumer Behavior through philosophical and religious perspectives rather than economically based or psychological ones. Nathalie maintains a freelance marketing practice with links to the hospitality, tourism, mining, retail, and service sectors <http://theinfinitegame.wordpress.com>.

Malcolm Cooper <coopermjm2004@yahoo.com.au> is pro-vice president for International Research and holds the position of professor of Tourism Management in the Graduate School of Asia Pacific Studies at Ritsumeikan Asia Pacific University, Beppu, Japan. He is a specialist in tourism management and development, environmental and water resource management and environmental law, and has published widely in these fields. He has held previous appointments at universities in Australia and New Zealand and has worked in the environmental planning and tourism policy areas for the government in Australia and as a consultant.

Peiyi Ding <p.ding@uq.edu.au> is a senior research officer and has a background in geography. He received his B.Sc. degree from Xinjiang University and M.Sc. degree from the Chinese Academy of Sciences in China, and his Ph.D. from the University of New England in Australia. He was a visiting research fellow at the Department of Geography and Environmental Sciences at the University of Melbourne, and a postdoctoral research fellow at The University of Queensland. His main research area is environmental management for tourism development with a particular focus on environmental auditing for tourism organizations.

Jonathan Edwards <jonedwards@bournemouth.ac.uk> is a Reader in The School of Tourism at Bournemouth University, United Kingdom. His research interests include issues relating to the development of tourism in the countries of the former Soviet Union, and he has worked in the Baltic States, Central and Eastern Europe, and Central Asia. He has recently led a tourism training initiative in Turkmenistan involving active cooperation with UNESCO and OSCE projects. He is a member of the Religious Tourism Special Interest Group of Association of Tourism and Leisure Education (ATLAS).

Yezheng Fan <fanyzh@263.net> received his Ph.D. in the Institute of Geographical Sciences and Natural Resources Research, China Academy of Sciences in 1998 and has worked in the Academy of Tourism Development, Beijing International Studies University since 2000. His research areas include tourism planning, professional development, informatization, destination management, and rural tourism. Currently, he is involved in a series of research projects on the development of tourism professionals in China with China National Tourism Administration (CNTA). Fan has published over 30 refereed journal papers, 10 book chapters, and 2 monographs.

Ebru Gunlu <ebru.gunlu@deu.edu.tr> is an assistant professor at the Department of Tourism Management, Faculty of Business Administration, Dokuz Eylul University, Izmir, Turkey. Her Ph.D. thesis was entitled *The Interaction Between Conflict Management and Organizational Culture in the Hospitality Industry*. Her research interests include hospitality management, human resources practices, and marketing of hospitality organizations. She has written articles and conference papers on topics including barter as a means to increase sales in the hospitality industry, importance of time management in the hospitality industry, and factors affecting communication in the hospitality industry.

Kevin Hannam <kevin.hannam@sunderland.ac.uk> is a professor of Tourism Development at the University of Sunderland, United Kingdom where he is the director of the Centre for Research into the Experience Economy. He has a Ph.D. in geography from the University of Portsmouth, Hampshire, United Kingdom and has published widely on cultural geography and conceptual aspects of tourism development, with a particular empirical focus on India and Scandinavia. He is the coauthor of the text *Understanding Tourism*, the book *Tourism and India*, and editor of the journal *Mobilities*. His research interests include: ecotourism, Third World tourism, European cultural and heritage tourism, and tourism theory.

Joan C. Henderson <ahenderson@ntu.edu.sg> has a Ph.D. in economics and social studies from the University of Edinburgh. She joined Nanyang Business School in 1997 and was previously involved in tourism education in the United Kingdom after working in public and private tourism sectors there. She is currently an associate professor and teaches in a range of hospitality and tourism programs and her research interests include tourism in South East Asia, crisis management, and heritage as an attraction. She reviews regularly for several journals and is a member of the editorial board of three tourism and hospitality journals.

Mazhar Hussain <mhussain@sesric.org> holds a master in economics from the International Islamic University of Islamabad, Pakistan and is currently working as a researcher in the Statistical, Economic and Social Research and Training Centre for Islamic Countries (SESRIC) based in Ankara, Turkey. His main research interests are the socioeconomic impacts of tourism, especially its role in poverty alleviation in developing countries; development of *halal* food industry; and climate change, agriculture and food security. He is also interested in interest-free banking and finance. Mr. Hussain has represented SESRIC at a number of international conferences.

Jafar Jafari <jafari@uwstout.edu> is the founding editor, *Annals of Tourism Research;* chief editor, *Tourism Social Science Series*; chief editor, *Encyclopedia of Tourism*; cofounder, TRINET; and founding president, *International Academy for the Study of Tourism.* A cultural anthropologist (Ph.D., University of Minnesota) and a hotel administration graduate (Cornell University), with an honorary doctorate from the Universitat de les Illes Balears (Spain) and the recipient of the 2005 UNWTO Ulysses Award, he is a faculty member of the University of Wisconsin-Stout (USA) and Professor Catedrático of the University of Algarve (Portugal).

Deborah Joanne Johnson <deborah@pscj.edu.sa> is the Vice Dean of the Ladies College, Prince Sultan College for Tourism and Business, Jeddah, Saudi Arabia. It is the first Ladies College based in Saudi Arabia focusing on tourism and business. It further offers streams in event and hospitality management. Deborah holds a Masters Degree in Post School Education. She recently completed her PhD in Tourism and Hospitality Management with a specialisation in sport tourism event management. She worked for South African Tourism, 1987–1996, involved with marketing, business development, tourist guiding, tourism development and event organising. She is also an accredited trainer in Responsible Tourism Development and Planning. Deborah has been involved with the tourism and event industry for the last 20 years. She has also worked for Cape Peninsula University of

Technology (CPUT), 1996–2008, and was the Head of Department for Tourism and Event Management. She developed and co-ordinated the tourism and event offerings of CPUT. Deborah assisted in developing event management standards for South Africa in association with the global event organization, Event Management Body of Knowledge (EMBOK), based in the United States of America. She was chairperson of the convenor council for Higher Education Establishments for tourism in South Africa 1996–2006. She further served on numerous tourism industry associations and councils. Deborah is owner and director of her own consultancy in South Africa, The Tourism Collaboration Network. Deborah has co-authored books on event management and tourism business development. She has been seconded by Prince Sultan College for Tourism and Business to serve as Vice Dean of their Ladies College and Head of International Relations for the Male and Ladies College.

Ayman Mounier Kassem < aymanmk62@yahoo.com > is the head of the Tourism Studies Department, and the vice dean of the Faculty of Tourism and Hotels, Minia University, Egypt. He is an expert for the Egyptian Ministry of Tourism focusing on Tourism Satellite Accounts and Human Resource Development. He holds a B.Sc. (Commerce), and a master's and doctor's degrees in economic studies. He is developing the Tourism Satellite Account for Egypt.

Ali Medabesh < alim@jcba.edu.sa > is the vice dean and the chairman for the Marketing and E-Commerce Department, College of Business Administration, Jazan University, Saudi Arabia. He specializes in services marketing and in particular customer comfort. He is an academic supervisor for all departments at the college. He is an executive board member of Community College. He is also a board member of Deanship of E-learning and Distance Education and board member of Deanship of Academic Development. He is an associate professor in marketing specializes in customer comfort as a new concept in services marketing.

Jamie Murphy < jamie.murphy@uwa.edu.au > is a professor at the University of Western Australia Business School. His industry experience includes owning restaurants, serving as the European Marketing Manager for Greg LeMond Bicycles and PowerBar, and freelance reporting for *The New York Times* and *The Wall Street Journal*. His academic experience includes almost 200 refereed publications; full-time positions in the United States and Australia; visiting positions in Austria, Canada, France, and Switzerland, and invited presentations on five continents. His latest initiative is cofounder and academic lead for Google's biggest business student initiative, the Google Online Marketing Challenge.

Norig Neveu <norigneveu@hotmail.fr> is a Ph.D. candidate in history at the Ecole des hautes études en sciences sociales in Paris, France. She is a research associate at the French Institute for the Near East in Amman. She focuses her research on changes in religious behaviors and practices in and around the holy sites in Southern Jordan between the 19th and the 20th century, using a micro-historical perspective.

Fevzi Okumus <fokumus@mail.ucf.edu> works at the University of Central Florida Rosen College of Hospitality Management, Orlando, FL, USA. He received his Ph.D. in Strategic Hotel Management in 2000 from Oxford Brookes University, United Kingdom. His research interests include strategic management of hospitality organizations and destination marketing. He is the editor of the *International Journal of Contemporary Hospitality Management* and also serves on the editorial board of nine international journals. He worked in the hotel business and held managerial positions before starting his academic career.

Dayangku Ida Nurul-Fitri Pengiran-Kahar <ida.kahar@itb.edu.bn> is a lecturer from the Faculty of Business and Information Technology, Institute of Technology Brunei and a recent master's degree of marketing graduate from the Business School, University of Western Australia. Currently, her teaching area focuses in two aspects on services marketing and selling and sales management. As a young researcher with a specific interest in tourism, she actively links tourism-related organizations in her teachings to gain and improve understanding of the dynamic industry. She also has great interest in consumer behavior changes due to presence of the ever changing technology.

Lisa Ruhanen <l.ruhanen@uq.edu.au> is the UQ tourism postgraduate coordinator with close ties to the United Nations World Tourism Organization (UNWTO). She now acts as a consultant for the UNWTO for their UNWTO.TedQual certification program and is a member of the UNWTO Education and Science Council Steering Committee. Dr Ruhanen's research interests include sustainable tourism, destination planning, and the impacts of climate change on policy and planning for tourism destinations. Dr Ruhanen has published in a number of academic texts and books and was a major contributor to *Oceania: A Tourism Handbook* edited by Chris Cooper and C.M. Hall.

Hassan Saad Sanad <hassansanad9@yahoo.com> is an assistant professor of International Law and Tourist Legislations, Tourism Studies Department, and the vice dean of the Faculty of Tourism and Hotels, Minia University, Egypt. He holds a bachelor of law, a master of public law, and a PhD in public international law. His current research interests remain in the area of public international law.

Noel Scott <noel.scott@uq.edu.au> is the author of several tourism books, and published over 130 academic papers. He has extensive experience as a senior tourism manager and researcher and over 25 years in industry research positions. He holds a doctorate in tourism management and master's degrees in marketing and business administration and is a senior lecturer at The University of Queensland, Brisbane, Australia. His research interests involve aspects of destination management and marketing.

Aishath Shakeela <a.shakeela@uq.edu.au> has recently completed her doctoral studies at The University of Queensland (UQ). Her thesis focused on tourism education and local employment in a small island developing state. She has over ten years of experience in teaching at tertiary institutions. Aishath has won a number of accolades including the prestigious Maldives Presidential Social Services Encouragement Award for her research efforts in preserving the Maldivian culinary heritage. She is currently involved as a research assistant at the UQ. Her research and teaching interests include sustainable development, tourism education, local employment, and island destinations.

Christian Steiner (Dr. rer. nat.) <c.steiner@geo.uni-mainz.de> holds a MaSc. degree in geography, political science, and law and a Ph.D. in geography. He is an assistant professor (Wissenschaftlicher Mitarbeiter) in the Department of Geography at the Johannes Gutenberg-University of Mainz, Germany. His research is focused on the impact of violent political unrest on the strategies of transnational tourist companies and on tourism development in the Arab world and on the political economy of tourism development in the MENA region.

Marcus Stephenson <m.stephenson@mdx.ac> read for his doctorate in the field of "social tourism" at Manchester Metropolitan University (United Kingdom). Marcus has published extensively in areas relating to tourism, race, ethnicity, and culture. He has studied the sociological dimensions of tourism since 1980s, and has conducted a range of ethnographic methodologies in the United Kingdom, Caribbean, and Middle East. He is the chair of research for Middlesex University Dubai (UAE) and heads the tourism management programs.

Sharifah Fatimah Syed-Ahmad <sfsa@um.edu.my> is an academic at the Faculty of Business and Accountancy, University of Malaya, Kuala Lumpur, Malaysia. She has a marketing degree from the University of Michigan, USA and masters in public relations from the University of Stirling, Scotland. Currently, a Ph.D. candidate at the Business School, University of Western Australia; her research focuses on Internet marketing—combining her interests in communication, tourism, and photography.

She looks forward in exploring the limitless research fields, specifically Islamic Tourism, social media and word-of-mouth.

David Tantow <dtantow@gmail.com> received his PhD in Geography from the National University of Singapore. His research focus is on heritage tourism and urban development in Southeast Asia. His doctoral work studied the cultural heritage of the Malay-Muslim minority community in Singapore. His main field site was the Kampong Glam historic district, which was declared a conservation area for Malay-Muslim heritage in 1989. Refurbishments there have only recently been completed, hence his interest in the recent representations of Islamic heritage in postcolonial Singapore.

Kazem Vafadari <mehrizi@ias.unu.edu> is JSPS-UNU postdoctoral fellow at United Nations University, Institute of Advanced Studies, Operating Unit, Ishikawa/Kanazawa, Japan. He finished his studies (MA) on theoretical economics in Iran and holds a Ph.D. in Asia Pacific Studies with a major in Tourism and Hospitality from Ritsumeikan Asia Pacific University. He is a specialist in tourism management and marketing and has published in these fields with a focus on Japanese domestic and overseas travel market. Dr. Vafadari is currently conducting research with Kanazawa University on the sustainable management of rural cultural landscapes of Japan focusing on Satoyama-Satoumi ecotourism promotion in Japan.

Boris Vukonić <vubor@efzg.hr> is a professor and the dean of the UTILUS Business School for Tourism and Hotel Management, Zagreb, Croatia. He has conducted research throughout the world on many aspects of tourism economics and religious tourism, including working closely with the United Nations World Tourism Organization and United Nations Development Program. He is a member of the Academy for Tourism and has authored many books including the foundational text, Tourism and Religion (Elsevier 1996).

Zhuo Wang <zhuo.wang@uqconnect.com.au> is a doctoral student at The University of Queensland. Her research interests include tourism planning, stakeholder collaboration, and culture route tourism. Before Wang began her Ph.D. research, she had worked for a tourism consultant company in Beijing for over 5 years, and completed more than one hundred tourism planning project in China and abroad. Wang achieved the China Outstanding Planner Award in 2006, and three of her tourism planning projects were assessed Gold Awards in recent years in China. In the research area, she has published over 20 refereed conference papers and book chapters.

Hamira Zamani-Farahani <hzfara@gmail.com> has worked as a tourism researcher, writer, and lecturer for several years and is the founder of Astiaj (Tourism Consultancy and Research Centre) in Tehran. Her publications include around 50 papers in Iranian tourism journals, two books, and several papers in international tourism journals. She has presented papers at international conferences and recently completed her doctoral thesis at the University of Malaya, Malaysia.

Author Index

Subject Index